More praise

'History can beat fic   ~ org.uk
should reach a wide puʊnc.'

Anne Crowther, *Times Literary Supplement*

'This authoritatively researched biography shows us the ugly side of late Georgian and early Victorian high society. In her propulsive narrative, Foyster reveals an aristocratic household turned upside down by scandal and mental illness. Taboos of sex, death and politeness are routinely shattered, with tragic, sometimes hilarious results. Unputdownable.'

John Guy, bestselling author of *Elizabeth: The Forgotten Years*

'[A] heartbreaking story, it works wonderfully.'   *Saga*

'Extensively researched and gracefully written.'

New York Times Book Review

'Foyster documents a family scandal ripped directly from early nineteenth-century headlines...The standing-room-only proceedings are exhaustively detailed, but equally as compelling are the stories of Wallop's family, friends, and servants, who contributed, one way or another, to his cover-up, his exposure, and his downfall.'   *Booklist*

'Ms. Foyster did a wonderful job...She really makes you look at how those with mental disorders or disabilities were treated in Georgian England and makes you wonder if it is any different than today.'

San Francisco Book Review

'One of the early nineteenth century's most notorious lunacy inquiries and a dynasty in turmoil...If this were a novel, no one would believe it.'

Sarah Wise, author of *Inconvenient People: Lunacy, Liberty and the Mad-Doctors in Victorian England*

'Extraordinary...A well-researched and vividly readable account.'

Catharine Arnold, author of *Necropolis: London and Its Dead*

'Portsmouth's story unfolds like a novel, filled with blackmail, abductions, adulter'' ~~~~~~ ~~~~~~~~~ ~~~~~~~~~ ~~~~~~~~~~~~ ~~~ f~mily scandals.

Reade₁

ity of Toronto

About the author

Elizabeth Foyster is a Fellow and Senior College Lecturer at Clare College, Cambridge. A historian specialising in family history, she explores the sorts of subjects that are often left out of the history books – childhood, married life, sex, relationships with siblings and parents, masculinity, old age and widowhood. She lives in London.

The Trials of the King of Hampshire

Madness, Secrecy and Betrayal in Georgian England

ELIZABETH FOYSTER

A Oneworld Book

First published by Oneworld Publications, 2016

This paperback edition published 2017

Copyright © Elizabeth Foyster 2016

The moral right of Elizabeth Foyster to be identified as the Author of this work has been asserted by her in accordance with the Copyright, Designs, and Patents Act 1988

Image credits and permissions can be found in the List of Illustrations, which constitutes an extension of this copyright page

ISBN 978-1-78607-178-1
eISBN 978-1-78074-961-7

Typeset by Palimpsest Book Production Limited, Falkirk, Stirlingshire

Printed and bound in Great Britain by Clays Ltd, St Ives plc

Oneworld Publications
10 Bloomsbury Street
London WC1B 3SR
England

For James and Emma

Contents

List of illustrations   ix

List of characters   xi

The Wallop/Fellowes Family Tree   xiii

The Norton Family Tree   xiv

The making of a king   xv

An unsound mind?   xix

HEIR

The gift   3

'Very backward of his Age, but good temper'd and orderly'   14

'Alarm'd at the Hesitation in his speech'   23

'The laughing stock of the school'   32

'One of the most sensible women in the Kingdom'   42

'His want of ordinary caution'   55

'Our family greatly indulges secrecy'   76

HUSBAND

'She was more like a mother to him than a wife'   97

'Lord Portsmouth surpassed the rest in his attentive recollection of
you'   109

'He must have been quite a natural'   119

'Black jobs'   129

'I was never with a gentleman of that kind before'   138

The 'company keeper'   148

A lack of 'proper feeling'   157

CUCKOLD

Mad, bad and dangerous to know?   167

'This unfortunate and devoted girl'   178

'Heir apparent'   187

Three in a bed   199

'That cursed woman'   211

'So long as he was sane, he took no part in politics'   224

He 'always expressed much anxiety about his Lady's health'   238

The King of Hampshire   244

KING

The plan   261

Family letters   281

Epilogue   296

Acknowledgements   301

Abbreviations   305

Notes   306

Index   325

List of illustrations

View of an event in Freemasons' Hall, Holborn c. 1810 (courtesy of London Metropolitan Archives/City of London)

John Scott, 1st Earl of Eldon by Sir Thomas Lawrence (courtesy of Wikimedia Commons)

Hurstbourne Park mansion, watercolour (courtesy of Hampshire Archives and Local Studies, Hampshire Record Office)

Farleigh House (courtesy of Elizabeth Vickers Photography)

Steventon Rectory, c. 1820 (courtesy of Jane Austen's House Museum)

Newton Wallop by Richard Livesay (courtesy of Elizabeth Vickers Photography)

Coulson Wallop by Richard Livesay (courtesy of Elizabeth Vickers Photography)

Urania Portsmouth, attributed to John Hoppner (courtesy of Elizabeth Vickers Photography)

Newton Fellowes by George Romney (courtesy of Elizabeth Vickers Photography)

The Very Reverend John Garnett, DD, Dean of Exeter (1810–1813) by John James Halls (courtesy of Dean and Chapter, Exeter Cathedral)

Lord George Gordon Byron by Richard Westall, 1813 (courtesy of Apic/ Getty Images)

View of St George's, Bloomsbury by George Shepherd (courtesy of London Metropolitan Archives/City of London)

John Hanson by John Charles Bromley, after Benjamin De La Cour mezzotint, 1820s–1830s (courtesy of the National Portrait Gallery)

A *voluptary under the horrors of digestion* by James Gillray, published by Hannah Humphrey 2 July 1792, (courtesy of National Portrait Gallery)

The Trial of Queen Caroline, oil on canvas, 1823, by Sir George Hayter (courtesy of Granger, NYC/Alamy)

Dr Matthew Baillie, engraving by H. Hook after J. Hopper (courtesy of Wellcome Images)

The Lunatic by Thomas Rowlandson (courtesy of Yale University, Harvey Cushing/John Hay Whitney Medical Library)

Marriage à-la-mode, Number 6, The Lady's Death by William Hogarth (courtesy of Universal Images Group/Getty Images)

Letter from Portsmouth to Newton Fellowes, 2 November 1851 (courtesy of Hampshire Archives and Local Studies, Hampshire Record Office)

List of characters

Fellowes family
Coulson: grandfather to Portsmouth.
Dorothea: aunt to Portsmouth.
Henry Arthur: uncle to Portsmouth.
Henry Arthur William: nephew of Portsmouth.
Isaac Newton: nephew of Portsmouth.
Mary: aunt to Portsmouth.
Newton: younger brother of Portsmouth, born Wallop but assumes the
    Fellowes name from August 1794. Marries (1) Frances, (2) Catherine.
Urania: daughter of Coulson, upon marriage becomes the 2nd
    countess of Portsmouth. Mother to Portsmouth.
William: uncle to Portsmouth.

Hanson family
Bridget: aunt to Mary Ann.
Charles: brother of Mary Ann.
Eliza: sister of Mary Ann.
Hargreaves: brother of Mary Ann.
Harriet: sister of Mary Ann.
John: father of Mary Ann.
Laura: sister of Mary Ann.
Mary Ann: 2nd wife of Portsmouth.
Newton: brother of Mary Ann.
Selina: sister of Mary Ann.

Norton family
Chappell, General: brother of Grace.
Fletcher, 3rd Lord Grantley: nephew of Grace.
Grace: 1st wife of Portsmouth.
William, 2nd Lord Grantley: brother of Grace.

Wallop family
Catherine: aunt to Portsmouth, wife of Lockhart Gordon.
Coulson: younger brother of Portsmouth.
Henrietta Dorothea: sister of Portsmouth.

Others
Alder, William Rowland: Mary Ann's lover.
Capy James: valet to Portsmouth.
Coombe, John Draper: family friend of Portsmouth's first wife.
Garnett, Reverend John: family friend of Portsmouth's mother.
Gordon, Catherine: cousin of Portsmouth.
Gordon, Lockhart, junior: cousin of Portsmouth.
Gordon, Loudoun: cousin of Portsmouth.
Seilaz, Jean: valet to Portsmouth.

The Wallop/Fellowes Family Tree

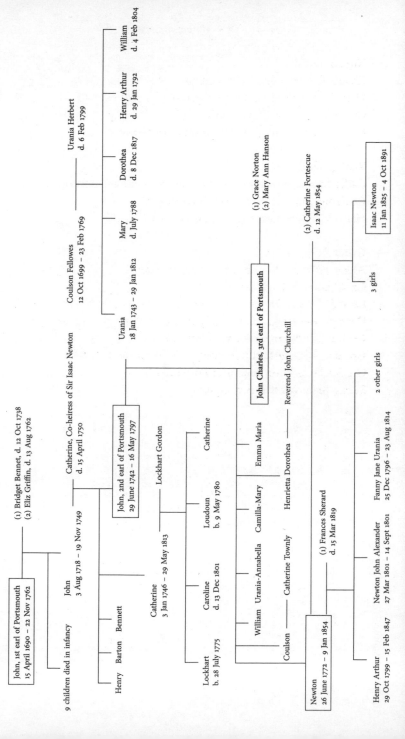

The Norton Family Tree

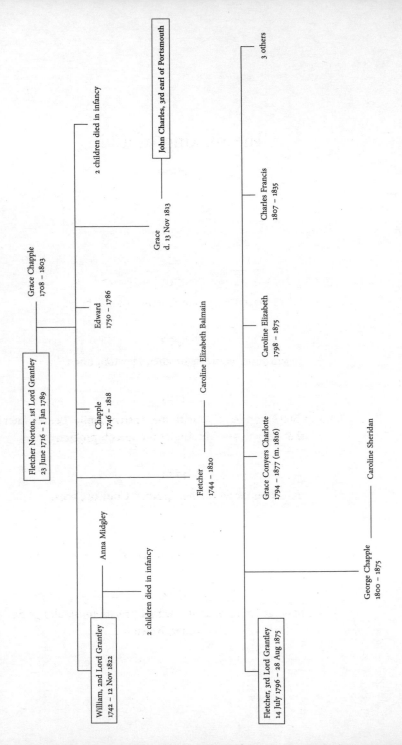

The making of a king

1767
18 December: John Charles Wallop born.

1772
26 June: younger brother, Newton, born.

1773
June: at Steventon Rectory with the Austen family. Leaves later that year to see Mr Angier for speech problems.

1774
19 September: younger brother, Coulson, born.

1775
Starts Odiham School.

1782
From May: at Hammersmith, with a private tutor, alongside his brother, Newton.

1790

July: travels abroad and meets Jean Seilaz.

1793

January: returns from travels abroad.

1797

16 May: father, 2nd earl of Portsmouth dies.

28 and 29 June: presented to George III as the 3rd earl of Portsmouth.

1799

22 July: 'abducted' by Seilaz and taken to London.

24 July: taken to Yarmouth, and 'rescued' from there at midnight.

19 November: marriage to Grace Norton.

1800

14 May: presented with Grace to George III at St James's Palace.

4 June: attends a ball to celebrate King's sixty-third birthday.

19 November: Jane Austen attends first anniversary ball at Hurstbourne Park.

1801

21 April: Seilaz writes a letter from Hamburg accusing Portsmouth of attempting sodomy.

1807

31 August: death of brother, Coulson, at Verdun, France.

1808

Summer: John Draper Coombe comes to live with Portsmouth at Hurstbourne Park.

1811

End of: Coombe leaves.

1812

29 January: mother, Urania, 2nd countess of Portsmouth, dies.

1813

11/12 March: Rev Dr Garnett dies in Exeter.

13 November: wife, Grace, dies.

1814

28 February: Coombe brings Portsmouth to London and leaves him at General Norton's house in Lincoln's Inn Fields.

7 March: marriage to Mary Ann Hanson.

22 November: Newton Fellowes, Portsmouth's brother, petitions the Chancellor to issue a Commission of Lunacy for Portsmouth.

1815

24 January: Portsmouth examined by the Lord Chancellor.

22 April: Chancellor refuses to issue the Commission of Lunacy.

Summer: Mary Ann begins her relationship with William Rowland Alder.

1820

August to November: attends Queen Caroline's trial in the House of Lords.

1821

Autumn: leaves for a tour of the North, arriving in Edinburgh in November.

1822

24 June: Newton Fellowes and William, 2nd Lord Grantley write to Coombe, authorizing him to take Portsmouth from Edinburgh.

26 June: Portsmouth seeks protection from his brother, whom he believes is planning to abduct him.

2 July: Portsmouth met on walk in Edinburgh and driven to Wonersh by Fletcher Norton and Coombe.

8 July: brought up by writ of habeas corpus issued by Newton Hanson from Wonersh to house of Mr Justice Bayley in Bedford Square, London. Bayley declares Portsmouth should have his liberty.

7 August: Mary Ann gives birth to a baby daughter, christened Lady Mary Ann Wallop.

7 November: Henry Arthur Fellowes, Portsmouth's nephew, petitions the Chancellor to issue a Commission of Lunacy for Portsmouth.

1823

16 January: Commission of Lunacy issued.

10–28 February: Commission of Lunacy held in Freemasons' Hall.

An unsound mind?

FOR A GRUB Street reporter, a news story did not get much better than this. It was Wednesday, 26 February 1823. Earlier in the month, northern England had experienced the worst snow storms for nearly thirty years. Despite the appalling weather, outdoor meetings were being held across the country to campaign for Parliamentary reform and to draw attention to the pitiful wages and miserable living conditions that left most working people facing grinding poverty. England looked nervously on at the prospect of another European war as France stood posed to invade Spain. Panoramas of the coronation of George IV two years before (minus his Queen who had been banned from attending) were still being sold, while the King himself recovered from another bout of luxury-induced gout at his opulent pleasure palace, the Royal Pavilion in Brighton.

But for two-and-a-half weeks the news story that held the attention of the British public was the trial of one man, John Charles Wallop, the 3rd earl of Portsmouth. Lord Portsmouth was the subject of a 'Commission of Lunacy', a legal proceeding to establish whether he was of 'unsound mind, and when he became so'. Commissions of Lunacy usually lasted a day, or maybe two, but, by 26 February, this Commission had entered its *fifteenth* day.

The mind on trial was Lord Portsmouth's, but the stories told to the Commission and then printed in the newspapers spoke volumes to readers about the society they had become. At a time of considerable change, and of political and economic uncertainty, the reports did not make comfortable reading. They told of the abuses of privilege, the corruption of power, and the breakdown of family life. It made for a horrifying but irresistible read.

From the time of King George III's episodes of madness, ending with his death on 29 January 1820, public interest in the mental troubles of the rich and famous had never abated. The shooting dead of Prime Minister Spencer Perceval by an insane assassin in the lobby of the House of Commons on 11 May 1812, and the suicide of Foreign Secretary Viscount Castlereagh on 12 August 1822, were reminders that power and wealth were no protection from the tyrannies of the mind.

To reporters, the Portsmouth case looked like another promising story of madness in high places. The course of his life story added extra spice to the tale. Over a hundred people, ranging from fellow aristocrats to domestic servants and agricultural labourers, gave statements to the Commission. On the side of those who brought the Commission were witnesses who told sensational stories of Portsmouth's lunacy. According to them, Portsmouth got sexual pleasure from blood-letting, enjoyed humiliating humble villagers by turning up and even officiating at family funerals, was routinely cruel to his servants, and allowed his wife to commit adultery in his own bed. One of his delusions was that he was the King of Hampshire, and he had ordered a throne to be built from which he intended to rule.

On the opposing side were an equal number of witnesses who were willing to testify that Portsmouth had a sound mind. Many had known him since he was a child, and while they thought him 'weak-minded', and certainly no great conversationalist, he had always been civil and well mannered in their company. He had performed his public duties well, and had regularly held and attended social functions. Had they got him so wrong?

At the centre of all the legal arguments and debates that would unfold was Lord Portsmouth himself. A shy, stammering man, he was in his fifties when the Commission against him was heard. He had already endured years of mental struggle as he tried to fulfil the role and responsibilities that came with his title and fortune. Now it seemed that members of his own family had turned against him, because it was they who had initiated the Commission.

This was their second attempt. The first call for a Commission had been issued in November 1814 by Portsmouth's younger brother, Newton Fellowes, within months of Portsmouth's marriage to his second wife, Mary Ann Hanson. Lord Byron submitted a written statement in support of Portsmouth, and said he saw no evidence that Portsmouth was insane when he married Mary Ann. Byron was a crucial eye-witness to events, for he had been a member of their wedding party. The statements of a large number of witnesses had been heard, and in January 1815 Portsmouth himself was questioned by the Chancellor, John Scott, the 1st earl of Eldon, in his private room behind the court. 'His Lordship being delicate in health,' reported *The Morning Post*, and 'to all appearance labouring under a cold', was supplied with 'a small stove filled with hot water under his feet as he sat'. He presented a pitiful image of vulnerability, shivering with the cold and, in all probability, fear. In April, Eldon, unconvinced that there was sufficient evidence of Portsmouth's mental instability for the case to proceed, refused to call a Commission. Portsmouth was left shaken and deeply upset. He was 'a good deal hurt' and felt the 'indignity' of the attempt, referring to it in a letter to his solicitor as a 'cruel application', that was 'most unbrotherly' of Newton. His responses were later recalled as evidence of his sanity: he was not a senseless fool but a man with feelings who could be hurt like anyone else.[1]

His family did not give up. Seven years later, in the autumn of 1822, they tried again, this time successfully. Byron was safely out of the country, and the Portsmouth family now had evidence of Mary Ann's adultery and cruelty towards Portsmouth to bring to the case. On this occasion, it was Portsmouth's twenty-two-year-old nephew, Newton's son, who made the petition.

By bringing the Commission, Portsmouth's family lifted the lid on a lifetime of secrets. They wanted to prove that Portsmouth was of 'unsound mind' so that they could place the family's considerable fortune and estates under legal protection. For years, it seemed, they had been covering up Portsmouth's bizarre, and sometimes disturbing, behaviour. In many ways, judging from the shock shown by some who thought they knew him, they had been successful. Portsmouth's mother, and then his first wife, had taught him how to control his conduct in public so effectively that he rarely drew attention to himself. But when both women died within a year of each other in 1812 and 1813, and Portsmouth married for a second time in March 1814, Newton Fellowes knew he had to act. Unlike his first wife, Mary Ann was a young woman and likely to bear children. Newton risked losing all chance of inheriting the Portsmouth title and wealth. He was willing to allow witnesses to reveal what they had known about Portsmouth for years, but were never before permitted to admit openly. What was private became public, and, most humiliatingly for Portsmouth, it was those who were closest to him on an everyday basis, his domestic servants, estate workers, and farm labourers, who dished the dirt. A nobleman was being sacrificed in the name of property, at the behest of his family, and by the words of ordinary, working people.

This was a domestic drama writ large. Mary Ann's family, by profession lawyers, helped Portsmouth put up a strong defence of his sanity. Portsmouth might have been odd, argued their counsel, and occasionally foolish, but no one, let alone a lunatic, could have put up such a convincing display of sanity in society, while continuing to be a madman at home. Such inconsistency of character, and for so many years, was simply impossible.

Sentimental attachment between wife and husband was never pretended. The couple had not lived together since Newton Fellowes had arranged the dramatic abduction of his brother from Edinburgh the previous July. Like the Portsmouth family, the motive for the Hansons was financial. The Hansons had to do everything to protect Mary Ann's stake as the countess of Portsmouth, and, since she had given birth to a baby girl in August 1822, the family's future. They had to prove that Portsmouth was sane so that both the marriage and the baby would be legitimate. Both families let others do the talking; neither the Hansons nor Newton and his son were ever present at the Commission or gave testimony. When the Commission had started on Monday, 10 February 1823, it was also unclear whether Portsmouth himself would be asked to appear. Others were set to determine whether he would be labelled insane, a madman, and a lunatic.

With such opposing views about the mind of Lord Portsmouth, and stories of family quarrels, private conversations, and bedroom antics, the newspapers could not print stories of the Portsmouth case fast enough. The personal and intimate level of detail revealed about Portsmouth gave reporters their best material. From the outset, national and provincial papers published full and daily coverage of the Commission. This was an ambitious undertaking, as the number of witnesses mounted, and the speeches of the lawyers could be long: Portsmouth's counsel gave an opening speech to the jury that lasted an incredible six hours. *The Sunday Observer*, usually a one-page broadsheet, advertised on 15 February that, as its report on the proceedings against Portsmouth already ran to eighteen columns, it would produce a 'special' edition with an extra page.

There was something about this man's life story that touched a raw nerve, and there did not need to be madness in the family for a reader to sympathize with Lord Portsmouth. In a society that placed such heavy emphasis on appearance, proper demeanour, and correct manners, there were few families without skeletons in the closet, or many people who did not worry about making social faux pas. But while readers were drawn to Portsmouth, in turn they found themselves being repelled by his sexual tendencies, insensitivity to the feelings of others, and violent behaviour. This dual response to Portsmouth made his story a compelling one.

The Commission was not held in any ordinary courtroom. Commissions of Lunacy were deliberately public affairs, open to anyone to attend, and were usually held in taverns or coffeehouses. This Commission of Lunacy, as perhaps befitted an earl, was held in the grand surroundings of the Freemasons' Hall on Great Queen Street, just a stone's throw from Holborn.

It was an ideal venue for packing in the crowds. The main room could seat eight hundred people, but such was the spectacle of Portsmouth's case that it became standing room only by its close. For *The Morning Post*, later mockingly called the *Fawning Post* by Mr Punch (because of its adoration of royalty and the upper classes),

Portsmouth's trial presented a welcome opportunity for describing a 'Who's Who' of London life. The jury alone was made up from a number of important figures in 1820s society. Twenty-three gentlemen had been selected to serve on the jury, under the foreman, Lord John Fitzroy. Fitzroy, as well as a number of other jury members, was an MP. There was also the banker Sir Thomas Baring and the architect John Soane. 'The Court was very much crowded,' the paper noted with much excitement on day six of the proceeding. 'We noticed several persons of distinction', 'several eminent physicians', and persons of rank, alongside men and women 'who look like peasants', preparing to be witnesses.

Incredibly, given what was being decided, Commissioners did not always call the subjects of their enquiries to be 'inspected', examined, and questioned. But Portsmouth and his side were adamant that he should have his say in court: it was his future that was being determined, after all. On the second day of the Commission, Tuesday, 11 February, Serjeant Pell, counsel for Portsmouth, asked whether his client would be called. He had visited the 'unfortunate' nobleman the previous day, he explained, and believed that only some warning of when an examination would take place would mean that he was 'as free from agitation as possible'. To judge the soundness of his mind, Pell argued, it was only fair that Portsmouth was in a calm state of mind, 'which could not exist, if he were called upon suddenly, and without previous notice'. The chief lawyer appointed by Eldon to conduct the Commission, Commissioner Trower, responded that he could not give Pell a date for Portsmouth's appearance, and that 'he did not know whether it would be necessary to see the noble Earl at all'.

This did nothing to calm Portsmouth's nerves. Waiting in a house round the corner from the Freemasons' Hall as his fate was being decided, and reading the daily papers that recorded the case that was being mounted to prove his insanity, he grew impatient for his moment in court. On Friday, 14 February, Portsmouth wrote a note to Pell requesting him to enquire again when he would be called. Pell received the note that evening on his return from the Commission, and, true to his client's wishes, asked the Commission at the end of Saturday's proceedings. Apparently having decided that Portsmouth would be examined, Trower said that he still could not say when that would be, as he wished all the witnesses for the petitioner (Portsmouth's nephew) to be heard first. Portsmouth should take some reassurance, however, that 'they would take care that his lordship should have such notice as would prevent his being taken by surprise'.

Following a day of rest on Sunday, the Commission heard another full day of witness statements on Monday, 17 February. Finally, on Tuesday morning, 18 February, the Commissioners decided that Portsmouth should attend the court at two o'clock that afternoon.

When Portsmouth arrived at the Freemasons' Hall that day, he knew that the eyes of the world were on him. His defence witnesses had yet to speak, and all that had been said in the previous eight days had been to prove his unfitness to govern himself and his property. There was an enormous amount at stake. If the Commission's jury reached the decision that his mind was unsound, he stood to lose everything. If declared a lunatic, he lost all his civil rights. This meant that he could not make any decision over his property, because he could not enter into any kind of legal contract. All management of his property would be handed over to a committee that would be appointed by the Lord Chancellor. Furthermore, the decision the jury made about when Portsmouth's mind became unsound, or the date they gave, determined retrospectively what contracts were invalid. Crucially, this included his contract of marriage. If Portsmouth was declared unsound before 7 March 1814, then even the validity of his marriage to Mary Ann would be placed in doubt. All Portsmouth's freedom to act, or make any kind of decision, whether concerned with personal or property matters, was in question. As a lawyer put it, Portsmouth's family wanted to make him a 'mere nonentity'. He stood to become a nobody with nothing.

The pressure was on, yet the judgment about Portsmouth would not just depend upon what he said. Personal appearance was believed to speak volumes about the person and the mind beneath. The face was particularly important: any kind of deformity was popularly regarded as an indicator of mental defect. Portsmouth needed to look sane.

To the spectators who saw his arrival, he presented a large, well-built man. He looked strong and, for a fifty-five-year-old man, physically robust. Yet, as a witness later put it, Portsmouth's appearance 'was very much to his disadvantage'. This was because of his eyes. One of his eyes was curved outwards in a convex shape, so it looked 'fixed off'. The other eye was described as being twisted or having a 'cart'. Portsmouth was left short-sighted, and in later years wore an eye glass. His sight could be corrected, but he was described as looking 'singular' and 'queer'. He did not look normal.[2]

Portsmouth was shown into a side room where he would be examined. Pell was permitted to leave the court to meet his client, and explain to him one more time the purpose of the Commission. A quarter-of-an-hour later, Pell returned, and said Portsmouth was ready to be examined, but had made one last request. He had asked – 'his lordship's eyes were almost streaming at the time' – that Pell and Mr Coombe might sit on either side of him. 'This he did,' explained Pell, 'because he would have some friends near him, whose presence would assure his mind before so many strangers.' Charles Wetherell, counsel for Portsmouth's nephew, objected, saying that granting such a request was totally unprecedented, and would prevent the effect of their questioning. But Pell won the argument. Portsmouth, a grown man already close to tears, and needing to be propped up on either side by his supporters, was ready to be questioned.

The gentlemen of the press rushed forward. But they were met at the doors to the examination room, and 'very politely' told to leave. Their presence, it was explained, 'would be incompatible with the delicacy which the Commission wished to observe to Lord Portsmouth'.

Three-and-a-half hours of questioning during one of the most sensational court cases of its time and no press reporting? Few from Grub Street would let this one pass by. Someone from inside that private room must be prepared to talk.

Sure enough, the next day, Wednesday, 19 February, *The Times* revealed 'some particulars' of what had gone on during Portsmouth's examination. Following its factual account of the morning's proceedings, it began a new section with revelations from inside the examination room. Portsmouth had 'notions in some instances highly confused; he thought women went nine years with child'. He 'scrupled not to relate many things against him which involved his own dishonour, without perceiving it'. However, he was 'partially adroit in hiding his follies', and, when questioned about some of them, he told the jury that he had given them up, in some cases, several years ago. 'He was generally coherent, and displayed minute accuracy of memory as to places, names, and dates'. Even counsel fighting for Portsmouth to be declared unsound admitted the next day that 'the manners of the unfortunate nobleman' had 'something of grace and deportment; his smile had more of expression in it than he could have expected in a man of defective intellect'. In conclusion, recorded *The Times*, 'the proofs of insanity upon the whole were supposed not to have been so manifest as to constitute of themselves a full justification for establishing the Commission'. Remarkably, Portsmouth's answers had led the paper (and perhaps the jury) to wonder why the Commission had even been called in the first place. Perhaps when he rejected the call for the Commission against Portsmouth in April 1815, the Chancellor had it right in the first place. Portsmouth was not so obviously mad.

Now the case looked like a cruel attempt by Newton Fellowes and his son to deprive Portsmouth of his freedoms and position. Taken by surprise when he married Mary Ann, and dismayed when she gave birth, it was easy to believe that this Commission had been brought as a first step to end the marriage and disinherit the child. If Portsmouth had always been insane, then why else had his family waited so long to bring the case? Newton's counsel argued that it was 'from motives of delicacy' that they had not brought Portsmouth in front of a Commission before 1815, and that they had wanted to protect the sensitivities of Portsmouth and those around him. But now they seemed prepared to abandon him to the lions.

Portsmouth had put up quite a performance, but, less than one week later, on Monday, 24 February, he requested a second examination. This was unheard of, and can hardly have been welcomed by members of the jury, who already had had to suspend their other business and social duties for two weeks. Pell said Portsmouth wished to be examined 'with a view to clearing up some misunderstanding which had occurred' during his first appearance. Sharing the impatience of others to bring the case to a close, and 'in consideration of the expense and inconvenience incident to the protracting of so considerable a suit', the Commissioner said that, as the Hall was needed for a dinner on Wednesday afternoon, the court could adjourn at 1p.m. that day, and Portsmouth be examined in another room.

The press could not believe their luck. They knew they had an insider who was ready to leak what happened behind the courtroom doors. Perhaps it was one of the lawyers, who were well known to supplement their incomes by supplying news of the cases they tried. Or it could have been one of the jury, lured by the promise of a handsome reward. The papers never revealed their source. There was no guarantee that *The Times* would win the story, and one week on the public interest in the Portsmouth case had only intensified. The fight was on to be the first to print Portsmouth's answers.

In the meantime, perhaps because Portsmouth's examination had gone rather better than they had hoped the first time, the legal team representing his nephew started objecting to the way it had been conducted. From the moment it became a possibility that Portsmouth could be examined, they suggested that he could be tutored and provided with prepared answers to the questions he was likely to be asked. The Chief Commissioner said that 'it must be most desirable that his Lordship should be presented with his mind pure and unbiased, that they might see clearly what sort of mind it was'. But with days of notice before each appearance, there had been plenty of time for preparation. Then on the morning of Wednesday, 26 February, a short time before his second examination, Wetherell dramatically announced that 'a medical gentleman, of the name of Lawrence, had gone into Lord P.'s room, and was engaged in conversation with him'. Also with Portsmouth were Pell and Mr Adam, his counsel. Surely this was an attempt to put Portsmouth's mind in a particular state before his examination, and this was 'an injustice to the Court, an injustice to the Jury, and an injustice to the lunatic himself', protested Wetherell. His charge to the jury, that 'were he on the Jury, he should know what to think of such a proceeding, and his conduct would be influenced accordingly', brought forth cheers from some of them. In this highly charged atmosphere, one juryman, Sir Thomas Baring, objected to the fact that at his former examination 'his Lordship almost uniformly turned round to Serjeant Pell, and from the expression of his countenance, answered affirmatively or negatively'.

As others agreed, and pointed out that Portsmouth had also turned to Coombe when he was asked questions, Pell re-entered the court-room. Affronted that his good name and professional conduct should have been questioned in his absence, he said that Lawrence was not with Portsmouth, but was waiting in a nearby room. He asked the jury to put themselves into Portsmouth's shoes. 'It was no easy thing for a man, being strong mentally, as was Hercules, corporally and physically, to have a series of questions put to him, by Gentlemen, with but few of whom he was acquainted.' This examination was, after all, also called 'an inquisition' of lunacy. Was it any wonder, under a barrage of searching and personal questions, that Portsmouth should look to his friends for support? 'In the distress of his feelings, with his faculties almost shipwrecked, under the pain of answering the questions of a crowd of strangers upon a subject the most distressing to our common nature', he had simply 'turned round, and looked for support under his trial, to the countenance of his friend sitting beside him.' To Portsmouth, Coombe was a friendly and familiar face in 'a crowd of strangers' who were set upon labelling him a lunatic. Wetherell and his team were forced to retract their statements about Lawrence, but, as the jury and the court retired to examine Portsmouth for a second time, the questions about whether they would discover anything about the real Lord Portsmouth remained heavy in the air.

When Portsmouth was examined on 26 February, a reporter from *The Morning Post* got the scoop. It took some time to persuade the insider to talk; and it was another two days before the paper printed the story. But it was worth the wait. 'His Lordship appeared perfectly prepared upon all the subjects upon which he was questioned,' they had been informed. The correction to his former answers that he had wished to make concerned the length of time his wife had been pregnant. It was nine months, not nine, or three years, as this newspaper believed he had stated at his first examination. Just as with the first examination, after the second, counsel revealed some of the questions

Portsmouth had been asked. Mr Adam, counsel for Portsmouth, said his client had been asked about the income he received from his English and Irish estates. Portsmouth said he could not give exact figures, as 'his income was at present uncertain, because the low prices of produce prevented his tenants from paying up the arrears'. These sounded like the words of a well-informed landowner who was experiencing the same economic problems as many of his fellow countrymen, not those of a lunatic who had no idea of what he was worth, or the value of money.

Portsmouth gave some strong responses to difficult questions, 'still', *The Morning Post* declared, 'various answers escaped him, which, from their incoherence or simplicity, are said to have made a strong impression upon the Gentleman of the Jury'. 'The general idea,' the report concluded, is that 'his Lordship's mind had been in some measure prepared for the occasion, and that notwithstanding...his Lordship's answers to the questions...were of such a nature as to involve considerable doubts of the Noble Earl's soundness of mind.'

While Portsmouth's second court appearance was not as strong as his first, newspapers were still hedging their bets about which way the jury was likely to swing. His performance had been ambiguous throughout, and suspicions remained about how far he had been coached by his legal team. There was discussion of whether Portsmouth fully understood what the court case was about. Some were concerned that he still thought the Commission had been brought to punish his second wife and her family for their cruelty to him. There was even the suggestion that Portsmouth deliberately acted mad because he believed that this would be a way that he could be rid of his wife and protected from her control.

Much as Portsmouth's two examinations added drama to the case, it had become clear that this was not going to be one man's struggle to prove his innocence of the charge of insanity. For Portsmouth's mind to be declared sound, evidence would have to be found from the words of others. The jury was still undecided, and there were another two full days of evidence to go before they would retire at 6p.m. on Friday, 28 February to consider their verdict.

They certainly could not rely on doctors to tell them whether

Portsmouth's mind was unsound. Such was the importance and complexity of the Portsmouth case that an impressive number of heavyweights in early nineteenth-century 'mad-doctoring', as physicians specializing in insanity were then known, testified. But there was no consensus among these doctors. While the majority opinion was that Portsmouth's mind was unsound, Drs Ainslie, Bankhead, and Latham each believed that his mind was weak, not unsound. They put up a strong defence of his sanity. Freed from the agitation, excitement, and stress of his unhappy second marriage, they argued, Portsmouth would be quite capable of managing his affairs. Bankhead, who counted the unfortunate Castlereagh as one of his former patients, said he had treated more than fifty lunatics in the course of his thirty-year career, but confidently declared to the court, 'I could not be in Lord Portsmouth's company three minutes without discovering that his is not an insane mind.'

The jury had to decide whether Portsmouth's mind was 'unsound', the legal term for insanity or lunacy. When each physician gave his diagnosis in the Portsmouth case, they were asked to provide the court with their definition of an unsound mind. It seemed a reasonable enough request, but the court got no clear answer. 'With respect to insanity, the definitions are always unsatisfactory,' said Dr Edward Thomas Monro. 'It is next to impossible to define insanity clearly, or separate it from weakness of mind. It is as difficult to define as to settle the precise boundaries of day and night.' How, then, could a jury 'declare a man to be insane, when they were unable to define what insanity was'? asked Portsmouth's defence team.

In Portsmouth's case, there was another complication to add to the imprecise and slippery nature of insanity. As stories about Portsmouth were told to the Commission, it became evident that his mental condition was one that was 'peculiar' or particular to him. He could not be easily labelled. Everybody agreed that Portsmouth had always been 'weak-minded'. During childhood, he had what we would now call 'learning difficulties'. Where his contemporaries differed was whether this mental weakness amounted to what they termed 'idiocy'. An idiot was someone who never developed the ability to reason, and whose mind could not be altered, shaped, or trained. Idiocy was a permanent, incurable, life-long condition. Did Portsmouth fit into this category? His weak mind had certainly limited his capacities, leaving him, as we would say, 'mentally disabled'. His behaviour was described as often being 'silly' or childish.

However, Portsmouth did not match the agreed legal notion of idiocy as someone 'who hath no understanding from his nativity'. Examining Portsmouth had shown the jury that he was no fool, and the stories they heard about his life demonstrated that his mental abilities were not fixed at childhood.

Instead, there were indications that Portsmouth had experienced episodes of mental breakdown and, more recently, delusions. These fitted more closely with what most people associated with insanity. Had Portsmouth's mind, weak as it had always been, now become insane? Had he become a lunatic? If he had not been born insane, then what had made him so?

In order to determine Portsmouth's fate, the jury first had to decide who or what was responsible for his mental condition. If it could be demonstrated that it was a particular individual or set of circumstances that had tipped Portsmouth's fragile mind over the edge, then simply removing him from this situation, rather than a verdict of lunacy, might be the answer.

If Portsmouth's mental state seemed more permanent, then the jury next had to agree upon at what point his bizarre behaviour had become so ungovernable and unreasonable that he had become 'mad', and so incapable of governing his own affairs. This was the big question at hand: when had this man become so different from everyone else that he could no longer be trusted with the freedoms that were common to all others?

The jury faced an unenviable task. With little to no help from doctors, they had to see into a man's mind. 'How difficult it was,' sympathized Pell, 'to detect the state of any man's mind – how nimbly the object eluded their touch.' Examining Portsmouth twice had only served to confuse the issue. But seeing Portsmouth in the flesh had brought it home that they were deciding on a person's whole future. Their verdict was not an abstract legal decision but one that could be life-changing for an individual who was all too human. Before them had appeared a man who was one of the wealthiest landowners in England, who had dined with royalty, and just two years before had sat and voted on constitutional matters in the House of Lords. He was no social pariah. His name had been proudly announced in the newspapers on the guest lists of fashionable balls and parties; he sat on the board of a London school; and he was a Governor at Middlesex and Queen Charlotte's Lying-In Hospitals. In his home county of Hampshire, he was High Steward of the Borough of Andover, and he had attended dinners and given speeches for the Corporation. He had sat with the judges at the assizes and was a member of a gentlemen's club. He had been married twice. He was someone who had a 'strong feeling of his Dignity and Station' in life. 'He was very proud of it and was very tenacious of his Rank and Right of precedence.' Yet here he was, a Peer of the Realm, visibly shaking and close to tears before a Commission of Lunacy. A large man, he had been reduced to a quivering wreck. Born into privilege and high status, this aristocrat was now suffering from a most spectacular fall from grace.

The Portsmouth coat of arms bears their family motto, '*In suiva la verite*', '*En suivant la vérité*': In following the truth. To find out the truth about Lord Portsmouth, the jury could not depend on doctors. 'I should not like to be examined by Doctors', admitted the Chancellor during the first attempt to get a Commission, for 'they generally find out you are a patient'. Instead, he said, 'I should like better the examination of men one meets within ordinary life.'[3]

To understand Lord Portsmouth, the jury would have to learn how he had become the man he was. That meant listening to the stories of and about his family, friends, and servants over the course of his lifetime. These were the men (and women) who Portsmouth had met 'within ordinary life'. Removed from the artificiality of the courtroom and the prying gaze of the physician, it was from these stories that the jury could learn how Portsmouth behaved in everyday situations. People had been judging Portsmouth all his life, and along the way deciding upon the boundaries of socially acceptable and unacceptable, sane and insane behaviour. The clues for discovering the truth about Lord Portsmouth lay within their stories, and these reached right back to his beginning.

Heir

The gift

~

T HE DAY-LONG JOURNEY from his Hampstead home to the village of Hurstbourne Priors in Hampshire gave a busy man like Coulson Fellowes a rare opportunity to stop and think. He set out on 14 January 1768, accompanied by his wife, Urania. Now aged seventy-one, he had owned Mulys House on the Belsize estate in Hampstead for the last forty years or so, and, like so many of his wealthy neighbours, he prized its location. Below him lay London, an ever-expanding urban sprawl, where he had made his fortune as a merchant. He had a home there too, in St James's Street, but in Hampstead he was removed from the pressures of trade, and the hubbub of city living. Here he could watch the prices and the duties to be paid on the goods he imported, from coffee, tea, and chocolate, to fabrics, brandy, candles, and paper, and reach London easily when decisions and deals had to be made. But he and his wife could also enjoy the benefits of the fresh air and open countryside that Hampstead offered, and socialize with their like-minded neighbours. He told himself that he had the best of both worlds.

Coulson was enough of a businessman to know that the safest investment in the eighteenth century was land. The commercial world was an unpredictable one, in which fortunes could be as easily lost as made. Coulson had been in his twenties when the South Sea Bubble, that gamble in stocks, shares, and overseas trade, had so spectacularly burst. His father's older brother had been involved rather too closely, becoming Deputy Governor of the South Sea Company in 1718. The scars were still felt, and Coulson's father, William, had played it safe, rejecting the world of commerce for that of the law to make his living. He had been successful, rising to the position of Senior Master in Chancery. William's marriage to an heiress was another shrewd move, for when her father died in 1718 he was left with sixty thousand pounds, with the stipulation that he should invest the inheritance in Devon. It was in this way that the Fellowes family had come to own the Eggesford estate in mid-Devon. The house that William rebuilt there was in red-brick and in Palladian style. It was a bold statement to society: we have arrived.

Inheriting Eggesford from his father, Coulson became a member of the new landed elite, whose wealth and good fortune was so vital in shaping Georgian England. Not only did he play a role in the expanding commercial economy, Coulson could also afford to participate in the many pleasures of eighteenth-century society. 'True' gentility, Coulson knew, was about polite manners and conduct. A man had to prove himself a gentleman; this was not something that could be inherited or bought. Coulson needed to demonstrate that he belonged. He set about this task with enthusiasm. He bought tickets to see plays and hear concerts. He read newspapers, purchased expensive volumes of maps and history books, and established a friendship with John Pridden, a bookseller based in Fleet Street. Relishing the opportunities on offer in Enlightenment London, he joined one of the most successful of learned societies, the Society of Arts. Once the new building of St John's Church in Hampstead was completed, he attended services and paid fees for a pew. In adjacent pews sat other successful city merchants, as well as respected physicians and leading lawyers.

Like his father, Coulson made a very good marriage. In April 1725, he married Urania, the daughter of Francis Herbert of Oakley Park. At seventeen years old, she was under-age, but, with a fortune of ten thousand pounds, quite a catch. They had two sons, William and Henry Arthur, and three daughters, Mary, Urania, and Dorothea. Coulson gave his wife a regular clothes allowance, with which she purchased silk and velvet gowns and coats. He bought her treats such as jars of raisins, and the couple enjoyed his purchases of venison and wine. Improvements were made to the house at Eggesford, and the family began to spend more time there after the birth of Mary in August 1729. Additional land was bought by Coulson in West Ham, Essex, and by 1731 he was paying for the expenses of stables and a coachmaker. In 1737, Coulson acquired the Ramsey Abbey and Abbots Ripton estates near Huntingdon in Cambridgeshire. Landed wealth brought political position; Coulson was MP for Huntingdonshire from 1741 to 1761, and was a sheriff in Devon for two years. With a growing family and so much responsibility, Coulson needed to take care of himself. Once or twice a year, he paid Mr Arnold Langley 'for bleeding' him, a fashionable practice that was thought to bring health benefits. He never neglected his appearance, and made payments to a barber for shaving, and for wigs and breeches. He looked and acted the eighteenth-century gentleman.[1]

Now on this long journey to Hampshire, Coulson could sit back in his coach (perhaps the one he had lined with a 'rich crimson Genoa velvet'), and reflect on his achievements. The greatest of them was the reason for this journey: the marriage of the daughter who shared his wife's name, Urania. On 27 August 1763, more than four years earlier, Urania had married John Wallop, the 2nd earl of Portsmouth. Their wedding had taken place at St George's Church in Hanover Square, and as a wedding present the groom had presented his wife with a pair of three-drop diamond earrings and a diamond pin. But his most important gift was his family's title: Urania Fellowes had become Lady Portsmouth, the 2nd countess of Portsmouth.

Despite all his business successes and landed wealth, it was Urania who had taken the Fellowes family to the very top of the eighteenth-century social ladder. Her marriage opened the door to the exclusive world of the aristocracy.

With Urania's title came all important lineage: the means of tracing power and status far back in time. The Wallops boasted that their family line descended from pre-Norman times, and certainly they had been landowners in Hampshire since at least the thirteenth century. But what interested Coulson most was their more recent family history. It was a story of prudent political choices, good fortune, and chance meetings. Coulson learned that the 2nd earl's grandfather was a loyal

Whig supporter, who had been appointed a Lord of the Treasury in 1717. In the 1730s, he had been rewarded by Robert Walpole with a series of positions in Hampshire, including Lord Lieutenant and Vice-Admiral. A 'grand tour' of Europe led him to the court of Hanover, where he met and befriended the Elector of Hanover, later George I. Royal support for Wallop continued with George II and George III, and he was first elevated to the House of Lords as Baron Wallop and Viscount Lymington in 1720, and then made the 1st earl of Portsmouth on 11 April 1743.

Coulson and his wife knew from the experience of their own family that position and wealth could not guarantee good health and personal happiness. Sickness and death were never far away, especially for the young. The 1st earl had been married twice, but, of the ten children born to his first wife, only one had survived into adulthood. That child, a son, also called John, became Viscount Lymington, and in 1740 had married Catherine Conduitt, great-niece and co-heiress of Sir Isaac Newton. Lymington and Catherine had five children, including Coulson's son-in-law, John. Neither of John's parents lived to see him marry Urania in 1763, and his grandfather had to endure the death of his tenth child before him. As the 1st earl outlived his son, Lymington never inherited the earldom. When the 1st earl died on 22 November 1762, his family recorded his many achievements on his memorial, but also chose to remark that 'thro' the several Chances and Changes of ye Concernments of this Life' (surely a reference to the death of all of his children before him), he had 'happily retained Tranquility of Mind'.[2]

A tranquil mind was a prized quality for the Wallops, but the significance of this was probably lost on Coulson, whose business brains were busy calculating how best to arrange a marriage between his daughter and the man who became the 2nd earl of Portsmouth on his grandfather's death. The 2nd earl inherited a fortune, which Coulson knew was far greater than anything he could ever own. The earl had lands in Buckinghamshire, Somerset, and County Wexford in Ireland, as well as many thousands of acres in Hampshire. This vast estate generated tens of thousands of pounds in rent each year, and provided valuable pasture, arable, and woodlands. The earl had two homes in Hampshire, one at Marlow in Buckinghamshire, and a castle at Enniscorthy in Ireland. This was the stuff of which dreams were made.

Coulson congratulated himself for securing his daughter's marriage to the 2nd earl in such a short period of time; the couple were married less than a year after the 1st earl's death. Of course, the fact that the Wallops were prepared to consider the notion of Urania marrying into their family was a credit to Coulson. He was a father who had invested in his children's education and upbringing, ensuring that Urania would not look or act out of place in the new social world she joined when she married. She was educated as a lady, which meant that she learned how to read, write, and conduct polite conversation with those she met. Coulson paid for his daughter to have dancing lessons, and she had the social skills and good manners that would be necessary as she crossed from her father's commercial world to that of the nobility. An eighteenth-century woman of her social standing would never work in a formal sense, but she could not afford to be an idle observer. Urania knew how to manage a household of servants, and, from her time at Eggesford, had gained insights into the operation of an estate. Time would show that she had inherited her father's business acumen, common sense, and financial competence. She had all the qualities to make her a perfect wife.

Urania had good looks on her side, and her beauty was long remembered. Both Urania and her husband were painted in later life by society artist John Hoppner. The painting of her husband, which unfortunately does not survive, showed 'an enormous stout old gentleman painted without any disguisem[en]ts…in robes with a red nose and face'. It was said that two tables in the hall of his house had to be hollowed out so that he could sit comfortably at them. Good living had to be accommodated.[3]

Marriages like Urania's were not intended to be love matches, although there was always the hope that affection would blossom after the knot had been tied. Instead, marriages at this level of society were business arrangements, negotiated between men, and involving significant transfers of property. Coulson secured the marriage of the 2nd earl of Portsmouth with his daughter because he offered a substantial dowry, which he paid as an annuity of four per cent, and, as he travelled to Hampshire that January in 1768, he may well have been calculating how to make the next payment that was due in February. Urania's marriage was an expensive investment, but one that Coulson had taken to ensure the future security of his family.[4]

It was probably getting dark by the time Coulson's coach reached the market town of Basingstoke in the north-east of Hampshire. Looking out of his window, he may have been able to catch glimpses of one of the earl's properties, Farleigh House, standing on a hill high above the town. The house there had been visited by Elizabeth I in 1591, but had burned down following a fire at some point in the 1660s. The house that Coulson could see had been rebuilt by the 1st earl in 1731. It was a large rectangular building, with a pleasing symmetrical front, and had been constructed using locally sourced flint and stone. Beyond its gardens stood St Andrew's Church, which the Wallop family used as their private chapel. Inside lay the remains and monument to the 1st earl of Portsmouth.[5]

It was around twelve miles from here to Coulson's final destination. Travelling west on the Basingstoke to Andover road, he passed fields where sheep grazed, and had long been valued for their wool. Farming was flourishing in this area, and the fair held at Weyhill near Andover was heralded as the 'greatest' in England for the sale of sheep, hops, cheese, and other rural goods. Good-quality soil produced crops of corn and sainfoin, a nutritious crop used to feed livestock. Woodland provided plentiful timber. Chalk streams were swimming with trout, and held their rainwater for a long time, creating ideal conditions for working mills.

As he entered the town of Whitchurch, Coulson crossed the River Test, and saw the paper mill that since 1712 had been making the bank notes that he had so often handled. Whitchurch was a small place (its population at the first census in 1801 was 1275), where most men and many women were employed in agriculture or the woollen industry. The White Hart inn at the town's crossroads, with its life-sized statue of a white deer above the doorway, had been providing weary travellers with welcome rest and sustenance since the fifteenth century. Coulson did not stop. Following the road out of town, his coach passed the Norman church of All Hallows, and travelled the short distance to his journey's end, his daughter's home at Hurstbourne Park.[6]

Hurstbourne Park was enough to make anyone gasp. In scale and grandeur it made Coulson's Eggesford home pale into insignificance. It had been the Wallop family residence for generations, and was now the chief seat of the Portsmouths. It dominated the tiny village of Hurstbourne Priors, which consisted of a small number of estate workers' thatched cottages. The mansion house stood just south of the church of St Andrew, and beside a stream of the river Bourne. The 1st earl had adapted the gardens to suit the fashions of landscape gardening in the early eighteenth century, using the water from the Bourne to create a rectangular canal, a grotto, and a small waterfall. Beyond the gardens the wooded park had eight avenues, and in the far distance lay hay fields and water meadows.

Coulson had visited Hurstbourne Park twice in 1766, so he knew what to expect. His daughter and her husband were keen to put their own stamp on the place, and had begun to discuss their plans. The house and gardens were thought old-fashioned by the 1760s, and the mansion's close proximity both to the busy Basingstoke to Andover road, and to the homes of the villagers was undesirable. Aristocratic distance from everyday life and ordinary working people was the goal. Coulson, who on a daily basis looked down on London from the heights of his Hampstead home, could understand that aspiration.

For Urania, building the new Hurstbourne would become her project. She certainly did not lack ambition. The architect chosen was James Wyatt, designer of the assembly rooms in Oxford Street, London, and known for his classical architecture. Urania changed the location of the family home, moving it nearly a mile northwards, away from the church, stream, road, and cottages, to a hill-top. South-facing, the new house was more secluded than the last. Many materials were taken from the old house to build the new, which consisted of a large central section from which curved colonnades led to east and west wings. The east wing held the library, chapel, and bedrooms; the west wing, the servants' quarters and estate offices.

Wyatt was an interior designer as well as an architect, and Urania was his ideal customer. No expense was spared. In the main wing, a great square hall was paved with white stone. Wyatt was commissioned to design the furniture for the drawing room, where guests were received, and Urania aimed to impress. There was red velvet furniture with gold painted legs, 'some beautiful tables and chests of drawers painted with peacock feathers and medallions containing landscapes and some very graceful gilt lamp-stands'. The ceiling was decorated with Adams mouldings. In the dining room hung a number of family portraits, including one of the family's ancestors, Colonel Henry Wallop, by Van Dyck. Dinners were to be grand affairs. Putting her name on the place, Urania commissioned a set of silver cutlery to be made with a mermaid (who appears on the Wallop coat of arms), and her initials, 'U.P.'

The library at Hurstbourne held many of the books and manuscripts of Isaac Newton, inherited by Catherine Conduitt, the earl's mother. This kind of legacy was reassuring to the educated Coulson. His daughter had married into a family, he told himself, that had respectable connections as well as money. Urania built a magnificent library in the new Hurstbourne to house Newton's collection. Bookshelves were supported by marble columns, busts of different authors sat above each shelf, and green silk curtains latticed every case.

There was no flower garden at Hurstbourne; the parkland began immediately in front of the house. To the side there was a kitchen garden, and a number of substantial, 300-feet-long glasshouses. Sheltered from the elements, all sorts of exotic fruit were grown inside, including peaches, nectarines, grapes, and pineapples. Urania, who was known for her love of birds, planted cherry trees close to the house, so she could watch them feed from the windows. An engine house was constructed to supply water from the Bourne to the house. The landscape surrounding the house was in the style of Capability Brown, and a lake was created by widening the Bourne with a dam. Visitors entered the park passing one of two newly built lodges from either the Whitchurch or Andover direction. Their carriages slowly wound their way up along the drives, allowing full views of the park with its ancient trees and plentiful deer, before reaching the grandeur of the house.[7]

It was ten years' work from start to finish, with the newspapers announcing in December 1788 that Lord Portsmouth's 'new superb house' was completed, and a grand gala ball held in celebration for the house that was described as a 'perfect palace'. Two years later, the earl estimated that the total cost of the new building, furnishing, landscaping, and other improvements to estate buildings had been a phenomenal £85,000.[8]

Urania would do her father proud, but when Coulson came to visit his daughter in January 1768 he was coming to congratulate her for a quite different reason. Coulson was not a sentimental man used to expressing his feelings. The only personal letters he wrote, and which survive, were to his son Henry Arthur, and concerned their shared interest in horses. The chief reason Coulson put pen to paper was to settle his bills and record his accounts. On 1 April 1731, he had written 'An Account how my Fortune then stood', a reckoning of debts owed and property owned. In careful detail and tiny hand, he kept another list of his expenses and income for the last four years of his life. Near the start of this account book he simply recorded the date and fact of his oldest son's marriage on 11 May 1765, and that he had given William two thousand pounds on this occasion. No other remarks about this marriage were made. The rest of the book recorded his life events through the payments he made for the things he bought and the luxuries he consumed.

However, on 18 December 1767, he wrote something quite different. This was so out of the ordinary that he recorded it on the left hand side of his notebook, separating it from the mundane list of accounts on the right hand side. Written as a memo, it stated:

Ld Portsmouth's son was born the 18th of Dec 28 minutes before 5pm in the afternoon.

A few pages later, again on the left-hand-side of his book, Coulson wrote:

1767 Dec the 18 little John Charles son of Urania was born, christen'd Jan 15th 1768.

Breaking with the convention of his account keeping, usually concerned with things, not people, Coulson recorded his grandson's birth. This was a momentous occasion in his family's history, of such importance that he carefully noted the very minute it had occurred. Coulson knew that this child, born to his daughter, would one day inherit the title of Lord Portsmouth. He could barely contain his excitement. An heir in place, his family's future was guaranteed.

He had waited over four years since the marriage of his daughter for this moment. For a young aristocratic couple this was quite a time-gap before the birth of children. There may have been another baby born before, that was either stillborn, or that did not live for more than a few hours. When Vicary Gibbs compiled the authoritative *Complete Peerage* at the end of the nineteenth century, he noted that John Charles was the '2nd but 1st surviving son and heir, born 18 December 1767'. No other evidence of the birth or death of this older brother survives. In December 1767, all had gone well, and there was nothing to indicate that Urania had experienced any problems in her pregnancy or during the birth of her child. John Charles was a healthy baby boy.

Arriving late on 14 January 1768, Coulson and his wife had just enough time to recover before the christening of their grandson the next day. The baby's christening took place, the parish clerk recorded, in the private chapel of 'his Father's House' at Hurstbourne. The child was named John Charles, and given the title Lord Viscount Lymington.

Back in London, Coulson reverted to recording the costs of the event: his travel to Hurstbourne cost eight pounds, he allowed his wife an additional ten pounds, perhaps so she could buy herself a new outfit for the occasion, and other expenses while at Hurstbourne amounted to just over three pounds. He used his connections to arrange for a parcel of fruit to be delivered to Hurstbourne the day before he arrived, and he gave a token ten pounds and ten shillings as a christening gift to the baby.

But he allowed his feelings about the birth of his grandson to show for one final time. A few months after his visit to Hurstbourne, on 2 April 1768, Coulson listed in his expenses the cost of 'a coral for little John'. Coral was a popular gift for babies. Its shape made it a good teether, and many mothers attached coral to a ribbon so their babies could wear it round their necks. Ever ready to be drooled, chewed, and bitten on, this was a useful, practical gift. But it was also a symbolic one. Coral had long been thought to hold healing properties, to bring good health, and to protect its owner from magic and bad luck.

'Little John' was the only grandchild Coulson ever knew. That spring and summer he made three payments to Mr Langley, the surgeon who usually let his blood, for advice 'about the ulcer in my face'.[9] As his illness grew worse, and more alarming, Coulson paid larger sums to Langley in hope of a cure. Blood-letting had cost him the same sum of one pound and one shilling for many years, but in August 1768 he paid Langley over one hundred pounds in fees for treatment to his face. The illness was terminal, however. Coulson made the last entry in his account book on 20 January 1769, and died just over a month later on 23 February. He would never see his grandson grow up, nor know just how appropriate his gift had been.

'Very backward of his Age, but good temper'd and orderly'

IN THE EARLY summer of 1773, a little boy arrived at the rectory in Steventon, a small Hampshire village, around eight miles south-west of Basingstoke. Now five-and-a-half years old, this was Viscount Lymington's first journey away from home. Surrounded by fields and gently sloping chalk hills, Steventon consisted of a single row of thatched cottages set in a valley. The rectory itself was positioned apart from the rest of the houses, and stood at the junction where the lane from the church met that of the village. The church of St Nicholas lay on a hill above, almost a mile away. The rector was George Austen, and Lymington had come to be tutored by him. For the next six months, the rectory was to be his school and home. Steventon was only about ten miles from Hurstbourne Park, but to Lymington it was worlds apart from the life he had so far experienced.

Everything was on a smaller scale. The rectory was a three-storey house, and when Lymington first arrived he was shown into the 'best parlour'. On the ground floor there was also a 'common parlour' for less privileged guests, a study for George Austen, a kitchen, and back kitchen. The next floor had seven bedrooms, and three attic rooms were on the top. Lymington, like other pupils who came to the Austen household, is likely to have been assigned an attic room. The house was big enough to accommodate pupils, and attractive enough as a country rectory, but was far removed from the grandeur and size of

Lymington's family seat. With its evenly spaced windows, and trellised porch over the front door, the Steventon rectory was thoroughly cottagey in feeling and appearance.

Outside space was too limited to allow for landscaping or extensive formal gardens. There was a sloped grass lawn, a small formal garden with a sundial, and to one side of the house, chestnut, fir, and elm trees. A kitchen garden with vegetable and strawberry beds, yard, dairy, and outhouses were where most of the activity took place. Chickens and ducks ran through the yard, and a newly fitted dairy housed a bull and six cows. Just beyond the garden lay fields where George Austen grew crops of oats, barley, and wheat. In June, everyone in the household, children included, was involved in haymaking, and in August there was the harvest to collect. All of life was tightly packed into a matter of three floors and a few acres.

Lymington was his parent's first child, but by the time he left Hurstbourne Park for Steventon he had two younger sisters, Urania-Annabella (born 1769) and Camilla-Mary (born 8 November 1770), and now a baby brother, Newton (born 26 June 1772). As the oldest sibling, he may have felt some pride, mixed with an understandable degree of nerves, as the first to leave home. While he was George Austen's only pupil at Steventon in June 1773, he had the rector's own children to keep him company. George and Cassandra Austen had three of their sons living at home when Lymington arrived. James was eight years old, Edward was five, and the two-year-old Henry had returned from his nurse the previous autumn. Cassandra, the couple's youngest child, who had been born that January, had been sent out to a local nurse in April. Jane, her famous sister, did not make her entry into the Steventon household until December 1775.

Lymington had come to be educated, and there was every indication that the Austens would provide him with a fine start in life. George Austen taught his pupils the classics, preparing them for later education at public school and university. George was fond of literature, and when he retired to Bath and auctioned his books, they numbered more than five hundred in total. The books in his library had been bought to be read, not just displayed. Their subjects were diverse, and reflected his wide interests beyond theology and the classics. He had a globe, which he used for teaching, and a microscope through which Lymington could study the wonders of the natural world. Austen was the kind of cultured man of whom Coulson Fellowes, Lymington's grandfather, would have approved.[1]

Mrs Austen did not offer Lymington any of the formal schooling for which his parents were paying, yet it is difficult to see how she could not have had an influence upon him. Her appearance was unremarkable; as described by her granddaughter, Anna, she was 'a little, slight woman, with fine, well-cut features, large grey eyes, and good eyebrows, but without any brightness of complexion'. Cassandra's family background, however, meant that at first she felt more at ease with her aristocratic pupil than her husband did. She came from a family of wealthy clergymen, the Leighs, and her mother was connected to the Oxfordshire family of Perrot. Proud of her family's history, she believed that the distinctive shape of her nose bore witness to her aristocratic roots.

She also placed a high value on education. Many of her family were Oxford academics, and her uncle, Theophilus Leigh, was Master of Balliol for fifty years. Brains were part of her inheritance, and she was undoubtedly a clever woman. She loved to write letters and read, and her keen sense of humour meant that she enjoyed composing witty verses, some of which she addressed to her husband's pupils. Cassandra laughed about her 'own sprack wit', an old phrase meaning 'a lively perception of the characters and foibles of others'; nothing passed her by.[2] She was sharp and, with a growing family and household to manage, well organized. She took to supervising her domestic tasks with enthusiasm. Bread was baked, beer was brewed at home, and the dairy kept her busy year-round. Outside, she was a hands-on gardener, enjoying time in her vegetable patch, and the challenge of finding recipes and ways of cooking the potatoes she loved to grow.

As his pupil was only five years old, Mr Austen concentrated on teaching and perfecting Lymington's rudimentary knowledge of reading and writing. As a clergyman, he also hoped to instil into his pupil a religious understanding and appreciation. As well as attending weekly services in Austen's church, Lymington witnessed at first hand the operation of a household with a strong sense of Christian duty and charity to their less fortunate neighbours.

Even if he was too young to be aware of it, beyond the church and schoolroom was where the Austens offered Lymington his most important lessons for life. Both Mr and Mrs Austen were involved in the running of their farm, dairy, and garden, and Lymington was expected to play his part in helping to tend, feed, manage, and gather agricultural produce and animals. As an adult, Lymington often appeared most at ease when he was outside in the fields and with his workers. It was in his early days with the Austens that this love of the outside was first nurtured.

Lymington also had other children with whom to play. After lessons were over, there was playtime a plenty in the Austen family. The eight-year-old James Austen was the big brother who Lymington would never have, and a role model to follow. The precocious James had yet to start composing the plays that in later years took place in the family's barn, but his love of words and story-telling made him an entertaining and captivating companion. Away from his two younger sisters and baby brother, Lymington also had Edward Austen, who was just two months older than him, to be a friend. As boys they were encouraged to play outside, where the children rolled down the grassy bank, climbed trees, and explored the country lanes near their home. It was boisterous, physical, and often competitive play. As the autumn approached, and the days became shorter, the Austen children listened to their mother or father read by the fire, played indoor games such as cards and charades, and even practised their dancing steps. It was free time spent together as a family.

Mrs Austen was pleased with the new member of their household. Soon after his arrival in June 1773, she wrote to her sister-in-law that 'Jemmy and Neddy are very happy in a new Play-fellow, Lord Lymington'.[3] George Austen needed to take in pupils to support the modest income he received as rector, and was able to charge the Portsmouths a good amount to tutor their son. Some wives might have resented this economic necessity, and the burden of taking care of another child, especially when the youngest of their own children was barely six months old. But Cassandra was ever the optimist, and immediately saw Lymington as more than a financial asset. He could occupy her two boys, and provide them with fun and pleasure. That, in her view, was what childhood was all about.

In the back of Cassandra's mind was also a painful memory of the first child she and her husband had taken as a pupil, the seven-year-old George Hastings. The boy had been born in India in 1757, the son of Warren Hastings, future Governor-General of Bengal. He was sent to England following the death of his mother, and in 1764 was recommended to the newly married Austens by George Austen's sister, Philadelphia. Cassandra and George were then living at Deane rectory while their home in Steventon was renovated. Cassandra was twenty-four years old, and quickly grew attached to little Hastings. But in the autumn tragedy struck, and the boy died of a 'putrid sore throat' (diphtheria). His father only learned of his death when he arrived in England the following June. The boy had died in Cassandra's home, and under her watch. She told others that 'his death had been as great a grief to her as if he had been a child of her own'.[4] A few months later, Cassandra's first child, James, was born and occupied her thoughts. But the experience of George Hastings had taught her of the fragility of child health, as well as the rewards of child care. Lymington was the first boy to be tutored by George Austen since Hastings. He and Cassandra were determined to do right by this child. And when Lymington needed affection, Cassandra was ready to give it.

For Lymington, the contrast between Mrs Austen and his own mother could not be greater. Mrs Austen had an ordered home and well-behaved children. As she told her sister-in-law, she liked the fact that Lymington was 'good temper'd and orderly'.[5] He was no threat to her way of doing things. Yet she achieved this in a less controlling and rigid way than Lady Portsmouth. She was at ease with herself and her role as wife and mother, and prepared to let her children be themselves and develop at their own pace. Muddy shoes, rough and tumble, and the odd accident in the yard did not ruffle her.

Lady Portsmouth was of an entirely different school of parenting. Twenty years later, when her young nephews had an unexpected school break from Winchester and stayed with her at Hurstbourne

Park, she wrote to her brother to reassure him that they were no trouble. 'We feel no sort of inconvenience,' she explained to their father:

> They are so mild, that they are to be seen, but not heard, save only when an answer is required, and that always given with great natural civility and propriety...I do think them very pleasant boys, not disposed to be running about anywhere.[6]

For Lymington's mother, manners were everything. Children were a potential disturbance, liable to disrupt the propriety of the adult world. They should be taught 'to be seen, but not heard'. Their conversation, even their presence, had nothing to offer. Children and parents should have separate lives, according to Lady Portsmouth. It was her nephews' silence, and their ordered conduct that made them 'valuable youths'.

When she was in her mid-seventies, one of Lymington's sisters, Henrietta Dorothea, wrote a letter to Eveline, the 5th countess of Portsmouth, in which she described the childhood she shared with her brothers (including Lymington) and sisters at Hurstbourne Park. Hurstbourne had no flower gardens, she explained, but the kitchen garden and range of glasshouses 'were magnificent'. However, as children they were not allowed to walk in this garden, or enter the glasshouses without their parents. It was only when they were attended by a governess or 'my mother's maid' that the children could walk in the 'pleasure ground'. Times had changed since then, Henrietta Dorothea acknowledged, and 'this will make you smile the regime being somewhat close but I know now it was wise and kind – altho' my volatile spirits bobbed a bit for less restraint'.

Henrietta Dorothea had to wait for adulthood to escape this 'close regime', where children could not walk (let alone run) outside without strict supervision. But his time with the Austen family gave Lymington his first taste of freedom. The Austens' home and grounds may have been much smaller than Hurstbourne Park, but the atmosphere was altogether less claustrophobic. Having arrived at the start of summer, he could run, play, and explore with two other boys, uninhibited by the presence of any adult. Joining the closely knit Austen family, he could feel supported, rather than stifled. While the children at Steventon were expected to show respect for their elders, there was none of that stiff formality between parents and children that existed in the Portsmouth family. Mr and Mrs Austen took pleasure in their children, and, when their work and duties allowed, joined in the fun. Henrietta Dorothea felt obliged to defend her 'Mother's management of things,' saying that it was 'graceful in her rank and most strickly [sic] supported by Christian influences'. Lady Portsmouth's style of motherhood was appropriate to her social position, and governed by her moral principles. But whether it left her children happy, Henrietta Dorothea did not say.[7]

Lymington's mother can hardly have approved of all that outdoor playtime, and her personality was so different from Mrs Austen that they were unlikely to have ever agreed about how children should be raised. So the choice of the Austen family to tutor the Portsmouth's eldest son and heir might seem surprising. There were plenty of other clergy families within a short distance of Hurstbourne Park who could have offered lessons and lodging. Why the Austens?

The Portsmouths would have been ready with an answer: Reverend Barton Wallop, Lymington's godfather and his father's brother, was friendly with George Austen. Barton was rector of Upper Wallop, a nearby Hampshire village. The friendship between the Austens and this branch of the Wallop family was long lasting, and, when Barton's daughter married the elderly Reverend Henry Wake in 1813, Jane Austen wrote a humorous poem about the couple.[8]

Family connections may have been important, but the experiment of sending a boy from the Portsmouth family to the Austens was not repeated with any of Lymington's other brothers. Lymington was a special case, and he was already receiving different treatment from his siblings. For the Portsmouths had a growing suspicion that all was not right with their oldest child. The real reason why the Austens were selected was that they shared a family problem.

Friends talk, and it is just possible that Barton knew more about Cassandra's family than even she was prepared to admit publicly. When he came to Steventon in the summer of 1773, Lymington met only three of Cassandra and George Austen's four sons. Their second eldest son, also called George, turned seven years old in August 1773, but had not lived regularly at home since he was four years old. He suffered from epileptic fits, and may have had problems communicating (this could be why his sister Jane learned sign language). Reverend and Mrs Austen both mentioned their son in letters. 'I am much obliged to you for your kind wish of George's improvement. God knows only how far it will come to pass,' wrote Reverend Austen in July 1770. 'Be it as it may,' he concluded with Christian resignation, 'he cannot be a bad or wicked child.'

Cassandra had her hopes raised when George did not have fits for nearly twelve months, but then cruelly dashed when they reoccurred. 'My poor little George is come to see me today,' she reported in December 1770.[9] For Cassandra, the problems of her son were a cruel reminder of the sufferings that had been inflicted on her younger brother, Thomas Leigh. His mind had never developed beyond a childish state and he remained what we would regard as mentally disabled all his life.

The Austens, then, were a couple who knew the pain and the difficulty of having a child who was not normal. How much the Portsmouths told the Austens about their son and their concerns before he arrived at Steventon we do not know. Possibly they said nothing, not wishing to prejudice their opinion before they met Lymington, and in order to test the Austens' reaction. But Reverend and Mrs Austen recognized the warning signs when they saw them. While many boys would have struggled to compete with the remaining Austen children in the intelligence stakes, especially with the quick-witted James, it was evident to Cassandra that, aged five, Lymington was already way behind. As she told her sister-in-law, Lord Lymington is 'very backward of his Age'. He was not developing as he should. Bitter experience meant that Cassandra was likely to be kind and sympathetic towards Lymington, while Reverend Austen's view of his own troubled son made him an understanding tutor. If Lymington got things wrong, it was not his fault; he could not be 'bad or wicked'.[10]

Though Mrs Austen's approach to mothering was in so many ways different from Lady Portsmouth's, for at least a short time both women followed the same course of action towards their troubling children.

They sent them away. They let others do the caring. 'Poor little George' was eventually housed with his disabled uncle in the village of Monk Sherborne, on the other side of Basingstoke. He was probably looked after by the Culham (or Cullum) family, for it was a member of this family who signed his death certificate in January 1838. He lived until he was seventy-two years old.[11]

If the Portsmouth family knew about these circumstances, then they would also have been reassured that the Austens would be discreet when caring for Lymington. After all, they placed considerable trust in the Austens. Talk of Lymington's emerging problems would have done untold damage to the Portsmouth's family reputation, but would have also discredited the Austens. Whether Lymington was visited by his parents when he stayed at Steventon we do not know. Given the sensitive nature of his case, it is unlikely that any letters were written between the two families. News of Lymington's progress (or lack thereof) was probably by word of mouth.

The Austen family perfected the art of secrecy when it came to family problems. After their two brief mentions of him in 1770, George Austen never featured again in his parents' letters. Realizing that their family was destined to be famous, their daughter Cassandra destroyed many of their letters following her sister Jane's death. If Jane, or any other member of her family, had ever mentioned the disabled George in their letters, they did not survive. Monk Sherborne was near to Sherborne St John where James, George's elder brother, was rector until his death in 1819. So perhaps James visited George and his uncle. Certainly, the Austen family made financial provisions for the two men. But otherwise they were excluded from the family circle. The silencing of this aspect of the Austens' family history was continued by later biographers, who simply erased George from the family tree.[12]

Unlike 'poor little George', Lymington was destined to inherit a title and vast wealth. The future of the Portsmouth family rested with him. If the Austens confirmed her worst fears about her son, then Lady Portsmouth knew she needed to act fast if there was any hope of remedy. Lymington never forgot his time at Steventon and the kindness of the Austens. In later life, their paths crossed again. But staying with the Austens long term was not an option.

'Alarm'd at the Hesitation
in his speech'

IMPEDIMENTS in SPEECH effectually cured by CHARLES ANGIER, in Wardour-street, opposite St Anne's-court, Soho, as can be attested by persons of the most reputable characters, who have been cured by him, people of known probity and honour. He does not desire his fee till what he undertakes is performed. He undertakes children of almost any age, who may be taught at the same time several branches of education.[1]

B Y THE AUTUMN of 1773, Lady Portsmouth knew her eldest son was not like other five-year-olds. The Austens had sounded the alarm bells: Lymington was a slow learner, and, most troubling of all, he was not talking in a normal manner. He had a 'hesitation in his speech', according to Mrs Austen, which was getting worse. Speech was the foundation stone for the rest of life. Schooling still depended upon oral repetition of everything from Latin verbs to times-tables, and, later in life, fluency in speech would be vital for Lymington's public roles as a Hampshire aristocrat. He had to learn to speak well.

The advertisements placed by Charles Angier in a number of newspapers throughout 1773 leapt out to Lady Portsmouth as beacons of hope. While perfecting the art of public speaking, or rhetoric, had long been held in esteem, and was an academic subject at university, correcting speech faults was relatively unknown in the eighteenth century. Speech therapy as we understand it did not exist and Charles Angier did not suffer from competitors in his field. But, in such uncharted waters, Lady Portsmouth did not want to be taken for a fool. The medical marketplace was awash with quacks and fraudsters who were all too ready to take patients' money in return for remedies that stood no chance of curing their complaints. Before she placed her confidence in Charles Angier, she needed to check his credentials.

Much of Angier's credibility, she discovered, derived from his father, Samuel. In the mid-eighteenth century, Samuel Angier spotted a business opportunity that was to be the origins of a family business. In a society in which polite manners and conversation were thought to distinguish the best from the rest, knowing how to speak appropriately became a key asset. Presentation was all: delivery was almost as important as content. Correct pronunciation, tone, countenance, and gesture while speaking commanded respect.

Here was Samuel's chance. Nobody was born knowing how to speak effectively, but he could teach the 'arts' of speaking to 'great perfection'. Rather than laying the blame of speech 'impediments, low voices, disagreeable tones, etc' on 'the badness of the organs, or weakness of the constitution', as others had done, he could demonstrate that these proceeded 'entirely from the irregular playing [of] some of the instruments of that art'. In other words, speech problems did not arise from physiological faults, but from bad habits. By practising and following the rules of speech that Samuel laid down, anyone might 'become an elegant speaker in a very short time'.[2]

Samuel realized that, while speaking with ease was desirable in polite society, it was a necessity for some professions, particularly for clergymen who had to deliver sermons, and barristers whose oral skills were vital for the defence of their clients. He started advertising his services directly to these professionals, wrote a pamphlet addressed to clergy on public speaking, and in 1751 achieved a remarkable coup by being permitted to deliver his lectures on pronunciation to the University of Cambridge.[3]

Samuel had not had a university education, but he gave his lectures five times in Master's Lodges and Senior Combination Rooms of

Cambridge colleges. In his audience were 'many Heads of Colleges, besides several Doctors both of Divinity and Physick, together with Professors, Masters of Arts, Fellows of Colleges'; these were the promising gentlemen of his generation. It was not difficult to understand the popularity of his lectures. He was playing to the insecurity of his audience: who would not want to learn how to present their ideas and arguments more effectively, or miss the chance of picking up a few tips that might give them the edge over their academic rivals? The delivery of Samuel's lectures was itself a test of his skill, but his audience apparently 'shew'd him a great deal of respect, and attended closely' to what he said. One Cambridge professor who simply attended the lectures, and another bachelor who saw Samuel privately for four consultations, were said to have 'alter'd so much for the better in their manner of reading publicly, as to surprise all their friends'. The Cambridge visit was such an important endorsement of Samuel's methods and ideas that his son, Charles, was still boasting about it ten years later.[4]

By the time Lady Portsmouth spotted Charles Angier's advertisements, Samuel had been dead for at least twelve years, but, on the back of his father's success, Charles had built a reputation of his own. He had been his father's assistant, inherited his manuscripts, and followed his no-nonsense approach. Like his father, he believed that, with the right tools and training, everybody could acquire the 'mechanical art' of speech. Furthermore, he thought that childhood was the best time to learn how to speak well. It was in childhood, Charles later explained, that any 'disorder was less fixed, and the docility of mind, irritability and contractibility of muscles, were greater'. If parents acted in time, faults could be corrected because children's minds and bodies were more pliable than in later life. Parents needed to take action before it was too late, argued Charles, because speech problems could hinder other areas of children's development. 'Impediments in Speech', ran one of his advertisements in January 1772, 'frequently prevent Children improving in several Branches of Education, as well as cramp and deject their Spirits.' Predating any language of psychology, Charles was nevertheless fully switched on to the emotional consequences of speech problems.

Without correction, he recognized that children would be left strug
gling to learn and could become painfully demoralized.[5]

Charles Angier was a perfect match for Lady Portsmouth's needs.
He took a positive view of the origins of speech problems, and he was
confident of his ability to fix them. So much so that could claim 'he
does not desire his fee till what he undertakes is performed'. He
promised results in a short time. 'Several Persons can assert that they
could speak plain, when they had been with him but two Hours', he
advertised shortly after his father's death. With experience, and no
doubt with an eye to the profits that could be made if treatment took
longer, his optimism was tempered, and he began to argue that a
two-month residential stay was most likely to yield results. He offered
'genteel accommodations' within his home, from his wife a mother
substitute for his young charges, and the continuation of children's
other 'branches of education' by himself, or by their nominated tutors.
This complete package, he assured parents, was all available at a very
reasonable price.[6]

On 12 December 1773, Mrs Austen wrote to tell her sister-in-law
that 'Ld. Lymington has left us'. 'His mamma,' she explained, 'began
to be alarm'd at the Hesitation in his Speech, which certainly grew
worse, and is going to take him to London in hopes a Mr Angier
(who undertakes to cure that Disorder) may be of Service to him.' It
was the last time Mrs Austen made mention of Lymington, who had
spent about six months in their home.[7]

At approaching six years old, Lymington was exactly the age that
Charles Angier thought best to begin instruction. Removed from the
comfort of the Austen family, the trip to see Mr Angier was probably
Lymington's first visit to London. It seems very likely, although we
have no positive proof that he stayed with Angier at his address, 99
Wardour Street, Soho. From the rural village of Steventon, Lymington
was thrust into the heart of urban life. Wardour Street was all noise,
smell, and bustle. Angier's rented house formed a pair with number
97 and John Tallis's illustration of it in 1838–40 shows it as a four-
storey home that was three windows wide.[8] It was a large dwelling,
but attached to another house and cheek by jowl with its neighbours.
Other residents in the street were grocers, carpenters, ironmongers,

upholsters, and builders. This was an area of London unfamiliar to most people of Lymington's social standing, and far removed from the streets and squares that he would come to know as an adult. For Lady Portsmouth, this was precisely its attraction: she and her son were unlikely to bump into people who mattered when visiting Angier. Lymington could be treated anonymously.

Lymington presented Angier with a challenge. Unlike many of his other clients, Lymington's mother was not consulting Angier for help to improve or polish her son's speech, but to teach him the more basic skills of forming and articulating words. Lady Portsmouth was a demanding woman, who wanted to see results, but also a desperately worried mother. To cure Lymington of his speech problems would give Angier a tremendous boost, even if his client's wish for confidentiality would mean that Lymington joined the long list of nameless individuals of 'known probity and honour' who had been assisted by him.

According to Angier's later treatise on the subject, hesitation in speech could be caused by an impediment in the lips, tongue, or throat, or a mix of the three. The problem might only surface when the individual sufferer tried to say a word beginning with a particular letter or sound. But, as a person with a stammer tried to speak, they presented a horrifying appearance. Flushing from a 'stagnation of Blood', they could suffer from a 'distortion of the Eyes', a struggling for breath, and an 'uneasiness in the Chest'. Sometimes sufferers had their throat open, and breath repeatedly taken in for so long that it could be ten minutes before they uttered a single word. All these symptoms would 'painfully convulse the Sufferer, and endanger Health'. In the meantime, they were individuals who were unpleasant both to hear and to see.[9]

We do not know what Lymington looked like when he spoke, but we can be sure that his mother wanted to cure him of such an un-attractive complaint. Likewise, we do not have direct evidence of how Angier treated Lymington, or indeed, any of his other clients. His cures were a trade secret that he and his father had perfected over many years. Charles probably followed his father's practice, as experienced by the philosopher and clergyman Joseph Priestley. When

Priestley consulted Samuel Angier for his stammer, he was made to take 'an oath not to reveal his method'. It was a promise that Priestley did not break even many years later when he wrote his memoirs.[10]

But we can tell what Angier did not do. Taking over his father's business in 1761, Charles was keen to state that his father had cured, 'not by those unnatural Methods which many are afraid of...For some have girted the Body to force out the Words by Violence; others teach them to speak in a doleful Manner, which always strain the Lungs'. Neither Samuel nor Charles followed these techniques. There is no evidence either that Lymington's speech problems were treated with bleeding. Nor did he suffer the blistering treatment administered to poor Samuel Johnson to cure him of his speechlessness following his stroke in June 1783.[11]

Fortunately for the young Lymington, Angier did not pursue any of these terrifying cures because they did not fit with his ideas of the origins of speech problems. Physical force or techniques designed to correct the imbalance of the body's humours would do nothing to correct bad habits. It is from Angier's ideas about the causes of speech impediments that we can surmise his methods. These were likely to be behavioural, and governed the 'rules' that Samuel laid down, and Charles adopted. Lymington probably underwent a kind of oral retraining, in which Angier encouraged him to correct the position of his lips, tongue, and mouth. Breathing and voice exercises taught him to manage his breath as he spoke, and use his vocal muscles efficiently. Perhaps he practised in front of a mirror making different sounds and faces, and was given tongue twisters and phrases to repeat. Angier may have tried to increase Lymington's self-confidence by encouraging him to believe that he had the ability to overcome his stammer. After all, once learned, many of these exercises were 'take-home' cures that could be practised alone, and revived if the problem reoccurred. In his publications, Angier could never resist mentioning Demosthenes, the ancient Greek statesman and orator who overcame the speech impediment he suffered as a boy by daily practice of oral exercises and hard perseverance. He was the Greek hero and obvious role model for Angier to use in his teaching of the six-year-old Lymington.[12]

Whatever Angier tried, it does not seem to have worked, at least in the long term. A number of witnesses in the legal trials that Lymington faced as an adult, when he held the title Lord Portsmouth, commented upon his speech. They included Thomas France, a lawyer who had known Portsmouth from his youth. Lord Portsmouth had 'an impediment in his speech,' he explained, 'a hesitation and stammering'. The impediment meant that it took longer than normal for him to answer questions. It was a 'natural and a permanent impediment', but it 'did not always exist to the same extent'. 'It became more observable when his Lordship was flurried: when he was at ease it was often hardly perceptible: but there was always a hesitation in his speaking.'[13]

Like others, France probably did not know that Lymington had been taken to see Angier. But the reason why witnesses were asked about Portsmouth's speech may have been related to Angier's failure to cure him. In eighteenth- and nineteenth-century Britain, there was enormous uncertainty and division of opinion about how to interpret stammering. Speech defects such as stammering were attributed to a variety of causes, and some of these were linked to mental development. On the one hand, stammering was seen as an indicator of extreme sensitivity, and a fault of genius, as exhibited by such notable individuals as Priestley, Charles Kingsley, and Martin Tupper. Samuel Angier did not cure Priestley of his stammer, but nobody ever questioned Priestley's intellectual capacity.

But, on the other hand, as listeners waited interminably for the stammerer to get their words out, it could be tempting to believe that a person who found speaking such a problem was in some way mentally deficient. Why else would they find a straightforward human action so difficult? Statistics seemed to support this view: as lunatics were collected in the growing number of asylums across the country, observers noted a higher incidence of stammering in their populations than outside their walls.[14] Were Lymington's problems speaking evidence of his mental weakness?

If Lymington's speech impediments were a symptom of a diseased brain, then Angier had no hope of curing him using his methods. Indeed, Angier and his father had but one qualification to their claims of offering a certain cure: they would take on 'any Person, except an Idiot'. Speaking may have been a 'mechanical Art', but people were not machines, and they needed to have sufficient presence of mind to understand how to correct their faults and be empowered to control their speech. Utterance, explained Charles Angier, 'is an Embellishment that adorns and sets off the Powers, and Accomplishments of the Mind': it was the means by which ideas and thoughts were communicated.[15] But if the mind remained underdeveloped, or became corrupted, then no amount of remedial speech education could help to counter its problems. Angier dared not turn away a son of a wealthy aristocrat, but how soon did he become aware that his treatments might not work for this boy, and was he ever prepared to admit this to his parents?

As Lord Portsmouth, Lymington found that his speech attracted attention, and added to suspicion about his mental state. Elizabeth James, a family friend of Portsmouth's second wife, had heard many rumours about Portsmouth before she met him. But when she did so, 'she did not find him so weak a Man as from previous report she had been led to believe'. He was 'remarkably polite and well bred'. 'If it had not been for a great hesitation in his Lordship's speech he might have passed exceedingly well in society,' she concluded. In her view, his stammer was the only thing that made Portsmouth stand out. It separated him from the rest.[16]

While others found having a speech impediment personally devastating, we have no evidence of how Portsmouth himself felt about this problem. However, there may be clues in another area of vocal expression: his singing. Portsmouth sang out of tune and time. Perhaps, like his younger sister, Henrietta Dorothea, who suffered from serious hearing problems when she was in her twenties, Portsmouth was tone deaf. It is also possible that Portsmouth's speech and singing difficulties stemmed from some fault with his hearing, although this seems unlikely. Lady Portsmouth wrote many letters expressing concern about her daughter, Henrietta Dorothea, but never linked her eldest son's problems to this cause.[17] Nor in all the years that Portsmouth was examined by physicians was there ever any mention of a fault with his hearing.

Nevertheless, when Portsmouth sang, he made an extraordinary noise. The rudest interpretation of the sound he made was given by John Godden, for over forty years the park keeper at Hurstbourne. Portsmouth fooled around with his farm workers at harvest time, Godden said, and start singing psalms. He sang them 'in a strange way: it was no more singing than a Bull's bellowing'. His singing in the church at Acton left the young girls in stitches of laughter, complained their school mistress. On occasion, even the church minister at Hurstbourne was reduced to laughter when he heard Portsmouth sing.

Most people would have been embarrassed and stopped singing, but not Lord Portsmouth. He enjoyed singing, and sang loudly. When he asked the school mistress why her girls were laughing, and she told him that it was 'because they were not attentive', he was 'satisfied'. He was the victim of humour, but he was blissfully oblivious to the fact.[18]

So, as with his singing, Portsmouth could have been unaware that his speech problems invited, as Angier put it, the 'uneasiness or pity, and too often the mockery and ridicule' of others. But this apparent lack of emotional response also condemned Portsmouth in the eyes of others. It showed an absence of feeling and sensitivity. A man who had so little self-awareness (or what we would term self-consciousness) was not normal.

He might have been spared the pain and embarrassment experienced by many of those who suffered from a stammer, but, when Lymington left Angier to be sent to school, he could not escape the attention of others. Having been sheltered and closeted by the Austens and then afforded the individual care provided by Angier, this would be Lymington's first step into the wider world. Special education had ended, and it now had to be seen how Lymington would fare alongside other boys in the schoolroom and playground.

'The laughing stock of the school'

IN 1775, WHEN he was seven years old, Lymington was sent to Odiham Grammar School, some twenty-five miles from Hurstbourne Park. He boarded there for the next seven or eight years, coming home for the school holidays, and was in due course joined at this school by his younger brothers, Newton and Coulson. Odiham was a quiet country place, later described by William Cobbett in his iconic *Rural Rides* as a 'nice little plain market-town'. The school there had opened in 1694, following the instructions contained in the will of Robert May, a local mercer. Some boys had their education paid for by May's benefaction, and were then apprenticed. A surviving list of pupils shows that forty-one boys received their schooling in this way between 1763 and 1787. Other boys, including Lymington and his brothers, were fee-paying, and by 1788 the charge was twenty guineas per year.

Odiham offered the typical grammar school education of the time, and, if required, the first step before public school and university. Advertisements in 1788 and 1789 declared that, at the school, 'young gentlemen are genteely boarded and tenderly treated', and 'taught the Classics, English, Writing and Accompts [maths] in all their Branches, the Use of Globes, etc etc.' By 1788, the headmaster was Reverend Jeston, but in Lymington's time the school was run by Reverend Benjamin Webb.[1]

Judging from the occupations of some of Lymington's school fellows, who went on to be tradesmen, surgeons, and barristers, those who needed an education so that they could earn a living when they grew older were well served by their time at Odiham. Whether Lymington was 'tenderly treated' by Reverend Webb we do not know, but the reminiscences of his fellow pupils show that the conduct of other boys was far from kind.

This was Lymington's first exposure to the world outside the narrow confines of Hurstbourne Park and the homes of Austen and Angier. He needed to show that he could stand on his own two feet, and in the schoolroom and playground defend himself when put to the test by boys who cared little for his title or status. But Lymington's failure to fit in made such an impression that, nearly fifty years later, other pupils at Odiham still remembered how he had behaved and been regarded.

Richard Bishop, for example, who later counted Lymington as one of his customers in the drapery shop he set up in Whitchurch, recalled first getting to know Lymington when they were both pupils at Odiham some forty-seven years earlier. Lymington was 'a big boy', about four years older than Bishop, who was in his final years of education at Odiham when Bishop joined the school. Bishop thought of Lymington, as all the other boys did, as 'a boy nearly void of all understanding'. 'He was the laughing stock of the school,' said Bishop, 'by reason of his singularly foolish silly ways and antics: the boys jeered him and ridiculed him as being a fool.' In the competitive environment of a boys' school, Lymington was an easy target. Even a boy who was struggling to learn could take comfort from the fact that he could do better than Lymington. Lymington might have been taught Latin, 'and used to stand up in a class with other boys' to recite their lessons, but, according to Bishop, this 'was only a matter of form', for Lymington 'certainly did not and could not learn as other boys did'. His 'very dull understanding' made this an impossibility, argued another former pupil. His stupidity was such that Latin verses were given to him 'which were full of nonsense', a fact that 'he himself was not able to discover'.[2]

To be a poor scholar was one matter, and in a boys' school this might have been forgotten and even forgiven if Lymington had shown himself to be physically strong and courageous. But he was a 'great coward'. 'Any small boy by holding his little fist' up at Lymington 'would frighten him and make him cry as though he was going to be half killed.' He was a cry baby who was 'the object of ridicule and the butt of the school', remembered John Bishop (possibly Richard's older brother). Night times afforded Lymington no escape from this mockery. He had 'so little sense of propriety that it was a common practice with him to dirty, not only wet but foul, his bed and clothes'. Here was a boy who had no control over his bodily functions, and locked into habits that most children outgrew. He was a 'big boy' to Richard Bishop, but he was still a baby in every other way. Perhaps his misery was shown by his persistent bed-wetting, but his fouling of himself was seen as beyond the pale. It showed a lack of 'propriety', or sense of acceptable behaviour. It could neither be hidden nor excused.

Who would want to be a friend to such a boy? Most children of Lymington's age longed to belong, to be accepted as part of a group, and even to be admired. Peer recognition was as important then as it is now. But there was no hope of this for Lymington. 'He seldom associated with any of the other boys or joined in their sports,' recalled John Bishop. No doubt he was the boy left on his own in the playground, shunned by the others. 'He was very timid,' said William Lovett, who was at school with Lymington for about three years.[3]

Timid here might well mean shy. There was little chance of Lymington developing his confidence or social skills in these circumstances. Of the half-a-dozen or so witnesses who later gave testimony about Lymington's school days, none said that they had been his friend. He had already become an outsider. Rejected by his school fellows, he sought other companionship. He 'had a propensity to low company', remembered one former pupil. For instance, he 'was in the habit of going to a low hovel to eat bacon and greens with a carrier of the name of Tom Boddy'. Off the school premises, perhaps Lymington found that he could relax and be himself, but he could not escape the censure of his fellow pupils. Did they follow him there one day, or did gossip about his meetings reach the school gates? Teasing him for meeting Boddy, the boys 'used to laugh at him to shame his Lordship out of it'. Mixing with the local 'low-life' was out of the question for most aspiring young boys.[4]

Yet for all Lymington's difficulties and peculiarities, none of his school fellows was prepared to declare that he exhibited the mind or behaviour of an 'idiot'. An idiot was a person who had so little reason, and whose mind was so underdeveloped that no amount of schooling would make a difference to their understanding. As a doctor who later examined Lymington explained, 'idiots cannot be acted upon by any impressions at all, still less is there the power of will, memory, and judgement'. Neither this doctor nor Lymington's school fellows thought he fitted this category. As John Bishop declared, although he thought Lymington's mind was 'uncommonly weak', he was 'not an idiot for he kept himself out of the way of harm and acquired some little education'. 'He was bordering upon idiotism,' thought former pupil Mr Vernon, but his common sense and ability to learn (albeit limited) prevented his acquaintances from being absolutely certain about how to label him.[5]

Lymington was already proving himself an enigma. While he fell far behind his peers in most subjects, he was uncommonly able at arithmetic. Giles King Lyford, a Winchester surgeon who would count Jane Austen as one of his patients, was at Odiham School for two years with Lymington. He remembered Lymington 'was considered to be a very good Arithmetician'. He 'well recollects' how Lymington 'was held up as an example by the Writing and Cyphering Master to the rest of the boys on account of his Lordship's quickness at figures'. Cyphering, or number work, was to prove a strength of Lymington's for the rest of his life. Lyford said Lymington was 'as sharp as any boy at a bargain, and could not be easily prevailed upon to part with his money'. Once his pocket money days were over, it was noted that he could spot errors on his estate accounts, complain about the high cost of a hotel bill as he settled it, and drive a hard bargain over the purchase of horses.[6]

His ability at figures could throw any attempt to prove him an idiot or insane off course. In July 1821, when Lymington (then Lord Portsmouth) was fifty-three years old, and facing a legal test of his sanity in the Chancery court, it was represented to the Lord Chancellor that he 'could not add five figures, by five'. In a comical, yet humiliating repetition of his school days, Portsmouth 'was obliged to go through' his sums in front of the Chancellor. It turned out that Portsmouth 'happened to be a better arithmetician than the Chancellor, for he did it very well, and I did it very ill', admitted Lord Eldon. Indeed, one witness to the occasion claimed that Eldon slipped up, and made a mistake, which Portsmouth corrected. The Lord Chancellor suitably humbled, was left wondering what else was 'not true' about what he had been told concerning Portsmouth's 'state of mind'?[7]

With this kind of ability, surely Lymington could not be called a fool? Mental arithmetic was not his only skill. According to Richard Bishop, at school Lymington 'learned to write, and made more proficiency in writing than in anything else'.[8] As an adult, writing letters would enable Lymington to manage the estate he would eventually inherit from his father, and give him a form of self-expression in the personal correspondence he sent to other family members. Surviving letters written by him show a clear and steady hand, and consistent spelling.

More remarkable than his writing, however, was his memory. When Dr Lyford met Lymington twenty years after they had been at school together, he recognized him by his unusual-looking eye, but Lymington went one better, and remembered Lyford's name. His good memory also meant that Lymington, then Lord Portsmouth, always asked after his acquaintances' children by their names. To doctors specializing in madness, this was proof that Portsmouth was not an idiot. 'Imbecility, idiotcy, has no memory', Dr Warburton declared. But 'memory may consist with lunacy…a lunatic may recollect'. As astonishing as Portsmouth's memory might be, what he remembered, and how he remembered, could still leave his mind open to question. Portsmouth had a memory for 'trifles' such as people's names, but not for 'great and considerable circumstances'. He had a 'sort of instinctive memory', thought Reverend McCarthy, which absorbed information without processing it. As one lawyer put it, 'His lordship remembered no material or worthy impressions, but those things only which good sound memories contrived to lose and throw out.' In other words, he could not distinguish between types of knowledge, and had no judgement about what was important. A good memory was no proof of soundness of mind, even if it meant idiocy was unlikely.[9]

There was enough about Lymington in his school days to mean that former pupils were divided over whether this period revealed anything about the man he was to become. William Lovett, who became a barrister, perhaps came closest of all Lymington's acquaintances to becoming a friend after they left school. Lovett and his father paid social visits to Hurstbourne Park, often met Lymington at county events, and 'friendly recognitions took place between them and they sometimes walked about together' when they met. For Lovett, there was nothing extraordinary about Lymington's time at school. He 'went thro' the routine of education much in the same way as other boys', he said. Similarly, although Lymington was 'not considered a clever boy, but rather weak', Lyford thought that at school Lymington 'was as capable as any boy there, of conducting himself in the ordinary occurrences of life'. 'I don't remember that his Lordship was laughed at by the other boys,' he claimed on another occasion.[10]

Could Lyford have been so detached and unaware of all the teasing and taunting that others described? Or did the legal and media attention on Portsmouth encourage those who knew him as Lymington to think differently about the boy they had known? Did they attach significance to events and habits that at the time were brushed aside? The later legal trials in which they acted as witnesses were opportunities for men like the Bishops to take the stage and show how they had taken a part in Portsmouth's extraordinary life. Would a bit of exaggeration and embellishment be surprising in these circumstances? Whose account of Portsmouth's school days was the closest to the truth?

By May 1782, Lymington and his brother Newton had both left Odiham School and were being privately tutored by a Reverend Dr Kyte at his home in Hammersmith. Lymington was fourteen, and Newton a month short of ten years old. Away from the school environment, we do not have the memories of other pupils to tell us about Lymington's experiences. But there are the beautifully written letters from Newton to his parents.

The earliest surviving letter from Newton dates from June 1780, when he was at Odiham, and was formally addressed to his father, 'Dear and Hond Sir'. All subsequent letters were sent to his 'Dear

Mama'. Each page had pencil lines to ensure that the carefully written script remained well presented, and it is clear that early letters from Newton were as much exercises in handwriting as means of communication. Given Newton's eagerness to give his father and mother 'satisfaction by the attention I have paid to the several Branches of my Learning since I last saw you', it is possible that these letters from Odiham were checked over, or even dictated, by Reverend Webb.

By the time Newton and Lymington moved to Hammersmith, the content of his letters became less closely supervised, and glimpses of life in the Kyte household emerge. 'Lymington and myself have both had little Coughs but we are very well now,' reported Newton on 1 June 1782. A few weeks later, he thanked his mother for sending him some 'very neat, and pretty' waistcoats. Soon afterwards, a tailor came to measure Lymington and Newton for some clothes. An uncle and aunt (possibly William and Lavinia Fellowes, their mother's brother and sister-in-law) visited them. There was a Mrs Kyte (Newton always concluded his letters by saying that 'Dr and Mrs Kyte send compliments'), who had a baby girl in January 1785, and possibly other children with whom to play. According to Newton, both he and Lymington looked forward to their summer holidays at Hurstbourne, and wanted to know how their sisters did at home.[11]

Kyte clearly had a good reputation for he tutored the son of another aristocratic family, John Parker, who became 2nd Baron Boringdon and 1st earl of Morley, at the same time as Newton and Lymington. John Parker's boyhood letters also survive, although unfortunately he does not mention Newton or Lymington in his correspondence. John told his Uncle Fritz, 'I do like school very well.' Kyte knew how to nurture his pupils' imaginations and enthusiasm for learning. Each year he took his pupils to see the play from Terence or Plautus performed by boys from Westminster School. Newton and John Parker both eagerly anticipated the occasion. On 16 October 1784, Kyte allowed Newton to attend the balloon flight by Jean-Pierre Blanchard and John Sheldon from Chelsea's military academy. 'I am just returned from little Chelsea,' wrote Newton to his mother, with breathless excitement, 'where I saw Mr Blanchard and Mr Sheldon ascend into the air, with which I was very much pleased.'[12]

When Newton wrote this letter, Lymington was being tutored elsewhere. Newton wanted to know in December 1784 when his brother broke up for the holidays, and hoped his mother had heard news from him. As Newton reported that he was studying Virgil and that his class had 'finished our Greek Part Book' in March 1785, he expressed hope that 'Lymington was very well when you heard from him last'. Lymington was now seventeen years old, and Newton twelve. Why Lymington had been moved from Dr Kyte, and where he was now living, we do not know. We can be sure from Newton's letters that he was with Kyte at Hammersmith in July 1783, but his whereabouts by the autumn of the following year is a mystery.

We can be certain that he was not at Eton, the destination of both his younger brothers, Newton and Coulson. Eton was the finishing school for many aristocratic boys of this period, and the artist Richard Livesay was given the commission of a leaving picture for both boys. Livesay was living in neighbouring Windsor, and made a handsome living painting portraits of Etonians, some of which were exhibited at the Royal Academy. Livesay's portraits of the young Newton and Coulson show them serenely confident of their attainment and wealth. Newton with his dark locks and Coulson with his fair hair look improbably tidy and well ordered for young men, yet ready to take on the world.

With no Eton we have no portrait of Lymington at this age. The unusual appearance of his eyes, which was already visible to his school fellows at Odiham, perhaps gave his parents a ready excuse not to have his portrait commissioned. But facial features could be disguised, and it is more likely that the real reason why no artist was asked to paint Lymington was because he gave his mother and father no cause to celebrate. He gave them nothing to boast about.

There are no surviving schoolboy letters written by Lymington either. This could, of course, be accidental. A fire tore through Hurstbourne Park on 1 January 1891, destroying many of the family's papers, and it may be that Newton's letters were a chance survival from a larger collection of letters home. We know that Lymington could write letters, and, when he went ahead of Newton to Dr Kyte's in the autumn of 1781, he wrote at least one 'short letter' to his brother who was still at Odiham. We also have evidence that Lady Portsmouth wrote letters to Lymington when he was at Hammersmith. But in March 1782 he was willing to delegate the responsibility of a response to his brother, Newton. 'Lymington desires his Duty and thanks for your letter,' Newton wrote to their mother. There are no surviving letters from Lymington's youngest brother, Coulson, either. Newton's letters suggest that he became the spokesperson, and letter writer, for both brothers. 'Lymington and Coulson are both well and join me in Duty to Papa,' Newton wrote to his mother from Odiham in November 1780, for example. From a young age, Newton was assuming a special role in his family, and one that might usually be taken by the oldest son. Perhaps Lymington was thought too unreliable a witness and Coulson too young to report back to their parents. We do not know how far Newton was aware that his eldest brother was causing his parents to worry, but they were giving him a significant degree of responsibility as a result.

There is, of course, another explanation for the absence of letters from Lymington and his youngest brother; their mother destroyed them. Letters from Newton were treasured and kept safely. They had an emotional value for Lady Portsmouth because he became her favourite son. Not that Lady Portsmouth let her high standards slip because of her attachment to Newton: she had clearly scolded him in 1782, when aged nine Newton had displeased her with one of his letters home. 'I hope you will approve of this Letter,' he wrote plaintively. 'I will take care for the future to conclude my Letters as you would wish,' he promised.

Newton grew into a man who earned his mother's approval. She was so proud of his good looks that she had another portrait commissioned of him, this time by George Romney, another well-known painter of Etonians.[13] Her other boys, Lymington and Coulson, caused her much disappointment. As a schoolboy, Coulson, named after Lady Portsmouth's father, still had a bright future ahead of him. As he left Eton, his portrait revealed nothing of the trouble he would later cause. Lymington, on the other hand, was already having a different upbringing from his brothers, and not because he was the oldest son and heir. Lord and Lady Portsmouth were forced to prolong

Lymington's education because he did not seem to be developing as he should. He spent more years at his first school and with tutors than was usual, and never progressed to a public school such as Eton. Urania, countess of Portsmouth, wanted no memory, written or pictorial of her oldest child from these years. But she knew that Lymington could not continue indefinitely to be instructed by others. As he entered his late teenage years, and approached his legal majority of twenty-one, Lady Portsmouth knew she had to take a more active role in preparing Lymington for his future.

'One of the most sensible women in the Kingdom'

WHAT WAS IT like to be the mother of Lord Viscount Lymington, the boy who never grew up? Described for the rest of his life as childish in his behaviour, and thought by some doctors to have a brain that never developed, how did Urania, 2nd countess of Portsmouth, feel towards her oldest son? She was the woman who had married with great expectations. She had risen up the social scale to the dizzy heights of the aristocracy, and had wealth beyond her parents' wildest dreams. There seemed to be no stopping her. But as each year passed since her son had been born, the reality of his limitations and problems were ever clearer. Deciding how to respond presented her with her greatest personal challenge yet.

For Urania, December 1788 was a good time to take stock. In her mid-forties, in the twenty-five years since she married the 2nd earl, she had taken to the aristocratic lifestyle with aplomb. After ten years of building work, and a multitude of decisions about its design, decoration, and furnishing, the new Hurstbourne Park was completed, and ready to be shown off to guests who attended a gala ball that month. Whether her marriage to the 2nd earl had been a happy one was not a matter that anyone thought appropriate to consider, let alone discuss. The relationship had certainly been fruitful. Urania had borne eight children: four boys and four girls. By December 1788, all eight children were still living, the youngest, William, aged four.

On 18 December, Urania's oldest child, John Charles, Lord Viscount Lymington, celebrated his twenty-first birthday. As he came of age, and reached his legal majority, Lymington's formal education ended. Urania had good reason to be worried about her son. Despite her best efforts to find a cure, he still stammered, his eyes gave his face an odd appearance, and after years of private tutoring he remained well behind his brothers in his academic attainments. The law determined that her first-born son inherited the family estate and title: there was nothing that Urania could do to alter this order of succession.

Yet Urania was never a woman to give up, or resign herself to despair. She was a fighter. There were glimpses of her strength of personality throughout her life. Writing to advise her son Newton when his wife, Frances, lay sick in April 1800, for example, Urania said that she hoped Frances would 'remember that her spirits are better than her strength and that she should Bottle up the one to preserve the other'.[1] A strong will would make her better. And who would know better than Urania, whose steely determination shone through the portrait Hoppner painted of her. Commenting a century later about a 'poor copy' of this portrait that hung at Eggesford, the 6th earl of Portsmouth said that the original captured Urania's 'keen look of intelligence' and her 'indomitable will'. Portraying her with 'the eyes not widely open' was to give the viewer 'the impression of a person who has a keen insight'.[2] She was all-knowing, but not necessarily understanding. She looks judgemental and critical: she was not a woman to cross. Urania's actions showed that she had pride and ambition for her family, and she let nothing, even her son's mental problems, get in the way.

There was much about Lymington's upbringing that had given Urania hope. He was good at some things. He was quick with figures, and he could retain information. His mind was open to impression, and as a child he could not be easily dismissed as an idiot. There were signs of development, and glimmers of light in his understanding.

This was what Urania needed to have confidence that she could prepare her son for his future life as the 3rd earl of Portsmouth. He could be shaped and moulded to fit. There were two chief parts he needed to play: one involved his property; the second his social role as an aristocrat and bearer of the family title.

With vast estates and several homes to inherit, Lymington needed to have a basic understanding of how his property was managed, and to keep an eye on the income it generated and expenses it incurred. Nobody expected any aristocrat in this period to spend their time being closely involved in the day-to-day decisions of farming or property maintenance. These tasks were always delegated to bailiffs who acted as estate managers, housekeepers, and a raft of agricultural workers and domestic servants. But Lymington needed to know something about the arable farming and the valuable timber business on his estates, and to oversee the accounts of his estates as they were submitted. There was big money involved. It was estimated that in 1799 the Portsmouth estates were worth up to eighteen thousand pounds per year.[3]

This role did not present Lymington with any difficulty. In fact, later in his life we have evidence that Lymington positively enjoyed talking about the price of corn and hay, and took pride in the quality of his farming land and animals. Although he would be subsequently deprived of much legal control over his estates, his family made sure that he was at least nominally in charge of the 'home farm', the one closest to the mansion at Hurstbourne Park. 'He was something of a Farmer,' said William Lovett, who saw Lymington in the years immediately following their time at school together. Lymington's attachment to his land could take on a patriotic spirit. On a trip into Wales in September 1819, Lymington (by then Lord Portsmouth) was so impressed by the sheep farming that he saw in the lands around Brecon that he sent instructions back to Hampshire for the purchase of sixty Dorset ewes and lambs for his land in England. Staying just outside Brecon, Portsmouth commented that 'it is so very pretty', and admitted that 'the land here is very rich but I would not exchange our English Land for any here'.[4] For a man who one day would call himself the King of Hampshire, his attachment to his land, and his identification with the place of his birth, began early.

Indeed, having ignited Lymington's interest in the workings of his estate, the problem could be that he paid too much attention to farming, not too little. The English people spoke with affection at this time about George III as 'Farmer George', but nobody expected him to get his hands dirty. The King's interest in agriculture was largely scholarly, and, when the image of him as a farmer was used widely during his first period of mental illness in 1788–89, it was designed to contrast with his son's more extravagant tastes and pastimes. King George was thought of as a man of the people, but he did not join them in their work. In contrast, as the 3rd earl of Portsmouth, John Charles' enthusiasm for farming meant that at harvest time he could not wait to get into the fields with his men. A local physician remembered being astonished on one occasion when he dined at Hurstbourne Park. At the dinner were the 3rd earl's first wife, and her brothers, Lord Grantley and General Norton. Lord Portsmouth entered the dining room last, and arrived 'heated and bloated with every appearance of having been hard at work all the morning. After eating voraciously he got up from the table, and saying he was wanted in the field went out.'⁵ His fellow distinguished diners were left aghast. Here was the 3rd earl of Portsmouth, red-faced, sweaty, and ravenous from a morning's outside work. His role was meant to be as landowner, and that meant organizing others to supervise the work of his farm. But, by becoming too closely involved, he had crossed the considerable gulf that was meant to be in place between aristocrat and rural labourer. The consequences for his relationship with both his social equals and his inferiors were to be devastating.

Urania did not know just how badly her son would pursue his role. His skills at mathematics meant that she was assured that he would not be fooled by figures. She invited Lymington to join her at meetings that she held with estate workers so that he could gain experience of overseeing accounts. Even during her husband's lifetime, and following his death when Lymington was earl, the principal gardener at Hurstbourne Park, Harvey Grace, presented his accounts to Urania. Harvey remembered Lymington 'used to look over the accounts and ask questions, relating to the work done, or charged for and used to add up the amount and sometimes detect little errors'. Once Lymington 'came to his title he used to be more particular and ask more questions than before'.⁶ With a head for figures, and an eye for detail, checking estate accounts was well within Lymington's capabilities. Yet, even when he became the earl of Portsmouth, Urania did not quite trust her son enough to let him take sole charge of the accounts. For the Hurstbourne gardens at least, she remained in control.

There were numerous 'conduct books' and periodicals published in this period, which taught parents how to instruct their sons so that they behaved appropriately in society. No doubt Urania had some of these in her library at Hurstbourne. But, as she helped her son prepare for this other aspect of his future role, she is unlikely to have needed to read them. Urania had not been born into the aristocracy, and had personal experience of adjusting to this world when she married the 2nd earl. She knew what conduct and behaviour was most essential for her son to exhibit so that he was socially accepted and, most crucially, did not draw attention to himself.

In the terms of the period, Lymington needed to know how to behave 'with propriety'. Most importantly, this meant being able to conduct civil or polite conversation with people of his social standing. He needed to exchange pleasantries, and to talk about 'the common topics of the day'. Such subjects as the weather, the condition of the harvest, horses and hunting were safe sources of conversation to which all people of Lymington's rank were expected to be able to contribute. Challenging and controversial subjects such as politics or religion were not seen as appropriate for everyday conversation. In due course, Lymington would be expected to offer hospitality and invite his wealthy Hampshire neighbours to dinners and balls. On these occasions, he was required to know how to make his guests feel at ease, as well as show appropriate manners at the meal table, and some knowledge of music and how to dance. Ideally, Lymington was expected to carry off these social requirements with such style that nobody would detect that they were skills that had been acquired. Such accomplishments needed to appear natural in their performance.

Like his father, Lymington was offered a number of honorary county positions because of his aristocratic title. These included being High Steward of the Borough of Andover, the governor of a charity school, sitting on the bench of judges at the quarter sessions and assizes, and being nominated a steward at the horse races held at Winchester. All of these positions required knowledge of how to behave at meetings, how to deliver a speech and vote of thanks, and how to act as a figurehead for each organization or occasion. This meant affording each role a gravitas and authority. Although Lymington was given these positions automatically, by virtue of his social position and family connections, he had to show that he was worthy of the honour.

The rest of Lymington's life was a test of how well Urania had prepared her son for his part. Time would prove that people who mixed with Lymington in society were as divided about whether he behaved appropriately as they were about whether he was a lunatic. But whatever conclusions they reached, as his mother, Urania could be held accountable. David Williams, a Hampshire surgeon, thought that, 'when in company', Lymington, who was then Lord Portsmouth, 'was from habit and education under a considerable degree of restraint and conducted himself with general propriety'. He had no doubt 'that this was the effect of restraint exercised upon him and habit acquired during the life time of his Mother: who was a very superior woman'. For Williams, Urania's skill had been to teach her son 'restraint', how to suppress those aspects of himself that others might find inappropriate, and present an alternative version that was socially acceptable. Manners here became a kind of disguise, hiding the less attractive person beneath, and Portsmouth was a type of social puppet, performing a role to order, but with no need for an understanding of what he was doing or why. There were many occasions when Urania's instructions for her son seemed to have worked. One female visitor who stayed at Hurstbourne for a fortnight in the autumn of 1816 found Portsmouth's conduct and attention to his guests faultless. He was 'remarkably polite and well bred', she said. If her son showed evidence of good breeding, then Urania could take the credit.[7]

At times Urania exercised control over her son by limiting his freedoms. Portsmouth's sister, Henrietta Dorothea, remembered wishing for 'less restraint' as a child. But the authority that Urania exercised over Portsmouth was even greater. John Baverstock, who had lived in Hurstbourne for sixty years, worked as a servant for the Portsmouth family, originally for the 2nd earl, and had known Portsmouth from his childhood. He said that, before Portsmouth's marriage, he was 'under the jurisdiction of his mother and she was a woman that kept him under: his Lordship could not then go about by himself or do as he pleased: he was not then indulged as he was afterward'. Portsmouth did not marry until he was thirty-one years old, yet until that time he was being kept under the strict (not indulgent) control of his mother. Urania's reason for such tight supervision was understood. His Lordship 'showed what he was after his marriage more than he did before, more publicly too,' said Baverstock. Under his mother's control, his true colours did not show and he could be shielded from the public eye.[8]

Lymington's father, the 2nd earl of Portsmouth, lived until 16 May 1797, but nobody ever commented on the part he played as a parent. Mothers were expected to take chief responsibility for the upbringing of their children, but Lymington was the oldest son and heir, so he should have been of especial interest to his father. Yet, since all of Urania's surviving correspondence dates from after her husband's death, we do not know if she talked to him about their children, or if he had particular views about how Lymington should be raised.

We have remarkably little information about the 2nd earl: even the portrait of him painted by Hoppner no longer exists. Few personal letters written by him survive, and his presence at social occasions is rarely mentioned in newspapers of the time. This absence of information, especially in the face of the abundant material and comment about Urania as a mother, suggests that he took a minor role in his oldest son's life. He may not have been an easy man or a particularly bright one. Of more than a hundred witnesses who would later be examined in the church courts about the 3rd earl's sanity, just one, a park keeper at Hurstbourne for nearly forty-one years, was asked to compare the 3rd earl with his father. The 3rd earl 'is not a man of equal capacity with his late father. He was bad enough, but the present Earl is worse,' he said. Capacity for what was left tantalizingly undefined.[9]

Without a strong male head of the family, Urania became the matriarch, overseeing the upbringing of her children and taking on some of the responsibility for estate management that would normally be reserved for her husband. She was so accustomed to being an authority figure that the death of her husband made very little differ-ence to her own or her children's lives. When Lymington became Lord Portsmouth, she should have retired into a dowager position, and let him assume control. But, as a further indication that all was not normal in this family's configuration, she just carried on, issuing instructions to the household servants and overseeing the estate's management.

She was not alone, and there was one man whom she trusted above all others to give her advice. Reverend John Garnett, although not a blood relative of the Portsmouths', nevertheless became one of their closest friends. Descended from a family of clergymen, including his father who was a Church of Ireland bishop, Garnett was a Fellow of Trinity College, Cambridge, and was ordained on 27 June 1779. Over his career in the church, he held a range of posts including the curacy at Hurstbourne Priors, Over Wallop, and the valuable living at Cliddesden and Farleigh Wallop, which was in the hands of the Portsmouths. He rose from being a Prebend and then Dean at Winchester Cathedral to being appointed a Chaplain in Ordinary to George III, and finally Dean of Exeter Cathedral. He seems to have never married or had any children, his will making special mention of a faithful servant and housekeeper, and leaving the bulk of his estate to his sister's children. The Portsmouth family saw Garnett as one of their own, and he spent much time living with them at Hurstbourne. Under the 3rd earl, he was described as 'the confidential friend and chaplain of Lord Portsmouth's family', and, as a 'most deserving man', he inspired the 2nd earl to write several times to William Pitt petitioning him for church positions. Garnett was held with such esteem that when he died a memorial to him was erected in pride of place within the Portsmouth family church at Farleigh Wallop. On a wall to the right of the altar, the plaque was to their 'generous friend', who had a 'manly and Christian Death: Attentive even in his last moments more to the good of others than his own sufferings'. His was the only non-family memorial to be erected.[10]

This apparently self-sacrificing individual was privy to all of the Portsmouth family's secrets, and unlike other friends seems never to have betrayed their trust. He was an understanding and sympathetic soundboard for Urania, and helped her through difficult times. Newton's letters make it clear that Garnett visited all three of her boys to check on their wellbeing while they were at school.[11] For the next twenty years, Garnett was present at the key moments in the 3rd earl's life, and at many of the family's points of crisis. He became a substitute father-figure for Portsmouth, especially after the 2nd earl's death. With no family of his own, Garnett may have valued his role in the Portsmouth one. But as locus parentis, as we shall see, he would attract the resentment and dislike of the 3rd earl.

Once Lymington had reached his majority in December 1788, decisions had to be made about the family's property. The 2nd earl was still in good health, but nobody could be confident that upon his death his son had a safe pair of hands to keep the family's fortune. Lawyers were brought in, including the family's solicitor, John Hanson. Over the next fourteen months, a legal settlement was negotiated, and finally agreed upon in February 1790. One of the signatories was Reverend Garnett. The settlement created a new entail, making Lymington an heir for his lifetime, and stating that, if he died without a male heir, the Portsmouth estate should be inherited by Newton, his younger brother. Family estates like the Portsmouths' normally descended through the male line so this document is noteworthy for stating the obvious. Lymington's mental state meant that his family thought they could leave nothing to chance: without a legal settlement, they could not rely upon him to follow the usual pattern. The stakes were too high to risk allowing him any freedom to settle the estates as he might otherwise wish. His hands were now tied.[12]

Being a mother is never easy, and raising a son like Lymington, who seemed to be exhibiting a range of mental problems, was particularly challenging. As any mother knows, winning universal approval for the way you bring up your children is well nigh impossible. But, because of the man he would become, more people paid attention to how Lord Portsmouth had been brought up than would have been usual. If all had gone smoothly, there would have been no need to look to his past for explanations.

There was only one witness in the legal trials that were to be brought against Lord Portsmouth who was prepared to suggest that Urania was partly to blame for her son's problems. That was Reverend Robert Wright, whose parish of Itchen Abbas was near to Hurstbourne, and who had known Portsmouth since 1794. Wright was a visiting magistrate to lunatic asylums, and claimed that he had 'made the character of the mind his study'. In his opinion, Portsmouth had a weak, but sound mind. Wright had seen Portsmouth over the years at a number of social functions in Hampshire and London, and thought him sharp in money matters, quick at figures, and an excellent judge of a horse.

'If Lord Portsmouth had not been kept in the background, but instructed in the management of his "secular" concerns', Wright did 'not know any man, who would have been more alive to the proper application of his income, and regulation of his expenditure: and he would have been capable of so doing.' Ironically, it was Portsmouth's weak mind that made him particularly capable of this role. 'The limited understanding of Lord Portsmouth led him to bestow his whole attention to an object,' observed Wright. The way that Portsmouth's mind functioned, which was to become fixated on particular tasks, and to mechanically apply procedure, could have meant that he managed his estates better than other noblemen. But Wright believed that Portsmouth was 'never fairly dealt with' by his family. With instruction, he could have controlled his estates. However, while Portsmouth's mother was alive, he was 'kept in the background'. Wright believed that Portsmouth was treated in this way 'because the old Lady Portsmouth looked upon his Lordship as inferior in understanding to his brother'.[13]

According to Wright, keeping Portsmouth 'in the background', teaching him the basics but expecting nothing more, and showing favouritism towards Newton, were ways that Urania responded to her oldest son's 'inferior' understanding. Given the frustrations she must have felt and the problems she confronted with Portsmouth, perhaps it was not surprising if Urania found it easier to be a mother to Newton. But did this mean that she failed to identify and develop her son's full potential? Was the effect of her control to stifle and even further limit her son's development? Knowingly or not, Wright raised the question of whether Portsmouth was destined for the trials of his sanity from his birth, or whether there was something about his upbringing that had pushed him in this direction. Even if Portsmouth had been born in some way mentally defective, had Urania made his condition worse? These questions were never developed or fully answered in the law courts. But the notion that Portsmouth might have been a different man if he had been treated in other ways as a child and young man was raised by Wright, and might well have been more widely discussed outside the courtroom environment. The strong personality of 'old Lady Portsmouth' and her central role in the upbringing of her son during his formative years is unlikely to have been forgotten.

If Urania found Newton a more rewarding child to raise, she still did not find it easy to show her affection for him. She found fault with his schoolboy letters and could inspire awe from him even when he was a grown man. The 6th countess of Portsmouth remembered how Newton, 'always spoke with the most profound reverence of "my mother"'. Newton may not have feared his mother as his older brother did, but, like all his brothers and sisters, when he was young he still had a formal relationship with his mother. She was, after all, described as 'one of the most sensible women'.[14] Urania did not let emotion cloud her judgement, even for those she favoured.

Newton was Urania's first child to make her a grandmother: he had four children with his first wife, Frances. Urania's letters to Newton show that being a grandmother brought back her memories of motherhood, and gave her a chance to think over the decisions she had made when her children were young. Responding to news from Newton that his son Harry was well again in January 1811, Urania admitted that 'I have cast more anxious thoughts for Him, than I own I ever did for you'. Urania wrote in this letter that, by the time Newton was thirteen years old (and Lymington eighteen), she knew 'you was to Bustle in this Life, and thought I was most Friendly to let you see, that Bustle early'.[15] In other words, she had decided that in his life ahead Newton would have to take responsibilities and learn to stand on his own two feet (perhaps because of her fears about Lymington's inadequacies), and she needed to toughen him up and let him experience 'that Bustle' while he was still young. At the same time that she was keeping a close watch over Lymington, she was letting Newton go.

Urania's letter to Newton defended her decision to let him experience the 'bustle' of life, but, if she had regrets about how she mothered him, she never altered her view of how she treated her oldest son. She believed that his weakness meant that it was imperative that she should take command. Indeed, she gave Portsmouth instructions even beyond the grave. Urania made a list of specific bequests for after her death. She left her two daughters, Henrietta Dorothea and Urania Annabella, a number of personal items, including mourning rings containing the hair of their father and dead brothers and sisters. There was no bequest for Newton. But John Charles, as earl of Portsmouth, was left a number of items, which Urania specified were for 'his life and after his death to go as Heirlooms' with the Hurstbourne estate. She gave him 'all the diamonds given to her Marriage with her late Husband', and listed each piece of jewellery. The Old and New Testaments, and a Book of Common Prayer that 'were in the Bookcase at Hurstbourne Park', and had belonged to Bridget, the 1st countess of Portsmouth, were given to him. Finally, Urania gave her son a number of pieces of 'Shell Work', all of which were kept in glass cases. These items presumably included the shell house that had been given to Urania by her brother, Henry Arthur Fellowes, following his travels abroad.

To be included in her final wishes, this shell work must have held special meanings and memories for Urania. As Urania wanted, they became part of the family treasures that were passed down through the generations, and were valuable enough to be rescued from the fire at Hurstbourne at the end of the nineteenth century. But, while they were in the 3rd earl's ownership, Urania wanted to ensure that her son kept them safely. After itemizing the shell work, she gave the order that it was 'to be placed in the South Dressing Room of Hurstbourne Mansion presently occupied by the Countess of Portsmouth'. So little did she trust her son, and so habitual and abso-lute had her control over him become, that Urania even directed the room at Hurstbourne where her bequest was to be displayed. Never mind that it was his house, his wife's dressing room, and now his shell work.[16]

Portsmouth was kept waiting for his mother's love. His emotional response to her was one of fear. 'He was afraid of her,' said a cook and housekeeper, 'he was very well behaved before his Mother', but 'as soon as she was gone he would abuse her in a shocking manner'.[17] After his father died, and as the 3rd earl of Portsmouth, his resentment at his mother's treatment grew. He was an adult, but his mother was still treating him as a child. Standing firm alongside his mother, Reverend Garnett was the type of male authority figure that Lord Portsmouth had never experienced in his father. Now this non-family member was helping his mother to control him, and interfering with his life. It was easier for Portsmouth to voice his discontent at his treatment towards Garnett than in front of his mother. But letting off steam by cursing his mother when she was out of the room was not enough for a man who had had his fill of being told what to do. Some might wonder whether Urania was doing the right thing by keeping her oldest son 'under' and 'in the background'. However, the consequences of allowing Portsmouth greater freedom would be seen in dramatic light within the space of the next few years.

'His want of ordinary caution'

SHAKEN AWAKE AT two in the morning, Lord Portsmouth was even more befuddled and confused than normal. Still half-asleep and barely able to see in the darkness, it was easier to go along with what was being asked of him than to resist. The voice telling him what to do was a familiar one, and his instructions about getting dressed had been repeated many times over the last nine years, albeit usually later in the morning. Portsmouth followed the directions he was given and was led downstairs and out of the house. Waiting for him was a chaise and horses. He was persuaded to get into the carriage, which then drove away at break-neck speed. Nobody in the house had been awoken by Portsmouth's departure. They slept peacefully within, as oblivious as Portsmouth himself that the first step in his abduction had just been successfully achieved.

Once Portsmouth's eyes had adjusted to the darkness, and the movement of the carriage had finally jolted him fully awake, he recognized one of the men who sat beside him: Jean Seilaz, his valet. Portsmouth had first been introduced to Seilaz in Basel in July 1790. While going to Eton like his younger brothers was out of the question for Portsmouth, his mother was keen that he should not miss out on another key component of a gentleman's education at this time, the 'grand tour'. The grand tour involved travel to European cities to view key classical sites, which for Portsmouth included those in Germany and Italy. During this time abroad, most parents believed it was as important whom their sons met, as what they saw. Tutors were employed to ensure that the young men in their charge mixed in the right kind of company. The overall aim of this foreign travel was that men would return to England more cultured, refined, and polished in their manners and conversation.

This form of finishing school had worked wonders for Portsmouth's great-grandfather; it was partly because of the connections he made with the court of Hanover that he was promoted to government posts and made an earl in 1743. Portsmouth's parents never had this kind of aspiration for his tour, but, if nothing else, it would keep Portsmouth out of the way for a few years, giving his family, and his mother in particular, a welcome break. He had hardly covered himself with glory during his school days, and sending Portsmouth away from home was something his parents had been doing since he was five years old. Out of sight was probably out of mind.

Portsmouth had two tutors who accompanied him on his tour, John Lawson and John Dougall. They were in charge of his education and itinerary, but they needed to employ a servant who would care for Portsmouth's everyday personal needs. Hence in Switzerland, at the start of their travels, they persuaded Portsmouth to employ Seilaz, a Swiss national from Berne, who worked as Portsmouth's valet for his journey into Italy, and back through Germany. How they first met Seilaz we do not know.

It was probably through spending time with Seilaz that Portsmouth increased his knowledge of the French language, first learned at school and now put into practice. He learned to speak it well. It was a language he did not forget, and used in polite circles back in England, conversing at ease, it was said, and with a good accent. For a man who found so many other aspects of learning a struggle, contemporaries found his ability to speak fluent French all the more remarkable. His stammer meant that he struggled to even articulate himself in English, yet, when speaking a foreign language, these problems seemed to evaporate.[1]

Travelling in foreign lands, far from home, and sharing as tourists in the discovery of new places, as well as the risks and exhaustion of the unknown, Portsmouth was heavily reliant on Seilaz for company and support. His peculiarities and social awkwardness made it unlikely that many fellow aristocratic travellers would want to socialize with him for long. He may have been lonely, but he had Seilaz.

When the time came to return home, in January 1793, asking Seilaz to come to England and continue as Portsmouth's valet seemed natural and the right thing to do. Seilaz accepted a generous pay package, which included the cost of travel back to Switzerland whenever he wished. But coming home for Portsmouth put him in a very different position to the one he had held abroad. Portsmouth at home meant performing his role as an English aristocrat, and being subject to the demands of his family. His social circle was determined by his mother, and his agenda left no room for keeping company with Seilaz. Portsmouth was back on duty.

There was something about Seilaz that Portsmouth's family did not like. This foreigner had a familiarity of manner with Portsmouth that left everyone who saw them together uncomfortable. Seilaz seemed to forget that he was a servant, and Portsmouth was his master. The problem stemmed from Portsmouth's lack of understanding about the proper form of relationship between master and servant. Portsmouth's 'easy open and unsuspecting disposition' meant that he was 'apt to place and repose confidence in individuals without discrimination'. Rather than maintaining a distant and formal relationship with Seilaz, Portsmouth was relaxed and familiar with him. Alarmingly, Portsmouth treated Seilaz as a friend, and that meant he saw him as his social equal, not inferior. Seilaz had such a hold on Portsmouth that Portsmouth never lost his respect for him, despite later events. 'I had reason to be satisfied with his character,' he told others in December 1802. 'I believed him to be, and I found him, a faithful servant...I always had a good opinion of him.'

For years, the Portsmouth family tolerated Seilaz living in their household. They persuaded themselves that he kept Portsmouth in good order. Making an enemy of Seilaz would only upset Portsmouth, they thought, and disrupt the calm equilibrium that had been achieved since his arrival in the household. Seilaz could be charming, but also 'cunning'. He seemed to know Portsmouth's weaknesses better than anyone, and told Portsmouth's parents that he could help. He warned them of 'the necessity of watching' their son, 'to prevent his suffering by the deceit and imposition' to which his 'credulity perpetually exposed him'. Portsmouth, he said, had a 'want of ordinary caution in his dealings with mankind'. Portsmouth's family needed him, he argued. He could be their protector. Seilaz knew their weakest link, and it would be best for everyone if the Portsmouths kept him on their side.

If Seilaz's persuasiveness won the 'favourable opinion' of Portsmouth's family, however reluctantly they gave it, he had far less difficulty convincing the 'credulous' Portsmouth. Slowly, but surely, he gained his trust. Portsmouth came to place 'the most unlimited confidence' in Seilaz. According to Portsmouth's family, Seilaz 'acquired such an ascendancy' over Portsmouth's 'mind and inclinations' that Portsmouth 'had not sufficient power or presence of mind to refuse to do any act' Seilaz 'prompted or advised him to perform'.

Would Portsmouth really do anything Seilaz asked? When Portsmouth's father, the 2nd earl of Portsmouth, died on 16 May 1797, Seilaz saw the opportunity to test his 'ascendancy' over Portsmouth. He accompanied Portsmouth to London at the end of June, when Portsmouth was formally presented at Court to George III at St James's Palace. Now the 3rd earl of Portsmouth, he also took his seat in the House of Lords for the first time. With Portsmouth newly ascended to his aristocratic title, fresh with excitement about the privileges that this brought, and removed from his overbearing mother, this was an ideal time for Seilaz to make his first move. They visited an attorney in Soho, who at Portsmouth's instructions drew up a bond giving Seilaz £999 and an annuity of £100 for the rest of Seilaz's life, which would begin on the day Seilaz left Portsmouth's service. Portsmouth put his signature and seal to this bond without hesitation.

Seilaz was later described as appearing 'elated' at the ease with which he had achieved this result. He began to plan other schemes by which he could defraud Portsmouth. While Portsmouth's family did not know of the Soho deed, when the two men returned to Hurstbourne, Seilaz was 'materially altered in his conduct and behaviour'. Gone was the charm. Instead, Seilaz was confident and arrogant in his manner towards Portsmouth and his family. 'Circumstances daily occurred' to 'create doubts and suspicions' in the minds of

Portsmouth's family about the 'honest intentions and faithfulness' of Seilaz. We do not know what those circumstances were, and perhaps Seilaz did not do anything in particular wrong, because if he had it would have given Portsmouth's mother the excuse she needed to have him dismissed. The problem with Seilaz at this stage was still intangible; it was a general disliking and uncomfortable feeling. Portsmouth's family continued to hesitate. Portsmouth remained loyal to Seilaz, blinded by his influence, and unable to see how his behaviour had changed. Seilaz was Portsmouth's servant, and Portsmouth could see no wrong.

By the summer of 1799, however, Portsmouth's family had decided that Seilaz had to go. Their patience with this suspicious foreigner had finally run out. Somehow Seilaz got wind of their intentions, and knew he had to act before it was too late. A year's worth of planning kicked in. He organized a chaise to be waiting outside Hurstbourne Park on the night of 22 July. He had awoken Portsmouth and pushed him inside. Waiting in the chaise was Gabriel Tahourdin, a Whitchurch attorney. Now all three men were making their way to London.

Fresh horses were waiting for them at different stages of their journey, so that they could continue without stopping. They arrived at Blenheim coffeehouse in Bond Street, London, between eight and nine o'clock in the morning. Seilaz asked for a private room, and took great care that Portsmouth's arrival was not seen by anyone in the street or in the passage of the coffeehouse. They were soon joined by Peter Tahourdin, Gabriel's brother, who was also an attorney. Peter brought with him two of his junior employees to act as witnesses to what was about to happen. A large number of ready-prepared legal papers and deeds were then produced. None was read over or explained to Portsmouth. Instead, Seilaz ordered Portsmouth to sign them. Portsmouth was 'so intimidated' by his circumstances, and threatened by the presence of the four men who were complete strangers to him, that he dared not refuse, and signed them.

Two were bonds, in which Portsmouth gave Seilaz one sum of £710 15s, and another of £400. In the second bond, Portsmouth also agreed to recompense Seilaz for the loss of any possessions that Seilaz had left that morning at Hurstbourne Park. The other documents were powers of attorney. In them, Portsmouth announced his intention of leaving the country, requested Seilaz to accompany him, and handed all legal control over to Gabriel Tahourdin. One paper that Portsmouth signed explained that, 'in consideration of the trust and confidence' Portsmouth had in Gabriel Tahourdin (he had never met him before that morning), he appointed him his attorney, giving him absolute authority over all his property and estates. Portsmouth put his signature to an order that all bailiffs, stewards, and tenants of his lands in Hampshire and Buckinghamshire should pay their rents to Gabriel. He gave Gabriel the power to make contracts on his behalf, and to sell timber, deer, horses, and sheep 'as he the said Gabriel Tahourdin shall think proper and most for my benefit'. Gabriel was given the authority to appoint and pay wages to all Portsmouth's servants and estate workers, and to deduct sums from the estate income as payment for being his attorney. This arrangement was to stay in place for Gabriel's lifetime. If Portsmouth died before Gabriel, then Portsmouth's heirs were bound to this deed. Gabriel would receive an annual salary of five hundred pounds for the 'trouble' of looking after the Portsmouth estates.

Fraud on a grand scale achieved, Seilaz 'put' Portsmouth 'to bed' at the coffeehouse, before locking his door and taking the key away with him so that Portsmouth 'might not be discovered and that no person might have access to him'. Seilaz, accompanied by the Tahourdin brothers, then went to arrange for a passport so that Seilaz could leave the country. They obtained a passport 'by false and fraudulent pretences', and returned to the coffeehouse. Portsmouth by this stage had become unwell. The cause and symptoms of his ill health were never described. He repeatedly told the men that he was not fit to travel. But Seilaz 'compelled' Portsmouth to get into another chaise that evening, using 'various threats', which 'greatly alarmed' him. Seilaz would not tell Portsmouth where they were going.

Now driven by four horses, the chaise left at great speed and headed towards Yarmouth. Seilaz used 'the most violent language to the several drivers…to make all possible haste'. Arriving at Colchester, Seilaz was told that they were too late for the next boat that was due to leave for Hamburg. So they dropped one pair of horses and proceeded to

Yarmouth at a 'more leisurely' pace, arriving on the afternoon of 24 July. For the whole of the journey, Portsmouth was rarely allowed out of the chaise, but was concealed from all possible 'spectators'.

On arrival at Yarmouth, Seilaz entered his passport with 'the Superintendent of Aliens', and got places for Portsmouth and himself on the next boat to Hamburg, which was due to leave the following morning. The two men retired to an inn for the night. Seilaz hired a 'double bedded room'. He dined with Portsmouth at the same table, in the same room, treating Portsmouth 'with the same familiarity as though he had been his equal'. The innkeeper certainly did not realize that one of his guests was an aristocrat. Having finished their meal, the two men went to sleep in their shared room. Seilaz 'never permitted' Portsmouth 'to be out of his sight but watched him very closely'. He was 'armed with two pair of loaded pistols', which he frequently showed to Portsmouth 'in so significant a manner as greatly to terrify' him. He put the pistols by the bed so that Portsmouth could see them.

Waking up at Hurstbourne Park on 22 July, and finding Portsmouth and Seilaz gone, the Portsmouth family had their worst fears realized. 'Being greatly alarmed', Newton Wallop, Portsmouth's younger brother, John Hanson, the family solicitor, and Reverend Garnett, the family's closest friend and adviser, set off for London. At five in the morning on 24 July, having just arrived in London, Hanson spotted Gabriel Tahourdin about to board the Hampshire coach. Somehow Hanson knew that Tahourdin was involved in the plot. He asked him where Portsmouth was, but Tahourdin denied that he had seen or knew anything. It was later discovered that Tahourdin was on his way to Hurstbourne, intending to 'turn out and evict' the whole of Portsmouth's family from his mansion. Tahourdin was carrying a list of the names of Portsmouth's family and servants, as supplied by Seilaz.

From London, Portsmouth's brother and friends followed him to Yarmouth. They arrived at midnight that same day. Having given a description of Portsmouth and Seilaz, they were told that the two men 'were gone to bed in a double bedded room'. On hearing this, it was only because the landlord told them that Seilaz was armed that they did not immediately burst into the room. They went to fetch a constable and a magistrate. To try to catch Seilaz off guard, the landlord then knocked on the door, telling Seilaz that the ship to Hamburg was 'getting under way'. The door was opened, and the rescue party rushed in. 'Upon seeing his friends', Portsmouth 'greatly rejoiced', and was much relieved. He immediately got out of bed, and left with them.

Seilaz was ordered 'in a very rough manner' to 'dress himself immediately'. Once dressed, the constable forced him to hand over his pocket book, in which was found the papers that Portsmouth had signed. Accusing Seilaz of having used a false name to obtain a passport, this document was also taken from him. His pistols were seized, and he was arrested and taken to the house of the town gaoler. The next day, Seilaz was transported back to London and committed to Cold Bath Fields prison. From there he was deported sometime later, under the terms of the Aliens Act of 1793.[2]

The relief of having returned to Hurstbourne after the high drama of the previous few days reinforced in Portsmouth's mind its association with safety and security. The world outside was a dangerous place. Meanwhile, Portsmouth's mother, brother, and friends took stock of what had happened. This course of events was a wake-up call to the vulnerable position their family now faced. Since the 2nd earl had died in May 1797, Portsmouth had inherited his title and nominal position as head of the family. But his mental weaknesses left him not only struggling to fulfil this role, but also perilously positioned to the exploitation by others. Just two years into his new role, Portsmouth had nearly lost all the family's fortune and honour to a daring foreigner. If there were lessons to be learned, they were that in the future Portsmouth needed to be protected. Scrupulous care was needed before anybody else was admitted to the family circle.

Seilaz had been removed, and Portsmouth had been rescued, but his family were mistaken if they thought the trouble with Portsmouth's valet was over. Nearly two years later, on 2 May 1801, Portsmouth was staying at a house in Lincoln's Inn Fields in London when he received a letter. The writing was in Seilaz's hand, and had been sent from Hamburg. It began:

My Lord, when an English Nobleman condescends to deny his own words he puts himself upon a level with the lowest subject in his Majesty's dominions.

Portsmouth, Seilaz said, owed him money, but he had not kept his word or bond by paying it. He continued with a sensational threat:

> If I have not by return of post a restitution made me of every Bonds security and money otherwise due to me from your Lordship I will expose to the World the repeated Sodomitical attempts you made upon me. Your Lordship I suppose well knows that penalty which attaches to an attempt to commit an act of Sodomy and that penalty is death and your Lordship's consciousness of guilt will point out to you the necessity of immediate compliance with the demand here made. My losses by your Lordship's family amount to near £2,000. Consult your own feelings and preserve if possible yourself and family from indelible disgrace by an immediate compliance with my request.

'Being dissatisfied' with the conduct of Mr Tahourdin, Seilaz informed Portsmouth that he was taking instructions from another solicitor, and would be returning to England where he would expect an immediate answer to his demands. 'My actions will depend solely on your Lordship's conduct' in response to this letter, he concluded.

Seilaz was right about the punishment for sodomy. The 1533 Buggery Act was still in force, and sodomy carried the death penalty. Fifty men would be executed for sodomy in England between 1805 and 1832. Being a member of the aristocracy gave Portsmouth no legal immunity. In the eighteenth century, it was largely the poor and working class who had felt the severity of the so-called 'bloody code' of law, many ending their lives hanging from Tyburn's rope. But the public execution of the 4th earl of Ferrers, and his failed attempt to convince the jury that he had been insane when he shot his steward dead in 1760, showed that every English man was subject to the rule of law.[3]

Men feared the pen of blackmailers like Seilaz because their threats to expose sexual secrets could lead to 'indelible disgrace': the loss of reputation, a good name, and social as well as financial ruin. In 1822, when Viscount Castlereagh committed suicide by forcing a small knife into his throat, rumour had it that blackmailers were hounding him with claims of sodomy. The stigma surrounding sodomy at this time gave Seilaz's attempt at blackmail its sting. He knew that, one way or another, he would get a response.

Portsmouth handed over Seilaz's letter to his lawyer, John Hanson, and it was probably a shocked Hanson, in consultation with the rest of the Portsmouth family, who decided upon his 'Lordship's conduct'. When he returned to England, Portsmouth took Seilaz to court, on the charge of sending a threatening letter in an attempt to extort money. In English law, Seilaz's offence was categorized as a mis-demeanour, and one that carried the penalty of transportation for seven years.

The case was heard before the court of King's Bench on 7 December 1802. The court sat in the vast space of Westminster Hall, adjacent to the Houses of Parliament. The judge was Lord Ellenborough, and John Hanson led the prosecution against Seilaz. 'A great number of lawyers were employed on each side, and the trial excited an uncommon degree of interest,' wrote one newspaper reporter. Hanson recruited an impressive legal team for Portsmouth, including Sir William Garrow, a barrister well known for his aggressive style of questioning and defence of his clients.

Portsmouth won praise for having the courage to bring the case. Lord Erskine, counsel for Portsmouth, told the court:

It must be seen how difficult it was to drag an offender of this kind to justice. These were crimes, of which it had pleased God, for the wisest ends, to implant in us such abhorrence that most men shrink back from the imputation of them, and though conscious of inno-cence, rather submit to extortion than appeal to the law.

Sodomy was such an 'abhorrent' crime that the newspapers which reported this case did not name it, instead obliquely referring to the accusation of an 'unnatural crime'. Seilaz's letter to Portsmouth was read out in court, before the jury, but newspaper reporters did not quote it in full, leaving out all mention of sodomy. For 'his firmness', and determination to resist the accusation, Portsmouth should be congratulated, the press argued. His legal action 'was honourable to him'. In bringing the case, Portsmouth 'performed a sacred duty to himself, but one of far higher importance to the public'. At a time of revolutionary fervour on the continent, Portsmouth was standing up for the rights of all Englishmen. He was a nobleman who would not be frightened and bullied into submitting to the demands of an immoral and socially inferior foreigner.

Portsmouth appeared in person before King's Bench. He swore that the letter was in Seilaz's hand, and gave details of how the two men had met. Portsmouth admitted that Seilaz had been a good servant. Nevertheless, his lawyers told the court how Seilaz was 'at the bottom of a foul conspiracy to deprive the noble Lordship of all his estates, and to drive his revered parent [his mother] and amiable sisters from under his roof' in 1799. Portsmouth's sudden departure to London and Yarmouth was described, and Seilaz's arrest and deportation was provided as a possible explanation for his subsequent extortion attempt. During a lengthy cross-examination, Portsmouth answered all the questions put to him. His responses took time, because of his stammer, which was always worse when he was under pressure. But, throughout his examination, Portsmouth's conduct was 'rational and sensible', and his responses were 'perfectly clear and consistent'. Many years later, Garrow remembered that Portsmouth gave his evidence 'in an intelligent and sensible manner', and was convinced that Portsmouth was at this time 'of sound mind'.

To everyone who saw him in court, and heard his testimony, Portsmouth seemed a man with nothing to hide. He was the innocent party in this case. He had been badly used by a servant whom he had previously employed and taken into his confidence. Seilaz's letter betrayed his depravity. 'In the usual course of inquiry, especially of this sort,' argued Portsmouth's counsel, 'the guilty party took care to conceal' their involvement in sodomy. 'But here the defendant had directly and plainly avowed his own guilt' by admitting to sodomy in the letter he had sent.

Having heard the evidence, and read over Seilaz's letter, Judge

Ellenborough announced to the court that 'he did not see that the Jury could hesitate in finding the Defendant guilty'. Given this direction, the jury did not even retire to consider their verdict. Instead, they immediately pronounced a guilty verdict on Seilaz.

Seilaz was not present in the court. Repeated attempts to call him to King's Bench to receive judgment failed. As a result, he was outlawed and banned from English society. This put an end to all his attempts to recover his pay and money owed to him, because he lost the right to use the civil courts. In theory, anybody who offered Seilaz food, shelter, or support could be accused of aiding and abetting a criminal. Seilaz's refusal to face justice betrayed him as a coward, and proclaimed his guilt.[4]

At least that was what Portsmouth and his family wanted everyone to think. It is the version of events that was presented by the best lawyers in the land, and was printed in the newspapers. However, Seilaz got to tell his side of the story at the court of Chancery the following May, when Portsmouth brought a bill to declare that the documents he had signed for Seilaz were false. Seilaz's account of what happened was quite different. Deciding who was the abuser and who was the abused in Portsmouth's friendship with Seilaz was altogether less certain.

Seilaz described his job as Portsmouth's valet after he was hired in July 1790. He had to provide Portsmouth with 'the most essential and important services on a variety of occasions'. This may sound grand, but it boiled down to providing routine day-to-day care for a man who was used to having everything done for him. Seilaz washed, dressed, and fed Portsmouth. Wealthy men expected to have servants attending to them, but Portsmouth was different. He was like a child because he was so incapable of looking after himself. As other servants would confirm, Portsmouth had no idea how to dress smartly or appropriately as a gentleman. If neglected, he dressed meanly, putting on worn clothes. He was said to have 'slept in and worn the same shirt for a week'. He cared nothing for his appearance. He did not shave every day. Servants even had to cut his corns and nails. He seldom used a toothbrush. 'He ate not like other people, but voraciously, and drank as if he would swallow glass and all.' Seilaz had to keep an eye on his consumption of wine, and mix it with water if he was becoming drunk. Without Seilaz's careful attention, Portsmouth would have smelled bad, his table manners would have been non-existent, and nobody looking at him would ever have guessed he was a nobleman.[5]

His personal habits were bad enough, but his temper made working for him even harder. His mood swings were unpredictable, and he could become violent when he was angry. Portsmouth developed an annoying practice of pinching Seilaz and his other servants, and pulling their hair. He seemed to think it funny when they cried out. His family said that he was 'of an easy, open and unsuspecting disposition', but there was nothing easy about living with Lord Portsmouth.

Seilaz argued that his hard work earned him a reward. In January 1793, and at Portsmouth's request, Seilaz came to England, a country far from his home. He worked for Portsmouth for four long years, gaining the confidence of Portsmouth and his family because of his loyalty. After the death of the 2nd earl, he went with Portsmouth to London. Portsmouth was excited at the possibilities now open to him. He could feel the thrill of being in control, believing that for the first time in his life his inheritance and title gave him the chance to act as he, and not others, wanted. In London, he told Seilaz 'that he then had it in his power to do that which he had long wished for an opportunity'. Portsmouth said he wanted to show Seilaz his gratitude for his 'many services and long tried attachment to him'. He had served him well abroad, as well as at home, he said, and Portsmouth particularly remembered Seilaz's part in 'preserving his life at Milan' when he became unwell. Seilaz had originally trained as a surgeon and dentist, a fact never mentioned by the Portsmouth family, who wanted to represent him as a simple servant. But his medical knowledge had obviously come in useful when they were on their travels. Exceptional service and care prompted Portsmouth's proposal to go to a London attorney so that an annuity could be arranged. When a bond was later delivered to Hurstbourne for Portsmouth to sign, Seilaz placed so little pressure upon Portsmouth that it lay unsigned for several months.

Seilaz told the court that he did not alter his behaviour after the 2nd earl's death. Portsmouth and his family could have dismissed him at any time, but they kept him on for another two years. Instead, Seilaz said that it was Portsmouth's mother who changed, not him. She knew that it was her son who was in charge now, at least in theory. After so many years of running the Portsmouth household, and ordering her son around, anyone who sought instruction had first to turn to him for orders now, and she found that hard to take. In practice, she found it impossible to let go. Portsmouth had taken Seilaz into his confidence, and complained to him about how he was 'treated by his Mother and others of his Relations'. Perhaps she suspected that her son talked to Seilaz about her, and resented their closeness. Her manner altered so much towards Seilaz that he asked her if he 'had offended her', saying that he was ready to quit if she was not fully satisfied. But she assured Seilaz that nothing was wrong. There was her opportunity to be rid of Seilaz, but she did not take it.

After Portsmouth's initial elation at succeeding to his title, reality kicked in. His complaints about his mother increased. He told Seilaz that he was 'particularly mortified at not being permitted to manage without control his own household or to give directions without restraint respecting his estates'. The restraint imposed by the 1790 legal deed, which gave Portsmouth control over the family's estates for his lifetime only, was beginning to show. In everyday terms, even if Portsmouth was manifestly incapable of managing a household, he was not unaware that this was something he should have been doing. He was in his early thirties, after all, yet he had no more authority than the youth Seilaz had first met on his grand tour.

Portsmouth's 'discontent' and unhappiness at his situation increased to such a point that by the summer of 1799 he had come to a decision. He wanted to leave England, he told Seilaz, and vest his legal authority in some 'confidential person' who could act for him in his absence. This course of action, he explained, would mean 'extricating himself from the unpleasant situation in which he had been so long'. It would be a way 'of obtaining the peaceful and comfortable possession of his Rights'. Portsmouth wanted Seilaz to go with him.

Seilaz said that he did everything to try to dissuade Portsmouth from this scheme, and repeatedly advised him against it. But Portsmouth would not listen. 'On account of the cruel treatment he experienced from his family he had made up his mind,' he said. Nothing would change his decision.

So, according to Seilaz, their night-time departure from Hurstbourne on 22 July 1799 was not an abduction arranged by him, but an escape plan orchestrated by Portsmouth. Portsmouth told Seilaz that he wanted Gabriel Tahourdin to act as his attorney, because he had heard his friend Reverend Williams speak highly of him. Seilaz acted as messenger and passed letters between the two men. Tahourdin would provide a copy of one of Portsmouth's letters to him in his answer to this Chancery case. In it, Portsmouth wrote of the 'ill treatment' he suffered, 'from my Mother and Mr Garnett and from almost all my own Servants and everyone of Lady Portsmouth's servants by whom they are encouraged'. This left him, he explained, 'miserably unhappy'. 'I am never consulted on any Business,' he complained, and he could only get small amounts of money to spend on himself. His mother and Garnett were still in charge of everything. 'I am not considered as Master of my own House,' he complained.

But he was Seilaz's master, and Seilaz was duty bound to obey his orders. Portsmouth told Seilaz and Gabriel to be ready at night with a chaise and horses. They had to leave secretly, which meant Seilaz was forced to leave many of his possessions behind at Hurstbourne. Portsmouth was in high spirits throughout the night-time journey to London. He was excited that they had managed to leave without being detected. He had so little money given to him by his mother and Garnett that he had to borrow money from Seilaz to pay for their travel expenses. When they arrived in London at the coffeehouse, Seilaz said that Portsmouth had no trouble signing the deeds because it was he who had arranged them. Exhausted from the journey, and having achieved what he set out to do, Portsmouth then retired to bed of his own free will. Seilaz vigorously denied locking Portsmouth in his chamber: this was something he would never have dared to do. Instead, Seilaz followed more of Portsmouth's orders while he rested, and went to arrange a passport.

According to Seilaz, Portsmouth was far from being made unwell by these events. Instead, Portsmouth said more than once on 23 July that 'he never had felt so happy and comfortable in his lifetime'. Indeed,

Portsmouth was in 'greater spirits' than Seilaz had ever seen him in the nine years he had known him. He was free from all that burden of responsibility and expectation. His mind relieved of the stress and pressure of performing a role that so ill-suited his abilities, he was a different man.

When Portsmouth got into the chaise to go to Yarmouth, he called Gabriel to him. He 'shook hands with him and begged him to carry on the business he had employed him in'. Gabriel left to return to Hurstbourne. It was Portsmouth, not Seilaz, who ordered the drivers to go faster on their journey, using 'violent expressions' to press his point. He insisted that Seilaz carry pistols. Portsmouth had often asked Seilaz to be armed when they travelled, but on this journey he had made this a 'particular request'.

At Yarmouth, Portsmouth was never 'compelled' to sleep in the same room as Seilaz. Portsmouth was the one who gave the orders on their arrival, as would be expected when a master and servant travelled together. Portsmouth told the landlord that he and Seilaz were to have a double-bedded room. He also asked that Seilaz and he eat together.

Portsmouth's happiness was brought to an abrupt end that night. The two men were rudely awoken in the early hours by a violent banging on the door. When the rescue party rushed in, Portsmouth was far from pleased to see them. Instead, he was much 'vexed'. Seilaz knew that Portsmouth was 'not on very good terms' with his brother, Newton. He had told Seilaz that Reverend Garnett and Mr Hanson were 'particularly obnoxious to him'. Portsmouth complained many times of their treatment of him, and he especially disliked Garnett.

Portsmouth was so little inclined to be parted from Seilaz that he did not even get out of bed to greet his visitors. His brother and Garnett had to go over to his bedside to talk to him. Seilaz heard them 'assure' him 'that if he would get up and go back with them everything at home should be made comfortable'. What an acknowledgement that all was not right at Hurstbourne! They treated him just like a naughty child who had run away, and for whom only promises of better treatment would ensure a return without a further scene.

While Portsmouth was gently coaxed to leave, Seilaz met with much rougher treatment. Having been deprived of his passport, papers, and pistols, he was marched off to the town gaol. From there he was sent to Cold Bath Fields prison. The name says it all. There he was held captive alongside some of the worst criminals in the country, a number facing charges of treason. Conditions were miserable. He repeatedly wrote to Portsmouth asking for help, but received no reply. He did not even have sufficient changes of linen or clothing, because this was all in the luggage that the Portsmouth family took away from Yarmouth. Some of Seilaz's papers were returned to him, but with all their seals torn off, rendering them useless.

Gabriel Tahourdin was busy trying to salvage his legal career. He put up a notice in Whitchurch, which was printed a few days later in the *Salisbury and Winchester Journal*. He said that reports that he had been imprisoned because of involvement with Lord Portsmouth were false, and that he intended to clear his name. Fortunately for Gabriel, nobody appeared to believe the Portsmouth family's version of events, which positioned him as a party to Seilaz's plot to deprive the family of their estates. Of course, everyone who was acquainted with Lord Portsmouth and his condition thought that it was only he who could have dreamt of such a crazy scheme. Within a short time, Gabriel and his brother were practising as lawyers again, and were conducting business in Chancery.[6]

At last, after several months, Seilaz was visited in prison by Mr Birch, a partner in Hanson's legal firm. He offered Seilaz a few pounds of relief, and tried to get him to sign a long document releasing him from Portsmouth's service. Seilaz refused to sign: why should he when Portsmouth still owed him wages and an annuity? A clerk from Hanson was sent with some clothes. But he also seized all the bonds and deeds Seilaz had relating to Portsmouth.

Seilaz claimed to not even know why he was imprisoned. He wrote to the Home Secretary, the Duke of Portland, several times demanding to know the reason for his confinement. He had been told when he was first arrested in Yarmouth that it was under the terms of the Aliens Act. But this was legislation that had been introduced by the government during the French revolutionary wars to protect Britain from political subversion. All foreigners arriving in Britain after 1793 had to be registered by their local magistrate. Any foreigner who did not notify the authorities of their arrival, or who was deemed to pose a political threat, could be held without bail, and deported. It cannot have been easy living in Britain as a native of a country that was an enemy. Seilaz was forced to prove his loyalty. 'Ever since his first arrival in England,' he told Chancery, he had been 'warmly and sincerely attached to the Government of that Country'. As evidence, he declared that he had given a sum of money towards the war effort. The Portsmouths had him arrested as an alien because they had nothing else with which to charge him, argued Seilaz. Even counsel for Portsmouth in King's Bench had to admit that Seilaz had been 'guilty of no political offence'. The Portsmouth family were forced to justify the decision to deport Seilaz from Cold Bath Fields to Hamburg, arguing that 'the object of the statute was to protect the natives against the misconduct of foreigners of every description'. Anybody could see that this was stretching the law to its limits, and well beyond its original purpose.

In February 1800, Seilaz was sent to Hamburg, a place where he was an 'entire stranger'. He was 'without friends and without money'. He made 'many appeals' to Lord Portsmouth by letter. Eventually, he applied to an English gentleman living in Hamburg for advice. Seilaz told him all that had happened. He wanted to get back the money Portsmouth owed him. It was this gentleman, Seilaz said, who composed the letter sent to Portsmouth, and which caused such an outcry. Seilaz simply copied out his words, and was 'entirely ignorant' of the English law he broke by writing the letter. Afterwards though, and once the heat of his anger had cooled, he decided it was an 'improper' letter to send. Seilaz begged the gentleman not to send the letter, and he promised to destroy it.

Seilaz was adamant that he never intended to extort money from Portsmouth. The only reason he returned to England was to recover 'what was justly due'. Since returning, he was imprisoned in Tothill Fields Bridewell, 'locked up among the common thieves' for four days. He had to raise five hundred pounds in bail to be released. When he attended the next Middlesex Quarter Sessions, as the terms of his bail required, he found that Portsmouth had moved his case to King's Bench. His solicitor had to repeatedly ask Hanson for his papers to be returned to him, and eventually King's Bench had to order him to do so. As well as the annuity Portsmouth had first arranged as a reward for his loyalty, these papers also contained character references he had written for Seilaz, in English and French. No wonder Hanson did not want to surrender them, for they would help Seilaz's defence. All this legal manoeuvre and delay was 'for the purpose of harassing and distressing me,' Seilaz lamented. It put him to 'great expenses' and loss, as he could not return to his home country and his 'professional concerns' as a surgeon and dentist.[7]

Seilaz's account of events fell on deaf ears. His statement was submitted to Chancery, but then buried within its mountains of paperwork. Nobody was interested in the grievances of a low-born French speaker when they stood opposed to the words of an honourable English nobleman and his family. Newspapers never aired his story. Seilaz was finished.

The key question about Seilaz and Portsmouth had already been asked during the trial at King's Bench. It was left hanging in the air, tantalizingly unanswered. Just what was the nature of the relationship between these two men?

If they were bedfellows, then at the start of the nineteenth century there was nothing particularly uncommon about men sleeping next to each other. Portsmouth considered and treated Seilaz as a friend. On that night in Yarmouth before they left England behind, the two men were about to embark on a new life together. In need of reassurance and protection, perhaps there was nothing surprising about Portsmouth wanting Seilaz to be with him.

But in Yarmouth the reaction of Portsmouth's brother and friends to news that the two men were sharing a room together, and their urgency to get into that room, may betray their suspicion that there was more to this relationship than friendship. Portsmouth's and Seilaz's escape from Hurstbourne was very like an elopement. Perhaps when Seilaz wrote his extortion letter to Portsmouth, he only put down in words what everyone dreaded to discover when the door opened. After all, being a gentleman's valet means caring for him in an intimate, personal way. It has to involve touch.

Later in his life many stories were told of Portsmouth's sexual preferences. There was nothing ordinary about what Portsmouth enjoyed. He had so little comprehension of what 'normal' relationships were meant to be like. If anyone had ever explained the facts of life to him, he had certainly not understood. Some would say he was impotent, but if he was then perhaps the problem was with women. He experienced sexual pleasure, but not in the usual way. He was quite capable of abusing his servants with words and violent blows, so forcing them to have sexual relations with him would not have been out of character. Many a master made his servant big with child; at least Portsmouth did not need to fear a little bastard as a consequence of his sexual relationships with men.

Or did Seilaz tempt Portsmouth to commit this crime? His French accent and foreign manners meant doubts were immediately raised about his innocence in this affair. Frenchmen, according to national prejudice, were too effeminate in their conduct, and likely to weaken the manly strength of Englishmen. Parents knew that spending too much time abroad ran the risk that their sons would return tainted by foreign habits. Worst of all, they might become morally corrupt. The French were always thought sexually immoral: it was not for nothing that the pox was called the 'Frenchman's disease'. If Portsmouth had come home with another sexual perversion, he would not have been alone.

Some might think Seilaz forced himself on Portsmouth. It was certainly easy to take advantage of him. Emotionally vulnerable, sexually naive, and mentally underdeveloped, he was a sitting target for sexual exploitation. If, as his lawyers argued, he 'had not sufficient power or presence of mind to refuse to do any act' that Seilaz 'prompted or advised him to perform', did this include sexual ones?

The timing of the arrival of Seilaz's letter was doubly embarrassing for Portsmouth (and some would say deliberately so), because by then he was a married man. It was important for him to clear his name. The newspapers reported how in King's Bench Garrow asked whether 'his Lordship might not be permitted solemnly to deny upon his oath the crime imputed to him'. But this was impossible, Ellenborough explained, because the trial was about extortion not sodomy. In response, Erskine said he 'regretted' that 'noble and honourable persons...could not be called to speak to the purity of his Lordship's life and character'.[8] The crime of sodomy was hard to prove in law, but it was equally difficult for Portsmouth to disprove. Seilaz's accusation was out in the public domain, and suspicion would always remain. Portsmouth's lawyers did their best to assert Portsmouth's innocence, but it may well have been for the best that Portsmouth himself was not asked to declare what had happened. Who knows what he would have said.

Nobody dared to voice the idea that sex between Seilaz and Portsmouth was consensual. To do so would be to recognize a relationship that had crossed social as well as sexual boundaries. But could Seilaz be condemned for showing affection and kindness towards a man who received so little of this from the family and friends who were nearest to him? Neither man belonged in English society: Portsmouth's mental problems and Seilaz's Frenchness separated them from others, but may have been what brought them together. They clung together in a hostile world. All the evidence points to Portsmouth's happiness with Seilaz. After Seilaz had given his answers to Chancery in May 1803, he disappeared from the historical record, and was not seen by Portsmouth again. In the years to come, many people would pore over the details of Portsmouth's life. But the complete truth of the time he spent with Seilaz will never be known. This at least will remain a secret.

'Our family greatly indulges secrecy'

~

BRAINS WERE NOT part of Portsmouth's family inheritance. For all that the Portsmouth family would name their children after him, Isaac Newton was no blood relative. His books and papers were proudly displayed at Hurstbourne, but they had been the legacy of Catherine Conduitt, who married into the family. Her marriage to John Wallop was such a disaster that it ended in separation, and was later claimed in family legend to have been the inspiration for Hogarth's series of paintings 'Marriage à la Mode'.[1] In Portsmouth's more recent family history, his uncle, Barton Wallop, had been made Master of Magdalene College in Cambridge. But this was no sign of academic distinction. According to one contemporary, Barton was 'totally illiterate'.[2] Closer to home, Portsmouth's youngest brother, Coulson, had attended Eton and would be elected MP for Andover in 1796. But he soon ran into debt, and drunkenness did little to enhance his limited abilities. By 1800, Pitt was receiving letters, approved by Urania, stating that he should step down before he made more of a fool of himself, for he was 'little better than an Idiot'.[3]

Even if Portsmouth did not descend from the brightest of family trees, few would have suggested that this set him on the path to lunacy. But, while Barton and, to a lesser extent, Coulson Wallop were public figures, there were other members of Portsmouth's family whose mental condition meant that they were kept hidden from sight.

Insanity in this family was so shameful that it was locked away, and for decades kept secret. Nobody wanted to admit that madness ran through the family line.

At some point in 1799, Portsmouth's mother ordered for him to be strapped down to his bed. Around the same time, and following a violent outburst from her son, Urania threatened to put him in 'the custody' of Dr Thomas Monro, chief physician at England's most notorious madhouse, Bethlem hospital. By 1799, Urania had been a dowager countess for two years, and Lord Portsmouth was thirty-one years old. Whether she gave these orders and issued this threat before or after Portsmouth's abduction-cum-escape attempt with Seilaz in July, we do not know. But something had happened to make Urania lose her cool: she was the 'most sensible woman' who had suddenly snapped. When she threatened her son with Monro, she told a person present that 'I have foreborn from having done this long ago from motives of delicacy'.[4]

Urania's words were remembered in the legal trials that Portsmouth later faced. That his mother had considered physical constraint and confinement for her son was a measure of how serious his condition had become, some argued. Her threats were presented as evidence that those closest to him had started to consider him insane well before any legal proceedings began. However, no servant could be produced to prove that Portsmouth had been strapped down, and, although Portsmouth was eventually examined by a Dr Monro, it was not in his mother's lifetime, and it was by Thomas Monro's son, Edward Thomas.[5]

Yet Lord Portsmouth was terrified when his mother uttered these words. For he knew that she had recent and personal experience of consulting with doctors for the insane, and that 'motives of delicacy' had not prevented her from confining her own sister, and his aunt, Dorothea, in a madhouse. His mother knew what she was talking about. To Portsmouth, these were not idle threats spoken in the heat of the moment, but an all too frightening possibility.

Urania was one of five children born to Coulson and Urania Fellowes. She and her two brothers, William and Henry Arthur, and sister, Mary (who died in July 1788), had been worried about Dorothea's mental health from at least August 1785. 'Our sister's unfortunate situation'[6] provoked many letters between the brothers and sisters, as they exchanged news of her condition, and debated what to do. Dorothea was unmarried, and living independently in a house on Twickenham Common. The challenge of responding to her illness was increased by her geographical distance from William, who lived at Ramsey Abbey near Huntingdon, and Haverland Hall in Norfolk, Henry Arthur, who, while having a house near Berkeley Square in London, was based at least some of the year in Eggesford, Devon, and Urania, who was at Hurstbourne in Hampshire.

While there were glimpses of hope and moments of recovery, with time, Dorothea's condition worsened. Dorothea suffered from delusions of several kinds. She became convinced that none of her servants was to be trusted, and that they were conspiring to steal from her and profit after her death. She took offence and gave offence 'anywhere, when the provocation seemed totally imaginary, in the street or in any public place', according to William. Her belief that she had been insulted led to some kind of public altercation (never detailed) on two separate occasions in Covent Garden and at Cheltenham. She was becoming an embarrassment: when Dorothea went to Bath towards the end of 1790, Urania and her brothers dreaded what might happen in this hub of society gossip. 'I am very fearfull that something shou'd happen to expose Her,' wrote Henry Arthur.

Finally, in the highly charged and politically sensitive years of the French Revolution, Dorothea became so emotionally involved in the unfolding events at home that she became convinced that her life was under threat from the 'common people' of Twickenham. Her interest in the Birmingham Riots of July 1791, which targeted Joseph Priestley, a former patient of speech therapist Samuel Angier, along with other dissenters and individuals thought sympathetic to the revolutionary cause, became obsessional. She followed events and the trials of the rioters in the newspapers, wrote letters to her sister Urania about them, and became so certain that the riots would spread, and her house (like Priestley's) would be burned, that she moved out.[7]

The Fellowes family were fortunate in where Dorothea decided to go. She took refuge from her imaginary foes in the home of John

Pridden, her father's bookseller in Fleet Street. Pridden, and then his son, who shared the same name, spent years looking after the affairs of Dorothea, apparently inspired by admiration for 'the venerable Coulson', her father, whom John Pridden junior credited with setting him on his career path as an antiquary and architect.[8] Dorothea was not an easy guest for the bookseller. In August 1791, William Fellowes recorded that, when he called in on his sister at Pridden's house, and found that she had gone to back to Twickenham for the day, Pridden 'told me, that she was hard to please, had affronted Mrs. P' by sticking out her tongue, and 'that his regard for the family induced him to put up with a great deal, meaning her temper'.[9]

Staying with Pridden long term was not an option, no matter how handsomely he was rewarded. Apparently unknown to Urania, in the autumn of 1788, her brothers discussed in their letters the possibility of Dorothea going to live at Hurstbourne. Portsmouth at this stage was still Lord Lymington, as his father was alive, and having finished school was probably living at home. It is a decision that Dorothea would have liked. She seems to have been in awe of her sister's position and success, asking William at one point if a servant-companion she had recruited was 'a proper person to sit at Ld Portsmouth's Table'.[10]

If William and Henry Arthur foresaw a problem with their insane sister living alongside her mentally troubled nephew, they did not specify it. The scheme was rejected because of Urania's health. Urania at this point was seriously ill. It was with some relief that in December Henry Arthur could write to his cousin, Robert Fellowes, 'Lady Portsmouth is quite well again and I hope to see her so in a few days – the loss of Her wou'd be great indeed.'[11] If her brothers thought the presence of Dorothea would only increase the strain Urania was already experiencing with her oldest son, they were discreet enough to never record it.

By August 1791, Dorothea was in a 'very deplorable situation'.[12] Urania in particular was anxious that a decision should be made about Dorothea's future. She later voiced frustration to her cousin about William, her oldest brother, and his inability to make up his mind. 'He is very apt to over Think himself, and to have little Patience, yet procrastinates everything...He never liked Trouble; or had firmness...

to give dispatch to Business – But thinking, ever thinking, without Resolution.'[13] William's procrastination is a gift to historians, however. In tiny hand, he meticulously recorded lists of questions that he and 'Lady P' had to resolve regarding Dorothea's care, a day-by-day account of his visit to London in August and September, and a remarkable document, dated September 1791, which he entitled 'Reasons for confinement'.[14]

William was the first to come to London, on 25 August. Urania arrived ten days later. Henry Arthur was too ill to travel (he died the following January), but, a few days before William's departure for London, Henry Arthur had written a long letter to him. 'I shou'd be heartily glad to hear that she was in a place of security where she might be taken good care of,' he wrote. A private madhouse was preferable to having a carer, or 'keeper', living with her, Henry Arthur perceived, 'because a single person about Her at home may use Her ill and we know nothing of it'. 'In my opinion there is not a doubt what to do,' wrote Henry Arthur, 'but the difficulty is – how to accomplish the end – with as little disturbance as possible.'[15] Having made up their minds, the public scene that Dorothea might make as she was confined in a madhouse was what most troubled her siblings. This was a family problem that they did not want others to know about.

William immediately set about getting Robert Darling Willis, a doctor who specialized in caring for the insane, to examine Dorothea. The rules governing the admission of patients to private madhouses had become much stricter since legislation in 1774. Private madhouses were institutions owned by individuals (who did not need a medical background), and operated as businesses for profit. Few were purpose built, but were private houses where troublesome but wealthy lunatics could be confined. Public alarm about cases of wrongful confinement, where perfectly sane people had been locked up by their relatives had led to the 1774 Act for Regulating Private Madhouses. This stipulated that all houses containing more than one lunatic had to be licensed and inspected once a year, and that patients should not be admitted without the order of 'some physician, surgeon, or apothecary'.[16] Willis was the perfect candidate for providing a certificate of Dorothea's insanity. He was the son of Dr Francis Willis, whose controversial methods of treating George III, including using a straitjacket, gag, and restraining chair, had produced a royal recovery in February 1789, and earned a handsome financial reward from the grateful William Pitt. Robert would attend the King during his second period of madness, and had established his own credentials as an expert on insanity.[17]

However, all did not go smoothly. William took Robert Willis to see Dorothea at Fleet Street on 27 August. Like her nephew, who would be examined by numerous physicians years afterwards, Dorothea was not told the truth about the identity or occupation of her visitor. Instead, William told her that Willis was 'transacting business' for him. Willis talked to Dorothea, and she confided in him her worries about being insulted by the 'common people'. But, having met her, Willis was not prepared to declare Dorothea insane, and told William that 'confinement under the present circumstances would be improper'. Two days later, Willis provided a written explanation. 'It appeared to me,' he wrote, 'that she was perfectly rational on all common topics', but 'she had taken up some peculiar ideas which made her act, in some points, much unlike herself.' 'This change in her mind' was 'probably dependent on a change of constitution owing to her time in life.' In Willis's view, it was Dorothea's 'change of life', the menopause, that provoked her occasional irrational behaviour. Hence, 'there is a probability of the symptoms wearing off by time alone', and the most he would recommend was that she should 'visit her relations or friends', or they visit her, to provide some distraction from her negative thoughts.[18]

This was an unacceptable diagnosis for William, Henry Arthur, and Urania. Responding to William's letter informing him of what Willis had said, Henry Arthur voiced what they all felt: 'I do not see how she can visit her Relations or friends – or they Her in Her present disordered state.' Her mental state rendered her unsuitable company. Only people used to being with 'persons in Her unhappy way' should be with her, thought Henry Arthur.[19] The last thing her siblings wanted was for her to stay with them and so risk her odd behaviour reflecting on them. They wanted distance from Dorothea and her mental problems, and that meant her removal from their company and confinement in a madhouse.

Urania was shocked by news of Willis's diagnosis, and hurried to London. Once there, she went with William, and their cousin Robert Fellowes, whom Urania had summoned to London 'on this sad business', to hear Willis's opinion for herself. At this meeting, Willis 'seemed to think Dorothea so little ill that he confessed, he did not know what to advise,' William recorded. Urania insisted that Willis visit Dorothea for a second time, which he did, but he continued to hold the same view.[20]

Unable to secure the signature they needed for the decision they had already reached, Dorothea's family simply shopped around for another doctor to see Dorothea. Dr Samuel Simmons, who had been a physician to Bethlem Hospital since 1781, was another hard-line physician whose cruelty to George III would provoke the King to label him that 'horrible doctor'.[21] When Simmons visited Dorothea, she told him about the houses that could be burned by rioters in Twickenham. He then informed her that he was not a lawyer, as he had been introduced, but a doctor. Dorothea was furious and told Simmons 'that if he would not leave the Room, she would'. She ran upstairs, and a servant was used to relay messages between the pair. Simmons had no hesitation at pronouncing that Dorothea's mind was 'deranged' and that she 'was not proper to be trusted without some person with her'.[22] He completed a form to say that she was insane, and advised the family to confine her in Mr Robert Holme's private madhouse, called Fisher House, in Islington.

The very next day, Urania, William, and Simmons met at Pridden's house in Fleet Street and followed Simmons' plan of pretending to take Dorothea to meet others whose property had been threatened in the recent disturbances. According to William, Simmons 'performed his part so well that Poor Dorothea was most effectually deceived'. Robert Fellowes went with Dorothea, 'and a most dreadful scene ensued upon their arrival' at Fisher House. 'Accusations of deception and much resentment followed', and from her questions and remarks it became apparent that Dorothea was well aware of into 'what sort of a House she had been introduced'.[23] Pridden was instructed to take care of all of Dorothea's affairs at her house in Twickenham, and to tell her servants that their mistress had gone on a visit 'into the Country'.[24]

Dorothea spent the next twenty-six years of her life confined in Fisher House. She outlived all her brothers and sisters, and Dr Simmons who continued to treat her until his death in 1813. If she was suffering from the menopause in 1791, then she must have been a very old lady when she died at Fisher House on 8 December 1817.

She was not forgotten by her siblings. Urania worried about her sister's living conditions, and confided in her cousin, Robert Fellowes, that Dorothea's case had prompted her to read treatises about insanity, including those by Dr William Perfect. 'I think she must lead a miserable Day!' wrote Urania, and, as the anniversary of Dorothea's confinement approached, she told Robert, 'I am sure there is not a Day that my Thoughts are not turned on the wretched Catastrophe!'[25]

Dorothea herself ensured that she was a trouble that did not go away because she wrote letters from the madhouse. She moved from imagining insults from her Twickenham neighbours to thinking her madhouse keeper had treated her with disrespect. But it was in 1799, the year that Urania threatened to strap her son to his bed, and send him to Dr Monro, that Dorothea's letters took a more disturbing turn. On 3 May, 22 July, and 27 September, Dorothea wrote three separate notes 'To the Legislature'. Of course, her notes never reached the authorities, but were forwarded to her family instead. In each, she complained that she was being poisoned. 'Three or four years ago, I complain'd that my Head was hurt every morning, by something in my Breakfast milk,' Dorothea wrote. She claimed to have informed Dr Simmons of her concerns, but nothing had been done. 'How many different Drugs I have to Complain of, I don't know; but, if the Poisons that are now mix'd with my Milk are continued, it is impossible that I can live,' she declared. By July, Dorothea was convinced that her food as well as her milk was being tampered with, so that she dared not eat. 'My fears for my Life have scarcely been interrupted,' she wrote in September. Convinced that her doctors were conspiring against her life she made the following dramatic statement:

I must set down the vote of the unlawful assembly of the College of Physicians to Destroy me, as the greatest act of Violence and oppression that was ever offer'd to an Innocent Woman. If there has been greater injustice, it has not come within my knowledge.[26]

If Dorothea's experience had taught Urania anything, it was that confinement in a private madhouse, and treatment with drugs did not always work. Dorothea had been neither silenced nor cured. It may have been as much exasperation with her sister's condition as with her son's that led Urania to issue her threats against him. But if Urania's threats to Portsmouth were never carried out, and she would describe her consent to have Dorothea confined as a decision that would 'ever bear very hard on my Feelings', Urania did not flinch from her resolve that confinement was a 'necessity' for Dorothea.[27] Urania tried to improve the comforts of confinement, but she never considered freedom for her sister. As Dorothea's condition worsened, in Urania's eyes, it became increasingly alarming, and the reason for her confinement more justified.

Portsmouth must have been aware of what had happened to his aunt, even if there is no proof that they ever met. For years, Dorothea's condition was the subject of family discussion, and while her independent wealth could meet the costs of her care, her bills and accounts had to be managed by other family members. We know that Dorothea also wrote directly to Portsmouth, as we have one surviving letter to him, dated 18 November 1800. Addressed to 'The Right Honourable The Lord Viscount Lymington', and asking that she be remembered to Lord Portsmouth, and 'the Mr Wallops' and 'Lady Wallops', Dorothea either did not realize or remember that the 2nd earl had died three years beforehand, and that Lymington was now Lord Portsmouth. Dorothea was well informed of her status, however: she signed herself, 'the unfortunate Dorothea Fellowes'.[28]

There was madness on both sides of Portsmouth's family. On his father's side it was exhibited through the children of Portsmouth's aunt, Lady Catherine Wallop. Catherine was the 2nd earl's only sister, who in October 1770 had married Lockhart Gordon, the son of the

3rd earl of Aboyne. Lockhart became a Judge Advocate for the British army in Bengal, and died there in March 1788. Catherine remained in London throughout her marriage, and bore four children who survived into adulthood: Lockhart, Loudoun, Caroline, and Catherine. As a widow, Catherine supplemented her income by tutoring and lodging young ladies in her Kensington home, including a Rachel Dashwood, the illegitimate daughter and joint heiress of Lord Le Despencer. Lockhart and his younger brother Loudoun became fond of Miss Dashwood, whom they saw in their school holidays. On leaving school, Lockhart trained for the ministry, and Loudoun, like his father, for the army. As a soldier, Loudoun travelled abroad to Martinique and the West Indies, but also fell into debt, and at one point was imprisoned in New Prison, Clerkenwell. Meanwhile, Portsmouth's widowed aunt, Catherine, and his cousin of the same name, paid visits to him at Hurstbourne in August 1802, and his cousin Catherine stayed with him again at some point between 1808 and 1810.[29] When in London, Portsmouth often called to see Lockhart and Loudoun: the cousins were on familiar terms.[30]

Scandal erupted soon after Loudoun's return from military duty in September 1803. Miss Dashwood had married Matthew Allen Lee, but had separated from him within a short time. She remained legally married, and, thanks to her inheritance and a generous allowance from her husband, a very wealthy woman. Both Loudoun and his brother Lockhart paid her many visits, and Loudoun declared his love for her, which he said she welcomed. Then, on 15 January 1804, the two brothers, both armed with pistols, abducted Mrs Lee from her home and took her in a carriage on a journey that they intended to end in Wales. Reverend Lockhart attempted to place a ring belonging to Loudoun on Mrs Lee's finger in an imitation of a wedding ceremony, and Mrs Lee was seen throwing a locket from the carriage with the words: 'the charm that has preserved my virtue hitherto is dissolved… now welcome pleasure'. They stopped for the night at Tetsworth in Oxfordshire, where Loudoun shared a bed with Mrs Lee. Her servants back in London had alerted the authorities to events, and the law finally caught up with the brothers in Gloucester, where they were arrested. They were brought back to London, and charged with the offence of forcibly abducting Mrs Lee, 'for the purpose of enjoying her property, marrying her, or defiling her person'. If found guilty, the brothers faced the death penalty.

Lockhart and Loudoun were tried at the Oxford assizes in March 1804. The newspapers had been following the case since the brothers' arrest in January. The courtroom and streets surrounding the court were so packed with eager spectators that the judge and lawyers had to push their way through the throng to reach their places. The trial opened with the case for the prosecution. Much was made of the social background of the brothers: they had 'the polish of gentility, and the refined advantages of high birth and elegant education', and so they should have known better. Greed and lust had won them over. A number of Mrs Lee's servants testified that they and their mistress had been threatened at gunpoint when she was abducted. Then Mrs Lee took the stand. Her evidence lasted two hours, beginning with an account of how she had stayed with Mrs Gordon when she was fourteen years old. But then the case against the brothers unravelled. Her answers to questions about the abduction made it apparent that she had been a party to the plan, and that she saw the journey as a romantic elopement not a forced abduction. She admitted that at Tetsworth she had intercourse with Loudoun, and had welcomed him into her bed. Rather than being a victim, she revealed herself to be a wicked temptress, who had no religion. When she said she 'did not believe in Christianity', the judge brought the case to a sudden halt. He ordered the jury to acquit the brothers because there was no evidence of force. As the acquitted brothers left the court, 'the mob cheered them with loud huzzas'. The disgraced Mrs Lee had to shelter from the crowds' insults and wait until it had dispersed before hastening away.[31]

In their letters to each other, the Portsmouth family remained resolutely quiet about this set of events. They were no doubt horrified about how the family name was drawn into the case. Witnesses and Mrs Lee were asked about the family connection between Mrs Gordon and her brother, the 2nd earl of Portsmouth. The story had become a public sensation, reported by newspapers across the land, and Loudoun, feeling frustrated that he had not had his turn in court to present his defence would not let it drop. A month after the trial, he published a lengthy attack on Mrs Lee, arguing that he and his brother were 'the dupes of an artful and treacherous woman'. In this publication, which went through several editions, Loudoun tried to boost his claims of respectability by boasting of his family ties with the Portsmouths. He wrote that their solicitor, John Hanson, acted for the brothers at the Oxford assizes, and Mr Serjeant Best had been sent to give them legal advice, 'at the express desire of the Earl of Portsmouth'. Three years later, Mrs Lee published her own 'vindication' of her conduct. The crowd at the Oxford assizes may have been on the side of the Gordons, but the press remained convinced that they 'had certainly no claim to popular respect'. As a clergyman, Lockhart's behaviour was particularly 'unpardonable'. The death of Lockhart's wife a few months after the trial was attributed to shock and grief.[32]

Loudoun and Lockhart had brought notoriety and shame to the family, but their trial in Oxford did not put an end to the troubles they would present. On 8 October 1810, Urania wrote to her son Newton to tell him that Loudoun 'has Relapsed'. At the breakfast table of Lord Grantley, who by this time had become a family member through his sister's marriage, and in 'Mixed Coy' (Company), Loudoun 'Broke Forth'. He said that he was the man who was described in the Book of Revelations as bringing peace on earth, and that he planned to fight Bonaparte in single combat on the plains of Almeida, and was confident of his success. Grantley met this outburst with a response that calmed the situation, according to Urania. He 'cooley told Him He was right, and He would go a part of the Way with Him to London, and promote his Journey'. If Grantley had started the journey with Loudoun, it ended with Loudoun being taken by 'two Persons to a Private House in London'.

Urania and Portsmouth now had two of their relatives confined in private madhouses. Since Urania described Loudoun's behaviour in 1810 as a relapse, it seems probable that he had experienced a mental breakdown before, and possibly had already spent time in a madhouse. Insanity may have been how Loudoun's family explained his abduction of Mrs Lee in 1804, although this cause was not one that was explored by the press coverage of the case.[33]

Like Dorothea Fellowes, Loudoun wrote letters from his captivity. Soon after the October 1810 incident Loudoun sent a letter to Lord Grantley's brother, General Chapple Norton, 'couch'd in very Sensible Language'. In his letter, he stated that 'He is sensible of his Malady, and…become very Well, and begs to be Liberated.'[34] The General shared the contents of the letter with the family, but, like Dorothea, Loudoun was never released. At some point, he was cared for by Dr John Warburton, and then moved to Laverstock House asylum, a large private madhouse near Salisbury, owned by the Finch family, which was renowned for the humane treatment of its inmates, and success at achieving their cure. Nevertheless, Loudoun was still there in January 1828. In June the previous year, aided by his brother, Loudoun had tried but failed to escape. Lockhart's claims that his brother's confinement was no longer necessary fell on deaf ears.[35]

In October 1810, it was left to Urania to 'Communicate this Sad Tale' of Loudoun's breakfast-time scene to his mother. Urania was sympathetic towards her sister-in-law, and admired her courage. Telling Newton of this meeting, she said Catherine Gordon 'bore' the news 'with feelings of One, accustomed to be…Burdened, and with the Resignation to Providence of "Give me Patience Thy Will be Done!"'. Perhaps Mrs Gordon won Urania's support because she was another mother enduring the consequences of having a mentally disturbed son.

When Urania spoke to Mrs Gordon about Loudoun, she had to 'conceal it from her Daughter, who is not to hear of it'.[36] Since Caroline Gordon had died in 1801, this daughter must have been Catherine. Why Catherine could not be told of her brother's fate is not made clear, but it may be because she too was in a fragile mental condition. By September 1824, Catherine was also confined in a private madhouse, in her case the one owned by Dr John Warburton. We know this because, once their mother died, Lord Portsmouth and his trustees became responsible for meeting the cost of the care of his two cousins. In June 1836, Drs Finch and Warburton were still chasing their fees.[37] Could this have been the case of one mad person supporting the care of two others?

* * *

'Our family greatly indulges secrecy', wrote Urania to her cousin Robert Fellowes on 14 January 1792. She had just received Robert's letter bearing the 'Formidable' news that her brother Henry Arthur had a 'Cancerous Complaint'. Henry Arthur had stayed with her at Hurstbourne in the early part of December, and she 'witness'd my poor Dear Brother Henry's ill-state of Health', but he never complained of pain and she did not realize that he was so seriously ill. 'That my poor dear Henry should conceal so afflicting a Malady from me… does not surprise me', explained Urania, because the family was so good at keeping secrets.[38]

There was no greater testament to this family's success at keeping secrets than the total lack of reference to the insanity and confinement of Dorothea Fellowes, and Loudoun and Catherine Gordon in the legal proceedings that faced Portsmouth. There were enough cases of insanity running through families for people to know that it could be inherited. When Newton first called for his brother to be subject to a Commission of Lunacy in November 1814, Dorothea was still alive, and Loudoun if not Catherine was confined in a private madhouse. Newton, and then his son, would hardly have wanted to bring attention to their other mentally troubled relatives, but they could not control what witnesses said, and no one made the connection between Portsmouth and his 'unfortunate' aunt or cousins. This was all the more remarkable given the doctors who were chosen to examine Portsmouth. Drs Francis Willis and Thomas Warburton were relatives of the physicians who had examined Dorothea and confined Catherine, and Dr Alexander Robert Sutherland had been put in charge of the medical care of Dorothea since the death of Dr Simmons. While each of these doctors thought Portsmouth was of 'unsound mind', none of them suggested that his condition was hereditary.

Family secrets have their costs, and Urania came very close to paying a high price for keeping Dorothea's condition a secret. Henry Arthur did not reveal the seriousness of his illness to his sister and brother, but, when he died on 29 January 1792, a much bigger secret came to light. Henry Arthur had never married, and controversially his father had left him, not his older brother, William, the Eggesford estate. By his death, Eggesford was said to be worth 'more than half a million'.[39] Henry Arthur had let his family know that he intended to repeat his father's decision of favouring Urania's second son, Newton, rather than her oldest, Lymington, by making him his heir. Since Lymington stood to inherit the Portsmouth estates, this should not be seen as any slight or indication of his uncle's regard for him. Lymington's future interests were already taken care of, and Henry Arthur was set to favour his next oldest nephew. Henry Arthur also led Urania to expect that he would leave her oldest daughter, Henrietta Dorothea, the jewels of her aunt, Mary Fellowes, which he had in his safe-keeping.[40]

The bombshell on his death came when his family turned the key attached to his watch to open his travelling case. Inside was his will, written in his hand, dated 16 September 1789, with a codicil of 5 January 1791. He left everything to a woman they had never heard of, Martha Brown, and her two children, whom he regarded as his own. Any child born to Martha within forty weeks of his death was also given a legacy of ten thousand pounds. When the shocked family investigated the identity of Martha Brown, they discovered that she was married to a soldier who had been in the East Indies for the last twelve years. In her husband's absence, she had been running a bawdy house for 'girls of the town', and was known as 'Mother Brown'.[41] That Henry Arthur had been conducting a secret relationship with 'so Bad a Woman' was truly shocking to Urania and her family. 'It seems hardly credible so sensible a Man could fall into such Deep laid snares,' wrote Urania to her cousin.[42]

The lawyers, led by John Hanson, and overseen by Reverend Garnett, were set to work. While nobody tried to deny that Henry Arthur had a relationship with Martha, however disgraceful this would have been, the family needed to prove that he had been duped into making this will. Demonstrating that Martha had deceived Henry Arthur by pretending the children were his own was fairly straightforward. Witnesses testified that Martha had not had any baby since her husband left the country twelve years before, and when Martha brought children to Hanson's house and claimed that their father was Henry Arthur, investigation showed that they were in fact the children of another woman. Martha was forty-nine years old, and when threatened with a search by midwives to determine whether she was seven months pregnant, as she originally claimed, she retracted her statement and admitted that she had not seen Henry Arthur since the previous July.[43]

Martha's claims on the Eggesford fortune were falling apart, but, for Urania to win it back for Newton, she needed to demonstrate that she was held in her brother's 'Esteem and Regard' up to the point of his death.[44] Written evidence of affection for his sister would show where Henry Arthur's true intentions lay. But this is where Urania had a problem: all the recent letters she had from her brother also discussed their sister, Dorothea. Proceedings in the court of Chancery had already brought unwelcome publicity to the family's affairs, and Martha's 'scandalous fraud' had been the subject of much newspaper reporting.[45] The last thing Urania wanted was the matter of her sister's condition to be dragged into the papers. She told her cousin that she could only feel 'great comfort in the thought of avoiding every step which will produce a Publication of so much unhappiness'.[46]

Urania went to extraordinary lengths to protect her son's inheritance without revealing her sister's case. She became so paranoid that her letters to her cousin could fall into the wrong hands that she stopped referring to Dorothea by name, and instead left a blank or inserted ellipses when she wrote about her.[47] Being pressed by the lawyers to produce a letter to her from Henry Arthur, she took her scissors to one that he had addressed to her, 'My Dear Raney', on 24 September 1791. She cut out all references to Dorothea and her doctor's opinions. Sending a copy of the letter to Robert Fellowes with boxes drawn around the sections she had cut out, Urania explained that she did this 'for my Conscience sake to my Brother Wm and my own Feelings on the Subject'. Such was her determination that Dorothea's fate should remain a closely guarded secret that she said 'I did not like even Mr Garnett should be left to Guess who the Doctors opinion was favourable to'.[48] Incredibly, Garnett, Urania's closest friend, who was fighting her cause in the courts, was not in on the secret of Dorothea.

Urania's actions were much to the annoyance of her lawyers, who decided that they could not use the letter that she had defaced. But their efforts to contest Martha Brown's claims on Henry Arthur's estate eventually paid off. 'No man was ever more imposed on by artifice and fraud than the Testator,' declared the Solicitor-General. Martha was confined in the Fleet while she was unable to pay off her legal costs. Newton, still a minor, was confirmed as his uncle's heir, and, in August 1794, a royal licence granted Newton the right to take on the surname of his great benefactor, Fellowes.[49]

Portsmouth's family was one that had shown itself more than capable of fighting over property and inheritance, and one that was prepared to lock up its mentally unstable members for decades at a time. Dorothea's condition had forced Urania to read up about insanity: if she was familiar with Perfect's works, then she was up-to-date with thinking about the causes and treatment of madness. Urania had also become aware of the legal options for protecting the property of the insane as she had been part of the family's discussion of whether they should seek a Commission of Lunacy for Dorothea.[50] Yet the idea of confining Portsmouth to a private madhouse was never suggested in all of this family's extensive correspondence, and comparisons between him and his aunt and cousins were never recorded. Why?

It could be because at this stage none of Portsmouth's family thought of him as mad. To be sure, during his childhood and youth he had shown many worrying indicators of problems to come. He had plentiful learning difficulties, and his early problems with toileting, as well as struggles with speech, bore comparison with many of the signs that other parents used to identify idiocy. His lack of self-awareness and social skills, as well as susceptibility to suggestion, we might associate with autism.

Yet, if Portsmouth had been subject to the legal tests for idiocy, which commonly included questions assessing memory for dates (such as his birthday), or ability to reason and complete simple arithmetic, he would have passed them with flying colours. He was nothing like the thirty-year-old Walter Long Warren who in 1735 was said to have 'so weak a judgement, capacity and understanding' that he would give away all his estate 'for a piece of gingerbread'. Portsmouth had been slow at school, but he had acquired some learning, unlike Fanny Fust, whose family protested against her marriage to Henry Bowerman in 1787 on the grounds of her 'total insanity or imbecility of mind'. Fanny had the mind of a three-year-old, it was claimed, and despite the best efforts of her mother and school teachers she could not read, spell, do needlework or hold any conversation 'whatsoever, even on the most trifling subject'.[51]

Portsmouth did not match the characteristics of those being labelled as idiots, but nonetheless his mind had not developed as it should. There was no obvious cause for Portsmouth's condition. No evidence suggests that there were problems with his birth, and there is no record of epileptic fits, which at this time were thought to trigger mental breakdown. Without a clear cause, coping with Portsmouth was never going to be straightforward. His family had time on their hands, and under Urania's watch they had tried a variety of responses. Quick-fix solutions failed (his stammer remained); time away at school or abroad only offered temporary relief. Legal protection was sought with the 1790 deed, but the Seilaz incident showed how easily Portsmouth could be subject to abuse and fraud.

Portsmouth was a liability but this did not make him insane. There is no evidence at this time of Portsmouth suffering from delusions like his aunt and cousins. He could be capable of rational thought, and controlled in his actions. In this context, Urania's threats to restrain her son and have him sent to Dr Monro could be understood as the words of a woman who was overwhelmed with worries about the mental health of her sister. With madness on her mind, and faced with her challenging, unreliable, and frequently irritating son, Urania had overreacted, and used words that reflected what was uppermost in her thoughts. She never intended for her threats to be carried out, and, apart from Portsmouth himself, nobody took her words seriously. It was only in later years, and after her death, that her words were remembered. For a woman who placed so much importance on keeping insanity a family secret, it is ironic that her threats would be used to raise questions about her son's mental condition.

Angry and exasperated, in 1799, it was clear to Urania that her son needed tight control if he was going to avoid incidents like the Seilaz one in the future. Confinement in a madhouse was not an option for her oldest son and heir. She started to seek another kind of keeper for her son: a wife.

Husband

'She was more like a mother to him than a wife'

ON TUESDAY, 19 November 1799, John Charles, 3rd earl of Portsmouth, was married to Grace Norton in the parish church of St John the Baptist, Wonersh, Surrey. Portsmouth was one month short of being thirty-two years old; his bride was forty-seven.

The woman who had married the 3rd earl of Portsmouth, and so became the new Lady Portsmouth, came from a respected and wealthy family in neighbouring Surrey, the Grantleys. Grace's father, Fletcher Norton, had been Attorney General for two years from 1763, and had served as Speaker of the House of Commons for a decade from 1770. 'Remarkable alike for the clearness of his arguments and the inaccuracy of his statements', he was a man with a tempestuous disposition, and an attraction to controversy. Awarded the title first Baron Grantley, he also earned the nickname Sir Bull-Face Double Fee.

The 1st Lord Grantley set about making improvements to his wife's family home in the small village of Wonersh, just a few miles south of Guildford, where he had been an MP. Wonersh Park was a large red-brick mansion, set in wooded grounds and a 'tastefully arranged' pleasure garden. It was where Grace and her four brothers who survived infancy grew up. Their father increased the Wonersh estate by buying more land in and around Guildford, and made Surrey his family home rather than Grantley, near Ripon, Yorkshire, where he had been born. Proud of the family's new aristocratic title, the Grantleys put their stamp on the place that they had made their home. When the parish church, which could be reached through a gate in the wall that surrounded the Park, was rebuilt, Grace's eldest brother, William, constructed a family mausoleum in the south chapel. By the time Grace married, her father had been dead for ten years, and William was the 2nd Baron Grantley, but her mother was still alive. With Reverend Garnett officiating, the couple exchanged their marriage vows within sight of the mausoleum, and then led the wedding party through to the bride's family home.[1]

Grace had become a Countess, but before her marriage we know very little of her life. Like her new husband, there was no portrait of her, or at least no surviving one. Nobody remarked on her looks, so perhaps they were unexceptional. At forty-seven years old she had probably given up all hope of marriage. Yet she did not have to take whoever made an offer. There was strong disapproval of forced marriages, and she held the power of veto. As a family friend described the marriage, Grace was 'at the time of life which made her able to judge for herself'.[2]

What Grace was thinking as she was led down the aisle, we will never know. If she had been worried about rumours that had begun to circulate about him, then it is possible that the earl's good manners and polite behaviour allayed her fears. Portsmouth's mother had certainly prepared him for such meetings, and, if Grace was reassured by his conduct, she would not be the first or last person to be taken in by his civility.

Even if Grace had no illusions about her husband's mental abilities, she cannot have thought him mad. The church, which governed the law on marriage, deemed that no person who was insane could enter a contract of marriage. For a marriage to be valid, each person had to be able to give their consent, and without understanding this was impossible. At least at the point when they exchanged their vows on 19 November 1799, Grace thought that Lord Portsmouth was sane. But perhaps that showed how little she knew him.

Grace's oldest brother, William, 2nd Lord Grantley, was pleased with the marriage. It took his unmarried sister off his hands, and her title increased the family's prestige. But one of her brothers (either Fletcher or Chapple Norton – reports differed) disapproved. Their friend, Justice Best, who also expressed his 'disapprobation' at the match, remembered that the family had heard Lord Portsmouth was 'a person of very weak intellect.'[3] Rather than acting as a boost to the family's honour, this brother thought that Grace's marriage to such a man would reflect badly on their family, and would perhaps encourage people to think that their father's money-grabbing tendencies had not died with him. Following this line of thinking, their sister's personal happiness was being sacrificed for family fortune and title.

This was a marriage of convenience for both sides. Once it had been decided in 1790 that after Portsmouth the next heir should be his younger brother, Newton, a young wife was deemed unsuitable for Portsmouth. If there was any concept that Portsmouth's condition could be inherited, then there was another reason why an older wife would be sought. Nobody wanted to risk another baby being born like John Charles. An older woman would not have any expectation of becoming a mother, and would perhaps make a less demanding partner in the marital bed. Grace's maturity, in understanding, patience, and ability to manage a difficult husband, would be her asset. Being 'a pleasant and agreeable lady, but of an age which did not promise prolific consequences' was Grace's key attraction.[4] Whether Portsmouth saw his bride, as she approached the altar on 19 November 1799, in anything like these terms was not recorded. Aside from exchanging their vows, both groom and bride were resolutely silent about the occasion.

The legal settlement that was agreed the day before the wedding was a sign that this was going to be no ordinary marriage. Lawyers always got to work before marriages at this level of society because they involved the transfer and protection of so much property. But the document signed on 18 November 1799 was an exceptional one, which would have repercussions for Portsmouth long into the future.

By this deed, Lord Portsmouth handed over all his estate to four trustees: Grace's brother, Lord Grantley; Portsmouth's brother, Newton Fellowes; Reverend Garnett; and John Hanson, the solicitor who had drawn up the settlement. By the terms of the settlement, Portsmouth could not enter into a lease or any other legal arrangement concerning his property without the signature of all four trustees. He could not draw a draft without it being countersigned by his wife. In exchange for a promised marriage portion of twelve thousand pounds from Grace, the trustees were empowered to raise a jointure of one thousand pounds a year for her should she be left a widow. Grace was also promised three hundred pounds per year as 'pin money', to spend as she wished. Several valuable household items, including Isaac Newton's manuscripts, were given to the trustees for their safe-keeping. As Dr Garnett and Mr Hanson were expected to do most of the work as trustees, and they were not family members, it was agreed that they should each be paid £150 per year out of Portsmouth's estates.

Why would Portsmouth have agreed to the terms of this settlement? As Best said, 'No one in his senses would have signed it.'[5] He was 'dispossessed of all control over his real and personal property', and was proof of his insanity, argued lawyers in the 1823 Commission of Lunacy, 'because he placed himself in such a situation that he could not possess himself of a £20 note.'[6] To draw up such a deed was evidence, thought the Chancellor in 1821, that the trustees saw Portsmouth as a man unable to act 'in respect to almost any trans-actions of human life, as far as related to his estate and property'. Incredibly, Portsmouth had chosen 'to put himself under fetters very similar to those which belong to a Commission of Lunacy'.[7] He was left with his hands tied; a man born into enormous wealth, but now without the power to spend it. He was beholden to his four trustees and on a day-to-day basis to his wife. Like a child, he was left finan-cially dependent. 'Is it possible then to believe that a man of competent understanding…could induce himself to give up his prop-erty in such a way as to be left with only that sort of pocket money which would be given to a school boy?' argued another lawyer.[8]

The marriage settlement brought rock-solid guarantees for the families of both Grace and Portsmouth. It gave Grace financial secu-rity for the rest of her life. At her age, there was no risk of Grace bearing a child who as Portsmouth's heir would deprive Newton of inheriting the estates that had been set apart as his by the earlier 1790 deed. But only the 1799 deed would ensure that during his lifetime Portsmouth could not sign away the family's fortune at a whim. In November, the painful memories of the summer when Seilaz had attempted to defraud the entire family were still fresh. Newton's lawyers later argued that the 1799 settlement was intended to protect the Portsmouth estate 'from imposition'. The family recognized that Portsmouth was 'a person of a weak and imperfect mind and of an extremely rash and irritable temper', and had a 'disposition liable to be imposed upon', and so was 'unfit' to be left 'in the uncontrolled management' of his estate.[9]

However, in time, the 1799 settlement, and the marriage the following day, became a thorn in Newton's side. To argue that in 1799 he and Grace's family thought Portsmouth was simply incapable rather than insane was extremely tricky when the deed meant such a wholesale transfer of power over property. Furthermore, Newton's lawyers became embroiled in complex legal manoeuvres as they attempted to prove that, while his older brother was 'weak-minded' in 1799, he had become insane by 1815. It was only by this later date, it was argued, that Portsmouth required a Commission of Lunacy.

Newton's self-interest in the 1799 deed was evident to everyone. Was it Portsmouth's state of mind that had changed or, given that by 1815 Portsmouth was married for a second time, his personal circumstances? Newton was left being asked by his solicitor to find evidence that would show that the marriage to Grace 'was a match of convenience' because this first marriage was 'the principal stumbling block' to proving that his second marriage was invalid.

Perhaps Portsmouth had always been insane, and in 1815 Newton just had to find new ways of protecting his inheritance. But if Portsmouth was insane in 1799, then 'it is the most scandalous deed that was ever executed', declared the Chancellor in 1815.[10] An insane man was not capable of signing such a deed, or entering into a marriage. The document would then become evidence that Newton had deliberately deprived his brother of his legal rights, and that Portsmouth's marriage to Grace was invalid from the outset.

To try to show that Portsmouth knew what he was doing when he signed the 1799 deed, and therefore was not insane, lawyers pointed to the fact that he made a number of changes to the document. He amended the papers by hand, and his changes were incorporated in the final document. Portsmouth increased Grace's pin money from two to three hundred pounds per year. Then in careful hand he wrote that 'Hurstbourne Park, House and Premises to remain for my occupation'.[11] The man who was to pass everything to four trustees on the eve of his wedding wanted the reassurance that his home, and the three hundred acres of land that immediately surrounded it, were to stay his own. This was his.

The marriage between Portsmouth and Grace was an arranged one, between two individuals who barely knew each other. It was a match based on comparable wealth and collective benefit, not personal compatibility. But once the legal documents had been signed, and the formalities of the wedding service were over, there was a limit to how far their families could intervene. Grace had been chosen for Portsmouth because it was thought she could take on a very particular (and, many would argue, peculiar) role as his wife. Now she had to perform.

And perform she did, with some aplomb. In public, the new couple led a busy life full of society engagements. Spending the winter months at her father's house in Lincoln's Inn Fields, and the summer at Hurstbourne, Grace and Portsmouth mixed with fellow aristocrats in town and country. There were balls and parties aplenty, and many social functions that provided the excuse for Grace to go shopping for a new gown. These were the pleasures of marriage to a peer, and the grand occasions that remained long in her family's memory. When Grace's mother died at Wonersh in 1803, at the advanced old age of ninety-five, she left her 'dear Daughter Grace now Countess of Portsmouth', the 'silver and gold gown and coat' that she wore at a ball held at Hurstbourne. With an endearing, yet poignant optimism, she also left her only daughter her 'childbed linen' and baby clothes, for her to use 'if she has one'.[12]

On a day-to-day basis, Grace assumed many of the responsibilities usually left to a husband in marriage. She managed all the household expenses, and tradesmen, estate workers, and servants knew that she was the one who would settle their bills. Servants were instructed to receive their orders from her, not Portsmouth. Grace 'always appeared to be on the watch lest his Lordship should commit some error of judgement', commented one of Portsmouth's former school fellows. She told servants and estate labourers to take care of her husband, to prevent him from coming to harm. A Hurstbourne gatekeeper was instructed by Grace to 'humour' Portsmouth 'in everything as far as he could'.[13]

Keeping Portsmouth in good humour was the principle that governed Grace's relationship with her husband. His bad and frequently changing moods were notorious, but being the daughter of 'Sir Bullface' had taught Grace a thing or two about how to live with irascible men. She could be visibly affected by her husband's anger. On one occasion, convinced that some poachers caught on his land should have been sentenced to transportation rather than imprisonment, Portsmouth became 'quite raving' with fury, and Grace was seen shaking with fear.[14] But most of the time Grace was able to control her emotions and focus on improving her husband's. Reverend McCarthy, who frequently visited the couple when they were at Lincoln's Inn Fields, was full of praise for how Grace managed her husband. She was 'eminently careful of him. She took care to have him soothed,' he remarked. If Portsmouth 'evinced a strong inclination to break out', she would pacify him, and encourage him 'to go to bed'.[15] Another trick was to try distraction. The wife of a Hurstbourne labourer recalled hearing Grace responding to Portsmouth's ill humour by cheerfully announcing, 'do now Lord Portsmouth come and look at this pretty baby'. Her best efforts were met on this occasion with Portsmouth deliberately turning his head away.[16]

Described after her death as a 'very pious' lady, Grace was the epitome of a virtuous wife.[17] At a time when moralists were busy constructing new ideals of femininity and domesticity, Grace embodied the qualities that would eventually be described in Coventry Patmore's *Angel in The House* (1854). This upper-class woman was a model of angelic patience, self-sacrifice, duty, and devotion to her husband. What she thought of her life as a married woman remains a mystery. Virtually nothing remains that was personal to Grace. Just two brief letters, one barely more than a rushed undated note to Newton Fellowes, enquiring whether he and his family will be joining her at Hurstbourne, survive in her hand.[18] Nearly everything we know about Grace comes from the reports and memories of others, and these were recorded after her death. In her lifetime, she was the invisible woman, subsumed by her husband's needs.

Grace seems too good to be true, but for some of those who knew her, it was her kindness to Portsmouth that was her main fault. She was just *too* kind. Her efforts to please her husband, to keep him in a good mood and make him happy made them both behave in ways that were inappropriate. Grace indulged her husband and allowed him to pursue some of his eccentric habits. The second surviving letter written by Grace was sent in August 1813 to Charlotte Maria, 8th countess of Banbury, and is friendlier and less functional in tone than the note to her brother-in-law. Grace began by describing attending a confirmation celebration for the daughter of a local family in Whitchurch, and the visit of her brother, Lord Grantley. But, since 'the weather has been very fine for the Harvest', Grace's main activity had been 'Dining out of Doors' with her husband. She breezily writes of sitting in the hay fields in 'some very pritty situations' as if that was an entirely normal thing for an aristocratic couple to do.[19]

But of course it wasn't, and nor was this couple's conduct when they dined indoors. Husbands and wives at this level of society usually sat at either end of the table, or opposite each other when they entertained. Grace, however, sat next to her husband. Several witnesses remarked on this as a 'peculiarity'.[20] It allowed Grace to control how much wine Portsmouth could drink, and perhaps ensure that conversation ran smoothly. But it also led to exchanges between the couple that fellow diners found astonishing. David Williams was a surgeon in Hurstbourne Priors who frequently dined with the Portsmouths when he visited London. 'A great many times', Williams witnessed Portsmouth stop eating, turn to his wife sitting next to him, 'and lay his head on her neck and fondle her and cry and make a great piece of work in a very ridiculous manner: she coaxed him as if she were humouring a fractious and spoilt child; and in a few minutes he began eating again very heartily.'[21]

The discomfort that Williams felt as he described this scene is palpable. There was a familiarity and display of dependence in this relationship that was altogether unnatural. Even if Grace knew what was required of her as a wife, Portsmouth appeared entirely ignorant of his role as a husband. He should have been at the head of the table, performing the 'honours of the table' to his guests, not fawning over his wife. He was her master, she his subordinate. But in this marriage, the roles had been reversed. As another frequent visitor remarked of the couple, 'her whole treatment of him was quite unlike the behaviour of a Wife to a Husband who was of sound Mind'.[22]

It was Grace's goodness that prevented her from taking advantage of her husband's dependence upon her. Many people who saw Grace together with Portsmouth would have agreed with his former school fellow's observation, that 'she was more like a Mother to him than a Wife'.[23] A bailiff at Hurstbourne believed that Portsmouth 'looked up to' Grace, 'somewhat as a little child does to a Mother or a Nurse', while a former servant said that 'his Lordship used to complain to her Ladyship as a Child would to its Mother'.[24] Being a mother figure meant Grace could exercise some kind of discipline over her husband. A footman observed that Portsmouth 'was plainly under some restraint in her presence but she was kind to him'. Grace 'spoke with authority to his Lordship, but mildly: she seemed to have the sort of command and direction of him that a mother has of a child'.[25]

But of course Portsmouth already had a mother. The fact that Urania pursued a very different kind of mother role from the one assumed by Grace inevitably brought the two women into conflict. The contrast between their different ways of managing Portsmouth could not be greater. Urania was the strict disciplinarian; Grace the indulgent carer. Urania knew her son needed a wife, but that did not mean that she had to like her daughter-in-law. She saw Grace as a figure with a function to fulfil, not a person whom she needed to get to know. This wasn't so much a case of rivals for affection (Urania may have been content to let Grace monopolize any feelings Portsmouth may have had), but a battle of wills over who had the greatest power over Portsmouth.

As early as the spring following her son's marriage, Urania was expressing her disapproval of Grace in her letters to her favourite son, Newton. 'I believe the Grandees of H.P. go on but strangely!' Urania wrote from London in April 1800. 'She holds a very Lofty Head, and this is the first time she has been here, and I paid my first visit Saturday.' Grace and Portsmouth's visit had to be postponed after Urania received a note from Grace to say, 'my P. was <u>rather</u> Fatigued', and so could not come. Married he might have been, but Portsmouth was still Urania's: he was 'my P'.[26]

Resentful that her daughter-in-law now determined when she could see her son, Urania was also critical of how Grace ran her household. Hurstbourne had become 'such a Pickle', Urania complained in January 1802. It was in disorder that was 'worse than a Stable. Nay many stables are in a more fit state for Human creatures to reside in!' Grace and Portsmouth were also neglecting the wellbeing of their servants, Urania believed. Newton, far away in Eggesford, Devon, was praised by his mother for sending relief to one sick Hurstbourne servant and his wife. In turn, Urania told Newton how she had intervened to organize medical assistance for a Hurstbourne coachman when he had caught a cold on a journey from London. 'The Want of Christian Feeling, to the Menial Servant who is known to have no resource, and should look up to, and be Protected by Master and Mistress' was shocking to Urania and a 'Disgrace' to Lord and Lady Portsmouth.[27] Although they had ample opportunity in the later legal trials that examined Portsmouth's life, not a single servant or other witness made the same critical comments about Hurstbourne under Grace and Portsmouth's management. This was Urania's particular bugbear.

Having controlled every detail of her son's life, Urania disliked being kept at arm's length when he married. Writing to Newton from London in August 1810 she said she did not 'know anything what is doing at H. Park. I had last week, a chip-in-porridge letter from her Ladyship: that told nothing on the subject!'[28] 'Chip-in-porridge' was a nineteenth-century phrase, meaning insubstantial. Such a lack of news was immensely frustrating. Urania had been a dowager countess since her husband died in May 1797, but it was only since Grace had become her son's wife in November 1799 that she had been made to feel like one.

Usurped she may have been, but Urania was ready to step in if the occasion arose. In January 1811, Urania wrote to Newton saying that 'owing to its being Wedn your Bro Breakfasted here': mother and son had got into some kind of London routine in which Portsmouth visited Urania once a week at her house in Harley Street. There he asked his mother to attend a social function with him, as Grace lay sick at their house in Lincoln's Inn Fields and could not go. Initially, Urania seemed reluctant, saying that she might not recognize the company and that she disliked going out in the cold weather. But then, she explained to Newton, she realized that 'a Time might come, when a more serious want of a Deputy to Gracy might happen,' and 'if I now complied, I might then be resorted too in such a Need'. 'In such a future Case, I should rejoice in being applyed too for assistance': so she agreed to go.[29]

Imagining a time when Urania might be able to resume her position of control over her son was not so difficult when we realize that Grace was only ten years younger than Portsmouth's mother. Grace was forty-seven when she married Portsmouth in November 1799, while Urania turned fifty-seven the following January. Comparisons between women of such similar ages were inevitable. John Godden, whose employment as a park keeper at Hurstbourne began during the lifetime of the 2nd earl, thought that, after the 3rd earl's marriage to Grace, Portsmouth 'had more liberty then than he had been allowed before'. Richard Poore, a wheelwright and carpenter at Hurstbourne, agreed, as he saw more of Portsmouth after his marriage than when his mother was in charge.[30]

But how wise was it for Grace to allow Portsmouth this greater freedom? Godden believed that Portsmouth, unaccustomed to living without the restraint imposed by his mother, grasped the opportunity that Grace offered him, and 'indulged in extravagancies of conduct, and showed more violence of temper'. Grace was always kind to Portsmouth, 'too much by half at times', thought Godden. Another employee, John Baverstock, believed that Grace's approach meant that 'his Lordship showed what he was after his marriage more than he did before, more publicly too'.[31] Grace's treatment of Portsmouth exposed his condition to a greater number of people. It made him vulnerable, and stored up trouble for the future. The insinuation was that Grace was just too kind for Portsmouth's good.

Being Grace, the wife of the earl of Portsmouth, cannot have been easy. Her husband's hands were tied by the terms of their marriage settlement, and her control over the Portsmouth's estates was limited. There was a suggestion in later years that the 1799 deed was in part drawn up to satisfy Urania, who was anxious to preserve the house and grounds that she had planned and completed, and who wanted to prevent Grace introducing any major changes.[32] Marriage to a man whose behaviour was unpredictable, interests and conversation limited, and needs for attention many, was demanding and exhausting, even at the best of times. All that patient endurance was bad enough without having to tolerate an overly critical mother-in-law. Perhaps it is not surprising that Grace ended up mothering Portsmouth. It was her way of coping with a difficult husband, and for Portsmouth it was the type of relationship that he was used to having with a woman of her age. For if Grace was Portsmouth's new, and possibly favoured, mother then that meant that her husband, who was in his thirties, continued to be treated as a child. Portsmouth was the child whom Grace would never have. The marriage between Grace and Portsmouth had been arranged, but their relationship was something that could not be managed. What nobody counted on was feelings. How Grace felt about her husband she never recorded. Portsmouth's feelings towards Grace were only examined when tragedy struck. Perhaps Grace found it impossible to set down her mixed emotions in words. But while she found a way of living with her husband that to the closest observer sometimes caused attention, the public image that Grace presented of the marriage of Lady and Lord Portsmouth was entirely without fault.

'Lord Portsmouth surpassed the rest in his attentive recollection of you'

O N SATURDAY, 1 November 1800, twenty-four-year-old Jane Austen sat down to write a letter to her beloved older sister, Cassandra. While she was visiting relations in Kent, Jane was eager that Cassandra should miss none of the local news and gossip. On Thursday evening, Jane had attended the ball at Basingstoke. She had done her hair specially for the occasion, but 'there was a Scarcity of Men in general, & a still greater scarcity of any that were good for much'. Still, there were a number of prominent Hampshire families in attendance, including the Dorchesters and the Boltons. The Chutes, whose home, the Vyne, stood in the parish of Sherborne St John where Jane and Cassandra's brother, James, was vicar, were also there, Eliza Chute recording that she thought the ball 'a very good one'. It was a conversation with Lord Portsmouth that Jane reported in most detail. 'Lord Portsmouth surpassed the rest in his attentive recollection of you, enquired more into the length of your absence, and concluded by desiring to be "remembered to you when I wrote next"', Jane reported. Lady Portsmouth 'had got a different dress on, and Lady Bolton is much improved by a wig'.[1]

As one of the keenest and sharpest observers of her time, there was not much that Jane Austen missed about the foibles of human character, either in her quick-witted letters or the novels that would make her famous. Yet when Jane described Portsmouth, who had lived at Steventon before she was born, but whose early connection with her family must have been discussed over the years, there was not a hint that she found his behaviour odd or disturbing. In fact, Portsmouth 'surpassed' the conduct of the other gentlemen who were present. His polite attention and memory of Cassandra were indicative of his good manners and, because he was the head of a key aristocratic family, flattering to Jane.

Three weeks later, on 19 November, Jane attended her first ball at Hurstbourne. This would become an annual event, held on the anniversary of Portsmouth's marriage to Grace. Jane had a great time. A female friend said she looked 'very well' in her aunt's 'gown and handkerchief, and my hair was at least tidy, which was all my ambition'. The wine was flowing. 'I believe I drank too much wine last night at Hurstbourne,' Jane told Cassandra, for 'I know not how else to account for the shaking of my hand to day.' Still giddy with excitement, she said it was 'a pleasant Evening...There were only twelve dances, of which I danced nine, and was merely prevented from dancing the rest by the want of a partner. – We began at 10, supped at 1, and were at Deane before 5.' Jane loved to dance and may have been disappointed that there were not more people, and hence dancing partners, present. 'There were but 50 people in the room; very few families indeed from our side of the Country, and not many more from the other,' she lamented.[2]

But in time the popularity of the Hurstbourne anniversary ball caught on. The Portsmouths may have become more practised at their invitations (Jane remarked that her invitation was 'very curiously worded', but did not elaborate), and the occasion became a feature in the county's social calendar that was reported in the newspapers.[3] While Lord Portsmouth opened the ball, its popularity had nothing to do with his dancing. Christopher Hunter, a surgeon from nearby Whitchurch who had seen Portsmouth dance, thought it 'without any idea of measure or time, and the most extraordinary way certainly: though by the concession that was made to his rank it was passed off'.[4] Social position might excuse poor rhythm, but a perceived lack of generosity was less easy to forgive. Jane Austen's great friend, Anne Lefroy, was very critical of her hosts when she attended the Hurstbourne Ball on 19 November 1801. 'It was not half so pleasant as the one last year' (the first ball, that had been attended by Jane Austen), Anne told her son. The dancing took place in the saloon, perhaps because the library had been such a cold venue the previous year. There were about a hundred people present (double the number at the first ball), but 'there was scarcely anything to eat at Supper and the Gentlemen complained that the wine was very bad and very scarce'. This poor show of hospitality could perhaps be explained by Lord Portsmouth, who was 'either out of health or out of humour and only stood up two Dances'. Portsmouth's mood was not improved when public curiosity at the event meant that 'four panes of glass were broke in the windows of the saloon by people who were looking in at the dancers'. Portsmouth threatened to find the culprits and make them pay for the damage. No doubt fed up with how things were going, Portsmouth talked of 'going to town to prepare for his wife's lying in' (or birth of their child). Knowing full well the age of Lady Portsmouth, Anne sardonically remarked to her son, 'I fancy he will have plenty of time to prepare before such an event takes place.'[5] Throwing a party was one thing, but if the host was in a bad mood it reflected on everyone.

No matter the merits of each ball, or the temperament of the host, people kept coming. Anne Lefroy had no hesitation about going to Hurstbourne the following year when her invitation arrived, and only stopped giving positive replies in November 1804 when her husband became too frail to attend.[6]

The Hurstbourne ball attended by Jane Austen in November 1800 came at the end of a year of social events that marked the introduction of Portsmouth and his new Lady Portsmouth to society. None was more formal than their presentation to George III at St James's Palace on 14 May 1800. Portsmouth had been presented to the King before, when he had inherited the title of Lord Portsmouth after the death of his father, but this time Grace, not Reverend Garnett, was by his side.[7]

Although it was not Portsmouth's first meeting with the King, it was nearly his last. A day later, on the evening of 15 May, as the orchestra played the national anthem, and the audience rose from their seats to pay respect to the King who was attending a play at Drury Lane Theatre, James Hadfield shot his pistol at the royal box. The would-be assassin successfully pleaded insanity (he had sustained head injuries while serving as a soldier), but was confined as a lunatic for the rest of his life. The celebrations for the King's birthday a few weeks later in June 1800 took on a new significance. A grand ball was the culmination of proceedings, and provided the press with the opportunity to give their readers a detailed description of what all the ladies were wearing. Portsmouth was there, along with Grace, the countess of Portsmouth bedecked in a 'royal blue silk petticoat…a drapery of rich brocaded gauze…cap royal blue crape, spangled with gold ornaments and flowers; train trimmed with blond; train royal blue, same as petticoat'. Henrietta Dorothea, Portsmouth's sister, was all in white, with a head dress decorated with pearls and white ostrich feathers.[8] Presence at this splendid occasion was a sign of membership of an exclusive club that depended upon wealth and title. Everyone who was anyone was there. The King himself was months away from another bout of mental illness, but for now the nobility were happy to congratulate him upon his escape from a violent madman.

Grace's dressmaker must have been busy that first twelve months of her marriage. The social engagements of the Portsmouths were regularly featured in newspaper columns listed under the heading 'The Fashionable World'. Lady Kinnaird's party at her house in Lower Grosvenor Street on 23 April 1800 was 'one of the most numerous and fashionable we have witnessed this season', reported the *Oracle and Daily Advertiser*. Top of the 'distinguished' guest list of some four to five hundred people were Lord and Lady Portsmouth.[9] A month later, the couple attended the Duchess Dowager of Chandos' Ball. The Prince of Wales and Prince William of Gloucester were only prevented from attending because of the assassination attempt on their father the previous evening.[10] When a 'select party' was chosen to play cards at the Duchess of Bolton's house in Grosvenor Square in June, the Portsmouths were invited.[11]

Portsmouth and Grace soon settled into a routine of social engagements that were divided by their winter months in London and summer at Hurstbourne. At Lincoln's Inn Fields, the couple were 'at home' and had a 'public day' once a week, generally on a Wednesday evening. 'Persons of rank and respectability' were invited to spend time with the Portsmouths, sometimes playing cards, but more often to enjoy music or dancing.[12]

Back in Hampshire, there were still balls and parties to attend, but also smaller affairs such as dinner parties at the homes of neighbouring families. The Portsmouths became involved in the annual music festival held at Winchester Cathedral, Lord Portsmouth joining other local nobility who gave their sponsorship to the event. In October 1800, they heard the newly composed oratorio *The Creation* by Joseph Haydn.[13] The audience crowded into a ball that followed its performance.

Not all of Portsmouth's socializing was done with Grace by his side. He belonged to the North Hants Club, a club 'composed of the Noblemen and Gentlemen of the County', which met several times a year for dinners in Basingstoke.[14] With his father's title, Portsmouth had inherited the position of High Steward of the Borough of Andover, and this also required attendance at meetings and dinners through the year. He was expected to pay for the cost of the wine at the Bailiff's feast in Andover, and to return a speech of thanks. He led the Andover corporation in procession through the town to the church, and afterwards to dinner.[15]

As a landowner with tenants, Portsmouth demonstrated due benevolence to his social inferiors. He called at the homes of his farmers when members of their family were ill, paid an annual subscription towards a soup kitchen for the relief of the poor in Andover, and at Christmas time arranged for food to be distributed to the poor in Hurstbourne parish.[16] The 'most respectable farmers' in the county asked Portsmouth to be godparents to their children.[17] In London, Portsmouth was a governor of the Middlesex Hospital and the Queen Charlotte Lying-In Hospital. He took especial interest in the children of the crowded and often economically deprived parishes that bordered Lincoln's Inn Fields. In February 1811, newspapers reported how Portsmouth had 'entertained' 130 'poor children, of both sexes' from the workhouse of St Giles and St George, with 'plenty of roast beef' and 'plum pudding'. 'His Lordship sat at the head of the table and carved for them; and after dinner was over he presented each of them with a silver sixpence.' The occasion was such a success that in April Portsmouth invited one hundred boys and seventy girls from the parishes' Charity Schools, where he was governor, to his house at Lincoln's Inn Fields. There the children received 'a good old English dinner, as well as a glass of pure ale, and a pecuniary donation each'.

Such ostentatious displays of charity were expected of noblemen such as Portsmouth. Few of Portsmouth's recipients of philanthropy regarded his behaviour as patronizing. Instead, his dinner for school children was described by the press as 'an excellent example of condescending benevolence'.[18] Portsmouth took to this role with ease. He attended meetings of the school and hospitals where he was governor, sometimes acted as chair, and on one occasion spotted an error in their minutes. Fellow governors commented that Portsmouth always acted rationally and with 'propriety'.[19]

While Portsmouth might have occasional mood swings, as witnessed by Anne Lefroy, the general impression that he gave was that, now he was married, he was enjoying life more. Before Grace, and living under the shadow of his mother, Portsmouth was 'more shy and reserved than he was in after times'. In contrast, after his marriage, Portsmouth became 'more talkative than in his younger days'. Marriage for Portsmouth brought him a new respectability, and it took him out of his shell. He could show the world of what he was capable, and in a way that was not possible with his overbearing mother. His public speeches passed muster; at the Bailiff's feast he 'returned thanks in an appropriate speech which was spoken as well as most Gentlemen unaccustomed to public speaking would have done'. No mention was made of a stammer; if this was in any way linked with his confidence, perhaps it was something that he had at least temporarily overcome.[20]

Bolstered by having a wife, in his early years of marriage Portsmouth engaged in one feat of gallantry that nobody can have anticipated. On 8 May 1801, after visiting his neighbours, Mr and Mrs Solly in York Place, Portman Square, Portsmouth saw a man running up the steps, and a silver salt-spoon fall from his pocket, which he did not pick up. 'Concluding that he had committed a robbery', Portsmouth 'ran after him, seized him by the collar, and drew him back to the house', where it was found that the man, John Lawrence, had two other silver spoons, also belonging to the Sollys, in his possession. A few weeks later, Lawrence was tried at the Old Bailey, and Portsmouth was questioned as the main prosecution witness. Lawrence, a Jew, had a Jewish physician, Dr Leo, testify to the court that he was insane when he committed the act. But Leo did not convince the court as suspicions were raised about his professional credibility, and it appeared that Lawrence had once before 'endeavoured to screen his delinquencies' by this plea. Lawrence was found guilty of grand larceny, and sentenced to be transported for seven years.

While accounts differed about the part that Portsmouth took in apprehending Lawrence (trial reports recorded that a 'labouring man' had thrown him to the ground), Portsmouth was long remembered as the man upon whose word a thief had been convicted of a capital offence.[21] His encounter with Lawrence coming just a few days after he had received the extortion letter from Seilaz, Portsmouth's experience at the Old Bailey may have helped to prepare him for his confident performance at King's Bench two years later.

In private conversation, Sir James Burrough 'never heard him say a foolish thing: the said Earl's conversation was neither literary nor profound, nor scientific but he spoke on ordinary subjects with intellect and propriety'. At his public days in Lincoln's Inn Fields, Portsmouth received 'his friends with great civility and good humour… he was remarkably attentive to the company, and chatted with them on ordinary topics'.[22] The Countess Dowager of Winterton thought Portsmouth always 'conducted himself with propriety' and that he 'passed very well in society'.[23] Years of his mother's training had come into play. A nephew of Reverend Garnett's said that he never saw Portsmouth behave without regard to the 'strictest propriety', and 'if there was a remark to be made, on this point, it was that he was ever punctilious in matters of form'.[24]

Good manners had become instinctive for Portsmouth. Reverend Newbolt shared a pew with Portsmouth for three hours during a commemoration event at St Paul's Cathedral. 'His lordship conducted himself with the greatest decorum', and talked with two royal dukes.[25]

Portsmouth was also invited to evening parties where members of the royal family, and the Dukes of Sussex and Norfolk, were present and behaved appropriately. 'His Lordship was of weak understanding,' said one host of such an evening. But, concluded this gentleman, he 'has met many, passing well in Society, of inferior intellect.'[26]

This stinging indictment of the upper classes in the early nineteenth century was made during one of the legal trials concerning Portsmouth's sanity. For when people looked back at the social occasions of Portsmouth's life they began to assess their significance not only for judging this man's mind, but also as a critical measure of the condition of their society. As evidence of Portsmouth's mental health, the statements of those who only saw Portsmouth in society 'have nothing to do with it,' argued lawyers, because 'it is obvious that a man is under restraint in public society.'[27] 'His behaviour in company is controlled by restraint,' argued Dr Francis Willis. Just six years into his practice as a mad-doctor, yet from a family whose name had long been synonymous with treatment of the insane, Willis was convinced that, 'if Lord Portsmouth were alone without restraint, he would exhibit his derangement'. 'I could place you at a table,' he told the jury of Portsmouth's Commission of Lunacy, 'and surround you with a company of lunatics, who would behave with the strictest propriety, and you should not know their state of mind.'[28]

But if propriety had become the shield behind which the real Lord Portsmouth could hide, then 'society' with its rules, expectations, airs, and graces, had participated in his deception. For years people had taken advantage of Portsmouth's hospitality, and were pleased when he had accepted their invitations. They wanted him as the figurehead for their charitable organizations, and as the name on their children's baptism registers. Examining Portsmouth's mind lifted the lid on the social world of which he was a part. In the first decades of the nineteenth century, just as political reformers sought to rid themselves of elite corruption and privilege, and moral reformers looked for a revival of true faith, Portsmouth's case revealed the full extent of the problems they faced. Beneath all the polish and refinement was a can of worms. Shallowness, hypocrisy, false friendship and generosity epitomized the social life of those whose lives were governed by pleasure and leisure. If Portsmouth was mad, then he came from a rotten core.

Yet were Portsmouth's contemporaries so blinded by his wealth and his title that they did not recognize madness when they saw it? 'It is impossible that forty persons in the county of Hants having had complete opportunities of judging could be mistaken' about Portsmouth when they declared him sane before the Chancellor in 1815, it was stated.[29]

When Portsmouth faced the legal trials for his sanity, his social acquaintances were asked by lawyers to think again about their encounters with him. Behaviour that had been dismissed as simply eccentric before, such as his style of dancing, was re-examined for indicators of his mental instability. Something as apparently trivial as how Portsmouth played cards was opened to scrutiny. An extremely popular pastime for the upper classes, friends were divided about whether Portsmouth was a good or bad card player. They were agreed that he understood the rules of whist, and his numerical aptitude meant that he could be a very good player at the gambling game of commerce. He was not the only gentleman to regularly lose card games; 'I have seen others play at whist as bad as Lord P,' remarked Reverend Newbolt. But was Portsmouth's poor play a reflection of the limitations of his mind? 'He seemed to have no plan,' concluded Newbolt. Without a game plan he was bound to remain only a 'tolerable player'. Portsmouth was certainly a bad loser. 'It was generally contrived that his Lordship should win,' commented another card player, 'for he was very much put out of his way and very miserable if he did not.'[30] Like a spoilt child, Portsmouth could not bear to take part in games unless he was the winner.

Questioning witnesses about Portsmouth's card playing was scraping the barrel for evidence of a man's sanity. Surely more weight, it was argued, should be given to the testimony of a witness like Elizabeth Crooke, who had known Portsmouth for nearly forty years when she testified in 1827. A Hampshire neighbour at Kempshott Park, Elizabeth and her husband had been formerly introduced to Portsmouth and Grace at a party held in Hanover Square soon after their marriage. In the country, 'friendly visits of several days at each other's houses, and in London, of dinner and evening parties' followed. Elizabeth had heard Portsmouth 'generally spoken of as of weak understanding' before she met him. 'His Lordship's manners in society however were polite and gentlemanly, and there was not any irrationality in his behaviour,' Elizabeth said. She found him 'by no means so weak a man as he had been represented. Lord Portsmouth was not a man of cultivated mind, but upon general subjects he conversed very rationally; particularly on topics connected with agriculture and the country.' In sum, 'he certainly did appear in some respects as not of strong understanding: but it was a fashion to laugh at what Lord Portsmouth did or said'.[31] Portsmouth, according to Elizabeth, was not mad, just weak-minded. For all of this society's faults, then, it could be tolerant of an individual who was mentally backward, just so long as he fitted in by behaving appropriately when in company.

Unable to prove that Portsmouth was insane by examining his conduct 'in society', lawyers had to turn to his behaviour away from the public eye. People like Elizabeth Crooke, Sir James Burrough, and the Countess Dowager of Winterton did not really know Portsmouth, it was argued. There were aspects of his character that were so shameful that Grace did all she could to keep them secret. At home, and out and about on his vast Hampshire estate, Portsmouth was engaging in activities that were both shocking and disturbing. The nature of these was revealed.

'He must have been quite a natural'

I T WAS THE autumn of 1802. Ann Pope was in her late forties, married to a labourer, and she worked hard as a weaver in Whitchurch. Every year she went with a group of other local women to the woods and coppices that were on the edge of Lord Portsmouth's estate to collect nuts. Strictly speaking, they were trespassing on his land, but few of the women saw it that way. They were simply harvesting a useful food source that would otherwise go to waste. There was no harm done to anybody, nor damage committed to any property. It gave Ann and her friends a chance to spend time together outdoors before winter set in, exchanging news and gossip. This was pleasurable work.

Except that this year the women were interrupted, and by Lord Portsmouth himself. His sudden appearance in the undergrowth surprised them all, and frightened a good many. Offended that the women were on his estate, he angrily turned them out of the coppice. But as they gathered their things, and started towards the road, Portsmouth stopped them and asked if any of the women could sing. Startled at his unusual request, but not wanting to cause any further offence, a young girl in their company offered to sing. When she had finished singing, Portsmouth reached into his pocket and gave the women a substantial sum of money, seven shillings, to share between them. He then asked them to return to the same place the next morning.

So began Ann's twice to three times a week meetings with

Portsmouth over the next two years. She, and 'as many as a score of women old and young about Whitchurch and Hurstbourne', became regular visitors to the estate. They always met Portsmouth outdoors among the trees and bushes, but his request for singing was never again repeated. Instead, Portsmouth wanted something altogether more intimate and bizarre. He started by asking the women if he looked well, and grew angry if they said he did. Saying that he was sick, he asked Ann and her friends to hold his wrist, and take his pulse. Then he took out a case of lancets, and ask them to bleed him. Ann declared that she never bled Portsmouth, and became so uncomfortable about his demands that she 'tied up her right arm to show him that she could not do it telling him that she had hurt it'. Portsmouth talked 'such stuff' as Ann was 'ashamed to repeat', about 'what sort of eyes, nose and nostrils such and such woman had'. He was obsessed with how women's pockets bulged out, and told Ann that these women carried basins under their skirts so they could collect the blood of the men they bled. On one occasion, Portsmouth ordered Ann and the others to put their hands in their pockets, 'and make them bulge out, and walk to the copse before him'.

Strange as Portsmouth was, Ann continued her visits. At the end of every meeting, Portsmouth gave the women money. The sums ranged from five shillings to half a guinea. 'It was such an easy way of getting a little money,' Ann later explained. The money 'did them good, and as they knew his Lordship had plenty it could do him no hurt,' she reasoned. Portsmouth's preferences became so notorious that:

> it was quite a common thing for women and girls about Whitchurch and Hurstbourne to go up toward the Park and try their luck if they heard that his Lordship was about there: and he might be seen in a high field on the lookout with his spy glass; and if he saw a woman going along one way or another he would be sure to go down to meet her and ask her to take blood from him.[1]

Stalking the women below him, Portsmouth found that not all were as difficult prey as Ann Pope. In time, both Ann and 'old Dame Curtis' persuaded their daughters to meet Portsmouth; this useful form of money-making ran through families. Sarah Adams, like her mother, Ann Pope, had married a labourer, and made her living winding silk. Described as a 'pretty woman', she started meeting Portsmouth when she was in her twenties, and he was in his forties. At their first meeting after she had taken Portsmouth's pulse, Sarah pleased him by saying 'he was very poorly'. Portsmouth agreed, and said 'he was very giddy in his head', and that 'he wanted to lose a little blood'. When Sarah refused to take his blood, saying she did not know how, he told her that she 'need not be afraid, for he had been bled by women in London'. He then slipped off his coat, rolled up his sleeve, 'and showed her his arms, and the places where he had been bled; and there were several marks, and on both arms'. At their next meetings Portsmouth had to make do with Sarah telling him his fortune, or with Sarah pretending that she, like her mother, had injured her arm and so could not let his blood. Believing Sarah would never bleed him, Portsmouth asked her to describe the appearance of a local doctor's three daughters, and, assuming they would know how to let blood because of their father's profession, asked Sarah to bring them with her.

But the doctor's daughters escaped Portsmouth's attentions because one day Sarah relented. Delighted to have got his way at last, Portsmouth took off his coat, and turned up his sleeve. He produced a long piece of white tape, about three yards long, with which Sarah tied his arm. She then used the lancet, provided by Portsmouth, to puncture his arm. Drops of blood were collected by Dame Curtis who held a basin below. Portsmouth said nothing during the whole procedure. Sarah then placed a patch of cloth over the place where she had let blood; Portsmouth put his coat back on, and gave Sarah and Dame Curtis seven shillings to share.

The occasion was repeated at least a dozen more times, Sarah becoming a clear favourite. Portsmouth gave her a present of a red leather case containing a collection of lancets, which she produced as evidence to show the Commission of Lunacy many years later. When Sarah pretended to Portsmouth that she had lost the case, he gave her another, this time silver mounted. She saw Portsmouth over the course of at least five years.[2]

Why did Portsmouth behave in this way? Were his encounters with these local working women evidence of his eccentricity, his simple-mindedness, or his insanity? People at the time struggled to find meaning in Portsmouth's behaviour, and to uncover some kind of explanation for it, in part because, if it was a sign of his madness, it was a symptom that was unique to him. Even other mad people did not behave in this way.

We can discount Portsmouth's blood-letting as a form of self-harm. Today people with learning disabilities or mental illness may exhibit signs of distress through forms of self-harm, which can include cutting and wounding. Yet Portsmouth wanted others to bleed him; he did not bleed himself. A few drops of blood did not amount to serious pain or harm.

Bleeding was used by respected physicians and by many individuals as a common cure for a range of ailments at the start of the nineteenth century. Many educated people believed that health depended upon the correct balance of the body's humours. Letting blood was a way in which an excess of fluids could be released, and the optimal temperature of the body restored. Portsmouth's own grandfather, Coulson Fellowes, had made regular payments to a practitioner to be bled.

Blood-letting was also used in treatments of people with mental health problems: it was one of a range of cures that was tried on George III during his mental breakdowns. John Haslam declared that in his extensive experience of treating patients that were mad or melancholic bleeding was 'the most beneficial remedy'. Those who were insane were often insensible to pain, he claimed, so they did not feel the impact of the lancet, 'the drawing of blisters, or the punctures of cupping'.

Yet bleeding also had its critics. It could do more harm than good, it was argued, and in some cases even cause an individual exhibiting insanity to degenerate into idiocy. 'Ideotism,' wrote one physician in 1806, 'may originate in…excessive use of the lancet in the treatment of active mania.'

It is feasible that, as a child and young man, Portsmouth's parents had treated him by bleeding. He had certainly learned to associate ill health with bleeding: he told the women that he was unwell and therefore needed to be bled, and on at least one occasion said that it was because he was 'giddy in his head' that he wanted bleeding. The more alarming possibility, that bleeding had caused Portsmouth's mental problems, and that its continued practice only worsened his situation, was never raised in the legal proceedings brought against him.

There was certainly something sinister about Portsmouth's meetings. Their secrecy and his odd beliefs about women with basins under their skirts suggested to those who later heard stories of these encounters that they were more than a habitual response to ill health. Most troubling was how to interpret the enjoyment that Portsmouth gained from being bled. The frightening possibility that Portsmouth was a masochist who got sexual pleasure from bleeding loomed large in later questioning about these incidents. In the nineteenth century, some believed that blood-letting increased virility: it gave welcome release of sexual energy as well as any bad humours. For Portsmouth, perhaps painful childhood experiences had become twisted into a form of sexual enjoyment.

It was a suggestion that preyed so much on the minds of the women who bled Portsmouth that they denied it before the accusation even arose. After her description of her copse meetings, the exchange between Ann Pope and the lawyer Mr Powell at the 1823 Commission of Lunacy went as follows:

Powell: Did he ever show you anything?
Ann: Oh, no! never (laughter)
Powell: You misunderstand me, woman. Did he take anything out of his pocket?
Ann: Yes, a lancet.

Ann went on to declare, 'During all these times Lord Portsmouth never took the least liberty with me or the other women.' Sarah Adams agreed, saying that Portsmouth 'never touched' her. Sarah made it clear that, although she started seeing Portsmouth when she was single, she continued meeting him after she was newly married. The implication was that, if there was something sexual going on, her husband would never have let her meet Portsmouth. Nobody suggested that these women's husbands might have connived in the arrangement.[3]

Yet Portsmouth's behaviour was so disconcerting that no woman ever met him on her own. There was safety in numbers. A sense that there was something wrong, and perhaps immoral, in their activities also meant that Sarah Adams refused to meet Portsmouth on one occasion 'because it was a Sunday morning'.[4]

Grace knew that her husband met local women on their estate. How much she was aware of what happened during these encounters is not clear, and whether Portsmouth ever betrayed his love of lancets to her is not known. It was about the time that Portsmouth first started meeting women on his estate that Seilaz had sent his letter accusing Portsmouth of sodomy; his wife was already busy dealing with the fall-out of his relationships.

But Grace was wise enough to know that village gossip about her husband's habits needed to be curtailed if she were to protect him. She instructed John Godden, a park keeper at Hurstbourne, to try to stop Portsmouth going into the coppices. She told Godden that she knew 'his Lordship was in the habit of meeting women there: and she was afraid that his Lordship might get into some mischief'. There seems little doubt that she confronted Portsmouth about these meetings, and told him that they could not continue. For one time Portsmouth 'came crying' to Godden, 'begging and beseeching him to intercede for him with a couple of children who he said had threatened to tell Lady Portsmouth of him'. When Godden found the children, who were young, they said that they had seen Portsmouth meeting the women again. Portsmouth had already given them a guinea to keep quiet. Afraid of the power of little children to condemn him, and knowing that Grace disapproved, Portsmouth acted guilty, and like a naughty child who had been caught in the act.[5]

Despite Grace's best efforts, Portsmouth's desire to be bled, and his interest in lancets, continued for many years. It was an addiction. He sent servants to buy cases of lancets when he was in London, and a gardener to the cutler to have them sharpened. A valet for Portsmouth for two years from 1822 described how his master folded up the waistcoat containing his lancets and slept with it under his pillow at night. Portsmouth was depicted as a solitary figure, standing for hours on end by the window of his house in Hanover Square, looking for women. Spying one, he would ask this valet 'if he did not see the basins she carried sticking out at her side'?[6]

The most damning evidence that Portsmouth got a sexual kick from bleeding came not from a woman, but from a man, James Capy. From March 1815 until the end of 1817, Capy worked as Portsmouth's valet. According to Capy, Portsmouth asked him 'almost every morning to bleed him'. 'His idea was that every woman carried a basin and lancets for the use of men,' Capy explained, adding that Portsmouth often asked him if Capy's wife 'did not carry them, both basin and lancets, and if the housemaid had not them and in which pocket they carried them and the like'. Sometimes Capy tied up Portsmouth's arm with tape and drew a lancet over the skin without touching it, and this satisfied him. Just the anticipation of the act seemed to be enough. The earl took an 'unnatural delight' in this, and, when his arm was tied, he watched 'the rising of the veins', and 'continued applying his other hand to himself in such a manner as to show that he felt a very depraved gratification from it'. 'His Lordship had undoubtedly the unnatural idea that bleeding was the act of copulation,' Capy told the courts.[7]

Even if Portsmouth's desire to be bled had not started as a sexual one, some of the doctors who examined him for the Commission of Lunacy thought it had become one. Portsmouth proudly showed Dr Sutherland his case of lancets, and told him that 'even the sign of the operation of bleeding being made, that of putting the fingers to the arm gave him pleasure'. He told Dr Tuthill that, when his arm was bound, the lancets produced 'a certain fullness of the parts of the generation', and that 'he knew not and never had known of any other means of producing the same effect'. Given a choice of giving up his wife or his case of lancets, he would rather abandon his wife, he said.[8]

Of course, by interpreting Portsmouth's behaviour and thinking as inspired by sexual desire, those who judged him could find a rational answer for something that was otherwise irrational. It did not help Portsmouth that, even twenty years on, Sarah Adams was noted by reporters at the Commission to be a 'pretty woman'. Few could imagine an encounter with such a woman that was not sexual.

For those who sought to prove that Portsmouth was insane, his blood-letting practices condemned him as a man with a sordid mind. This behaviour showed that he had crossed the line from the sexual naivety usually associated with idiocy, to the perversion and immorality of insanity. Rather than the helpless victim of fate, he was the maker of his own misfortune. There he was, creeping around in the shadows and the dark corners of his estate, mixing with village women, while Grace, in the house high above him, remained pure and innocent. Sex for Portsmouth had become so detached from a human relationship that it was immaterial to him whether the person holding the lancet was male or female. It was the inanimate object of a needle and the sign of his body's response to it that turned him on.

Yet this argument was introduced to the courts and largely rested on the evidence of one man, Portsmouth's valet, Capy. Capy's description of Portsmouth proved contentious on a number of points, and it stood as a lone voice among the others who had been asked to bleed Portsmouth. The village women were all adamant that Portsmouth had never behaved 'indecently' before them. Lawyers warned the jury at the Commission of Lunacy that 'things very obscene might sound extraordinary; but they must not infer madness too hastily'. Other aristocrats engaged in dubious sexual practices. The jury were reminded of the case of the exotically, yet reassuringly foreign-sounding Kutzmanoff, who had been found 'hanging and dead, after being placed there for the gratification of his abominable desires by a common prostitute'. This was worse than anything alleged against Portsmouth, 'yet it was never construed into a proof of insanity'.[9] Sane men might be perverse.

Portsmouth's habits became notorious. Lord Byron joked to a friend that to Portsmouth:

> we owe...the greatest discovery about the blood since Dr Harvey's; – I wonder whether it really hath such an effect – I never was bled in my life – but by leeches – and I thought the leeches d-----d bad pieces – but perhaps the tape and the lancet may be better – I shall try on some great emergency.[10]

Yet while Portsmouth's behaviour could trigger a range of responses from humour to horror, he himself remained ignorant of why this behaviour might attract such attention. Others took over from Grace in tutoring Portsmouth that his love of bleeding was wrong. When Portsmouth appeared before the Commission of Lunacy that had been brought against him, 'there was a crafty attempt at delusion', it was claimed. Portsmouth tried to convince the jury that 'he never had been bled but by professional gentlemen', and, when pressed upon the point, Portsmouth claimed 'that he had given over the use of lancets for several years'.[11] It was better that Portsmouth deny the practice altogether, his lawyers clearly thought, than be drawn into the types of questions that had been posed by the doctors who had examined him.

By the time he was brought before the Commission in 1823, Portsmouth was well rehearsed in the wrongs of admitting to being bled by the women on his estate, but whether he understood why it could be seen as wrong was less clear. Hannah Curtis and her friends clung to their view that Portsmouth was a harmless idiot, not a dangerous madman. They told the Commission he 'must have been quite a natural', the popular term for a fool or idiot. He was 'altogether simple,' Ann Pope said. His requests exploited nobody, but when granted gave him pleasure and the women financial reward.

It was twenty years or more after their first meetings that the women's stories were told, and the private fascinations and habits of Portsmouth became public. When they did so their words were explosive because they threatened to expose a man who bared his flesh and allowed himself to be vulnerable to women well below his social status. Even if these were not sexual liaisons, Portsmouth's meetings were inappropriate social encounters. Collectively described as 'unskilful and ignorant persons', Sarah Adams, Ann Pope, and Hannah Curtis could not even sign their names at the end of their witness statements.[12] These village women should have been Portsmouth's social and intellectual inferiors. But Ann Pope, Sarah Adams and their company punctured not only Portsmouth's skin but the illusion that Portsmouth was a normal, functioning aristocrat.

There was a dark side to Portsmouth's character that for many years remained hidden. So when stories of Portsmouth's blood-letting activities were first told they were hard to believe. How could a man maintain such utterly different personas, one in public, another in private, for so long a time? At the first attempt to call a Commission of Lunacy in 1815, lawyers for Portsmouth asked the Chancellor:

> Did your Lordship ever hear of so strange a kind of madman as a man who could personate everywhere a person in his senses except in his own Park, a lunatic of this description must be an admirably good player in order to perform all these characters.

If Portsmouth only showed his weaknesses in front of his social inferiors, then he 'is a man who shows very good discretion and caution, in short he is no madman', it was argued.[13]

But now a jury had to decide which of the 'characters' that Portsmouth had played was the true Lord Portsmouth. Who was telling the truth, and who had the greatest insights into his state of mind? For the jury of fellow peers and wealthy men, this meant listening to the stories of women and men whose working lives had brought them into most frequent and closest contact with Portsmouth. It was these ordinary, often poor and illiterate people, who had seen Portsmouth off his guard. Unaccustomed as they were to paying attention to the words of their social inferiors, and as uncomfortable as their stories could make them feel, the jury felt compelled to listen. And given a public platform and the opportunity to speak, ordinary people just kept those stories about Portsmouth coming.

'Black jobs'

I T WAS A common enough experience for a father, but that did not make it any less painful. In May 1807, William Litchfield was watching his daughter die. There were a host of diseases to which children could fall prey, and very little that a parent could do to prevent their being lethal. Wealth did not always act as a protector. As well as an older brother who probably died within the first few hours of life, Portsmouth had a younger brother and a sister who did not live beyond their childhood, and a further sister who died just before her seventeenth birthday. For the rich, children stood a greater chance of survival by the early nineteenth century than they had a century earlier. Of the ten children fathered by the 1st earl of Portsmouth, only one lived to adulthood, and even this child died before his father in 1749. But by the nineteenth century, as the population of England increased, and towns swelled in size with little regard to sanitation, the divide between the life expectancy of the rich and poor grew greater. Attention was eventually given to the plight of the urban working classes, but the squalor and appalling living conditions of the labouring poor in rural counties like Hampshire was all but forgotten. Babies and children paid a high price for this neglect.

By the standards of the time, Litchfield could afford a good quality of living for his wife and children. He had a steady income working as a carpenter on the Hurstbourne estate. With plentiful supplies of timber, and a wide range of farm and outbuildings, stables and cottages as well as the mansion to maintain, he was never short of work. He had been employed at Hurstbourne all his working life, beginning with service under the 2nd earl. This Lord Portsmouth had rewarded him with a cottage on the estate, about half a mile from the mansion. It was here that he brought his young wife to live, and where his children were born and raised.

But in spring 1807, Litchfield's daughter became seriously unwell. Over the course of a fortnight her sickness grew worse, each day the girl growing weaker and suffering more pain. Desperate to help her, Litchfield approached his mistress, Grace, Lady Portsmouth. Grace 'did everything she could for her', sending her family's physician, Dr Ludlow, to see the girl. But the doctor told Litchfield there was nothing he could do: as so often at that time, even if medics could diagnose the illness they could not offer a cure. A nurse was sent to tend the girl. It was obvious to everyone who saw her that she was dying, and all Litchfield and his family could do was sit and wait.

Litchfield had already been taken aback when Portsmouth had abruptly asked him during his meeting with Grace if he thought his daughter would die. The carpenter had known the 3rd earl since he was a boy, seeing him about the estate during his school holidays, and on his return from his tour abroad. In Litchfield's opinion, Portsmouth was 'nothing better than a fool', a weak-minded man who had 'no understanding'. It was Grace who always paid his wages and settled his accounts, but, because Portsmouth 'was very fond of giving orders', he would pretend to follow his instructions, 'for peace and quietness'. Portsmouth was forever getting in the way of his work, so on one occasion Litchfield gave him a nail to drive, to try to keep him occupied. With this one nail, Portsmouth was 'as well pleased as ever he was in his life'. Litchfield knew that Portsmouth was simple-minded, and was perhaps ready to forgive his direct questioning about his daughter, as long as his curiosity stopped there.

Now the girl was hours away from death. Nobody thought she would live to see another day. As she lay in the cottage, surrounded by her loving family, and cared for by a nurse, this tender deathbed scene was suddenly disturbed. Portsmouth, accompanied by the parish clerk, arrived at the cottage. The nurse went to the door and told Portsmouth that the girl was dying and was not fit to see him. But

Portsmouth would not budge. So Litchfield came to the door, and Portsmouth repeated his request to see the dying girl. Litchfield refused, and asked both men to leave. The clerk went to stand on the other side of the hedge that surrounded the cottage, but Portsmouth remained on the doorstep. Litchfield 'would not let his Lordship into the cottage; and so he stood at the door'. For 'above an hour' there was a stand-off between Litchfield and Portsmouth. This was a terrible battle of wills. Portsmouth was Litchfield's master and social superior; he literally held the keys to his livelihood. His displeasure could result in unemployment and homelessness. As Litchfield stood his ground, and refused Portsmouth entry, he protected his family from an awful abuse of authority, and allowed his daughter to die in peace away from the prying eyes of a stranger. Yet he could not do what every father would have wanted, and be with her in her final moments. Having shared the agony of her dying over the last few weeks, he missed his child's death. She died without him.

Portsmouth's intrusion into Litchfield's family tragedy continued. On being informed that the girl had died, Portsmouth went with the clerk to the parish church of St Andrew, Hurstbourne, to toll the bells for her. Portsmouth took pleasure in ordering and inspecting an expensive coffin, but left Litchfield to pay for it. Then, on the day of the girl's burial, he met the small procession of Litchfield, his wife, and other children as they took her body from their home to the church. Complaining that they were quarter of an hour late, Portsmouth was dressed scruffily in a 'common blue coat'. He took position in front of the body as if he were the undertaker, and led the party to the church. Once there, Portsmouth acted as a clergyman, singing the 88th Psalm, and then repeating six of its verses as the girl's body was lowered into the ground. Many years later, as a seventy-four-year-old man, Litchfield testified in the legal proceedings that were brought against Portsmouth. The words he spoke as he concluded this story of his daughter's death, and the part that Portsmouth played, spoke volumes. He 'was very much hurt at it all: but what could he do,' he declared. Deep pain, humiliation, and sheer helplessness cry out from manuscripts now hundreds of years old.[1]

* * *

Portsmouth's habit of turning up uninvited to funerals, or 'black jobs' as he called them, became well known to his servants and estate workers. They knew that they could get Portsmouth out of a bad mood just by mentioning that there was to be a black job. On one occasion in London, Portsmouth disappeared all day after they told him a funeral was going to take place in Holborn. When he returned, 'he said that he had got in as chief-mourner, and got some turkey and wine for lunch'. Servants fooled around with Portsmouth, placing a log on their shoulders 'in the manner that a coffin is usually borne', and he then followed them singing psalms.

Portsmouth's fascination with funerals meant that, when the servant Samuel Osborne lay sick, he made frequent enquiries about him, and 'expressed his hope he would die observing that then we should have the Blacks here'. When the head coachman's wife was ill, Portsmouth visited the stables to see if she was dead, and when she did die, he went to the church to toll the bells for her. Portsmouth compared the number of funerals in Whitchurch and Hurstbourne, and liked to believe that there were a greater number in Hurstbourne, meaning 'he was ahead'.[2] In London, he knew all 'the principal hearse drivers about the town', and visited undertakers to ask if there were any funerals. If there were, Portsmouth would 'join them in his phaeton, and drive so close as to touch the wheels of the mourning coaches: he would then laugh, and shake his whip at the coachman'. Coachman Charles Webb attended at least thirteen funerals with Portsmouth, and saw 'his Lordship on foot walking by the side of the procession'.[3]

Portsmouth showed interest in the burials of those well below his social status. A former servant of Grace's mother, who had gone blind in old age, was allowed to remain in the house at Lincoln's Inn Fields where he died. Portsmouth was 'Chief Mourner' at his funeral, 'not out of respect for the deceased', another servant explained, 'but because he liked to attend these things'. Portsmouth went to extraordinary lengths to pursue his interests. He was seen setting off in heavy rain to walk the mile from his house to the church at Hurstbourne to ring the bells when someone died. A former Hurstbourne servant 'becoming insane was placed in the asylum at Bethnal Green where he died'. Portsmouth went to the undertakers in London 'where the body lay and thence he followed it to the grave'. If the sight of a peer following the body of a poor lunatic was not unusual enough, then his payment for a poor woman's coffin when she died in St Martin's workhouse or his presence at the burial of a former mistress of St Giles' workhouse was bound to be remembered.[4]

It was Portsmouth's behaviour at these funerals that caused the greatest offence. 'There was a box which was used as a privy in the churchyard' at Hurstbourne, the carpenter Robert Wright explained. When his father-in-law died, since it was snowing 'his Lordship had it brought down to the foot of the grave, and he and the clergyman got into it; his Lordship acted as clerk'. Portsmouth gave the responses in the service instead of the clerk, and said the 'amen' before him. Others saw him playing tricks and messing around until the corpse arrived, and then look sorrowful, twisting his face 'into all manner of forms'.[5]

Park keeper John Godden was already appalled after he told Portsmouth that his wife was very ill and 'his Lordship said he was glad of it and hoped she would die soon'. But it was his conduct at the funeral of another servant who died at Hurstbourne that he found most unbearable. Portsmouth 'stood as Clerk with the Book in his hand, his Lordship was winking his eye at one and the other and laughing in such a shameful or at least in such a sad way' that Godden 'was obliged to leave the place, he was so much hurt at his Lordship's ridiculous conduct at such a time'.[6]

Godden's response to Portsmouth was telling: he walked away. Nobody challenged Portsmouth's presence at these burials. His behaviour broke with all common decency and respect but it left people so aghast that they felt powerless to act. At an event that was already emotionally charged, no one wanted to risk making a scene or causing further spectacle by trying to stop Portsmouth. It was as if the horror and shock of what was unfolding froze everyone who witnessed it.

Those who saw Portsmouth at these events were left with the impression that he was a man stunted in emotional growth. A person with a 'feeling mind' would not want to be constantly attending funerals, but for Portsmouth these events were 'a mere trifle'. If one of his horses was ill, he would cry his eyes out, but show no sorrow at the funeral of a little girl. Portsmouth was so immature that, instead of sadness, he experienced pleasure at a funeral. He talked to his servants about funerals 'in a way that showed that he had a great delight in them'. To Wetherell, a lawyer who was fighting to prove Portsmouth was insane at the 1823 Lunacy Commission, Portsmouth's response to the death of Litchfield's daughter showed a 'savage joy'. His haunting of the dying and his appearance at funerals was nothing less than an 'imitation of foul and obscene beasts of prey', and showed the disposition of a vampire.[7]

Away from such colourful comparisons, Portsmouth's behaviour was troubling because it could also provoke inappropriate responses from other people. Funerals were not just social rituals but were intended to be deeply serious religious occasions. Portsmouth officiated and read psalms at funerals 'in such a manner as to excite other feelings than one would desire on such an occasion', coffin-maker Richard Poore explained. 'Every person's countenance showed it'; as they stood around the grave, people stifled laughter as their attention was drawn to Portsmouth's antics. The awkwardness of the moment could produce giggles rather than tears. 'It was quite a mockery of what should be solemn if anything should,' Poore concluded.[8]

Portsmouth's social position meant that there were occasions when he was expected to take a lead role in directing the religious worship of his household, estate, and local community. In the early nineteenth-century, the Church of England was under threat from dissenting groups, Catholic incomers, and reformist pressures. Aristocrats like Portsmouth were meant to form the backbone of the Established Church, upholding its traditions, hierarchy, and order. Yet, aside from the disruption he caused during funerals, Portsmouth's behaviour during church services and at home when he conducted household prayers undermined the Church. He sang hymns out of tune, gave responses too loudly and too soon, and gabbled through prayers in front of his servants at breakneck speed. Portsmouth set the school-girls at the church in Acton 'a laughing' at his loud 'hems!' and they commented 'what a fool he was to make such a noise in the church'. Instead of setting an example by showing respect to clergy, Portsmouth laughed at them. One Sunday on his return from a service conducted by an elderly clerk at Andover, 'his Lordship continued all the way home mocking the old man, repeating his words, and imitating his manner'. Portsmouth once proceeded reading the evening prayers in the chapel at Hurstbourne immediately after he had finished the morning ones, leaving at least one servant unable to stay; 'I could not bide for laughing'. He paid so little attention to the meaning of what was being said that, when the parson had a cold and cough during a service in the church at Hurstbourne, Portsmouth copied his coughs and splutters in his answers.[9]

Portsmouth had gathered enough religious instruction from his childhood and schooling to know what was expected of him, and to some church ministers he presented no problem. He could conform. Reverend Pedden said that Portsmouth's conduct in church was 'most exemplary'; Reverend Heslop shared a pew with Portsmouth and thought 'he prayed with devotion'. Reverend McCarthy observed that Portsmouth was 'very attentive to the service', and, along with other churchgoers, only complained and grew restless if his sermons were too long.[10]

But whereas outward conformity was not always an issue for Portsmouth, his behaviour raised difficult questions about the relationship between religious practice and belief. What did the weak-minded Portsmouth understand about religion, and could he develop a religious faith? The jury at his Lunacy Commission wanted to know whether any clergyman had refused to give Portsmouth the sacrament. Did his immoral and irreverent conduct or his simple-mindedness mean that he should be prevented from being a communicant? The Reverend Antrobus answered that, if Portsmouth had ever wanted to receive communion, 'I should have felt very much distressed how I should act'. Antrobus thought Portsmouth 'utterly incapable of knowing anything of a matter so serious', was uncertain whether he understood 'the nature of the Lord's Prayer', but believed Portsmouth was not wholly ignorant of 'a future state and a Supreme Being'. The extent of Portsmouth's ignorance could be astonishing: he was very fond of singing a psalm that began with the words 'The Lord Himself, the mighty Lord', because, it was claimed, he thought that the 'Lord' was himself. But other clergy stuck to the principle that no man had the right to deny the sacrament to any person seeking it, except perhaps to 'evil-doers'.[11]

While his limited intellectual abilities did not disqualify Portsmouth from participating in this key Christian ritual, some thought that they should have prevented him from assuming a prominent place in the worship of his household and community. It made a mockery of religion to have a man with so little understanding taking prayers and being allowed to direct religious services. Just as the Portsmouth case exposed the shallowness that underlay so much of the elite social calendar, so his conduct relating to religious affairs revealed the problems facing the Established Church. Having a title and an estate had come to take precedence over religious knowledge and spiritual experience. So long as Portsmouth went along with the routine forms of worship, it did not matter if he had little sense of what he was doing, or what the words he repeated meant. Religious devotion had become measured by adherence to a number of routine practices, and it could take a fool to jolt people out of their familiar but mindless performance.

Portsmouth's conduct upon religious occasions and his love of black jobs forced people to confront the depths of their beliefs. Sex and death were the taboos that Portsmouth disregarded with such insensitivity that, while some were left feeling alarmed, hurt, or simply numb, others were faintly amused. While a good number of the lunatics who were confined in madhouses across the country exhibited a morbid fascination, Portsmouth was unusual because he was more interested in the funeral that would follow than in death itself. His desire to see Litchfield's daughter die was never repeated, but he remained a follower of funerals until he was called before the Commission. For Portsmouth, a funeral was a social occasion with bell-ringing, procession, and ceremony. It was a time when he delighted in the attention he could attract, and he appeared oblivious to its reason or the person who was being laid to rest. The feelings of others did not seem to cross his mind. By taking the emotions and the religious faith out of the ritual of burial, Portsmouth left people with a sense of hollowness that was as horrifying as the grave itself.

After listening to stories like Litchfield's, the jury had to decide what caused Portsmouth to behave in such socially unacceptable and insensitive ways. Did his actions arise from the weak mind of a fool, or the perverted mind of a lunatic? Fundamentally, was Portsmouth capable of understanding the differences between right and wrong?

'I was never with a gentleman of that kind before'

WORKING FOR LORD Portsmouth, whether as a household servant or as an estate labourer, was certainly a unique experience. Charles Green had trained as a shoemaker, but times were hard so he had gone into service, working in at least one other household before his position at Hurstbourne began in 1808. Service was a full-time occupation, and meant living as well as working in the same house as the employer. So servants like Green saw Portsmouth on a daily basis, and at close hand. 'I observed his manner much,' Green later stated to the Lunacy Commission. He was initially shocked at how the Hurstbourne household was run. Everyone took their orders from Lady Portsmouth, not her husband. Grace held the purse strings, and Lord Portsmouth had only 'pocket money' to spend. Lord Portsmouth was master and head of the household in name only. 'I was astonished at the manner of the servants to him,' Green remembered. 'They would take such improper liberties with Lord Portsmouth. I was astonished they would attempt to behave so to a man of his rank. I soon found out why it was.'[1]

Portsmouth spent his time in places usually reserved for working men. It was funerals of workers and their families that attracted Portsmouth, but another reason why he rushed to church whenever a person died was because he wanted to ring the bells. Indeed, as soon as any church service at Hurstbourne was over, Portsmouth rushed out of his pew, and hurried up the steep stone steps that led to the belfry. Once there, Portsmouth threw off his hat and coat, and stripped to the waist just like his fellow bell-ringers. Calling himself 'Jack', and declaring that he was the head bell-ringer, Portsmouth would excitedly announce, 'come Boys we must have a peal!' Portsmouth ordered that several days a year were bell-ringing days, including his birthday. At weddings, Portsmouth stood at the Communion Table with the Minister until the ceremony was over and then addressed the congregation by saying that he hoped they would remember 'us poor ringers'. If any payment was made, Portsmouth insisted that the sum was divided equally, much to the annoyance of his fellow bell-ringers, who were all working men, some of them his servants.

Unsurprisingly, perhaps, for a man who could not sing in tune or time, Portsmouth was a 'very bad ringer'. One Hurstbourne labourer who heard Portsmouth ring the church bells thought he did not know the difference between 'doing well and ill'. He did not understand the idea of ringing in a peal, so another man always had to stand beside Portsmouth to catch the rope and hand it to him when it was his turn to pull. Portsmouth seemed blissfully unaware of his lack of ability, and bell-ringing became one of his many pleasures. Along with pretending logs were coffins in an attempt to keep Portsmouth amused, his servants strung ropes across hooks in the stables to let Portsmouth pretend that he was ringing bells.

Green knew that his master loved music, for he was invited to play in his household band. Portsmouth took their performances very seriously, and gave all the band members special clothes to wear. Yet all the musicians knew that their patron was a fool. If Portsmouth asked what key they were playing in, they would answer 'O', and 'he was satisfied'.

Portsmouth's lack of attention meant that even an apparently inno-cent pastime such as ringing bells could be dangerous for others involved. He constantly messed around, sometimes using his rope to hit his fellow bell-ringers. But he caused greatest alarm when one day he placed a rope around another man's neck, and 'someone removed it, or, as the bell was going up, he would have been hanged'. Following this near-fatal incident, 'my Lord laughed', remembered the man's father.[2]

Portsmouth also spent time with his men when he visited the stables on his estate. He derived enormous enjoyment from riding his phaeton, a light four-wheeled horse-drawn carriage that was very popular at this time. This could be viewed as merely eccentric, as was the case with Portsmouth's Surrey neighbour at Clandon Park, the 2nd earl of Onslow, whose passion for driving four-in-hand was captured in one of Gillray's caricatures. Onslow favoured black horses and, because he also had his carriage painted black, 'the whole turn-out had more than the appearance of belonging to an undertaker'.

But whereas Onslow's macabre appearance had something in common with Portsmouth's pursuit of funerals, Onslow was commonly thought of as strange, and as a source of mild amusement, never concern. Portsmouth, on the other hand, took his interest in horses to new extremes. Coachmen and stable workers saw Portsmouth whipping his horses mercilessly. He had a large collection of whips for this purpose. Charles Webb, who was head coachman for Portsmouth from November 1808, thought that it 'was a sort of childish mischievous sport to his Lordship to cut them as he did. It was not from passion or malice in his Lordship; but it was what a mischievous boy might do.' But if whipping his horses was the childish play of an idiot rather than a madman, then Portsmouth's orders to have his horses bled seemed far more sinister. His servants simply pricked the animals with a pin, and made it look like they had been bled, and Portsmouth did not know the difference.

Although Portsmouth said that he was fond of horses, in the words of George Twynam, his gentleman neighbour, 'he was no sportsman'. He drove his phaeton in such a fast and furious manner that there was surprise that he did not cause an accident. To Webb, Portsmouth was too much of a coward to know how to manage a horse. If a horse started to kick as he whipped it in the stables, he ran away. At the slightest sense of danger while riding his phaeton, Portsmouth threw down his reins. And if 'any little thing happened to carriage or harness when they were out his Lordship would begin to halloo and cry, and call and beg to be let out, like a big blubbering boy'.

Horses were needed on the Portsmouth estate for work as well as leisure. To all his farm hands, it was extraordinary that Portsmouth insisted upon driving the heavy well-built cart horses around his farms. This was the occupation of a labouring man, not a peer. Portsmouth even drove dung from his stables to the fields, and such was his thoroughness at this task that a gardener needing manure was forced to get up early in the morning to beat Portsmouth to the stables.

While Portsmouth could prove himself a competent dung remover, he got in the way of other farm labour. Portsmouth was unable to distinguish between play and work; everything was a source of fun to him. Portsmouth acted as a young child, oblivious to danger. He went 'within the sweep of the scythe' as grass was being mowed; had to be pushed out of the way as carpenter Litchfield sawed off a beam; stood in the path of a tree that was about to be felled; and got too close to other farm carts as they were passing.[3]

Portsmouth was in his forties, but he was still behaving like a little boy. He played 'the most silly and absurd tricks'. 'If a servant had a new coat on Lord Portsmouth would find some means of spoiling it'; and he thought it amusing to try to stick rabbit skins and dishcloths to the back of their clothes without their noticing. If a servant was cleaning the plate, he would tarnish it; pinch the tools of a worker to slow his progress; throw water on to a fire that had just been lit; and blow out the candles in the parlour and servants' hall. In the fields he put a halter around the neck of one of his favourite labourers and said that he had a dancing bear, and he thought it was funny if he pushed the men into nettles or ditches. If he wanted to play hide and seek with his farm workers, they pretended that they did not know where he was so that he left them alone for a time. At least one bailiff was forced to employ a group of labourers specifically to keep Portsmouth amused and out of the way so that farm work could continue uninterrupted. Portsmouth was particularly fond of pulling the ears of his servants. One labourer, who started work at Hurstbourne as a boy under his father, told the courts that it would take him a year 'to tell all the childish foolish tricks he has witnessed in Lord Portsmouth'. He 'did not much like it' when Portsmouth pinched his ears. Portsmouth's conduct mocked and demeaned his workers; at the time it was mildly irritating and tiresome, but with repetition it could become unbearable.[4]

Many found his treatment of animals disturbing. He flogged his horses until they were 'mad' and 'did not know' what they were about. He not only mistreated his horses on occasion, but also took an unnatural interest in the slaughter of his cattle. Whenever butcher John Pottecary drove the cattle from the Hurstbourne estate to be slaughtered, Portsmouth met him and beat the animals severely with a large stick. Once at the slaughterhouse, Portsmouth started knocking the ox on their heads with an axe he had made specially for this purpose. In his eagerness to be part of the killing, Portsmouth started hitting the animals before they were properly secured, meaning he put himself and others at risk of being trampled. Among the blood and gore, Portsmouth 'mangled' the animals, and 'put them to great torture'. As the animal was 'struggling and roaring thro' pain', Portsmouth 'seemed much pleased and laughed', shouting out above the din, 'It serves you right you vicious Devil.' Pottecary could do nothing to prevent this bloodbath. When he told Portsmouth 'it was a shame to beat the creatures so', even arguing that 'he would spoil the meat', Portsmouth grew angry and threatened to fire him.

Describing Portsmouth's behaviour at the slaughterhouse, the grieving father William Litchfield bitterly remarked, 'anything cruel and death of any kind delighted him'. 'He was very cruel to dumb creatures,' reported a lodge keeper at Hurstbourne. In the hay fields and water meadows 'where there are a good many frogs', Portsmouth 'used to stick them with the prong of a fork'. 'The poor things' would cry out 'almost like a child'. If anyone objected, Portsmouth would shout, 'Damn them!' and 'Serve them right: they eat plenty of them in France.'[5]

Not all of Portsmouth's employees stood by as their master inflicted such cruelty. But if they intervened, they risked becoming the targets of his violence. When a coachman objected to Portsmouth trying to make a horse pull a load that was immoveable, 'smack went the whip in his face'. Grace arranged for the man to receive five pounds in compensation. Litchfield seemed to be right: Portsmouth enjoyed inflicting pain on creatures or people who he believed were less powerful than himself. He ordered a mix of jalap and mustard to be put into the beer of servants he did not like, and held the men down while they were forced to drink. The cook was told to feed servants who had fallen out of Portsmouth's favour with nothing but water-gruel and mustard for a week, and, if he found that she had not followed his orders, he whipped her out of the kitchen with stinging nettles.

Yet any power-kick that Portsmouth may have gained from these occasions was short-lived. Beneath a thin veneer of bravado and self-importance (he scolded any servant who addressed him as 'Sir' rather than 'Lord') was a giant coward. Just as he ran away from any horse or bull that threatened to trample him, he was easily intimidated by the words and actions of his servants. When Portsmouth tried to strike his valet, Charles Lee, because he said 'the servants should not burn his candles', Lee resisted and Portsmouth was 'cowed'. Coachman Webb put up with Portsmouth whipping the horses, but he could stop Portsmouth trying to strike him, by threatening to go to Bow Street to get a warrant against him. Green experienced his master's unpredictable behaviour and unwarranted anger one day as he followed Portsmouth, Grace, and Miss Gordon around the garden at Hurstbourne. Portsmouth suddenly turned and hit him so hard on the head with a stick that Green fell to the ground. Green was taken to bed, where Grace sent him some white wine and whey to aid his recovery. 'I was not much hurt,' Green later admitted, 'but I thought to frighten his Lordship' by pretending to be more seriously injured. Servants like Green were well aware of their rights, and with Portsmouth they were not afraid to voice them. 'I knew it was not fit that a gentleman should knock down his servant,' stated Green, 'so I said to my Lord, the next time he offered to strike me, I will put you in the Crown-office and take away all your property from you.' At this, Portsmouth 'was very much frightened', and his violence towards Green was never repeated. His servant had put him in his place.[6]

Who would work for a man like Portsmouth? Servants like Green were told when they were employed 'that they were to put up with a great deal'. Suffering 'pulling of the ears' and suchlike would have to be endured, but in compensation they were promised greater wages than most. However, the Portsmouths were not known to be generous employers, and, as working-class agitation mounted in the first decades of the nineteenth century, the labourers at Hurstbourne joined many others across the country by going on strike for better wages. Trouble lay ahead.

Of course, servants and labourers were always free to give their notice and seek work in a more conventional setting. Some did so, such as the valet, Lee, who left sometime after his master had tried to strike him. Lee was 'much about Lord Portsmouth's person, and observed his conduct', he later explained to the Lunacy Commission. 'I quitted his Lordship's family because I felt myself uncomfortable', he said.

But whether out of fear of unemployment and hunger, or from loyalty towards Grace, who was universally admired by the Hurstbourne workers, the majority remained. These working-class men could show a patience, tolerance, and understanding of Portsmouth's behaviour that was remarkable. William Lock spent the whole of his working life as a labourer on the Hurstbourne estate, first for Portsmouth's father, and then for Portsmouth himself. In Lock's view, Portsmouth 'knew no more than a child what was proper to be done about the Farm...all he cared for was having his day's amusement'. Lock saw Portsmouth at funerals when he helped to carry the bodies to the grave, and stood next to Portsmouth in the belfry as a fellow bell-ringer. Yet, describing an incident when Portsmouth cut him across the back with a long cart whip as he was lifting hay, he told the Commission, 'it could not be from malice'. Portsmouth was the boy who had never grown up. He was 'always of the same description', explained Lock, 'for he was the same man and behaved in the same way day by day and year by year'. When Portsmouth talked 'foolishly' about how the whip strike could not have hurt, it took all of Lock's willpower not to respond by hitting Portsmouth back. But there was no retaliation because he did not believe Portsmouth had intended to harm him. Like Webb, who did not think Portsmouth whipped his horses out of malice, Lock had decided that Portsmouth was too simple-minded to be cruel. Cruelty required a state of mind that Portsmouth did not have. So Lock kept his fists by his side, and plainly told Portsmouth that 'he would not stand it'.

While such forbearance earned the gratitude of Grace, who trusted Lock sufficiently to ask him to keep a special watch over her husband, over time it was wearing. 'It was the hardest matter in the world to keep him in any tolerable humour,' Lock later explained. 'Hundreds of lies were told him almost daily to keep him quiet: such as telling him that somebody was ill and likely to die. No one could hardly believe the nonsense and lies they were obliged to talk to his Lordship.' Green remembered putting a broomstick between Portsmouth's legs, and getting him to chase him around a room; lifting his master on to a pole and carrying him about like a horse; and taking hold of Portsmouth's 'pig-tail', rapping it against his neck or shoulders 'as he would a knocker', and calling out, 'is anybody at home?' At the time this was great fun for Portsmouth and perhaps for his servants, but, on reflection and when they were asked to describe their work for Portsmouth in his trials, such playful antics caused deep embarrassment. Green later admitted that this was the last way he would behave with another master, and that he was 'almost ashamed of having done it'.

The problem with Portsmouth's relationship with his workers was that he did not behave as their master. His personal habits left everyone appalled. When out riding Portsmouth told his postilion that 'he must get off and have a piss'. Once off his horse 'he turned round and showed his private parts' to his servant, 'in the most plain and gross manner', telling him 'to look at him'. On other occasions, he would 'whistle to the labourers and they to him (just as to a horse) when they and he have been making water'. 'His Lordship had no more sense of decency in that respect than a little boy in petticoats,' declared park keeper Godden. 'He used to stand and do it in the middle of a field exposing himself to the labourers at the time,' Godden remembered.

Servitude, with its expectations of deference and obedience, could only function while there was respect for those in command. As lawyers in one of Portsmouth's trials explained, 'All persons look up for example to those who are in higher stations in life…this Nobleman forgets all that belongs to high rank and great opulence.' Portsmouth's mental limitations reduced him to the capabilities of a child, but they also prevented him from exercising authority over his social inferiors. At Hurstbourne, 'all distinction of Master and servant was lost', remarked one observer. 'I knew how to manage him,' Green told the Commission: in this upside-down household, it was the servants who controlled their master, not the other way round. Portsmouth, according to Green, was not a 'perfect madman, else I should be afraid of him. I was never with a gentleman of that kind before. I considered him strange, but not mad. I consider a madman one who does all sorts of things and is not conscious of it, and cannot be ruled.' But 'we used to rule my Lord'.[7]

So far, the only non-family members who really knew Lord Portsmouth were the servants and workers who lived alongside him. They saw him for the man he was. But their social position meant that they just had to put up with it. For decades they had to tolerate his bizarre behaviour, or else quit and find work elsewhere. Within the Portsmouth household, the reversal of roles, where servants like Green could rule their master was maintained for so long as there was a mistress who inspired loyalty. That mistress was Grace, Lady Portsmouth.

It was not until 1815 that Portsmouth's servants and estate labourers were asked to provide accounts of their experiences working for him. Testifying during legal proceedings that aimed to obtain a Lunacy Commission, they were put in an unenviable position. Unconvinced that there was need for a Commission, the Chancellor refused to call one. A raft of employees who had given evidence in favour of a Commission were dismissed for daring to call their master's sanity into question.

Even when the Commission was called in 1823, the words of working men were more likely to be questioned than Portsmouth's better-off acquaintances. Were the stories of ordinary working people really to be believed over those Lords and Ladies with whom Portsmouth mixed socially? The character of working-class witnesses could be questioned to raise doubts about the reliability of their accounts. In bereaved father Litchfield's case, friends were asked if he was addicted to drinking. No credit should be given to the words of the blood-letting women Sarah Adams, Ann Pope, or Hannah Curtis, it was argued. These women 'were and are persons of bad fame, character and reputation, who for gain or reward' could be persuaded to say anything.

Telling a convincing story was not easy when for so long they had been expected to keep silent. Called to travel to London, and then being asked to speak before a room crowded with people, and to answer questions posed by highly educated lawyers could be an over-whelming experience. Still, having bottled up these stories for years, perhaps only sharing them with friends and family, working men and women could finally speak out. Some jumped at the opportunity. Green had no hesitation in declaring that Portsmouth's mind 'did appear to be like a boy four or five years old'.

Yet the unsophisticated way in which Green and other workers spoke provoked mockery. When Green explained he knew 'how to humour' Portsmouth, he chose a metaphor with which as a former cobbler he was familiar: 'I found the length of his Lordship's foot'. This, *The Times* noted, caused laughter to break out in the Freemasons' Hall. Laughter was frequently heard during Portsmouth's lunacy trials, usually in response to some answer or expression given by one of his workers. In what should have been a serious matter, laughter provided a welcome release. For, while men such as Green were questioned and their responses recorded, a deep sense of unease filled the room. Portsmouth's trials were an occasion when the social order was thrown out of place. Just as Portsmouth's mental condition reversed the usual roles of master and servant in his household, so these legal proceed-ings permitted working people to give their views about the conduct and future life of a social superior. When Green provoked humour by comparing how he measured his master's capabilities with the way he would a customer's foot, or following his testimony about Portsmouth a Hurstbourne carpenter declared, 'I am a married man and so is my wife', the laughter they caused was almost a relief. It allowed the jury and audience at the trials to put these witnesses back into their place: these were humble, unsophisticated, and ill-educated people. What did they know of the workings of an aristocrat's mind?[8]

The 'company keeper'

By January 1808, Grace Portsmouth had had enough. Approaching her fifty-sixth birthday, she was thoroughly disillusioned with marriage, and the demands of her husband were becoming too much for her to bear. Their social life was still good, but the strain of trying to hide her husband's faults, and the need to keep a constant watch over him was beginning to show. She was living a double life; in public presenting the dignified appearance of a wife married to a Peer of the Realm, while in private dealing with the daily consequences of being married to a man who was far from normal.

The events that made up the social calendar, characterized by formal exchanges of hospitality and expectations of good manners, ground on. At each occasion, Grace worried that Portsmouth would commit some social faux pas. Her husband could not be trusted to manage the simplest of tasks. Grace planned a party at her home in Lincoln's Inn Fields for the night of 27 January. 'Numerous persons of distinction' were on the guest list. But as Portsmouth was dressing he carelessly got too close to the fire, and his clothes caught alight. Grace heard his screams, came rushing into his chamber, and as she attempted to extinguish the flames, also set fire to her clothes. Grace and Portsmouth were both 'severely burnt', and were left suffering from shock. The unusual and dramatic reason for the party's cancellation was reported in the newspapers the next day.[1]

Grace was aware of her husband's meetings with women on his estate, and she heard about his attendance at funerals. She saw him rush off at the end of church services to ring the bells, and she knew he loved to ride his phaeton. It was easier for her to accommodate some of her husband's obsessions than dispute them, so she joined her husband in the fields with his men, and took an interest as he talked about his horses. But so often she had to pick up the pieces when things went wrong. She was left to apologize, and to try to make amends when his servants or labourers got hurt. They knew that she was the person to listen to their complaints, and to offer compensation in return for their continued patience and silence.

There was no way for Grace to escape this marriage. Divorce was only granted on the grounds of adultery. A legal separation with the right to live apart was only possible if she could prove cruelty or adultery. For all of Portsmouth's faults, he was never violent to Grace, and his sexual habits included nothing so ordinary as an extra-marital affair. Even if Grace could demonstrate that Portsmouth was insane, this would not get her a divorce. A marriage could be annulled, or declared legally void, on the grounds of insanity. But that insanity had to exist at the point the marriage vows were exchanged. It was irrelevant if Portsmouth had become insane since his marriage day. Grace had promised Portsmouth to remain his wife 'in sickness and in health' and 'till death do us part'. Never had those vows been so sorely tested.

With so much pressure upon her to cope and with little apparent affection in return from her husband, Grace may have felt desperately lonely. Her dear mother had died in October 1803, and her brothers were busy with their political and military careers. Her mother-in-law, Urania, was the one other woman who knew Portsmouth best. But in recent years Urania had been distracted by troubles caused by her other children. Coulson, Portsmouth's youngest brother, had turned into a scoundrel. Jane Austen knew him as a cad, who was notorious for his indelicate language and drunken habits. Marriage in 1802 had not sobered him up or made him more respectable, and for years he played hide and seek with his creditors. Facing imprisonment for debt, he was finally forced to flee to France, where he died in August 1807. Faced with a son who had so openly defied her authority, and rebelled against his strict upbringing, Urania was also confronted with worries about her daughter, Henrietta Dorothea. Newton Fellowes received numerous letters from his mother who had an 'anxious time' trying to find a cure for Henrietta Dorothea's deafness. She was sent to spend time at the seaside, saw physicians in Bath and then Exeter while she stayed with Newton at Eggesford, and experimented with hearing aids. Whether this amount of trouble and expense ever led to a permanent cure is not known, but at least her deafness did not prevent Henrietta Dorothea from making a good marriage to Reverend John Churchill in June 1815.[2]

Given Urania's critical stance towards her daughter-in-law, especially in the early years of her marriage, she was probably the last person Grace would have invited to come and help at Hurstbourne. Urania was a prolific letter writer, but no letters survive between the two women. Grace had remained silent about what she thought of her husband when she first married him, but, by the time of the January party in 1808, she was voicing concern that her husband's condition had worsened. With no family confidante or friend, the nearest person she could talk to was Godden, the longstanding park keeper at Hurstbourne. Grace found marriage to Portsmouth 'more than she was equal to', believed Godden; 'she was pretty well tired out with his Lordship'. 'Poor man,' said Grace to Godden about her husband, 'what a misfortune it is for him to be in this way.'

Grace remained the sympathetic wife, but, according to Godden, she described Portsmouth as being 'ruled by the moon'. Her language, if remembered correctly by Godden, was significant. For it meant that, even if she thought she had married a weak-minded man, she believed that he had become a lunatic, since 'lunatic' derives from the Latin term for moon. Had Portsmouth changed, or had Grace just got to know him?[3]

Grace thought Portsmouth had become more violent, and one incident in 1808 confirmed this to everyone. George, a coachman, broke his leg in an accident, and Grace with her typical kindness allowed him to stay within the house at Hurstbourne to recover. He was tended to by her family doctor, Dr Ludlow. John Baverstock, a servant who had worked for the 2nd earl as well as the 3rd, attended George during the day, and a female servant was employed to care for him at night. If Urania and Newton had any justification for their criticism of how Grace provided for the Hurstbourne servants in the early days of her marriage, there could be none now.

But about a month after his accident, and without any warning, Portsmouth entered the room where George lay, and ordered him out of bed. 'George, get up and go to work,' he demanded. When George said he could not, Portsmouth threw himself across the bed and landed upon George with such force that he broke his leg for a second time. 'I heard the bone crack,' said Baverstock in his chilling recollection of events. The sound of the bone cracking and a 'terrible scream' from George were heard by Baverstock and another servant in the next room. They rushed in, Baverstock pulled Portsmouth off George, and asked him 'how he could do such a thing'? When Baverstock said he was sure he had broken George's leg again, Portsmouth remarked, 'I'm glad on't, serve him right', and, in response to Baverstock declaring that 'you've ruined the man', Portsmouth said, 'I don't care for that.'

Baverstock led Portsmouth out of the room, leaving George with an injury from which he would take another six weeks to recover. As he lay defenceless on his bed, George felt so terrified that he asked Baverstock for something that he could use to 'guard himself' against his master. He was provided with 'an old broom handle'. The other servant who had been with Baverstock, and had witnessed these events found Portsmouth's conduct so 'inhuman and unfeeling' that it made him 'sick'. When Portsmouth met Dr Ludlow a while later he made no attempt to deny that he had broken George's leg, but said it 'served him very right'.

What became of George we do not know. He may not have been alive by the time Portsmouth's trials began as he never appeared as a witness. Despite solicitor enquiries, nobody even seemed to be able to find out or remember his surname. But the memory of his treatment by Portsmouth lived long in the minds of his fellow servants. There was something undeniably shocking about this event, and Portsmouth's response to it. Initially, lawyers argued that if George had been seriously injured then he would have brought an assault case against Portsmouth, but none was lodged. Yet by the time of the 1823 Lunacy

Commission there was sufficient evidence that the injury could not be denied, and lawyers for Portsmouth represented it as a one-off incident that was cruel, but was not evidence of madness. Many masters were violent to their servants, and this was wrong, but it did not prove insanity.[4]

To Grace, this event marked a new level of violence from Portsmouth that might be repeated, but more worryingly signalled how little her husband understood about the consequences of his behaviour. His reaction to both Baverstock and Dr Ludlow seemed to indicate that he was unable to comprehend why his actions were wrong. He was showing a callous disregard for others. Here was a man who had no moral boundaries. He had overstepped the mark, and even Grace's endurance.

Grace knew that she had lost control, and that she needed to take urgent action. In the summer of that year, she invited John Draper Coombe to live with her and Portsmouth. For the three years that followed Coombe's arrival, there was relative peace and harmony at Hurstbourne. No further occasions of Portsmouth's violence were recorded, and there were no dramatic incidents that anyone could remember. Grace had her confidence restored, and she could even dare to feel happy again.

The man who achieved this miracle of domestic transformation was in his early thirties, originally from Hampshire, and was a distant relative of Grace's family, the Grantleys. Trained in the medical profession, it was said that he had served as an assistant surgeon in the regiment of General Chapple Norton, Grace's brother. He was certainly known to Grace's brothers, and she may have been advised by them, as well as their family friend Justice Best, to take him into her household.

Just what role Coombe was expected to assume later became a matter for debate. He was more than a family visitor, because he was paid a handsome salary. Coombe was a crucial witness in Portsmouth's Lunacy Commission (he was the first to be called), but was evasive about why he had first come to Hurstbourne. He was with Portsmouth 'to direct his mind, and to regulate his conduct in general,' he said. He had no experience or special training for treating patients with mental problems. He was there, it was claimed, to assist Grace with her general domestic concerns, and to attend the whole household, not just Portsmouth.

Yet for all who saw Coombe at Hurstbourne he appeared, as one former Whitchurch surgeon put it, 'very much of the same description as that of a keeper over a lunatic'. When Coombe first arrived at Hurstbourne, servants were told that he was a 'visitor', the bailiff Mark Swait explained, but, when he stayed, they were informed that he was to be 'a company keeper for my Lord'.[5]

If Grace had recruited Coombe as a 'keeper' for her husband, then that was evidence that she thought her husband was insane. Employing individuals to live alongside and control their unruly relatives within their homes was a popular choice for wealthy families who had an insane member. It avoided the stigma of confinement in a private madhouse (the fate that befell Portsmouth's aunt and cousins), while it allowed for maximum discretion and secrecy. If Portsmouth's behaviour was going to get physical and more violent, having a strong man beside him might limit its effects.

But Coombe's arrival in 1808 was not absolute proof that Portsmouth was irrevocably insane. When Coombe left in 1811 to get married, he was not replaced; surely evidence that the position of 'keeper' for Portsmouth was not regarded as a permanent necessity. Grace was the type of woman who never gave up hope. She may well have believed that with Coombe's help she could restore her husband to his former self. Her faith in Coombe was not misplaced.

When he first arrived at Hurstbourne, Coombe wondered why he was there, for Portsmouth received Coombe 'with great politeness'. Indeed, like others who were socially acquainted with Portsmouth, Coombe found that Portsmouth 'could at times conduct himself with perfect propriety'. He watched Portsmouth 'not only enter a room with the manner and apparently conscious dignity of a nobleman: but also for hours together behave with as much propriety as any man could have done'.

It was necessary to see a great deal of Portsmouth 'to form a round and satisfactory opinion respecting him', Coombe discovered. He watched Portsmouth far more than he was aware, and learned about his many 'eccentricities'. Within days, Portsmouth 'betrayed great peculiarity of manners', and Coombe's job had begun.

Coombe described himself as 'managing' Portsmouth. Others in the household observed, and usually admired his methods. Coombe had a commanding presence, and soon had authority over Portsmouth. He could stop any inappropriate behaviour with just a look. The cook at Lincoln's Inn observed that Portsmouth 'was very bad before Mr Coombe came: he was too much for her Ladyship at times'. But after Coombe's arrival his behaviour improved. He stopped fooling around if the cook or other servants threatened to fetch Coombe. Servants at Hurstbourne also noticed a change, coachman Webb remarking that, 'when Mr Coombe was in sight', Portsmouth stopped playing pranks. Coombe came to the slaughterhouse twice when Portsmouth was there. Coombe said not a word, but Portsmouth immediately left, 'just as a school boy would with his Master who had found him where he was forbidden to be'.

How this younger man could have achieved such a measure of control over Portsmouth was a subject of speculation. He had been hired by Grace, but he was critical of her treatment of Portsmouth. Asked by the 1823 Commission if she was kind to her husband, he responded, 'Certainly; I might say to a fault', her 'kindness and attention to him were beyond anything'. He insisted that nobody told him how to manage Portsmouth, but that he devised his own plan after he had observed his charge. He decided that by being firm and by demanding respect he would gain results. In Coombe's view, Portsmouth 'had the mind of a child with the passions of a man'. Just like a child, Portsmouth could be controlled and restrained through fear; 'I managed him by terror sometimes, and sometimes by kindness,' Coombe told the Commission. He might threaten force, but he was seen exercising it only once by a servant, when Portsmouth refused to leave Lincoln's Inn to go to Lord Grantley's seat, and Coombe seized him by the collar. Usually his control was more subtle. William Pitman, an Andover surgeon who saw Portsmouth several times for minor injuries, was full of praise. Coombe's methods were 'the best mode' of control for Portsmouth, he thought. Coombe was 'cool, collected, determined: he had a commanding eye and Lord Portsmouth plainly felt and…by his conduct acknowledged the ascendancy and control which Mr Coombe…quietly exercised over his Lordship'.[6]

Portsmouth did not like Coombe, and, given that he was told that Coombe was a prize fighter and a very strong man who could kill with his bare hands, he was unsurprisingly afraid of him. 'Lord Portsmouth was seldom in good humour when Mr Coombe was with him,' remembered one Hurstbourne bailiff. Coombe stopped Portsmouth having fun. His tough 'bad cop' approach was diametrically opposed to the kindness of Grace, and left Portsmouth feeling frustrated and unhappy.

Just like a boy who had been too tightly controlled at home, as soon as Portsmouth could sense freedom, he ran wild. Much to Coombe's irritation, his authority was confined to Portsmouth's stays at Hurstbourne Park, and when Portsmouth was in London he 'mixed in society and he went about London alone'. Trouble was bound to follow.

Thomas Davis was a trustee and inspector of the charity schools of St Giles in the Fields and St George's, Bloomsbury, where Portsmouth was a governor. He already knew about Portsmouth's mental limitations, and had watched astonished as he voted both ways during a governors' meeting. But a number of times during 1809 and 1810, Portsmouth turned up at the school unannounced and struck fear into all the pupils.

If he saw any child laugh at him, he insisted that the teachers flog the child. If a child who saw Portsmouth in the street did not raise their hat, Portsmouth ordered that they be given twelve stripes with a cane, six on each hand. The children appealed to Portsmouth for mercy, 'but without effect'. 'His Lordship was insensible to it,' remembered a music teacher, 'and was evidently gratified by seeing the punishment inflicted.' Portsmouth went 'round the school and if he could find a boy that had a hole in his coat or a dirty face' he ordered punishment 'far exceeding the fault'. Hundreds of lashes were commanded, and, if a teacher remonstrated with Portsmouth, he grew furious. The teachers refused to mete out such extreme discipline, and at least one complaint was made to the Board of Trustees about Portsmouth's behaviour. The mere mention of Lord Portsmouth's name 'was a terror to the school'. Any child who attended one of Portsmouth's conspicuous displays of charity in 1811, when he offered them a meal, was filled with a mix of fear and dread. Even for a hungry child, the presence of Portsmouth at these events was a sure impediment to healthy appetite and digestion.

At some point in 1811, Coombe left Hurstbourne and the employ of Grace to get married. He had done his job well, but he may have been relieved to quit. His position in the household was never an easy one. He was not a servant, and he was described as a gentleman, but his salary meant that he was in a position of dependence. He was given so much power and authority that Portsmouth regarded Coombe as his master. A distant relation he may have been, but he was not treated as a family member. Much like a tutor or governess who resided in a family's home, he was put in a position of considerable trust, but in return all he could expect was a salary. Getting married gave him the chance to be the boss of his own household and family.

Grace was devastated when Coombe left. She had come to rely on him as Urania had on Reverend Garnett. To Grace, Coombe's qualities and skills were unique, and it is entirely possible that there was no new 'company keeper' because she believed he was irreplaceable. Grace did not see Coombe again, but Portsmouth and his family turned to Coombe for help in the future. He had not escaped this family's problems for good.

Without Coombe, Grace was left alone to control her husband. She begged park keeper Godden 'to look to Lord Portsmouth as much as he could'. For, as she explained, 'there was no one now but myself'.[7]

A lack of 'proper feeling'

SOMETIME ON THE evening of 13 November 1813, Portsmouth entered his wife's bedroom in Lincoln's Inn Fields to go to bed. Grace was kneeling by the bed, as if in prayer. But as he approached her and saw her face he realized that she was dead. She was sixty-one years old, and her death was attributed to an apoplectic fit, or what we might today call a stroke. She died alone.

Grace had been complaining for some time of 'a giddiness in the head'. Portsmouth said that he had advised her to see Dr Matthew Baillie, one of the leading physicians of the day. But in 1813 Baillie was occupied with his most famous patient, George III, as he suffered from another of his episodes of insanity. Over the course of the regency, which had begun two years earlier, Baillie visited the King at Windsor several hundred times. Never able to resist the opportunity to take on a new fee-paying patient (it was said Baillie was so much in demand that he regularly worked sixteen-hour days), Baillie sent a note to Portsmouth appointing a time when he would see Grace. Grace resigned to wait and 'see whether she in a few days might not get better'.

In the end, the doctor never arrived because Grace died before her appointment. Portsmouth had demonstrated his concern for his wife's health; Baillie did not come cheap. The irony that Portsmouth had recommended Baillie to examine his wife's head could not have been lost to the Commission of Lunacy years later. At the Commission, Baillie was one of a number of physicians to declare Portsmouth insane. But when his wife had been sick, who better than a man with head problems of his own to know that Baillie was the doctor his wife should see?

In the days immediately following his wife's death, Portsmouth withdrew from society, and returned to Hurstbourne. Edward Phillips, an Andover physician who had become friendly with Portsmouth while playing cards with him, came to give his condolences. Initially, Phillips was told that Portsmouth was not seeing anyone, but, after Phillips presented his card, Portsmouth warmly invited him in.

Portsmouth was eager to talk to Phillips and to get his medical opinion about his wife's death. He told Phillips how Grace had died, and that he had tried to get Baillie to see her. As he spoke, Phillips considered that Portsmouth's 'manner was collected'. Like any person who had lost someone who was close to them, Portsmouth wanted to know if he could have done anything to prevent his wife's death. In particular, Portsmouth asked if that cure for all ills, and his own peculiar obsession, bleeding, would have made any difference, and prevented the fit. Phillips answered all his friend's questions, and then 'endeavoured to divert his Lordship's mind, as he seemed much affected'. Phillips was confident from his experience treating patients with disordered minds that Portsmouth had a weak but sound mind, and this conversation confirmed his opinion that Portsmouth was not insane. He spoke 'with a tenderness and intelligence equal to a person of the strongest mind', and his conduct was 'uniformly correct and proper'.[1]

Death had taken away the three people who had the closest interest in Portsmouth's welfare in less than two years. On 29 January 1812, Portsmouth's mother, Urania, had died at her home in Harley Street, aged sixty-nine. Buried in the family vault of the church within the lands belonging to Farleigh House, she was laid beside her husband, and three of their children who had died before her. Fourteen months later, in March 1813, Reverend Garnett, close family friend and one of Portsmouth's trustees, also died. Portsmouth attended his funeral, and oversaw the erection of a memorial in the Farleigh Wallop church.

Now Grace was also dead, and for the first time in his life, aged forty-six, Portsmouth was without anyone to tell him what to do or

Even the vast interior of Freemason's Hall could not accommodate all who came to hear Portsmouth's trial for lunacy.

John Scott, first earl of Eldon and Lord Chancellor, found Portsmouth's case 'the most painful business' of his legal career.

Hurstbourne Park, the 'perfect palace'.

Farleigh House, the Portsmouths' other home in Hampshire.

Jane Austen's family home at Steventon, where Portsmouth was sent as a boy.

Portsmouth's younger brothers, Newton and Coulson, painted for their proud parents when they left Eton.

Urania, 2nd countess of Portsmouth – who would dare to cross this woman?

Urania's favourite son, Newton.

Urania's trusted friend, Reverend John Garnett.

Byron, the hopeless romantic, was cared for by the Hanson family as a child. He was all too ready to return the favour.

St George's, Bloomsbury. The wedding party climbed the front steps on their arrival, but following the service made a hasty exit through the back door.

The aspiring John Hanson: could that be the grounds of Farleigh House through the window?

A VOLUPTUARY under the horrors of Digestion.

Left: The Prince Regent and future George IV, representing the very worst of the upper classes.

Below: A case of 'spot the woman' amid a sea of men: the trial of Queen Caroline in the House of Lords.

A physician for the great (and wealthy), Dr Matthew Baillie.

Did Portsmouth fit this caricature of madness? (*The Lunatic* by Thomas Rowlandson)

Or was Portsmouth more like the idiot depicted in Hogarth's painting? The gormless servant who fetched laudanum for his suicidal mistress has no comprehension of his error.

Hurstbourne Park, Nov.ʳ 2. 1857

Dear Brother

I shall never part with this house
and premises as long as I live here
for not letting your son Newton to
come to it at all over again and I
cannot spare it at all as long as I live
I will never let your son have it at all
to come to it nor will I be at the expense
of the repairs he has occured to defray
the expences at his own expence I will
not send him any money at all to do it
it was done unknown to me quite so
I did not know it was going to be done
any thing to do it quite unknown to me

Yours &c &c
Portsmouth.

'I shall never part with this house': Portsmouth's heartfelt letter to his brother.

how to act. While Dr Phillips was impressed by Portsmouth's conduct, there were others who were appalled by his response to his wife's death. Once again, it was the servants who saw his other side.

To date, Portsmouth's interest in funerals had been confined to those of working people who were unrelated to him. But Grace's death gave him a chance to organize and participate in a funeral of an altogether different kind. By now an expert on undertakers and hearse drivers, a day or two after Grace's death, Portsmouth visited Webb in the stables. It had been decided that Grace's body should be returned to her family home at Wonersh, to be interned in the church where she had got married. 'His mind was full of it,' remembered Webb. He came 'in great glee', 'joking and laughing and enjoying it very much'. Daily visits to the stables followed, as Portsmouth tried to guess which 'black-job coachmen' would drive the hearse. He was sure 'old Joe' would be one of them. Portsmouth told Webb that if he was right, then Webb was to give the drivers 'a flogging all round; and when they got to Lord Grantley's to give them a ducking in the horse pond'. Discovering that Webb had never driven a coach in a funeral before, Portsmouth said Webb should pay him five shillings.

As the day of the funeral dawned, Webb and the other coachmen who knew Portsmouth wondered just what would happen. If they were expecting a funeral with a difference, they were not disappointed. Mr Page, a London undertaker, had been instructed to take charge of the funeral. He already knew Portsmouth, as he had been employed by him to bury 'a poor woman' who had died in St Martin's workhouse. On this earlier occasion, he did not think Portsmouth's interest peculiar, as he believed that the woman had some connection with a servant in the Portsmouth household. This was 'not foolishness but an act of charity', he later declared.

The funeral for Grace was one fit for a countess. Her coffin was laid in a funeral carriage, with her coronet on a cushion before her. The cortège consisted of a large number of coaches that made its slow procession to Wonersh. This was intended to be a solemn and dignified occasion, reflecting the high social position of the deceased, her husband, and their family. But when Portsmouth first saw the hearse, he immediately asked Page, 'How much will that come to Sammy?'

and also enquired about the cost of his wife's coffin. Such matters, especially to a wealthy man like Portsmouth, should have been far from his mind. The funeral was in November, but the following May Portsmouth was still disputing its cost with Page, and saying that he had been overcharged.

On the day of her funeral, Portsmouth was delighted to find that two of the coachmen he had predicted would drive the hearse were present. One was 'old Joe'. As they went along the road, Portsmouth looked out of his coach window several times at Webb, and 'laughed, pointing with his fingers towards old Joe'. About twenty miles into their slow journey, Webb, driving another coach, 'accidently came close to the mourning coach' in which Portsmouth was sat. Portsmouth 'made signs' to Webb to 'flog the coachman' who was driving Grace's carriage. When the procession stopped at Guildford, a short distance from Wonersh, Portsmouth came up to Webb, 'knocked him on the elbow', and said, 'Charles, go and…give a good one', meaning that Webb should now carry out the flogging.

Of course, Webb did no such thing, but Portsmouth was persistent. The day after the funeral, Portsmouth visited Webb in the stables and asked him if he had flogged the coachmen. He demanded the five-shilling fine from Webb, and would not give up on it. Webb eventually paid Portsmouth half a crown three weeks later.

Summarizing his account of Grace's funeral, Webb said, 'his Lordship did not appear…to grieve at all after his Ladyship, or show any reasonable or proper feeling on the occasion of her death'. Gatekeeper William London agreed. As he sat by his fire in the Lodge at Hurstbourne a few days later, Portsmouth chatted to London about who had driven the hearse, and complained that he could not get Webb to pay the five shillings. 'Who do you think carried her?' Portsmouth asked London, commenting, 'She was damned heavy.' 'His Lordship could not have showed less sorrow than he did on that occasion', remembered London, than 'if he had been talking of any poor person in Hurstbourne parish of whom he had known nothing.'

Portsmouth's words and behaviour were so shocking that those who heard or witnessed them struggled for explanations. Why would a man who had been so well treated by his wife be so apparently lacking in sorrow at her death? 'The late Lady Portsmouth expressed the utmost tenderness for his Lordship,' said Webb, 'notwithstanding which, he mentioned her death with great glee.'

Those who had observed Portsmouth with his wife pointed to his inconsistency of affection when she was alive. 'At times Lord Portsmouth appeared to be very fond of her Ladyship,' a bailiff remembered. 'He would hang over her and kiss her and call her his dear and his love', but after a few minutes 'he would be altogether as cross with her'. 'He would change like the wind', and he showed no more certainty of affection than a 'baby in arms'. So it followed that, after his wife's death, Portsmouth could not maintain any display of grief. He told a butler that 'he had lost his best friend when he lost his late wife', and his bailiff 'that he had lost his poor wife'. 'He whimpered a little', recalled the bailiff, 'making a sort of mock cry for a few moments', but he then took the man's ear and pinched it, 'in his usual way, laughing all the while just as he had used to do'. Grace's death appeared to have so little affected Portsmouth that he behaved just as normal. Most witnesses agreed that Portsmouth was fond of Grace, and that he had 'some sort of regard for her'. But there was such shallowness to that regard that it evaporated as soon as Grace was dead and buried. As park keeper Godden put it, 'he is convinced that his Lordship would have lost all feeling for her in the pleasure of tolling the bell for her and attending her funeral if she had died at any time'.

Many people had been astonished at Portsmouth's lack of sensitivity towards the feelings of others, especially when he had disrupted the funerals of people he did not know. But after Grace's death it was Portsmouth's own emotions that came under scrutiny. His response to the death of other family members had been a foretaste of what might happen. After the death of his father he had a 'serious conversation' with a clergyman in which 'he expressed deep regret at his father's decease', but also sought advice about how he should live his life now that he had inherited a 'great estate and fortune'. While he maintained a level of formal composure on this occasion, some twelve years later, when he joined in some manual work drawing gravel on his estate and suddenly started crying, he surprised his co-worker by saying that he was thinking about his father. Another time, Portsmouth was seen crying when he heard that his brother Coulson had died abroad. But William London said that 'the next minute it was all over and he was in good spirits again'. As a result, London did not believe Portsmouth 'felt anything at losing his brother'.

No love was lost between Portsmouth and his mother, so perhaps it was not surprising that nothing was recorded of his reaction when Urania died. But Grace's death should have mattered to him. If this man did not show emotion about the death of a woman who had been his wife for fourteen years, then could he ever develop an emotional attachment? Did he lack the emotional maturity for an adult relationship? Some were ruthless in their assessment. Godden did not believe that Portsmouth was 'capable of any proper feeling of affection', for example. To local doctor Daniel Ludlow, Portsmouth 'was attached' to Grace 'much in the way that an animal is attached to one who is kind to it, no exercise of reason being necessary to the existence of such attachment'. Portsmouth's regard for Grace was mindless in Ludlow's opinion. It was an instinctive response to her kindness, but there was nothing more. There was an expectation that at this level of society, where arranged marriages were common, relationships between husbands and wives would be forged and developed after the knot had been tied. But with Portsmouth's limitations this was impossible. He had no love to give.

This trial of a man's mind was becoming a test of his feelings. But what was the relationship between the head and the heart? Was it fair or 'proper' that Portsmouth's mind was being judged by his emotional reactions, or lack of them? People responded to death, for example, in infinitely varied, and often surprising and unpredictable, ways. Feelings, especially if they were deeply held, could make anybody act in an irrational way. Truthful, honest feelings were tricky to measure. Outward behaviour, especially when it came to a complex emotion like grief, might not be an indicator of inner feelings. Just as Dr Phillips was impressed by the measure of control that Portsmouth demonstrated when talking about the death of his wife, so also Dr Ainslie, who knew Portsmouth socially as well as a patient, was ready to defend Portsmouth's reluctance to talk about his grief in an emotional way. When Ainslie saw Portsmouth a few weeks after Grace's death, 'after the usual exchange of civilities, the Earl shaking his head' said to him, 'in a serious manner', 'You know I have lost Gracey?' Portsmouth 'conducted himself in a perfectly rational and sensible manner', Ainslie argued. Indeed, in a period when some people were condemned for indulging in grief, and grieving to such excess that they lost their reason (this was listed as a frequent 'cause' of insanity for those admitted to public asylums), Portsmouth could be praised for his measured response to his wife's death. If he was not overly emotional about his wife during her lifetime, it would be hypocritical of him now to display feelings for her. Ainslie thought Portsmouth was a classic case of a man who found it difficult to show his feelings. He believed Portsmouth:

> felt much more than he outwardly appeared to do: the Earl was not a polished man, but he showed as much feeling on that occasion as his general habits permitted him to do: it was evident that he regretted the loss of his...Wife, and that he was aware of the loss he suffered by her death.

There was nothing sophisticated about how Portsmouth expressed himself, but his name for his wife, 'Gracey', was evidence of his affection for her. He did feel love, even if he struggled to show it. 'He certainly was as fond of her as he could be of anyone', concluded gatekeeper London.[2]

Even if Portsmouth's behaviour following his wife's death could be explained, or excused, as being exhibited during special circumstances when any man would be put under strain, it alerted the Commission jury to his emotional difficulties. This was a man whose slow mental development seemed to have affected his ability to feel and demonstrate affection. Although they never complained, the experience for both his mother and Grace of caring for someone who could give so little in return must have been devastating. For Portsmouth himself, his apparent inability to feel, and the death of both his real mother and his substitute one, left him in the future vulnerable and exposed to the abuse of others.

We do not know who was present from Portsmouth's side of the family at Grace's funeral in November 1813, but we can be sure that word quickly travelled about his alarming behaviour. Grace's brother, Lord Grantley, was one of Portsmouth's trustees, and he, along with the three others, Newton Fellowes, Justice Best (who had taken over from Reverend Garnett after his death), and John Hanson, met in London at the end of the month. They had seen just how badly things could go wrong if Portsmouth was left unsupervised. It was decided that Portsmouth should stay at Hurstbourne, and that Coombe would be invited back to take care of him. Coombe was installed by the end of December, and Henrietta Dorothea, Portsmouth's sister, who was still unmarried at this stage, took position as a useful female presence with responsibility for domestic concerns.[3] Portsmouth's first taste of freedom was curtailed, or so his trustees thought.

Cuckold

Mad, bad and dangerous to know?

A T MIDNIGHT ON Monday, 7 March 1814, Lord Byron sat down to start writing his journal. It had been a long day. He had risen at seven that morning, somewhat bleary-eyed, and still hung-over from attending two balls the previous night. 'Very reluctantly', he got dressed, and by half-past eight he was ready to leave the house. Outside it was a misty, cold morning. The London streets were still sprinkled with snow that had fallen several days before, and a hard frost made the pavements hazardous for walking. But neither tiredness nor the freezing temperatures would deter Byron. For he had an important appointment to keep with his solicitor, John Hanson.

Byron's meeting with Hanson was not a usual one between a solicitor and his client. But, ever since Byron could remember, his relationship with Hanson had been personal as well as professional. John Hanson was the solicitor recommended to Byron's widowed mother when he inherited his title and the Newstead and Rochdale estates in May 1798. That summer, Hanson and his wife had stayed with the ten-year-old Byron and his mother for three weeks at Newstead. By the time the Hansons returned to London, they had earned the trust of both mother and child.

John Hanson set about protecting Byron's estate by making him a ward in Chancery. A legal guardian was formerly appointed, but this was in name only, for in every other way Hanson took responsibility for the young Byron. The following summer, Hanson returned to

Newstead for another two-week visit. When he left for London in July, he took Byron with him.

Byron was warmly welcomed into the Hanson family home in Earl's Court. John had bought the house a few years earlier from the executors of John Hunter, the famous anatomist and surgeon. There was much excitement within the Hanson household about Byron's arrival, particularly among Hanson's children. Hargreaves was the Hansons' oldest son and was the same age as Byron, Newton a few years younger, and sisters Mary Ann and Laura were part of a growing family that would later include another boy and three more girls. John and his wife had talked so much of their young charge that they 'had somewhat piqued the curiosity of my elder brother and my sisters and myself', remembered Newton. 'My Father brought Lord Byron into the room in his hand – all eyes were upon him.' Seven-year-old Laura, 'after examining Lord Bryon from head to foot', exclaimed, 'well, he is a pretty boy however!'

At eleven years old, Byron was a shy boy, who gripped Hanson's hand very tightly on this first family occasion. He had been born with a deformed right foot (it was 'inverted and contracted'), and was often in acute pain, and self-conscious about his lameness. His mother wrote to John Hunter about her son, but had not been able to afford to carry out the treatment he advised. One of the first things that Hanson did was to take Byron to see Dr Baillie. After several consultations, Baillie declared that it was now too late to correct the shape of Byron's foot, but advised that a special boot should be made to aid his movement. Byron responded to this disappointment by withdrawing into the world of reading, often spending all morning 'upon the sofa quite lost in his book'.

Hanson's attempts to find a remedy for Byron's foot may have struck a chord for a special bond developed between the pair. Byron had never really known his father, and his relationship with his mother was always fraught and frequently volatile. His early childhood had often been unhappy, and there was a fragility and vulnerability about him. But Hanson showed such interest and concern in Byron that Byron could not help developing a fondness for him, and came to refer to him as his 'pater'. In turn, Hanson wrote to Mrs Byron with news of his 'honourable little companion', telling her, 'I entertain a very great affection for Ld Byron.' He became increasingly proud of 'his little protégé'. In time, Byron relaxed into the Hanson family's routines, and played with the Hanson children. Hunter had conducted many of his experiments at home, and reminders of his eclectic interests, such as the thirty-foot replica Egyptian pyramid that he had built in his garden, provided endless sources of games and fun. When Byron confided to Hanson that for years he had been subjected to the cruelty of his nurse, Mrs Gray, Hanson believed him, and saw that she was dismissed.

It was Hanson who put arrangements in place for Byron's education. He found a school for him in Dulwich, run by Scot Dr Glennie, and from there, in September 1801, Byron entered Harrow School. Hanson sent his oldest son, Hargreaves, to Harrow at the same time, and they may even have been in the same class. The two boys became close friends. Each school holiday, Byron returned to the Hansons' home, stating a preference to this over spending time with his mother. He was introduced to friends of the Hansons', the Grantleys, and shared in the delight of their annual Christmas gift of a huge cake and tub of Grantley butter.

A visit of Mr and Mrs Hanson to a speech day at Harrow entered family legend. John decided to wear a 'most curious', and 'triangular kind of judge's hat', which was turned up at the sides, with a silk strap and buttons. If Hanson was trying to look important, the effect was the opposite. Byron, Hargreaves, and their school friends roared with laughter, and, if ever in the future the family needed amusement, the story of the hat would be rolled out. The hat itself assumed a 'sort of immortality', remembered Newton, appearing in the upper storeys of the 'dark huge mansion' in Chancery Lane where Hanson worked, or next to the pyramid at Earl's Court. Mr and Mrs Hanson had become substitute parents for Byron, and, by sharing in their family jokes and memories, Byron had become one of the family.

Byron stayed with the Hanson family in the month before his studies began at Trinity College, Cambridge, in 1805, and he kept in touch with them by letter while there. As a young man Byron was dependent upon Hanson to release his funds, and Hanson was quite prepared to scold Byron for his irresponsible behaviour. But on the whole Byron took Hanson's reprimands in good humour, and the tone of the letters between them remained warm. When Byron travelled abroad for his grand tour, he missed both Mrs Hanson, 'who has often been a mother to me', and John Hanson. 'I have travelled a good deal, and seen a good deal,' he wrote to Hanson from Athens in January 1811, but wistfully he looked forward to the day he could 'take a bottle of your port in Chancery Lane', and talk about the old times. When Hargreaves died in May that year, Byron was devastated.[1]

So, when John Hanson invited Byron to witness the wedding of his oldest daughter, Mary Ann, and as an old 'family friend' gave him the honour of giving her away at the altar, he could hardly decline. He had been present and shared in many of this family's key moments of happiness and sadness. For the last sixteen years, Mr Hanson had been much more than a guardian of his financial and legal interests, and Byron felt indebted to him. 'I could not very well refuse without affronting a man who had never offended me,' Byron later recalled.

Yet, a few days earlier, when Hanson told him of his daughter's wedding, Byron might have been expected to be surprised at the man Mary Ann was due to marry. For Mary Ann's husband-to-be was none other than Lord Portsmouth. Portsmouth was another of Hanson's clients, and Hanson was his trustee. There was a twenty-four-year age gap between the young Mary Ann and the forty-seven-year-old Portsmouth. She was a solicitor's daughter, he a Peer of the Realm.

But Hanson knew Byron well enough to rouse his interest and guarantee his support. He told Byron that there was a plot by Portsmouth's brother, Newton Fellowes, for Portsmouth to marry 'some elderly woman...by whom no issue could be reasonably expected' so that 'the title and family estates might thereby eventually devolve to Mr. F[ellowes] or his children'. Since Portsmouth had already been married to an 'old Lady', Newton's plan was for him to marry 'another old woman'. Portsmouth, however, who had grown attached to Mary Ann, 'had expressed a dislike to old women and a wish to choose for himself'.

Byron, the romantic whose personal life would rock the establishment, liked nothing better than the idea of throwing Newton's scheme off course. His mother's reduced circumstances, and his father's debts when he was a child, gave Byron a 'quick sense of iniquity and a spirit of defiance', which would last a lifetime, according to Hanson's son. Here was a worthy cause for his rebellious nature. Portsmouth's 'preference of a young woman to an old one – and of his own wishes to those of a younger brother – seemed to me neither irrational nor extraordinary', Byron later stated. Hanson had him hooked.

Byron arrived on time, and as expected that cold Monday morning. By 1814, Hanson had moved his London home closer to his offices, and was living in one of the elegant houses on Bloomsbury Square. So many of Hanson's neighbours were lawyers that the area had become known as 'Judge Land'. A few hours passed before the wedding party left for the church. Mary Ann, with Charles and Eliza, her younger brother and sister, and Mr Buckworth, a young man who was a family friend, all travelled in Mr Hanson's coach. Mr Hanson remained at home, while witnesses could not agree later whether or not Mrs Hanson, Mary Ann's mother, went with her to the church. Charles whispered the destination, St George's, Bloomsbury, to the coachman. Since St George's was only two streets away, and the carriage was full, Byron walked the short distance with Portsmouth.

The two men talked. If Byron needed reassurance that Portsmouth wanted this marriage, he got it. Portsmouth told Byron that 'he had been partial to Miss Hanson from her childhood'. 'Since she grew up', and particularly since the death of his first wife, 'the partiality had become attachment'. This all seemed very probable; Portsmouth, like Byron, had known John Hanson and his family all his life. Hanson had been such a trusted adviser to Portsmouth's father that he had been a beneficiary of his will, and he was an executor of his mother's will. He had arranged and witnessed all the important legal decisions made by his family. Hanson was the link to his past and now to his future. Mary Ann was 'calculated to make him an excellent wife', Portsmouth told Byron.

The wedding party were so keen that they arrived at the church too early, and before the morning service had ended. They were shown to the rector's pew near the altar. St George's, which some would laud as Nicholas Hawksmoor's finest achievement, had been consecrated in 1731, its statue of George I surrounded by lions and unicorns on the tower, ensuring that it fast became a London landmark. It was a familiar church to Portsmouth, who had visited when attending meetings for the nearby school of St George's, and he had called in several times to make enquiries about funerals when he heard the bells tolling.

When the wedding service began, aside from Reverend William Gilbank, who officiated, the only additional witnesses were John Harrison, the parish clerk, and Jane Colborn, the church sexton. Byron gave away the bride, as requested. Portsmouth's behaviour appeared to Byron to be 'perfectly calm and rational on the occasion – he seemed particularly attentive to the priest and gave the responses audibly and very distinctly'. Byron thought the latter was especially important to note, 'because in common conversation his Lordship has a hesitation in his speech'. Indeed, rather than hesitating, at times Portsmouth seemed rather quick with his answers. 'Portsmouth responded as if he had got the whole by heart,' Byron recorded in his journal, 'and, if anything, was rather before the priest.' This eagerness to get married amused Byron, but it caused him no concern. 'The Ceremony passed without any thing remarkable,' Byron told his friend John Cam Hobhouse. 'The women cried a little as usual – but Lord P's deportment was quite calm and collected.'

Everything about the service seemed routine. Reverend Gilbank was dead by the time questions were raised about the marriage, and the sexton also may have shared his fate, for she never gave her account of the wedding. But Harrison, the clerk, was alive, and he could remember nothing unusual. Portsmouth 'conducted himself throughout the ceremony with great decorum', he recalled, and acted in a 'perfectly rational and sensible manner'.

Indeed, the only point when things did not go according to plan was when Byron gave the bride away at the altar. 'Made one blunder,' Byron wrote in his journal, 'when I joined the hands of the happy – rammed their left hands, by mistake into one another. Corrected it – bustled back to the altar-rail, and said "Amen."' Byron's mix-up of hands meant that by accident he was 'nearly married himself,' he laughingly told Hobhouse that afternoon.

Having signed the register, the parties left the church by a back door, and met their carriage in a street behind the church. Byron went back with them to Bloomsbury Square. They had been absent for only half-an-hour. On their return, Byron congratulated the family, and 'drank a bumper of wine'. He was asked to stay for dinner, but could not. The remaining party had a cold lunch, and then bride and groom left in Mr Hanson's carriage for their first night of married life at the Windmill Inn, Salthill, in Buckinghamshire. They were accompanied by Mary Ann's father, mother, sister, and brother.

The next day, 9 March, Mr Hanson held a dinner for the newly married couple in Bloomsbury Square. Thomas Halls, a nephew of Reverend Garnett, and a close friend of the Hansons' (his sister would marry Charles), was one of the many guests. He thought Portsmouth 'conducted himself in the same manner as a newly married man might be expected to do: he appeared in very good spirits'. Sitting next to his wife, he seemed 'very fond' of her, and enjoyed introducing her as the countess of Portsmouth. He told Halls that his brother had 'wanted me to marry an old woman, but you see, I liked a young one best'.

Byron saw the couple and the Hanson family on 10 March. 'Received many, and the kindest, thanks from Lady Portsmouth, père and mère, for my matchmaking,' he wrote. He noticed an immediate change in Mary Ann. 'She looks the countess well, and is a very good girl. It is odd how well she carries her new honours. She looks a different woman, and high-bred too. I had no idea that I could make so good a peeress.' Byron felt very pleased with himself and had no regrets about his part in the marriage. 'I thought that if Ld. P. got a good plain quiet homekeeping wife – young too – instead of the tough morsel prepared by his brother – it was no bad bargain for either party,' he later wrote to Hobhouse.[2]

At the time, and in the years that followed, Byron emphasized to his friends that he saw nothing 'remarkable' or 'particular' in the marriage between Portsmouth and Mary Ann Hanson. His witness statement to this effect, which was submitted to Chancery in written form around December 1814, was crucial in establishing the validity of the marriage and ensuring the rejection of Newton Fellowes' first call for a Commission of Lunacy against his brother. Byron was adamant that Portsmouth was 'rational' in his conduct. Portsmouth was no 'more insane than any other person going to be married', Byron told Lady Hardy.

Byron insisted that he barely knew Portsmouth. 'I have never been very intimate with his Lordship,' he told Chancery in 1814, 'and am therefore unqualified to give a decided opinion of his general conduct.' But there was one incident in Byron's childhood that might have given him some warning about Portsmouth.

In 1799, when the eleven-year-old Byron had first come to live with the Hansons in Earl's Court, in the period before his wedding to Grace on 19 November, Portsmouth had also chosen to stay there. 'One wet morning just after breakfast,' remembered Newton Hanson, everyone took sanctuary in the conservatory. 'We were lounged about in this retreat when Lord P took the liberty of pulling Ld Byron's ears in his usual rough way tho' in fun.' Byron did not see the joke. Enraged, he grabbed one of the large shells that was on display (perhaps a piece of Hunter's collection), and threw it across the room at Portsmouth. It narrowly missed Portsmouth, but shattered a window. Byron's reaction not only frightened Portsmouth, but everyone else in the conservatory. Mrs Hanson frantically started apologizing on Byron's behalf: 'Lord Byron did not do it intentionally my Lord,' she told Portsmouth. But Byron kept repeating that he *did* do it intentionally, and 'he would teach a fool of an Earl to pull another Noble's ears'. It seemed to take an age for the two to be reconciled, and shake hands.[3]

While this occasion gave the Hansons an early insight into Byron's fiery disposition, for Byron it was an indicator that this fellow nobleman was a bit of a fool, with irritating habits that he would not tolerate. Writing to John Hanson following Portsmouth's marriage to Grace, Byron hoped that 'his lady when he and I meet next will keep him in a little better order'. A good wife would keep this man in check. Mary Ann Hanson fitted the bill, just as Grace had done.

As far as Byron was concerned, Portsmouth was a prize 'fool of an Earl', but not insane when he married Mary Ann. As Byron told Hobhouse, 'I could not foresee <u>Lunacy</u> in a Man who had been allowed to walk about the world five and forty years as Compos – of voting – franking – marrying – convicting thieves on his own evidence – and similar pastimes which are the privileges of Sanity.' He knew nothing of horsewhipping and blood-letting. Like so many of Portsmouth's social contemporaries, Byron was in the dark about his less savoury occupations. In March 1814, Byron did not know and could not predict what would follow.

But Byron was quickly affected by the consequences of his part in Portsmouth's second marriage. In September, Byron became engaged to Annabella Milbanke, and wanted John Hanson, as his solicitor, to make arrangements for their marriage settlement. But by this point Hanson was busy defending his daughter's marriage to Portsmouth, and trying to ensure that the Chancellor rejected Newton Fellowes' call for a Lunacy Commission against Portsmouth. Byron was initially sympathetic with Hanson's position, reassuring him 'with regard to Mr Fellowes...you are well able to cope with and curb him – what <u>can</u> he do that can seriously molest you or your son-in-law?' But as the weeks passed, and Hanson did not return to his London offices from Hurstbourne, both Byron and Annabella became frustrated at his lack of attention. In December, Annabella wrote to Byron's half-sister complaining of Hanson's 'procrastination'. 'I know from good authority that he has taken an unreasonable and unnecessary time for the completion of settlements,' she told Augusta. He was too preoccupied by 'the troubles of his own family', and his frequent reference to 'Lord Portsmouth' when she saw him, instead of 'Lord Byron', showed 'what was uppermost in his mind'.

All this delay only served to increase Byron's doubts about his forthcoming marriage, but, unfortunately for both parties, they did not prevent it. Byron married Annabella on 2 January 1815. The couple had planned to take their honeymoon (or 'treaclemoon' as Byron liked to call it) at Farleigh House. Whether it had been promised by Mary Ann or Portsmouth as a favour to the man who had been the chief witness of their marriage is unknown. But since 'Lord Portsmouth and his brother have gone to Law about intellects,' Byron explained in a letter to Annabella in November 1814, 'it would be no proof of mine if I were to take Farleigh as a tenant until it is ascertained unto whom the brains and buildings actually belong'. 'This explosion among the senses of the Portsmouth family,' Byron wrote to Annabella a month later, 'has set me off about another house – as I would rather dwell among the reported sane.' They settled for her father's house, Halnaby Hall, in Yorkshire, instead.

Byron kept in touch with Hanson following his wedding, and with news of the Portsmouth case. He was convinced that his written statement about the Portsmouth–Hanson wedding, which had been submitted in December, would persuade the Chancellor to refuse the Commission. 'I shall hope soon to hear you have given Master Fellowes his reward,' Byron wrote to Hanson with optimism in January, but in early February was dismayed to hear rumours that the case was turning against him. When the Chancellor finally ruled that a Commission would not be called, Byron felt vindicated. Hanson's gratitude to Byron was obvious, and he was still sending Byron gifts of venison from the Hurstbourne estate three months later.[4]

When a second attempt was made to call a Commission in autumn 1822, this time initiated by Newton Fellowes' son, Henry Arthur, Byron was not called as a witness. He was perplexed about why this was the case, and stated his willingness to travel back to England to give his evidence. But by the time the Freemasons' Hall opened its doors for Portsmouth's Lunacy Commission in February 1823, there was no possibility of Byron making a credible witness for Portsmouth's sanity. For Byron's personal reputation was in ruins.

His marriage to Annabella in January 1815 had been a disaster from the outset. Byron's tempestuous nature, his love of wine and women, and uncertainty about the extent of his intimacy with his half-sister, all contributed to his marriage breakdown. On 10 December, the couple had a child, Ada, but by January 1816 Annabella was convinced the marriage was over. She thought that Byron had become insane. 'He believes himself to be guilty of a dreadful crime,' she wrote to Dr Baillie, the expert on insanity and brother of one of her friends. While she was probably unaware, or not prepared to state the suspicions of others that Byron had committed incest with Augusta, Annabella supplied Dr Baillie with a list of Byron's 'insane ideas' and practices. According to Hobhouse, Baillie came to examine Byron, the patient he had treated as a young boy for his deformed foot. He would not give a 'decided opinion'. When Annabella arranged a secret meeting with John Hanson, he was horrified to discover that she was so certain of Byron's insanity that she 'might have a design of <u>resorting to personal restraint</u>'. Hanson told Annabella that he had known Byron since he was ten years old and that, although he had many 'eccentricities', he had never seen any signs of insanity. As for restraining Byron, Hobhouse believed that Hanson warned Annabella 'most seriously against such a desperate and, as he thought, mistaken measure, which might produce the very mischief which she dreaded, or perhaps a more terrible catastrophe'.

Hanson protected at least one of his clients against an accusation of insanity, for, while Annabella and Byron signed a private deed of marriage separation on 15 April 1816, she never publicly aired her suspicions about Byron's state of mind. She did not need to, for all but one of the newspapers took Annabella's side in their separation proceedings. Byron was vilified for his personal failings and what was perceived as his lack of morality. He was hounded by the press, and jeered at in the streets. On 24 April, Byron left England, never to return, not even for the Portsmouth case.

In the autumn and winter of 1822–3, Byron watched from the side-lines as Portsmouth's trial progressed. He told one of his correspondents that he found it all 'vastly amusing', but he was power-less to affect what happened. 'My name I see by the papers has been dragged into that unhappy Portsmouth business,' he wrote, for some were claiming that Mary Ann had been one of Byron's many lovers. This was quite untrue, Byron wrote, for 'my liaison was with the father – in the matrimonial shape of long lawyer's bills'. Yet the lies that were being told about Byron were indicators of his diminished status in the public eye. There was no longer any point in listening to Byron's version of events about the wedding day of Portsmouth to Mary Ann Hanson. For who would believe a man who was 'mad, bad and dangerous to know'?[5]

'This unfortunate and devoted girl'

JOHN HANSON. HE had always been there. As a newly qualified solicitor, he had worked as the 'confidential legal adviser' to Portsmouth's father and mother. He had spearheaded the dowager countess's efforts to secure Newton Fellowes' inheritance from his uncle Henry Arthur. In July 1799, he was one of the rescue party for Portsmouth when he was abducted by Seilaz, and he led the prosecution against the valet in King's Bench. In 1804, he acted for the Gordon brothers during their trial at the Oxford assizes. The Portsmouth family trusted him completely. They 'laid open' their 'family situation' to him, and he offered them reassurance and protection. He was the author of the 1790 and 1799 legal deeds that were designed to safeguard the family's fortune and future. It was said 'no business of importance' relating to the Portsmouth family 'was done without consulting the said John Hanson', and 'unlimited confidence was reposed in him by the whole family'.

He could be relied upon at moments of crisis, and he found practical solutions to emotional problems. He remained clear and level-headed when things went wrong. He went that extra mile for this family, and well beyond what his job description as a solicitor required. He knew all their secrets, and they told him of their worst fears. Byron thought of Hanson as a benevolent father figure, and as someone who cared for him at his weakest moments. To the Portsmouths, Hanson also appeared to be a man who was dedicated to the needs of their most vulnerable member.

But the events of 7 March 1814 shattered this illusion. By marrying his oldest daughter to Portsmouth without the knowledge of any of the other trustees, and most importantly his brother, Newton Fellowes, Hanson revealed himself in an entirely different light. For years he had been in the shadows, gathering information and earning trust – waiting. On Monday, 28 February, Coombe brought Portsmouth to General Norton's house in Lincoln Inn's Fields. Norton was absent, and the only member of the family present was the nineteen-year-old Fletcher (future 3rd Lord Grantley). For reasons that never became clear, Coombe made the fateful decision to resign his post, and to leave Portsmouth, 'as a man would hand over a bale of goods', to his trustees. Hanson saw his chance. Within the space of one week, he had put arrangements in place for the marriage of his daughter to Portsmouth. Far from being the kind and devoted family adviser, Hanson's true character, as a ruthlessly ambitious man driven by greed and an overly inflated sense of his own importance, was now exposed. If Portsmouth, the man who would be subjected to a Lunacy Commission, had mastered the art of hiding his real self, then this was well within the capabilities of Hanson. But it was Hanson's conduct towards Mary Ann that was hardest to believe. Surely no father, however great his ambitions, would sacrifice his daughter to a man like Portsmouth?[1]

Mary Ann had grown up knowing about Lord Portsmouth. As the eldest girl in a family of eight children, she had seen how closely her father's career was tied to his relationship with the Portsmouth family. From modest, middle-class beginnings, he had expanded his legal practice, becoming a partner with a Mr Birch and setting up offices in Chancery Lane. He was well known within the legal profession, and held a number of government posts. In October 1794, he was appointed Receiver-General of the Land Revenue, and from 1807 he became solicitor to the Board of Stamps. But it was his income from his private clients, most notably the Portsmouths, which had the greatest impact on his family life. Even without the many legal disputes that arose because of Portsmouth's condition, Hanson would have been kept busy, and well paid, by managing their vast estates in several English counties, and in County Wexford, Ireland. From November

1799, he also received an annual payment of £150 as Portsmouth's trustee.

Mary Ann was ten years old when Portsmouth married Grace. Her father's success and increasing financial confidence meant that in 1802 the family moved from Earl's Court to Bloomsbury Square. The perks of her father's work for the Portsmouths were not just financial, however. Farleigh House had become Urania's dower house in her widowhood, but she had no desire to live there, preferring to be in London. For a short time Urania let the mansion to Newton Fellowes, and he and his wife Frances bought furniture from London for it in May 1802. But by 1804 Urania was looking for a new tenant as Newton and his family moved to make Eggesford in Devon their permanent home. It was offered to John Hanson. Farleigh House was a beautiful home. More manageable in size than Hurstbourne, the house had been substantially restored by Viscount Lymington, later the 1st earl of Portsmouth, in 1731. Hanson jumped at the chance, and even purchased the new furniture from Newton. Five years later, Hanson was also given the opportunity to rent the farm there, negotiating a competitive rate that was offset against his legal costs.

Mary Ann and her family found themselves pursuing a lifestyle that was more akin to their aristocratic patrons than their humble origins. Mrs Hanson and her children spent the winter months in London, but in the summer moved to Farleigh for 'the season'. There they enjoyed entertaining their affluent Hampshire neighbours. Byron looked forward to staying at Farleigh in the September before he started Cambridge. With excitement he wrote to Hargreaves Hanson, who shared his love of shooting, that 'I hope we shall be the cause of much destruction of the feathered Tribe, and great Amusement to Ourselves'. Such was the ease with which the Hanson family fitted into the county set, a later biographer of Byron assumed that Farleigh House was owned by them. John Hanson saw himself as a country gentleman whose residence in the country as well as in the town was a measure of his success. In later years, when he commissioned a portrait of himself, the country scene depicted through the window behind him may well have been from Farleigh. If the man standing in the book-lined office was the John Hanson of Chancery Lane, the place shown through the window was where he believed he was destined.[2]

Hanson was proud, but he wanted more. When Portsmouth was left a widower in November 1813, and then arrived in London on 28 February, he could see a way in which through the marriage of his daughter he could achieve much more than just a resemblance to an aristocratic family. As a solicitor, he knew what legal documents were needed for a marriage, but he left everything to the weekend before the marriage on the Monday morning. Everything was done in haste, and, in hindsight, with a suspicious irregularity. First there was the marriage settlement. Oliver Turner, a law stationer on Chancery Lane, never before employed by Hanson, started receiving parts of the settlement to copy on Saturday. In the forty years of his working life, Turner had never seen a deed so full of blanks. He delivered it back to Hanson on Sunday. The original was not produced at Portsmouth's trials (the Hansons refused to surrender it), but it was said to have given Mary Ann one thousand pounds a year for the rest of her life, even if she outlived Portsmouth; John Hanson and Lord Byron the same annual sum; and, within eighteen months of the marriage, ten thousand pounds plus an annual payment of one thousand pounds until the total reached thirty thousand pounds to Byron and Charles Hanson.

On Sunday, Charles Hanson was sent by his father to a clerk of a lawyer in Doctors' Commons, the church court that administered marriages. He failed to get a marriage licence there and then, but persuaded the clerk to come to Bloomsbury Square with the necessary documentation the following morning. So, when Byron arrived at the Hansons' home around nine o'clock on Monday, 7 March, there was work to be done. If Byron knew of how he would benefit from the marriage settlement, his role in the wedding no longer looks so altruistic. But, although Byron witnessed the signing of both the settlement and the licence, there was foul play afoot. Both John and Charles Hanson planned to falsify the documents. The group assembled in the drawing room to witness the necessary signatures and oaths was certainly an odd one, deliberately so. It included John Dell, a watchmaker, who only vaguely knew Charles Hanson as a customer. Dell made the audience at the Commission laugh with his remark that 'there was nothing in the affair which required the aid of an eminent watch-maker; there was no stop-watch. Mr Hanson did not seem to require winding up.'[3]

Jokes aside, John Hanson had every reason to feel wound up and tense that morning. Although he had got everything in place for the wedding, the behaviour of his daughter and her husband-to-be was difficult to predict. At twenty-three years old, nobody thought Mary Ann was attractive. 'She was not pretty,' Byron wrote, perhaps offended that others thought he had an affair with her. The best that a guest at the dinner held by Hanson the evening after the wedding could say was that Mary Ann was a 'well-informed person; not, as I think, of a good figure; very genteel in her manners, and of uniform decorum'. He may as well have said nice, but ordinary.

Mary Ann was head-strong; her future life with Portsmouth would prove that. She might have enjoyed her stays at Farleigh House, but that did not mean she wanted to become a countess by marrying the earl of Portsmouth. Indeed, her marriage to Portsmouth took so many by surprise that questions were raised about how willing she was to become his wife. The first that Elizabeth James, an old friend of Mrs Hanson, knew of the wedding was when she received some wedding cake and a card announcing their marriage. Meeting Portsmouth at a concert given by Mr Hanson in Bloomsbury Square soon afterwards, 'she did not find him so weak a man as from previous reports she had been led to believe'. Still, she felt compelled to address the rumours that Mary Ann had been forced into the marriage. She found a moment in a quiet corner to ask her if it was true, but Mary Ann denied anything of the sort. Similarly, although the Hanson's chambermaid Elizabeth Wiseman knew nothing of Mary Ann's wedding until it was over, she had not heard that Mary Ann 'was with great difficulty prevailed upon by her father', or that she did not give her consent 'until very late in the night previous to the said marriage taking place'.

If Mary Ann was up late on Sunday, 6 March, then by the next morning she wanted nothing to do with the wedding arrangements. She was not present in the drawing room when the documents sealing her future were being signed, and she later claimed ignorance of their contents. To Portsmouth, she seemed a reluctant bride. 'Old Hanson had not got her in the humour to have me,' Portsmouth told his coachman the day later. In the future most people focused upon whether her husband had been tricked into the marriage, with far less attention given to Mary Ann's feelings. It took Byron, in private correspondence to Hobhouse, to remark about the wedding, 'It struck me as so little an entrapment for Ld. P. that I used to wonder whether the Girl would have him – and not whether he would take the Girl.' For what young girl would want to marry a man more than twice her age, and who was notorious for being 'weak-minded'? Were the riches that Portsmouth offered enough?

Hanson knew that Portsmouth would also need careful handling if he was to achieve his goal. At first he tried the charm offensive, inviting Portsmouth to Bloomsbury Square numerous times in the week before the wedding. Portsmouth was there so often that gossip below stairs in the Hanson household was that he was intending to marry one of the Hanson girls, although nobody seriously thought it was going to happen.

If the Hanson servants did not know a marriage was afoot, neither did Portsmouth. Telling Portsmouth beforehand ran the risk that he would talk, and news of Hanson's plans would reach the other trustees. But not telling Portsmouth meant that he did not look or behave like a husband-to-be. After the marriage, Portsmouth told all the people he knew best, which in his case were his servants and workers, that, even on the morning of Monday, 7 March, he did not know that he was going to get married that day. Joseph Head dressed him. Portsmouth did not have a clean shirt, and wore a black coat and waistcoat, breeches, and hessian boots. His hat still had the mourning band on it to mark the death of his wife, Grace. He had not shaved. As he left, he told his servants that he was invited to breakfast at the Hanson's house in Bloomsbury Square.

Witnesses thought Portsmouth was perfectly calm during the signing of the marriage documents. He read them through, paid attention as oaths were administered, and gave his signature without any problem. But whether Portsmouth understood what was happening was another matter. In some ways, he seemed unaware of the importance of the occasion, repeatedly asking the Doctors' Commons' clerk if he had heard news of his friend Mr Farquahar.

It may only have been after ten o'clock, when Charles Hanson was sent to the church to tell the clerk to prepare for a wedding, that John launched his offensive. As Portsmouth later told a gardener in the stables at Hurstbourne, Hanson said that he must marry his daughter, 'otherwise I never should have a wife, and my brother would take me into Devonshire and shut me up'. Newton Fellowes was planning to confine him in a private madhouse owned by Mr Clay, Hanson warned.

Hanson knew exactly how to scare Portsmouth. He could have been aware that Urania had threatened to lock her son up, and over the years she may have even discussed the possibility with Hanson. Hanson was certainly privy to the family secrets surrounding the confinement of both Portsmouth's aunt Dorothea, who was still confined in Fisher House, and his cousins, Loudoun and Catherine Gordon. As Newton Fellowes was a fellow trustee, and because he thought his brother held no affection for him, Portsmouth was all too willing to believe that Hanson had gained some advance knowledge of his brother's plans for him. He was left terrified. Marriage beckoned as an attractive escape route.

Hanson had played his trump card, and it worked. Portsmouth agreed to marry one of his daughters, but asked if he could marry Laura, the 'pretty one'. Hanson would not accept, and said that 'the eldest was the one he had looked out for me'. The bully Hanson pushed Portsmouth out of the house, and along the passage to meet Byron for their walk to the church.[4]

In the future legal trials of Portsmouth, people had to decide whether his marriage to Mary Ann was valid. To be so, there had to be evidence that both bride and groom gave their consent freely. It also had to be demonstrated that Portsmouth understood what he was saying as he made his promises at the altar, and that he had the mental ability to give his consent. Insanity took away the right to enter into any kind of contract. This is why the detail of events on the wedding day was so critical. It even meant that a key witness like the parish clerk, John Harrison, was examined twice by the church courts to ensure he had got his story right.

Harrison was adamant that Portsmouth was sane on 7 March 1814. Portsmouth was 'perfectly rational and sensible', and he saw no evidence of 'coercion or restraint'. 'I saw no appearance of entrapment or compulsion,' Byron insisted to Hobhouse. Marriage arranged over the course of a week, within four months of the death of a first wife, to a woman twenty-four years younger and of nowhere near the same social status might be surprising, but it was no indicator of insanity. Indeed, that Portsmouth did not tell his family of his plans was even construed as 'strong proof of soundness of mind'. In the past, Portsmouth felt his family 'had very much interfered in his affairs', and so he was 'desirous of keeping them in the dark'. He was in control now, and could make decisions for himself. John Hanson did not force Portsmouth or his daughter to get married. 'It would have been an act of insanity in Mr Hanson to have married his daughter to a lunatic,' it was argued a year later. No father was so cruel.

In March 1814, eyebrows might have been raised about the marriage of Lord Portsmouth to his solicitor's daughter, but for the moment only the domestic servants, gardeners, and coachmen whom Portsmouth had befriended had any indication that its arrangement hid sinister intentions. Portsmouth had been married before, and there was no reason to believe that this marriage would not work. The success of this marriage could not be judged on just its beginnings.

As for Mary Ann, was she simply a pawn for her father's ambitions? 'This unfortunate and devoted girl was dragged on by her own family to lend herself to this project of fraudulent and cruel iniquity,' the lawyer Stephen Lushington argued in Portsmouth's trials. Lushington's emotional speech caught the attention of reporters and was printed in the newspapers. Mary Ann was 'the victim of the wicked designs of her own family,' he said, 'whose parental and family duties to her, should have preserved and protected her from entering upon the fatal paths into which they compelled her to venture'. Let down by her family, she was pushed into a marriage she did not want, and with a man she did not desire. Lushington knew well enough how to win public support. Arranged marriages might be tolerated, but forced unions filled everyone with horror.

Yet, when stories were told of the marriage that followed 7 March,

Mary Ann's status as a victim looked less certain. In the space of a couple of days Byron already saw a change in Mary Ann. From being the young girl he once knew, crowded out by her seven brothers and sisters, and perhaps overshadowed by her prettier younger sister, she had been transformed into a countess. Marriage brought her a new confidence, an opportunity to assert herself, and be herself. Even a father like John Hanson could not determine the kind of wife she would be.[5]

'Heir apparent'

NEWTON FELLOWES KNEW nothing about his brother's marriage to Mary Ann Hanson until it was too late. When he heard the news, he was staying with his wife and three children at Hurstbourne. They often stopped at the family seat on route to Eggesford. 'He and all his family were going to quit Hurstbourne Park pack and package,' he said to a neighbour, for he had heard that Portsmouth and his new wife were 'coming down and should want the house'.

Newton had become 'heir apparent' to the Portsmouth title and fortune by the terms of the 1790 deed, a position that was confirmed nine years later when he became one of the four trustees entrusted to protect the estate. But his future inheritance was only assured if his older brother had no children. By marrying a much younger wife, and a woman who was from a 'known breeding family' (she had seven brothers and sisters, after all), for the first time Portsmouth was in a position that seriously threatened his brother's future. Leaving Hurstbourne, Newton felt that he was being forcefully evicted, from both title and home.[1]

Newton was less than five years younger than Portsmouth, but his life had followed a very different path from his older brother. From an early age, Urania had pinned all her hopes upon him. He crossed the hurdles of aristocratic education without a problem, progressing from Odiham to the tutorage of Dr Kyte in Hammersmith, and on to Eton. He had a spell as a student in the Middle Temple, and then finished at Trinity College, Cambridge, where Reverend Garnett was a Fellow.

Newton's future looked bright after he inherited a fortune and the mansion at Eggesford following his uncle's death in January 1792. The will was disputed, and even in the 1820s Newton was still receiving letters from his solicitor, Henry Karslake, about this inheritance. But the sums made the trouble worthwhile. 'I came into ten thousand a year and £200,000 ready money,' Newton boasted to a relative, 'and didn't I make it fly!'

Like Portsmouth, Newton loved spending time outside, and took an active interest in farming his estates. He also liked his coach and four, and had a favourite coach, 'of original design' that he insisted on driving himself from Eggesford to London. He certainly enjoyed the good life, suffering from gout for much of his adulthood as a consequence. But his greatest pleasure was hunting. Family legend had it that he was out hunting for such long days that, when he returned, ravenously hungry, he could not wait for the cooks at Eggesford to prepare a meal, but set to boiling eggs over the open fire in the dining room. He could eat six eggs in succession.

If eccentricity was a family trait, then so too was rebelliousness. Much to his mother's annoyance, Newton did not always conform. As an idealistic young man, he was not always willing to tow the family line in political affairs. On 29 May 1797, Urania wrote to Newton, thanking him for his condolence letter following his father's death on 16 May (Newton does not seem to have attended the funeral), and telling him that she had ordered a mourning ring for him to wear. Moving swiftly on from matters relating to her husband's death, Urania then wrote that she had been really upset by what she had read in the newspapers about Newton's conduct at the Hampshire County Meeting the previous month. The meeting had overwhelming support from gentlemen for a petition to be presented to the King calling him to dismiss his corrupt ministers, and for an end to 'the present improvident and unfortunate war' against France. Newton's uncle, Robert Fellowes, gave his support for a similar petition at a County Meeting that was held in Norfolk. But in Hampshire, Newton seconded an amendment to the petition and spoke to defend the government and its actions in the war with France. Urania had already written to Newton on this issue, but he had not replied. 'You have adopted a line of public conduct so diametrically opposite to that of your great Benefactor [presumably Urania's brother, Henry Arthur],' she angrily wrote, 'and every Principle entertain'd by your Ancestors, on both sides.' While Urania was willing to pay lip-service to her son's independence of thought and actions: 'you retain your opinions,' she wrote grudgingly, but such 'non-compliance with my sentiments' meant that he lost her support. Visiting Newton at Eggesford was out of the question: she had once spent three happy weeks there, but now, she told him, it would only increase her sorrow to be in his company.

Newton was equally wilful over matters of the heart. Two years earlier, in January 1795, and at the tender age of twenty-two, Newton had married the woman of his choosing, Frances Sherard. 'This marriage his mother strongly disapproved,' remembered a relative. No wonder. Frances was the youngest daughter of a Huntingdon clergyman, and decidedly middle class. Perhaps the couple had met when Newton visited his uncle at Ramsey Abbey. It was certainly not a marriage that had been arranged by Urania or her husband, who no doubt had a far grander and wealthier bride in mind for their second son. With the inheritance from his uncle, and legal arrangements in place for the day he would assume his older brother's title and position, Newton could have felt that he had his destiny set out for him by his parents. His marriage was the one big decision in life that he wanted to make for himself.[2]

Newton had a freedom of choice in marriage that he never thought his older brother should exercise. He had grown up with Portsmouth, spent time with him in the playground, and had begun taking responsibility for him from an early age. As he quickly out-performed his older brother academically, he also became aware of his parents' wider concerns about Portsmouth's development. For years, he was the recipient of the many letters written by his mother in which she agonized about how best to manage Portsmouth. He was the family representative who was sent to Yarmouth to seize his brother from the clutches of Seilaz. He knew Portsmouth was trouble and that he needed to be managed with care, and there seems little doubt that he approved of his marriage to Grace, and may even have played some role in arranging it. After her death, Newton was instrumental in organizing Coombe's return to keep a watch over Portsmouth. But whether he had plans to marry Portsmouth to another older woman, as Hanson told Byron, is unclear. There is no evidence to prove it, and he certainly would have expected Portsmouth to spend a longer period in mourning before another marriage was arranged. Everyone recognized that Grace was an exceptional woman, and finding her replacement was not something that could be done easily or in haste.

Newton knew his brother's weaknesses and limitations. When he heard about Portsmouth's marriage to Mary Ann Hanson, he never considered it a love match. This was a sham of a wedding, and his brother had been tricked or forced into it. The exchange of vows tied his brother to a lifetime's commitment, and potentially overturned the plans for the Portsmouth estates that had been set in place nearly a quarter of a century earlier.

The person who lay behind this marriage was John Hanson. This is what hurt Newton most. Portsmouth had not been abducted by an opportunist to be married against his will to a stranger. There were a scattering of marriages like this to the insane or weak-minded in the eighteenth and nineteenth centuries, provoking law cases and inspiration for sensational novels. Instead, this was personal. The marriage of Portsmouth was arranged by the family solicitor, trustee, and friend, and the bride was his own daughter. Hanson took advantage of his position, and his knowledge of the Portsmouth family's situation. Newton was left feeling slighted and utterly betrayed. News that Hanson, the new countess, and Portsmouth 'came in triumph and made a cavalcade' with colours to mark their arrival at Hurstbourne was a further bitter blow.

Newton inherited his mother's spirit of determination, and there was no way that he was going to abandon the Portsmouth name and fortune as easily as he had left Hurstbourne Park. He was in for the fight. Portsmouth had married Mary Ann, but Newton remained one of his trustees. What followed was a battle of legal wills, as Newton sought to prove that John Hanson still had to obtain the consent of the three other trustees before making any decisions about the

Portsmouth estate. Newton acted quickly, and by August had filed a Bill in Chancery charging Portsmouth with 'committing waste' by cutting down ornamental trees at Hurstbourne with no prior warning to the trustees. So began a legal process about trees that was to last at least another five years. An injunction was issued to stop further felling, but this was breached and challenged a number of times. Business at Chancery was notoriously slow, and this case dragged on as lawyers argued about the definition of an ornamental tree, and whether a gamekeeper needed to have a clear view of the estate from his cottage. Even the Chancellor (perhaps with lunch on his mind) started discussing the merits of different types of trees: 'old trees are like old cheese, often the best of their kind'.

While the case could descend into farce, the intent was deadly serious. This was about who was in charge: of Portsmouth as a person, and of the Portsmouth family estate. Of course, Newton's opponent was a lawyer, and Hanson knew the best people in his profession to come to his aid. When Newton later tried to obtain a Lunacy Commission, it was tricky to maintain that he thought his brother a lunatic when earlier that same year he had thought him mentally capable of being sued at Chancery, and swearing his oath before giving answers to a Bill. Newton raised the issue of the 1799 deed, but Hanson responded by arguing that this document, signed the day before Portsmouth's marriage to Grace, was simply a marriage settlement. As a result, the deed and its terms had ceased upon her death.

In September 1814, the feud between Portsmouth, Hanson, and Newton moved from the dusty offices of Chancery to the very gates of Hurstbourne Park. In a provocative step, Newton stationed himself in nearby Whitchurch, and on a daily basis entered the Hurstbourne estate to kill game, 'sending it away every night in large baskets'. This 'was meant as an insult to Lord Portsmouth,' Hanson argued to Chancery, and was 'a mode of exercising Mr Fellowes' authority as a Trustee'. Portsmouth, no doubt directed by Hanson, retaliated by printing trespass notices that the farmers at Hurstbourne were to issue on sight of Newton. Newton had no right to do sport at Hurstbourne; he had become a trespasser on the lands that belonged to his ancestral home.

Hearing that the leases of many of the tenants at Hurstbourne had come to an end, and that Hanson intended to raise the rents, Newton began his own paper campaign. He distributed handbills stating that Hanson was only one of four trustees, and that he had no power to let the farms or raise the rents at Hurstbourne without the agreement of the other trustees. Newton visited many of the tenants in person, telling them not to quit, and to continue to pay their rents at the old rate. A number followed his instruction.

For the Hurstbourne tenants, utter confusion about who had control followed when Portsmouth issued another set of handbills later in the month. These read as follows:

> Notice: Mr Fellowes having taken upon himself to assume a power over my property and circulated hand bills pretending to be one of my Trustees, I give this Public Notice that Mr Fellowes is no longer one of my Trustees and has no right to interfere in any manner whatever in my property or concerns, the Trust in which he was originally named a Trustee and that only nominally having ceased with my former marriage.

The words meant nothing in law: Chancery never revoked the 1799 deed, and the trustees remained in place despite Hanson's best efforts and the many years of legal argument that were to follow.

But the exchanges in September 1814 showed Newton what Hanson was about. Newton had been summarily dismissed as a trustee, and treated as a trespasser on his family's lands. Hanson had no intention of allowing him any control over the Portsmouth estates, not even to decide whether a tree should stand or fall. As the fight between the two men became a confrontation on the very land that was at stake, each had shown their hand and the battle lines had been firmly drawn.[3]

On 22 November, Newton issued a petition to the Chancellor to call a Commission of Lunacy for his brother. If the Chancellor agreed, and the Commission declared Portsmouth a lunatic, all his property would be handed over to a committee. Of greater importance to Newton, given that the 1790 and 1799 deeds protecting the Portsmouth estate were still in place, was that a verdict of lunacy would ensure that the validity of his brother's marriage to Mary Ann became questionable. If Portsmouth was insane on 7 March, then his marriage vows and his signature on the marriage contract and register meant nothing.

Portsmouth's ability to manage his property had already been seriously curtailed, but a Lunacy Commission could take away the most fundamental right to enter into personal relationships. Retrospectively and in the future, if declared a lunatic, Portsmouth would lose the liberty to form any kind of legitimate relationship with a woman. He could not love, or be loved, as a husband or a father. His mind would separate him from the rest of society, and condemn him to isolation.

The legal process that could lead to this damning verdict of lunacy was designed to be rigorous, thorough, and fair. No Chancellor was expected to make the decision alone. Instead, he would hear arguments from both sides, for the petition (Newton), and against it (Portsmouth and Hanson). The Chancellor, Lord Eldon, did his job well, hearing statements from over 130 witnesses, and arguments from the lawyers for both parties.

It is the statements lawyers made in 1814–15 that survive today. They show how quickly the case became a bitter family feud. Newton was accused of wanting to make his brother a 'mere nonentity', and it was said that he was only petitioning for a Commission because he wanted to protect his own interests. Concern for the Portsmouth estate was secondary to Newton's selfish desire to 'set aside' his brother's marriage to Mary Ann, and to 'bastardize' any children that might follow. For years, Newton had been content to let John Hanson take the lion's share of managing the Portsmouth estates, and he had only started to take note and exercise his authority as a trustee when he felt threatened by his brother's marriage. Portsmouth had not told his brother of his forthcoming marriage to Mary Ann because he was sick of his interference in his life. Now jealousy and greed were prompting his brother to pursue the cruellest of legal actions.

Counsel for Newton presented a very different picture of their client, of course. Newton was a reluctant petitioner, who was only pursuing this legal remedy because he had been provoked by the actions of John Hanson. For a long time, Portsmouth had been a proper subject for a Commission, but Newton had held back, 'from motives of delicacy'. All families desired 'to avoid such a proceeding if possible, not only with respect to the individual but with respect to the feelings of those who are connected in family relation'. Seeking a Lunacy Commission was always going to be a last resort. It would have been insensitive to the feelings of Grace and her family to have sought such a Commission in her lifetime, and Newton's own family circumstances 'made it inconvenient if not highly revolting to their feelings to apply' before now. What family wanted to expose themselves to the scrutiny of others, especially when lunacy was the issue, without good cause? Hanson, with the marriage of his daughter to Portsmouth, was a veritable traitor who had committed 'fraud' on a grand scale, and forced Newton to act. Hanson had acted immorally, and Newton had to right that wrong. Only a Commission could protect Portsmouth from the designs of such a man.

Knowing a bit more about Newton at this time helps to put his decision into perspective. He and his wife Frances had their share of personal tragedy. They had lost two of their children within their first year of life, and as grieving, 'afflicted parents' they erected a monument to the first, Newton John Alexander, in St Peter's Church, Over Wallop. They chose the words 'Sacred to departed innocence' as its heading, continuing that it had 'pleased the Almighty to translate' Newton 'from a sinful world to an Heavenly one at the early, but immaculate age of five months'.

The death of two babies in 1801 and 1803 was undeniably painful, but accepting God's will was even harder when it deprived them of the life of their oldest daughter. Fanny Jane Urania was seventeen years old when she died on 23 August 1814. Newton was in the midst of his legal struggle with Hanson, and, in what might have been seen as an ill omen, Fanny was said to have hit her head when she fell jumping from her father's coach on to the front steps of Hurstbourne house. She appeared fine immediately after her fall, but shortly after the family's return to Eggesford became seriously ill, and died within four days of 'water on the brain'. The devastation felt by her immediate family was visible. Newton's only surviving daughter, Henrietta Caroline, just turned sixteen years old, had rested her head in the hands of her dying sister, 'stunned by the suddenness of the shock'. It was said that the hair pressed by Fanny's fingers 'was perfectly white' ever after. Frances, Newton's wife, who had always suffered from poor health, became seriously unwell. Henrietta remembered her mother being paralysed and bed-ridden for a number of years thereafter.

Newton had his own cross to bear in 1814. With the death of his daughter and the illness of his wife, he could scarce afford the time for his brother's affairs. But Newton had been instilled with a strong sense of family duty. From his school days, he had been taught the importance of his family's name and property. This had shaped his upbringing, his mother admitting that she had toughened him by letting him cope with the 'bustle' of the world while he was still young. When Portsmouth married Mary Ann, he had acted in a way that put him beyond brotherly sympathy from Newton. For Portsmouth had put himself before family interest; his marriage, unlike Newton's to Frances, could alter the course of the family line. Now Newton had to put his own family sadness to one side, and act decisively to save and then secure the Portsmouth legacy. He owed that much to the memory of his father and mother. As a lawyer later put it, as the 'heir apparent to this Noble family', Newton could 'not lose sight of his duty' to protect 'those honours and great estates'. 'Whenever that inheritance is in danger of annihilation', as it surely was by Portsmouth's marriage to Mary Ann, 'it is his duty to stand forward and protect it not only for himself but for his noble brother.'

Newton may have believed that petitioning for a Lunacy Commission was the only course of action available to him, but his decision was presented by John Hanson as deeply hurtful to Portsmouth. Hanson kept a letter that he claimed was written by Portsmouth to him in January 1815 in which Portsmouth referred to Newton's 'unbrotherly manner' and his 'cruel application'. Robert Bird, a Winchester solicitor employed by Hanson to oppose the Commission, remembered how Portsmouth 'seemed to feel the indignity' of the case. 'He bore it very patiently and in a manner dignified,' Bird recalled, and 'he was by no means insensible to its effects'. Portsmouth was not such a fool or a madman to be unaware of what was happening, or the meaning of his brother's actions. He did have feelings and sensitivity, even if his naturally shy manner meant that 'he subdued his feelings,' Bird thought.

Actions can speak louder than words, and Bird witnessed a scene of tenderness between Portsmouth and Mary Ann that he thought showed where Portsmouth's true feelings lay. At dinner a few days after Newton had first petitioned the Chancellor, Mary Ann was 'much depressed'. Portsmouth 'in a very kind manner bid her raise her spirits, and invited her to take a glass of Madeira with him'. When Mary Ann struggled to carve the turkey, Portsmouth said she should be relieved of this task, and, 'referring to Lady Portsmouth's depression', asked Bird to take over. Feeling the strain of what lay before them, it was Portsmouth who was in control of his emotions and could help his wife to overcome hers.[4]

No doubt Portsmouth felt less assured a few months later when he had to face the Chancellor in his chambers on 24 January 1815. Ill with a cold, a hot water stove was brought to warm Portsmouth's feet. What Eldon asked Portsmouth was not recorded, and at the 'earnest request of the parties concerned' the press were asked not even to report that the examination had taken place. Not all abided by this call for secrecy, but the press had to be content with reporting Portsmouth's cold symptoms, rather than the detail of his examination. But that was enough. Word was out: the sanity of Lord Portsmouth was being questioned.

In the autumn and winter of 1814–15, if Portsmouth felt betrayed, it was by his brother, not John Hanson. He had 'harassed' him on his estates and now humiliated him by requiring him to be examined in front of the Lord Chancellor. All his life Portsmouth had been taught the importance of keeping his mental weaknesses in check and hidden from public view. Now Newton had exposed him for all to see.

As the legal arguments continued, the decision that Eldon was likely to take was far from predictable. Both sides made convincing arguments for and against a Commission, and Portsmouth's personal appearance seemed to have done nothing to bring a speedy resolution to the issue. For everyone involved, the wait seemed interminable. Finally, on 22 April, Eldon reached his decision. He would not call a Commission. The arguments that Portsmouth was insane were not convincing. A Commission was not warranted. 'This is the most painful business that I have ever been concerned in in the course of my judicial life,' Eldon commented. Eldon, who had been called to the bar nearly forty years earlier, and whose support for and close relationship with George III during his periods of insanity had earned him the nickname 'keeper of the King's conscience', knew what he was talking about.

The relief of Portsmouth and the Hansons was tremendous. John Hanson threw a celebration dinner party in London for Portsmouth and his daughter, attended by Lord Grantley (Grace's brother), Lord Bolton, and a number of other distinguished guests. A toast was made to Portsmouth to mark the Chancellor's decision. In Hampshire, John Hanson's brother-in-law, who owed his position as rector of Farleigh to Hanson's connections with Portsmouth, set about organizing a triumphant return of Portsmouth and Mary Ann to Hurstbourne. All of the estate's tenants and workers gathered to meet Lord and Lady Portsmouth on their journey back from London. They assembled in the tiny village of Mapple Durnell, just outside Basingstoke, and accompanied Portsmouth 'by way of congratulation' on the road back to Hurstbourne Park. Once the crowd arrived at Hurstbourne, a dinner was provided in a number of rooms for as many as could be accommodated. There had been almost an entire change of staff over the previous few months as Hanson had dismissed anybody who had dared to speak in favour of the Commission, so there was much confusion as loyal members of the household showed newer members where to find such basic items as knives and forks for the many guests. But it was a happy occasion, when Portsmouth moved from room to room, talking to everyone. Around twenty-five Hampshire gentlemen joined the party. After dinner, Portsmouth invited everyone into the dining room, where guests squeezed for space and strained to get a view of their host. Portsmouth gave a speech 'saying how happy they had made him, and that he was only sorry that the short notice he had, prevented showing them greater hospitality'. 'He did not say much, but what he did say was to the purpose,' recalled John Twynam, Portsmouth's gentry neighbour. Locksmith and mender of bells Robert Long, who had been on the welcoming procession from Mapple

Durnell, remembered events far more warmly: 'Everyone present was quite delighted at what Lord Portsmouth said on the occasion.' With free food and booze, and a Lord and master so obviously pleased to be back home, what reason was there to feel otherwise?[5]

With two triumphant arrivals to Hurstbourne in less than a year, the Hanson family had symbolically laid claim to the Portsmouth estate. Now that the Chancellor had rejected Newton's call for a Commission, Mary Ann was also confirmed in her title and place as Lady Portsmouth. Newton never recorded his response to the Chancellor's decision. Shattered and exhausted he may well have been. He had revealed doubts about his brother's mental health, fuelled society's gossips, and lost forever the affection of his brother, yet to no good end. He never thought he would dare to risk an attempt to get a Commission again.

Three in a bed

IN AUGUST 1817, some two years after the Chancellor had ruled in her favour, Mary Ann gave her husband's valet permission to take a day's leave from work. The servant in question, James Capy, was used to taking orders from Lady rather than Lord Portsmouth. He was one of the many servants who had been hired by John Hanson in the spring of 1815, replacing those dismissed for giving evidence supporting a Lunacy Commission. Three days into his new position, Capy was ready to give up. Portsmouth had pinched him and pulled his ears, and tried to flog him. Capy told Lady Portsmouth and her father that he would not stay another day working under these conditions, but both persuaded him to continue, 'saying they would make it worth my while'.

Capy remained, and spent enough time with his master to conclude that Portsmouth was 'half an Idiot and half a Lunatic'. Portsmouth soon revealed his fascination with bleeding and lancets, and asked Capy to bleed him. Capy obliged, and witnessed the pleasure Portsmouth gained. Sent to fetch Portsmouth from the slaughter-houses of the towns they visited, Capy entertained his master with stories of 'black jobs'. '[I] never saw anything like capacity or a sound mind in him,' Capy later testified, 'never for one minute – everything marked entire weakness from first to last and unsoundness too.'

In London, Capy lived with the Portsmouths when they stayed in rented houses in upmarket Wimpole Street, Harley Street, and Portland Place, since Lord Portsmouth had lost access to his previous

London home in Lincoln's Inn Fields after Grace's death. But the recently married couple also set up a new home, Fairlawn Grove, at Acton Green. The house was 'approached by a lodge and a carriage sweep to a portico entrance and a flight of stone steps to the hall'. There were twelve bedrooms, a conservatory, and a billiard room. The house was surrounded by twelve acres of land, of which eight were pleasure grounds, laid out 'with every regard to good taste, and at considerable expense'. There was a double coach house and stables that could accommodate eight horses, as well as a cow-house, piggery, and fruit-house. Fairlawn's location was its prime attraction. It was close to Chiswick High Road, and the main westerly route out of London, and thus ideal as a stopping point between central London and Hurstbourne. An area that had been known only for its market gardening became in the early nineteenth century the building plot for a number of substantial homes for the wealthy elite. Fairlawn combined 'all the advantages of a town and country residence', a later sales pitch said, and the Portsmouths could count the Rothschilds at nearby Gunnersbury Park among their neighbours.

Like his master, Capy was a newly married man when he started working in the Portsmouth household. As well as generous wages to compensate him for the difficulties he faced at work, Mary Ann regularly allowed Capy leave to return home to his wife in London. But Capy soon became suspicious that there was an ulterior motive for his dismissal. As Portsmouth's valet, like his predecessor Seilaz, Capy was the servant who had the closest and most regular contact with Portsmouth. He helped him wash, get dressed, stood by him as he ate, accompanied him wherever he went, and at the end of the day helped him to bed. Capy was always by Portsmouth's side, and knew all his routines and his many foibles. Nothing escaped his notice.

But every time Capy was sent home, the household routine at Fairlawn was broken, because his dismissal signalled the arrival of another man, William Rowland Alder. Alder was a Northumberland-born gentleman from Horncliffe, on the border with Scotland, about fifty miles south of Edinburgh. He was roughly the same age as Portsmouth, was said to have been a school friend of Mary Ann's father, and had trained as a barrister. Alder had been a frequent visitor to the Portsmouth household ever since Capy had been hired, often staying overnight. It was obvious that, to Mary Ann, Alder was more than a family friend. But just what were they up to when he was out of the way? Capy was 'determined to know'.

So when Mary Ann dismissed him one afternoon in late August 1817, Capy 'made as though he went home', and left the house, 'but took with him a key which would enable him to let himself in quietly'. He stayed at a neighbour's house until nine or ten o'clock at night, and then crept back into the house. Capy's bedroom was on the floor above Portsmouth's dressing room. The dressing room was positioned in the middle of the house, with doors leading to Portsmouth and Mary Ann's bedroom on one side, and on the other, doors to the guest bedroom occupied by Alder. Capy 'lay still' in his bed, rigid with excitement, listening for every sound. At around midnight, he heard Lord and Lady Portsmouth, and Alder each retire to their rooms for the night. All fell silent. Then, about an hour later, there was the 'distinct' sound of Alder's door into the dressing room opening, and footsteps of someone passing through into the Portsmouth bedroom.

Capy waited. It was the middle of the night and the house was shrouded in darkness. He wanted to be certain about what he might see. With considerable willpower, he 'lay still till it was light'. At around four in the morning, 'as soon as light', Capy slipped out of his bed and down the stairs, not putting on his shoes, for fear of alerting someone that he was coming. He went into the dressing room, and saw that the door of Alder's room was open. He then:

> opened one of the folding doors of Lord and Lady Portsmouth's room as quietly as he could and went in. He had at once a view of the bed: the curtains of it were partly drawn; but on the side where [Capy] entered they were undrawn and he had full view of the bed within.

Capy saw 'all three lying in bed together'. Alder was lying closest to Capy, under the covers, and undressed. Mary Ann was in the middle 'lying with her right hand in Mr Alder's bosom'. Portsmouth was on the far side, and lay with his back to his wife and to Capy. Mary Ann had her eyes closed, and was probably asleep. But Alder, lying on his back, and facing towards the dressing-room door, was awake. Capy said nothing, but stood still, surveying the scene. For 'scarcely a moment' the two men looked straight at each other. Time stopped. In that electrifying moment words were not needed. The look said it all: 'I know that you know'. Capy, 'satisfied that Mr Alder saw him', bowed, and went out of the room.[1]

Capy's testimony at Portsmouth's Lunacy Commission in 1823 was dynamite. *The Times* printed it on their front page. For a husband to be made a cuckold by his adulterous wife was bad enough, but for him to allow that adultery to be committed in his bed while he lay there was intolerable. Such was the 'brutalized state of his mind' that Portsmouth submitted 'to what no sane man could have endured', it was surmised. Portsmouth knew that adultery had been committed, it was argued by those who sought to prove him insane, but he was 'incapable of feeling the indignity or of attempting to resent or prevent it'. He was motionless beside his wife and her lover not knowing how else to act. A terrible insult was happening right next to him, but he just lay there. His mind had frozen him to the spot.

Unsurprisingly, Mary Ann and her family did everything they could to discredit Capy's statement. Soon after Capy had witnessed Alder in bed with Mary Ann and Portsmouth, he was permanently dismissed from the household. The Hansons claimed that Capy was ordered to leave after 'he had the audacity to attempt the honour of Lady Portsmouth'. Yet, when Capy sought a character reference from Mary Ann a year or so later, she could hardly refuse. When his good name was questioned in court, Capy even claimed that he had been intending to leave, and that he did so when a friend had married one of Mary Ann's maidservants and needed the position.

Capy went into business soon after he left the Portsmouth household, and, with his wife who was a milliner, set up as a haberdasher and draper in London. The Hansons alleged that Portsmouth's brother, Newton Fellowes, had offered Capy three hundred pounds for testifying at the Lunacy Commission, with Capy boasting to friends that as a consequence he would be 'provided for for life'. Capy was represented by the Hansons as a dishonest individual who had stolen goods from Fairlawn when he worked there, and a man whose word could not be trusted. A business partner, who told later legal proceedings of a fallout with Capy that resulted in charges of assault, did not hesitate to brand him as a 'bad character'. This character assassination had begun within weeks of Capy's statement to the Commission. Mary Ann's brother, Newton Hanson, wrote a letter to the editor of *The Times*, incensed at the 'foulest and most malignant aspersions on my Lady Portsmouth's conduct and reputation'. Capy had 'the effrontery to pretend that he could distinctly see everything that was going on in a bed, with merely a part of the curtains undrawn, and only the upper half of the window-shutter open, at four o'clock in the morning', he fumed.

Newton Hanson's letter had a desperate air about it: did it matter if Capy could not 'see everything that was going on' in a marital bed, if there were three people in it? Mary Ann was reported (surely not using her exact words) to have responded to reading Capy's account by exclaiming, 'I have criminal intercourse with the schoolfellow of my father! It is monstrous.' Yet the fact that her father had been content to marry her to a man of a similar age would not have been missed by many.

Certainly, by the time of the 1823 Commission, attempts by the lawyers employed by the Hansons to dismiss Capy's account were clutching at straws. They even tried to argue that, if Portsmouth was asleep in the bed, he might not have been aware that Alder had entered it. As the Chief Commissioner responded incredulously, 'What! Not of a third person being in the same bed with him and his wife?' and the case risked descending into farce, the importance of what Capy saw was only further highlighted.[2]

Capy's story was so sensational that it would never go away, but haunted the Hanson family for years to come. Much later, when they declared that Capy's statement was false because for the whole of 1817 the Portsmouths had been unable to stay at Fairlawn due to renovation work, their claims fell on deaf years.[3] It was too late. With Capy's testimony, Portsmouth's trial for sanity at the Commission had changed irrevocably. This was now a case about sex as well as madness. It was Capy, after all, who was first bold enough to assert before the Commission that Portsmouth's interest in bleeding was all about sexual desire. Now that he added an account of adultery, the spotlight was on Portsmouth's wife, Mary Ann, as well as on Portsmouth himself.

Even if Capy was a born liar, and the three-in-a-bed story a figment of his crude imagination, there were plenty of other witnesses who were prepared to come forward and give their versions of Mary Ann's relationship with Alder. Alder was a trustee of the marriage settlement made between Mary Ann and Portsmouth on 7 March 1814, but there is no evidence to prove that he was present in the Hanson household on the morning of their wedding, or at the church. There was plenty of opportunity in the legal proceedings about Portsmouth's marriage that followed to speculate that Mary Ann's affections were already tied elsewhere, but nobody ever suggested that her relationship with Alder had begun before her marriage. Instead, it seems likely that their sexual liaison began in the summer of 1815. Portsmouth and his wife had gone to Southend, the seaside resort on the Essex coast, for a holiday. Alder visited them there, and Mary Ann, as well as one of her sisters, joined him on a boat trip across the Thames estuary to Kent. Portsmouth was not invited, and the party were gone for three or four days.

Frequent overnight visits by Alder to Fairlawn followed. Neighbours saw Mary Ann and Alder taking walks on the common together, sometimes alone, and on other occasions with Portsmouth walking behind them. There was no attempt by Mary Ann and Alder to conceal the nature of their relationship: they walked openly arm in arm. People remarked, 'Here's Lady P. and her flash man', and did so within Portsmouth's hearing, but he did not react. In turn, Mary Ann went to London three or four times a week, alone. A housekeeper remembered how Mary Ann left Fairlawn soon after breakfast, in general more dressed up 'than usual'. She took gifts of 'venison, game, poultry, and fruit' with her, and returned in the evening exhausted, and then went straight to bed. The visits to town stopped as soon as Alder was at Fairlawn.

Witnesses saw a transformation in Alder's appearance. In his late forties, and 'not a comely looking man', one servant at Hurstbourne Park mistook Alder for a tradesman when he first visited in the autumn of 1817 because he was dressed so 'shabby'. But over the course of time, Alder smartened up. He had a 'handsome brown coat, military trousers, and spurs'. As their relationship developed, Alder and Mary Ann became ever more confident about displaying their affection for each other in public. To the servants who saw them, they acted more like husband and wife than Lord and Lady Portsmouth. An upholsterer thought Alder was Lord Portsmouth when he first came to work in the household. At mealtimes, Alder sat next to Mary Ann, with Portsmouth removed to the bottom of the table. According to Capy, Alder and Mary Ann played the equivalent of footsie under the table: 'they would set knee to knee, and foot to foot', and 'he would pick a bit off her plate, and she would pick a bit off his'. All of this was in the presence of Portsmouth: Alder 'put his hand round her ladyship's waist', but 'his lordship never complained of this'.[4]

Accounts of Mary Ann's relationship with Alder demonstrated that their adultery was blatant, and carried on in the face of Portsmouth. Mary Ann was not the sweet, innocent girl who had been dragged into an arranged marriage by a cruel father. Instead, she was a woman who delighted in the pleasures of sex, and took little effort to hide her real feelings. If Portsmouth's first wife, Grace, had been an angel, then Mary Ann was surely a harlot.

Evidence of Mary Ann's relationship with Alder was crucial in determining that the call for a Lunacy Commission succeeded in late 1822, when the first had failed in 1815. But when the Commission met, it was interested not so much in how Mary Ann's adultery had destroyed her marriage, as in why Portsmouth seemed to be 'insensible to such pollutions'. People began to ask what Portsmouth knew and understood about sex, as well as what he could do. Did Portsmouth have either the physical or emotional capacity for sex? Was it shock or ignorance that left Portsmouth in an apparent state of stupor before a man who should have been his rival?

Portsmouth's naivety and gullibility could be breathtaking. He said that Alder had been introduced to him as a medical man. His wife, Portsmouth told a family friend, 'was subject to hysterics' (a generic term used to describe female complaints), and 'had a bad state of health'. When this friend told Portsmouth that Alder was no medic, Portsmouth insisted that he must have been 'for he was in the habit of attending her ladyship at night'. Portsmouth even defended Alder's night-time visits, telling Capy that, as Alder was a doctor, 'it was proper that he should attend Lady Portsmouth at night'. Portsmouth was also ready to believe Mary Ann and her brother Newton when they told him that 'Alder was so ruptured that he could not get a child'. 'His lordship was pleased at the idea of Alder not being able to do it,' commented a friend.

Portsmouth's routine was disrupted by Alder's visits. He complained that his sleep was disturbed by Mary Ann getting out of bed in the middle of the night, or that he was forced to sleep on the sofa because Mary Ann turned him out of their bed. He was sufficiently aware of his wife's intimacy with Alder to start referring to her as 'Mrs A'. But Portsmouth told the doctors who examined him that he could do nothing to stop Alder. Alder, he argued, was a stronger man, and he was right to be afraid of him.

Intimidated by Alder, Portsmouth seemed to have little idea of what Alder and his wife were doing when they were in bed together. Portsmouth appeared to know neither how babies were made nor how long a pregnancy was expected to last. In earlier historical times, Portsmouth may have been called 'an innocent', a kinder term than the 'idiot' label that was used by the nineteenth century. Sexual innocence was certainly a description that could be applied to Portsmouth. According to Capy, when he asked Portsmouth 'if he knew anything of the intercourse of the sexes, he said not'. Capy obliged by telling Portsmouth the facts of life, but Portsmouth did not believe a word, telling Capy that he was a 'foolish fellow' for thinking such things. When doctors examined Portsmouth for the Lunacy Commission, they were astonished that a man in his fifties, who had been married twice, could have so little knowledge about sex. Dr Latham told the Commission that he thought Portsmouth had 'no more idea of sexual intercourse, gestation, and pregnancy, than a blind man has of colours, or a deaf man of sound'.

The full extent of Portsmouth's sexual ignorance was revealed when the Commission asked him about Mary Ann's pregnancies. At his first examination, Portsmouth declared that he thought a woman was pregnant for nine years, only correcting his mistake at his second appearance before the jury. His confusion may have arisen from the fact that Mary Ann fell pregnant soon after beginning her relationship with Alder, but she suffered a series of miscarriages, of which Portsmouth was not always aware. When she became pregnant again, to Portsmouth, his wife seemed to be permanently expecting a baby. So Portsmouth told Dr Baillie that Mary Ann was pregnant for fifteen months at one time, and that the child should have been born in January, but Newton Hanson, Mary Ann's brother, had told him that 'it was put off for a little while, and so it did not come till March'. This baby was probably stillborn, or miscarried, for Mary Ann never gave birth in March to a child that survived. There were witnesses that stated that Mary Ann had a miscarriage in Bognor, Alder being the first person allowed in her room to see her. Another probably occurred around the time Portsmouth, Alder, and Mary Ann stayed at the Abercorn Arms in Stanmore, where Mary Ann 'appeared to be very low' and servants were told that they should not 'go near the Countess's room'. Portsmouth could show kindness to Mary Ann on these occasions, and concern for her health, but he remained convinced that she was suffering from nothing more serious than the perennial female symptoms of hysterics and nervousness. When he was later told of the truth behind these confinements, Portsmouth was content to repeat a popular myth about miscarriages, that they were 'in consequence of the child being ill-begotten'. How any child was 'begotten' he did not know.

Portsmouth did not make the connection between sex and pregnancy. He told some doctors that he never had sex with Mary Ann, but that he believed the babies she bore were his. 'I firmly believe,' stated Capy, 'that when Lord Portsmouth saw the vein rise, from the arm being tied, that was all the idea he had of sexual intercourse.' Portsmouth's sexual world was about lancets and blood. According to Coombe, Portsmouth 'had the mind of a child with the passions of a man'. He sought to satisfy those passions. When he told the eminent doctor Sir George Tuthill that he had been to Mrs Wood's brothel in London, he said that he had taken his lancets, and that he believed other gentlemen went there with their own lancets, 'and for no other purpose'. The idea that sex could be about having a loving or physical relationship with a woman did not enter his mind.[5]

Marriage gave Portsmouth neither sexual knowledge nor experience. Mary Ann took no interest in enlightening her husband. The early signs were not good. As well as noting that the clothes of the ladies still had their shop-tickets attached (indicating a rushed wedding), the chambermaid at the inn where Portsmouth and Mary Ann spent their first night of married life together thought their bed showed a suspicious absence of activity for a newly married couple.

Portsmouth's lack of initiative and interest may have been a relief for Mary Ann, but it was incomprehensible to others. The explanation must lie, it was assumed, in Portsmouth's own inadequacy. It was concluded that Portsmouth was impotent. His impotence meant that he allowed Alder to enter his bed, 'to perform those operations which it was supposed nature had inhibited to him', as a lawyer so delicately put it. 'Being so impotent,' Dr Latham told the Commission more directly, 'it is not unreasonable that he should feel no curiosity upon the subject of sexual intercourse.' If he couldn't do it, then why should he want to know?

We will never discover the truth behind the claims that Portsmouth was impotent. Portsmouth in turn admitted and then denied them. He did not even know what impotence meant, telling Dr Monro that he was impotent in one breath, and then saying that he had sex with Mary Ann in the next. Impotence was certainly a convenient label, which allowed people to align sexual with mental incompetence. It gave them an easy way of understanding a man and his sexual preferences that were otherwise so out of the ordinary. With his stories of blood-letting, Capy had raised the frightening spectre of Portsmouth as a man who was sexually capable but mentally unable to know how to behave. But to argue that Portsmouth was impotent was to return him to a childlike state of both physical and emotional immaturity.

Byron, a man whose own sexual reputation was never free from suspicion, took great delight in the suggestion that Portsmouth was impotent. Writing to Hobhouse from Genoa, following news of the Portsmouth Commission, Byron said he 'knew nothing of his ignorance of "fuff-fuff-fuff"'. As Portsmouth was 'of a robust[i]ous figure – though not a Solomon', Byron 'naturally imagined he was not less competent than other people'. But now it turned out that this big man could not perform. The only sexual arousal he experienced was from 'the tape and lancet', a fact that Byron said he would remember and 'try on some great emergency'. Portsmouth the fool and sexual weirdo had become a laughing stock.

But the story of his marriage to Mary Ann could also invite sympathy. She made no attempt to hide her relationship with Alder from her husband. Instead, she taunted Portsmouth about it, making him post letters to Alder that appointed times and places for their liaisons. While she fawned upon Alder, she neglected Portsmouth. Then, one day, Capy said Portsmouth ordered him to fetch the book entitled *Aristotle's Master-piece* from Mary Ann's bedroom. *Aristotle's Master-piece*, not by Aristotle at all, was the sex manual of the day. It had already gone through at least twenty editions. Mary Ann, Portsmouth said, had asked him to explain the contents of the page that she had turned down. On fetching the book, Capy saw the section that she had selected. It was on 'the insufficiency of man'. Mary Ann, who 'was in bed at the time', twice sent for Portsmouth to join her, asking him to come with the book. But Capy told Portsmouth, 'it was not a fit book for him to read', and that he was 'certain Lady Portsmouth did not want it'. No respectable wife would.[6]

That a wife might attempt to teach her husband what to do in bed was unthinkable in the early nineteenth century. It signalled how Mary Ann's adultery had led to a total breakdown of order in the Portsmouth household. Mary Ann should have been subservient to Portsmouth's wishes, not the other way round. Alder had taken Portsmouth's place at the meal table, and in his bed. Mary Ann enjoyed humiliating her husband. The horror for everyone who witnessed this, and for those who later heard about this marriage, was that Portsmouth did nothing.

Mary Ann knew she was in the wrong. She had lost her mother to typhus within a month of her marriage to Portsmouth. Her brother, Newton, was said to blame their mother's death on the shock of Mary Ann's marriage. Without her mother, the kindly figure beloved by Byron as well as her own children, Mary Ann had no moral compass. She was certain that her relationship with Alder would invite criticism from her father. Servants were ordered to hide Alder's hat and coat when John Hanson came to stay at Fairlawn. On an occasion when her father's visit was unexpected, Alder made away in a coach so he would not be seen. Her pregnancies were more difficult to keep secret. There may have been some truth to a story that Portsmouth told a doctor about one of his wife's miscarriages. Mary Ann had lost the baby, Portsmouth said, after Newton Hanson had run up against her, knocking the unborn child on the head. Mary Ann risked bringing shame on the whole family if she bore a bastard, and this may have provoked her brother to take the most extreme steps to end her pregnancy.[7]

But Mary Ann had no intention of ending her affair. She had obeyed her father by marrying Portsmouth, but that did not mean that she had to love her husband. She was not prepared to sacrifice her happiness, or to assume the role so often admired in women at this time of patient resignation. Mary Ann would be neither victim nor martyr. Impotent, perhaps, in body as well as mind, Portsmouth was treated by Mary Ann with scorn, not pity. As her feelings for Alder became ever more intense, her frustration with Portsmouth increased. Her cruelty to Portsmouth became more pointed, and took forms that even Portsmouth could not miss. This was a couple and a marriage that was heading for catastrophe.

'That cursed woman'

THERE WERE WARNING signs. Within hours of their marriage, the nature of Mary Ann's intentions towards her new husband were being made clear. No clean clothes were fetched for Portsmouth before the couple set off to Salt Hill for their first night of married life, and when Portsmouth returned to London the following day he looked 'more slovenly and was very dirty'. By the evening he was better dressed, and, to those attending the dinner held in Bloomsbury Square to celebrate the wedding, Portsmouth appeared to be proud of his young wife. Still, 'Mr Hanson seemed to exercise more interference and influence over Lord Portsmouth than one gentleman is entitled to use to another,' observed one guest. The dynamic of relationships in this family seemed all awry.

The servants saw everything, of course. James Palmer was in John Hanson's service when Mary Ann married Portsmouth, but then became Mary Ann's footman. It was a promotion for him, but his new position was not a happy one. 'The squabbles between them were not like other squabbles I have seen in other families,' Palmer later declared about Mary Ann and Portsmouth. Portsmouth was heard screaming in his room.

Quarrels began between the couple soon after their marriage. One took place at the dinner table in Bloomsbury Square, in front of Mr and Mrs Hanson. Portsmouth's father-in-law intervened, threatening to send for a person who would confine Portsmouth in a madhouse. 'Alarmed' and intimidated by Hanson, Portsmouth 'begged and prayed to make it up, and offered to shake hands with the Countess, which was refused'. Speaking 'in a commanding sort of manner', Hanson 'ordered' Portsmouth out of the room, and Portsmouth obeyed. There were no doubts among the servants about who was the master of this household.

Mary Ann had little tolerance for Portsmouth's eccentricities. The summer following their marriage, the couple took a trip to Worthing. Mary Ann and one of her sisters sat inside the coach, while Portsmouth sat next to the coachman. There was nothing that Portsmouth liked better than to drive, but the coachman had 'received strict orders from her ladyship not to give up the reins'. This put Portsmouth 'in a great passion', and as the journey continued he became more and more frustrated. He 'stamped with his feet on the foot-board' but this meant that the horses were thrown into a gallop, scaring the ladies within. Mary Ann called the coachman to stop, and, once they had come to a halt, she 'ordered' Portsmouth to come inside the carriage. As Portsmouth was climbing in, 'her ladyship pushed him, and he fell into the road in the dirt'. Getting to his feet, he started to walk away from the carriage, at which Mary Ann and her sister told the coachman to continue. Portsmouth was left dishevelled in the middle of a dirt road to find his own way. His new wife had abandoned him.[1]

As under butler to Lord Portsmouth when Grace was alive, Joseph Head was the faithful servant who had dressed his master on the morning of his marriage to Mary Ann, little knowing that Portsmouth was to be wed that day. Having remained in Portsmouth's service, in the autumn of 1814, he entered the dining room at Hurstbourne during one of the quarrels between Portsmouth and Mary Ann. Mary Ann ordered Portsmouth out of the room, but he was not ready to comply. 'The room was his' and 'she ought to go,' he angrily retorted. Nevertheless, she won out, for Portsmouth retreated to the dressing room. When Head told his master that dinner was ready, Portsmouth told Head that 'he had supper, breakfast and dinner by ill treatment', and that 'he wished he might drop down dead as his late wife did, as he was treated like a dog'. He burst into tears several times, and said Mary Ann had threatened to fetch Mr Coombe. He was utterly dejected and miserable. 'That cursed woman has been here again,' he complained, telling Head that 'he lost his best friend when he lost his late wife'. Only now did he realize how special Grace had been.

If there was a thaw in their relationship once Newton Fellowes had called for a Lunacy Commission in November 1814, it was a temporary one. The bitter arguments were simply put on hold until the Chancellor turned down the application in spring 1815. By then, all of Portsmouth's closest servants, including Head and Palmer, had been dismissed by Mr Hanson for 'telling the truth', as Palmer put it, to the Chancellor. When Palmer was recruited by Newton Fellowes, he was accused of being a spy by the Hansons.

Capy, one of the replacement servants recruited by Mr Hanson for his daughter, was present when Mary Ann and Portsmouth dined in Bloomsbury Square in June 1815 after they had spent the day at the royal court. Portsmouth was 'in very high spirits, and having more wine than he was accustomed to do, he became intoxicated'. After dinner, Mary Ann and her tipsy husband returned to their house in Wimpole Street. According to Mary Ann, as they began to get undressed for bed, Portsmouth turned upon her and seized her by the neck. Responding to her cries for help, Mary Ann's aunt, Bridget, rushed into the room. When Bridget tried to separate the pair, Portsmouth 'violently pushed' Bridget so that she fell to the floor. Depending upon which account was to be believed, Bridget was left with either a bleeding nose, or two black eyes.

Drink had lessened Portsmouth's inhibitions. He was no longer afraid of his wife, but was bold and violent. But Mary Ann responded in kind. She ordered Capy to whip Portsmouth, and, according to Capy, she 'beat' Portsmouth in bed. She had often threatened to whip her husband, but now her anger meant that there was no stopping her. She whipped Portsmouth 'when without his clothes with very great severity'. Capy did not deny whipping his master on this occasion, or others: 'Sometimes it was necessary to chastise him, to keep him in some degree of order,' he argued. Yet he did not beat him 'with the same degree of severity as her Ladyship'. Capy was left to deal with the after-effects of her violence. He applied ointment to Portsmouth's bruised bottom and thighs. Preserving the modesty of their readers, reports of Capy's testimony to the Commission left a blank when he described the exact location of Portsmouth's injuries: 'All about his __ were always black and blue,' he said.[2]

There was something disturbingly cruel, even sadistic, about the violence that Mary Ann directed towards her husband. She was rumoured to have kept a whip under her pillow to use against her husband, beating him in bed when he was naked and most vulnerable. She deliberately humiliated and degraded the man she had married, showing him no respect or regard. In her marriage, Mary Ann was rarely without the company of other members of her family living alongside her, either her brothers Newton or Charles, or one of her four younger sisters. But whereas there might have been family disapproval of her relationship with Alder, they simply joined in with her violence.

Taunting Portsmouth became a Hanson family pastime. In Southend, Charles was seen striking Portsmouth with a whip, leaving Portsmouth with a swollen face, and at Hurstbourne servants saw Newton hitting him with a stick. Laura, who was 'quite a little girl' when her older sister married Portsmouth, threw dirt and water at Portsmouth, provoking a full-scale and undignified quarrel when Portsmouth retaliated by throwing the same back. Laura and the younger Selina both attended boarding school near Fairlawn, and were frequent visitors. On several occasions, Laura spat in Portsmouth's face, and Mary Ann encouraged her sister and Newton to make faces at him. 'Even the little one Selina would point at his Lordship and make game of him: tantalizing and teasing him,' remembered a bailiff. 'They behaved to his Lordship as children do to poor idiots in the street,' he recalled.

The Hansons denied Portsmouth the freedoms he had enjoyed during his marriage with Grace. Estate workers saw him out and about less often. At Fairlawn, his team of horses was taken away from him, reportedly to make room for the horses owned by Alder. This 'hurt his spirits very much,' thought one servant, 'for that had been his principal amusement'. Kept to the house, he had to find a way to 'slip' out without causing attention if he was to make his way to the stables. Those who had known Portsmouth since he was a child noticed a change in him. He no longer attended as many funerals, and, when he did so, he stood quietly by the grave. 'Anyone could see that he did not feel himself at liberty as he had done,' remarked an elderly gatekeeper at Hurstbourne. 'He always appeared as if he thought that somebody was after him and watching him.' Living in a state of perpetual fear, Portsmouth was no longer himself.

As Alder got smarter, Portsmouth became scruffier. Before now, Portsmouth's mother and Grace had ordered his clothes and ensured that he always looked decent before company. But Mary Ann disregarded these needs. According to Capy, who as Portsmouth's valet knew his master's wardrobe well, Portsmouth was reduced to wearing and sleeping in the same shirt for a week as Mary Ann refused to buy new ones. His drawers became so worn that Capy resorted to sewing their tears, while Mary Ann's brothers wore Portsmouth's dress shirts and silk stockings. Although one member of the Hampshire county set thought Portsmouth was better dressed after his second marriage, the people who saw him on a daily basis at or around his home were agreed that his appearance had taken a turn for the worse. One employee at Fairlawn thought Portsmouth looked so dirty that he was 'more like a scavenger than a nobleman'.[3]

Diminished in spirit, and reduced in appearance, Portsmouth was in no state to refuse anything the Hansons asked of him. In August 1815, while staying at Southend, Portsmouth gave the solicitors Thomas France and George Palmer a list of instructions for his will. The will was a short one. He desired to be buried in the family vault at Farleigh, next to his father and mother. Then he gave everything he possessed to Mary Ann, with the exception of two legacies of one thousand pounds each to his sisters Henrietta Dorothea and Annabella, five hundred pounds to his cousin Barton, and 'to my old friend and relation' John Hanson two thousand pounds. Mary Ann was to be the sole executrix. When he came to read and sign the will a day later, Portsmouth added a codicil. He said that he had forgotten to leave a legacy 'to a gentleman who had been very kind to him': five hundred pounds was designated to Charles Hanson.

At the Lunacy Commission, Portsmouth's will making was initially given as evidence of his sanity. Both solicitors testified that they would never have allowed a lunatic to make a will; their reputations would have been in tatters if it could be proved otherwise. Over the years they had known Portsmouth, they had received many written instructions from him, and these were always 'perfectly rational'. They believed him to be of 'sound' but 'weak' mind. Palmer even raised a laugh from the Commission when he declared that he 'had seen men with weaker minds than Lord Portsmouth, and noblemen too'. His other clients would not have thanked him for that.

Yet, once the terms of the will were read out (no surviving written copy survives), suspicions were immediately raised. The presumed heir to the Portsmouth estates, Newton Fellowes, was written out of his inheritance. With a pen stroke, Portsmouth's brother was wiped from history. While he got nothing, and his sisters and cousin tokens, the Hansons, wife, father, and brother, got it all. The intentions of the other two legal deeds concerning the Portsmouth estate, of 1790 and 1799, were blatantly disregarded to favour the Hanson family. The other trustees had not been consulted. The only thing that would be returning to the Portsmouth family upon his death was his body.

The very coherence of the written list of instructions, Palmer later admitted, made their composition by Portsmouth unlikely. The handwriting looked a lot like Mary Ann's. Rather than evidence of sanity, this will showed how much Portsmouth needed legal protection. He could not manage his own affairs, and, as the will demonstrated, was vulnerable to the coercion and exploitation of others.[4]

The arrival of Alder had done nothing to lessen Mary Ann's cruelty to Portsmouth. In fact, Portsmouth's misery increased as Alder joined in. A gardener at Fairlawn who saw Mary Ann give Portsmouth a violent slap on the face in the garden in 1816 saw this followed by Alder whipping him. Alder then pushed Portsmouth down a flight of stone steps towards a gravel walk. Portsmouth cried 'murder', fell on the bottom step, where he was whipped by Alder again. After picking himself up, Portsmouth then ran about the grounds in great distress. The gardener was ordered to lock one of the gates to prevent Portsmouth escaping. For the next month, Portsmouth was seen by a surgeon for a knee injury caused by the fall.

Sometimes the cries of Portsmouth caught the attention of people beyond Fairlawn's gardens. On one Sunday in 1818, Alder struck

Portsmouth twice on the chest, and, when Portsmouth cried murder, Alder 'took him by the collar and shook him against the gates – he again cried murder'. These gates led on to the common, and many people who were taking an afternoon stroll there came to look 'over the wall'. At this, Mary Ann and Alder ran away and hid in the shrubbery. They had some shame.

Inside the house, they felt able to behave how they wished. The presence of household servants never inhibited them. But to many observers of their violence, whether witnessed inside or out, what was most astonishing was that Portsmouth never fought back. He was clearly strong enough, his physical stature often being remarked upon. He could even verbally argue his position; Mary Ann's physician told lawyers that he had often heard Portsmouth 'assert his right to a freedom of action, and to carry his point against the present Countess of Portsmouth even better than some husbands of unquestionable capacity might do'. But Portsmouth was so frightened by Alder and his wife, and was of such a cowardly disposition, that he could not stand up for himself. He was bullied and 'kept in awe and subjection by severity', as his knee surgeon put it. Fairlawn was a place where the world was turned upside down; where a wife and her lover ruled over the man who should have been in command. A carpenter who saw Portsmouth being beaten by Mary Ann and Alder 'thought it was scandalous Lord Portsmouth did not attempt to return the blows', or even 'appear', as far as he could see it, 'to resent it: but took them patiently'. Did he have no manly pride?

There was one time when Portsmouth reacted and sought outside help. Sir Richard Birnie had acquired a house and lands adjoining Fairlawn when he married, and had often seen his neighbour at church in Acton. During the services, he thought Portsmouth 'very quiet' and a man who only drew attention to himself during the hymns, when he sang 'in a strange way'. But late one Sunday afternoon in August 1819, Birnie had a surprise visit at home from Portsmouth. Portsmouth was 'much agitated', and asked Birnie to issue a warrant against his wife. Birnie was a magistrate at Bow Street, and had much experience of dealing with women who sought protection from their violent partners. But this home visit was highly unusual: didn't

Portsmouth know that it was shameful for a husband to seek protection from his wife? His request was an embarrassing admission of weakness. Birnie asked what had happened. Lady Portsmouth had flogged him with a whip, Portsmouth said, while her two sisters, Laura and Selina, had held him. Sure enough, there were whip marks on his face and neck.

This was shocking evidence of a breakdown of household order, but the last thing Birnie wanted to do was to turn a domestic incident into a public drama. 'From the general character of the family, I did not grant the warrant,' he later recalled. It would not do to issue a warrant to keep the peace against a countess. Instead, Birnie tried to calm things down: 'I endeavoured to make him forget it,' he explained. By talking about their gardens, Birnie found a way to achieve this, and the two men walked across from Birnie's property into Fairlawn's grounds.

There they were met by three ladies, one of whom approached and addressed Birnie. 'She was astonished,' remembered Birnie, that 'I should have the impudence to come into her grounds without her leave'. Birnie turned to ask Portsmouth: was this Lady Portsmouth? When he said yes, Birnie remarked 'that I was not in the habit of being treated in that manner'. Portsmouth had invited him in, after all. He left with a warning to Mary Ann: on this occasion he had 'studiously avoided interfering in the family disputes', but 'the next time Lord Portsmouth applied to me for a warrant, I should not be so delicate'. He seemed pretty confident, from what he had seen and heard, that there would be a next time. Mary Ann, however, remained defiant. She told Birnie that he should not have paid attention to anything that Portsmouth had said, for 'it is impossible that you can be ignorant of Lord Portsmouth's situation'. Madmen could not be believed, even if they had visible scars from violence all over their faces.

There was no next time. Mary Ann was sufficiently worried about Birnie's opinion that she had Capy lie to him by saying that Portsmouth was drunk when he made the accusations of her violence. Portsmouth never approached Birnie again. Birnie was probably relieved. Settling ugly family quarrels was something that he dealt with at work in

London. At Bow Street, there was a clear social distance between him and the majority of poor and desperate women who sought his help after domestic violence. He did not want the tranquillity of his weekend retreat disturbed by the arguments of his neighbours. This was not how people of his quality were meant to behave. Portsmouth and his wife were best left alone.[5]

Isolated, Portsmouth turned to his servants and estate workers, as he had always done. Some were sympathetic and kind, allowing him to fool around and indulging him with conversations about horses or the latest funeral. But many were new employees, who had been recruited by the Hanson family and were more likely to follow their example by showing Portsmouth little or no respect. Benjamin Goose, a coachman at Fairlawn, admitted when he was examined by the Commission jury, 'I never took the liberties with any other master that I did with Lord Portsmouth; I treated him as one of my fellow servants.' Servants took their orders from Mary Ann or Alder, and joined them in their petty cruelties. 'When it rained very heavy, and Lord Portsmouth wished to get into the house by a particular door,' recalled a carpenter, 'the servants would be ordered to lock it, and send him round to another, and so treat him till he was wet through.' In Portland Place, the outside door was also locked against Portsmouth, and, on at least two occasions, Mary Ann ordered that Portsmouth be locked inside the house while she went out. Capy was not the only servant who beat his master; Mary Ann's footman, Charles Want, was also seen striking him. By 1821, an observer thought the servants took no more notice of Portsmouth than the dog that lived in the household. 'His Lordship appeared… to be quite like an outcast,' he remarked. 'There was not the least appearance of respect or of his being treated as the head or master of the family,' it was said. Lord Portsmouth had been replaced and then ejected by Alder. He was a family misfit with no role to play, and no place in the social order.

Not everybody was prepared to continue working in these circumstances. Jones the gardener explained to the Commission that he 'felt very uncomfortable' by what he saw. He and his wife left the service of Lord and Lady Portsmouth voluntarily in March 1819, he explained, because they 'disliked the treatment of Lord Portsmouth'. They could not stand by, but nor was it appropriate for them to intervene.

In the years following the 1823 Commission, Mary Ann did everything she could to deny or downplay her violence towards Portsmouth. He was often drunk, she said; Alder was simply defending her after Portsmouth initiated violence by pinching or attacking her; or injuries were the result of accidents. But the weight of the evidence was against her. Her whole attitude towards Portsmouth was wrong. She treated him in a 'very sad way,' remembered Jones. 'She did not ever appear to be sociable with him', and hardly even spoke to him. She regarded Portsmouth 'with a sort of disdain: if his Lordship came near her she pushed him off in a contemptuous manner'. 'She behaved like an unkind nurse for a child,' concluded Jones.

Over the years, the disdain grew, and malicious cruelty towards Portsmouth became habitual. As a carpenter was working in the conservatory at Fairlawn, he overheard voices in the saloon. He 'peeped under one of the blinds' and saw Mary Ann flogging her husband, telling him 'he would wipe his shoes another time'. He could see that Portsmouth had been collecting dung, and that he was very dirty. Mary Ann whipped and talked to Portsmouth 'just as if he had been a little boy that had come into the room without wiping his shoes,' the carpenter thought. Portsmouth 'cried out' and 'begged like a child not to be punished, and held up his hands to keep off the blows'.[6]

In the early nineteenth century, Mary Ann epitomized an attitude and behaviour towards the mentally ill and disabled that many found distasteful, even unacceptable. For by this time public attitudes towards those who suffered, whether in mind or body, had softened. A new understanding was shown towards the poor and destitute, the criminal, and the insane. Mad people were still fascinating, but they were expected to inspire feelings of sympathy, not the pointed jeers and base pitilessness of old. Thus, Mary Ann was out of touch with her own time and represented an intolerance and insensitivity that many had come to associate with the past. This was a new century and a period for change and reform. Where was her humanity, understanding, and sensitivity to the less fortunate? She was also a shameful example to her own sex. In her lust and greed, she had forgotten all the feminine virtues that should have belonged to a wife. She was a ready figure for vilification.

By the time of the Commission in February 1823, it suited Newton Fellowes and his son Henry Arthur for Mary Ann to be represented in this way. They wanted the jury to find Portsmouth a lunatic, and they produced witness after witness to show that Mary Ann, Alder, and her family had treated Portsmouth as if he were insane from the day of his marriage. Mary Ann could only behave in the way she did because Portsmouth was mad; no sane husband would have tolerated her adultery and violence for so long.

Mary Ann's conduct also offered a convenient explanation for Portsmouth's alleged lunacy. Portsmouth's brother and family wanted to remove any idea that his condition was hereditary. Idiocy or lunacy from childhood was far more shameful than madness that had arisen because of the ill-treatment by others.

Evidence of Portsmouth's reaction to Mary Ann's behaviour was useful in suggesting that it was she who had made him mad. Repeated ill-treatment meant that even a man like Portsmouth, who ordinarily did not react or resist, eventually snapped. The surgeon who saw Portsmouth after his knee injury in 1816 contended that Portsmouth 'might at length be exasperated, and that then like an animal under similar circumstances he would be violent and dangerous'. Sometimes, argued Jones, the Hansons would deliberately act so that Portsmouth was 'worked up into a rage'. Then Portsmouth would 'rave and stamp and be very violent', at which the Hansons 'ran away as they would from any animal that they had teased till it was dangerous to be in its way'. Tormented and taunted, Portsmouth had become a raving madman.

The jury was left wondering just what impact marriage to Mary Ann had had upon Portsmouth. Could treating Portsmouth as mad, especially over a number of years, have made him crazy? How often did a person have to be told that they were mad, and be responded to by everyone around them as if they were mad, before indeed they became mad, and the person others thought they were? 'It has been said', quoted Serjeant Pell at the Commission, that 'oppression will make a wise man mad'. Most people who knew Portsmouth well thought he was weak-minded, even before he met Mary Ann. But did her violence and cruelty push him over the edge into lunacy? 'Imprisoned within those hated walls,' argued Pell, 'and corroded by the daily torture to which he was subject, no wonder if a mind, originally weak, should become violently deranged.'

Presenting Mary Ann as the cause of Portsmouth's lunacy was not straightforward, however. It left Newton and Henry Arthur Fellowes with two problems. First, there was the awkward question of why they had left Portsmouth in a position of suffering for so long. It was improbable that they had remained wholly ignorant of the conditions he endured from the Hanson family. After their first call for a Lunacy Commission was rejected in the spring of 1815, it was more than seven years before another Commission was sought. After this long wait, there were bound to be questions about what had then prompted their request. A disinterested concern for the wellbeing of their family member would sound pretty hollow.

Secondly, if Mary Ann was the trigger to Portsmouth's insanity, then she was the obvious solution. Remove Mary Ann and Portsmouth's sanity would be restored. 'Kind and proper' treatment would make Portsmouth sane again, argued lawyers opposing the Commission. Portsmouth did not need a Lunacy Commission, just a good divorce lawyer. There was plenty of evidence of Mary Ann's adultery, so why didn't Portsmouth's brother and nephew help him pursue this legal option? The answer, it was easy to deduce, was because a Lunacy Commission would serve more of their interests. If legally declared a lunatic, Portsmouth would be permanently prevented from posing a threat to the family name and fortune.[7]

Mary Ann's confidence had grown with time. She transgressed moral codes and nobody stopped her. She had a lover, and tormented her husband when she wished. At and around Fairlawn, she felt that she could behave with impunity. But she had married an aristocrat, and as a countess there was an expectation that she and her husband would have public as well as private lives. Grace managed to keep Portsmouth's behaviour in check through kindness. In society,

Portsmouth had conducted himself with such good grace and manners that many thought there was nothing out of the ordinary about him. But this façade required patience and hard work on the part of his wife. What would happen now that he was married to Mary Ann?

'So long as he was sane, he took no part in politics'

∼

LORD PORTSMOUTH INHERITED power as well as a fortune in property when he became the 3rd earl. As a member of the landowning elite, he was entitled to positions in local society, and as a peer a seat in the House of Lords. For most of his life, Portsmouth, like many of his fellow peers, took a minimal role and interest in political affairs. There was no expectation that he should. But because his trial for lunacy in 1823 coincided with a period of heightened political tension, the part he had taken attracted special attention.

In the first decades of the nineteenth century, the establishment was facing mounting criticism and the charge of 'Old Corruption'. Calls for a wholesale reform of politics and the franchise looked ever more attractive in the shadow of the French Revolution. Radicalism and popular unrest were of daily concern to those in authority. While Parliament continued to pass legislation that served to protect the landed interest, such as the much reviled Corn Law in 1815, thousands of agricultural workers were facing a bleak future of hunger and distress. The massacre of demonstrators at St Peter's Field, Manchester, on 16 August 1819, followed by the arrest, trial, and imprisonment of the radical 'Orator' Hunt in 1820, exposed a government that was willing to harness violence and intimidation to maintain its position. In this context, the revelation that a man of doubtful mental capacity could be entitled to vote in Parliament, simply by virtue of his title, was a glaring admission of all that was rotten about the 'ancient regime'. It was Portsmouth's additional misfortune that the one occasion when he participated in Parliamentary politics was when the position of the monarchy itself was at stake. Portsmouth's indecision and inappropriate conduct during the trial of Queen Caroline in 1820 condemned him when he faced his own trial three years later.

In Portsmouth's lifetime, land and wealth brought entitlement. Portsmouth's father wrote letters to William Pitt seeking positions in government for his friends, and a church living for Reverend Garnett. The peers not only ruled the House of Lords, but they also dominated the House of Commons. As the Portsmouths' Hampshire neighbour William Cobbett noted of Parliament, 'one house filled wholly with landowners, and the other four fifths filled with their relatives'. It followed that, as soon as he was of age, Coulson Wallop, Portsmouth's youngest brother, became MP for Andover. Coulson was not even present at his election, and his drunken, irresponsible behaviour did not stop Portsmouth seeking further favours for him. Within months of their father's death, Portsmouth was writing a letter to Pitt wishing 'to promote' the 'advancement' of his brother Coulson, and asking that he be placed in 'some situation which may give an addition to his income'. When Coulson's problems with debt made a public life impossible, his older brother Newton Fellowes simply took over as MP for Andover.

While Coulson and Newton both qualified to be MPs just because they were the brothers of a peer, in this world of political favours, the Portsmouth family knew they held a trump playing card: their Irish estates. Close to thirteen thousand acres of land had been granted to Sir Henry Wallop in 1598 in County Wexford, south-west Ireland, along with a Norman Castle in Enniscorthy. The Portsmouth family paid precious little attention to their Irish property: only Newton Fellowes ever bothered to visit or make attempts at agricultural improvements. Yet the rental income from their Irish estates made a valuable contribution to the family's income, and ensured that the reports from the bailiffs and receivers of rents in Ireland were carefully scrutinized.

The 2nd earl of Portsmouth did all he could to remind Pitt of his 'interest' in County Wexford, offering to support any candidates put forward for election there, and insisting that he had assisted the government's cause 'both with my purse and influence'. Such loyalty should 'entitle me to expect some degree of attention', he concluded in a letter seeking an appointment for one of his friends in July 1790.

Appointments, promotions, pensions, and even peerage creations were the bread and butter of politics at this time. They were the way to win friends and influence people, and Pitt's in-tray was stuffed with letters like the 2nd earl's. Perhaps he should have taken greater note of Portsmouth's special pleading, for when the United Irishmen rose in 1798 they did not do so in Dublin, as had been anticipated, but further south in County Wexford. The surprise slaughter of a hundred militia by the United Irishmen at Oulart was followed by the storming of Enniscorthy and Wexford at the end of May. But as the rebels camped at Vinegar Hill, on the other side of the River Slaney from Enniscorthy Castle, they were surrounded by an army of some twenty thousand heavily armed men. On 21 June, a bloody battle was fought, with the rebels suffering defeat and heavy losses. What was 'quite unprecedented' about the 1798 Irish rebellion, a recent historian has concluded, 'was the element of holy war'. In one example of sectarian violence, up to two hundred men, women, and children, most of whom were Protestant, were rounded up and either shot or burned alive in a barn at Scullabogue, County Wexford. Horrified at the scale of the violence, and increasingly fearful of French attempts to become involved, Pitt's response following the Irish rebellion was to push for tighter control over Ireland, resulting in the 1801 Act of Union.

The Portsmouth estates were situated at the very centre of the 1798 rebellion. Enniscorthy Castle became a prison for the few surviving rebels who were caught and not immediately slaughtered on the spot. Within a week of events at Vinegar Hill, Portsmouth, who had succeeded as 3rd earl the year before, was writing to his uncle, Bennett Wallop, about the rebellion. 'The long dreaded misfortunes have at length taken place on my estate in Ireland,' he began. 'Within this month the greater part of my tenants there have been murdered, every building on my estate burned and the whole laid completely waste by the Wexford rebels.' But then Portsmouth reached the point of his letter:

> should peace be restored to that unhappy country tomorrow, I cannot expect to receive my rents for many years to come! It is therefore utterly out of my power to give you any pecuniary assistance. The loss of the better half of my property reduces me to a state of the greatest distress – and after payment of the existing burdens on my English estates, will…leave me a subsistence on the most contracted scale.

What mattered to Portsmouth about the rebellion was how it would impact upon his finances. Loss of life, and the destruction to homes and land that would burden everyday existence for the survivors, was of no interest. Events in Ireland simply served to excuse him from extending financial support to his uncle. Portsmouth's claims that his Irish estates represented more than half of his income, and that he would be left on a subsistence, were preposterous. A year later, in March 1799, Portsmouth was still using the 'heavy misfortunes' he had suffered due to the Irish rebellion as a reason for not giving pecuniary help to his relatives. In a letter to Pitt, Portsmouth asked that his brother Coulson be given a post 'tenable with his seat in Parliament', to 'render his situation comfortable'. Since the rebellion, he argued, he could not afford to support his brother himself.

Portsmouth's letters epitomize the very worst of the English absentee landowner. They are staggering in their insensitivity and selfishness. But it is significant that Portsmouth's letter to his uncle ended up in Pitt's correspondence files. Pitt needed to know what landlords of Irish estates were thinking. Portsmouth's letter to his uncle and his subsequent one to Pitt showed that Portsmouth was a man for whom politics only became relevant when matters of self-interest were at stake. This was valuable information. Portsmouth might be of use to Pitt in the future as he held lands that were strategically important, and because he was open to receiving favours in return for support.

For Portsmouth's letters betrayed him as a man devoid of any political consciousness: his allegiance could be easily bought.[1]

Throughout his life, despite his control over his property being restricted, or perhaps even because of it, Portsmouth maintained a keen sense of his social position. He insisted upon his social inferiors addressing him correctly, and was easily offended if others did not acknowledge him, or show the respect that he was owed because of his title. Indeed, he could show an inflated sense of his own importance and capabilities, at one point taking initial steps to become a magistrate, which, fortunately for all concerned, was never carried through. It was Portsmouth's right and privilege to sit with the judges at the Winchester assizes, and, in London, Portsmouth frequently spent several hours at a time on the Bench of the Old Bailey. There is no indication that Portsmouth ever attempted to influence the decisions of the judges he sat beside, but, in hindsight, his interest in the trials of violent thieves, murderers, and rapists appeared odd, even voyeuristic.

Portsmouth proudly took his position in the House of Lords. Driving his phaeton in Piccadilly one day in 1812, Portsmouth stopped when he saw his Hampshire neighbour, the magistrate and clergyman Robert Wright. When Wright enquired why Portsmouth was in London, Portsmouth told him that he was there to vote on the 'Catholic question'. Parliament was debating whether there should be an emancipation Bill, allowing Catholic Irish MPs to sit at Westminster. At this point, a friend of Wright's, who was walking with him, and whom Wright knew held opposite views to Portsmouth, declared, 'a very pretty judge, you are, my Lord of the Catholic question'. Whether this was intended as an insult that questioned Portsmouth's ability to vote because of his limited intelligence, or because he was a Protestant landowner in Ireland, we do not know. But Portsmouth did not hesitate with his rebuff. 'I think Sir I am as well qualified to give a conscientious vote on that subject as you are!' he replied, and this was spoken 'with a great deal of spirit,' Wright remembered. A raw nerve had been touched: Portsmouth's sensitivity about his rights was clear, and he was ready to defend them.[2]

In the House of Lords, so far, Portsmouth's attendance had passed unnoticed. He took advantage of his privilege as a peer to appoint domestic chaplains, and he occasionally delegated the right to sit in the House to proxies. His company could be valued precisely because he did not talk politics. Long-time family friend and Hampshire neighbour Sir James Burrough never talked about political affairs with Portsmouth, but liked him the more for it. 'I have frequently laughed with him,' Burrough told the Commission. 'I like merry company; that is my taste.' Burrough was no unreformed country gent: he had earned his knighthood through his career in the law, and had acted as counsel for Portsmouth during the Seilaz trial. He admitted that Portsmouth's conversation was about matters that 'did not require any mental exertion: that is to say on topics connected with farming, horses and the common transactions of the neighbourhood'. Yet this respected judge, who was known for his straight talking, presented a convincing case for Portsmouth's sanity. 'The more I saw of his mind the more I was convinced that his mind was perfect,' he told the jury. A clever and successful man such as Burrough would not waste his spare time with a fool.

Portsmouth's position in the House of Lords might never have attracted comment if it had not been for the events of 1820. For much of this year, the nation was gripped by a fever of excitement, curiosity, and scandal as George IV tried to divorce his wife, Caroline of Brunswick. 'Since I have been in the world,' recorded one diarist, 'I never remember any question which so exclusively occupied everybody's attention, and so completely absorbed men's thoughts and engrossed conversation.'

George had loathed his wife from the moment they met, but their arranged marriage went through in 1795. He had no intention of giving up his lavish lifestyle or lovers, frequently quarrelled with Caroline, who was no shrinking violet, and gave up living with her altogether after their daughter, Charlotte, was born nine months later. Irritated by her very existence, George falsely accused Caroline of adultery in 1807, and piled on the pressure for her to leave the country. This she did in 1814, in return for £35,000 per year. When Charlotte died three years later, nobody thought to inform her mother, and Caroline was not invited to the funeral. 'A more contemptible, cowardly, selfish, unfeeling dog does not exist,' wrote one political diarist about George; 'the worst man he fell in with in his whole life,' the Duke of Wellington was recorded as saying.

On 29 January 1820, the insane and elderly George III died, and his son became King. Much to his horror, Caroline prepared to return to England. He might not want her as his wife, but Caroline was determined to be his Queen. George thought divorce was his only option, but his own infidelities meant that seeking legal recourse in the church courts was a non-starter. Instead, he pursued a Bill of Pains and Penalties in the House of Lords, which charged Caroline with adultery, and if successful would have stripped her of her royal title and position.

The proceedings, which quickly became referred to as a 'trial', began on 17 August. All peers were required to be present. There was plenty of evidence that the Queen had committed adultery while abroad, and, by having relationships with her Italian servants, she had chosen her lovers unwisely. But the trial was still a public relations disaster for George. Testimony from low-born foreigners was always going to raise popular xenophobia, and the underhand way in which evidence was gathered against Caroline, such as the use of spies and common thieves to steal her personal papers, did nothing to strengthen the case against her. Outside the Lords, publicity about the trial mounted as the Queen gathered support from a vast range of people, many of whom had never been engaged by politics in this way before. Women sympathized with her position as a wronged wife and mother; the respectable middle classes, affronted by the immorality of the monarchy, debated the case; and political radicals latched on to her cause as a convenient way in which they could criticize authority and corruption. All the while, the air of blatant hypocrisy hung heavily over George.

Portsmouth did his duty and attended every day of the trial. This was no mean feat: the trial lasted until 9 September, when the House adjourned until 3 October, and then continued until 10 November. Henry Brougham, counsel for Caroline, gave a speech that lasted two whole days, and was so charged with emotion that at its close Lord Erskine was said to rush from the chamber in tears. The record keeper for the House of Lords remembered that Portsmouth's behaviour 'was perfectly proper, and did not excite remark one way or the other'. Portsmouth looked attentive. Burrough, who served as one of the judges in the trial, recalled seeing Portsmouth in the House of Lords, and, while they never talked of the trial, they often had some 'trifling conversation' as they passed. All appeared orderly and correct.

But then came the votes. On 6 November, the Lords had to decide whether to give the Bill a second reading. In effect, the vote asked the Lords to choose between the King (in which case the trial would proceed) and Caroline (which would require a vote against a second reading and the end of the trial). Which way would Portsmouth vote? The King stood for authority, hereditary power, the establishment, and tradition: the very essence of all the peerage represented. At a personal level, the King, like Portsmouth, had an adulterous wife but was not free from sexual scandal himself. Yet Portsmouth also had much in common with Caroline. Like her, he had been an embarrassment, and he had also suffered the consequences of being excluded from exercising the powers that should have come with his social position. As Caroline stood in the House of Lords, the only woman in a sea of men, Portsmouth may well have understood what she was feeling, and sympathized and identified with her. He had been in her position for much of his life.

On 6 November, Portsmouth voted with the majority, in favour of a second reading. The majority was a small one, of twenty-eight members. The Bill continued to be debated until 10 November, when the Lords were asked to vote whether the Bill should be read for a third time. Knowing how tight the majority had been days earlier, the atmosphere was tense. 'Public expectation hung upon every vote,' counsel for Portsmouth remembered. Brougham bent forward 'with breathless anxiety, to listen to the votes as they were delivered', marking down on paper as each vote was cast. The votes were looking equally divided, and too close to call. With so much at stake, every vote mattered. At last, the Chancellor reached the bench of earls. Each stood in turn to declare his vote. They reached Portsmouth. He stood. He paused. 'There was a solemn stillness – a death-like silence pervading the house – it was only broken by a whisper of "Give him time – Give him time."' The wait was long and painful. Finally, Portsmouth cast his vote. This time he voted for Caroline.

Portsmouth was not the only person to change his mind. Four others, including two bishops, also voted for the second reading, but against the third. This shift sealed the fate of the Bill. With a Lords majority of only nine votes in favour of a third reading, the Bill could not continue, and Caroline was acquitted, much to the delight of her supporters. Celebrations broke out across the country, as Portsmouth's name, along with the others who had joined the debate on 10 November and voted for Caroline, was printed in the newspapers.

But Portsmouth would be remembered for 'voting both ways', while others would be forgotten, because of the manner in which he cast his vote. That hesitation was fatal. He appeared muddled. He later told Coombe that 'he did not know for what he voted: he believed he voted both ways'. It was not the quality of the debate that had convinced him to vote differently, but genuine confusion. A man whose basic ignorance of how to vote had previously led him to vote both ways at school governors' meetings had now been publicly exposed in the highest political setting. Under pressure, and with all those eyes looking at him, he panicked, and ended up voting a different way simply to get the moment over. Afterwards, he could not be certain what he had done.

When Portsmouth came to face his trial before the 1823 Lunacy Commission, more evidence came to light that cast doubt upon his understanding of the importance of the occasion. Two letters that Portsmouth had written from the House of Lords were produced. The first was an affectionate one to Mary Ann, expressing pleasure that her health was recovering (she may have just had a miscarriage), and hoping to see her at Fairlawn when the House adjourned in September. 'I am my dearest Love your affectionate love', Portsmouth signed it. The second was an angry note, headed the House of Lords, 5 October, and addressed to Reverend Antrobus in Acton. Portsmouth complained to Antrobus that his clerk, John Markham, had objected to his singing and prevented him from attending church. Portsmouth therefore directed that Antrobus should give him 'a severe reprimand'. There was nothing to the complaint: the clerk certainly did not appreciate the 'loud' and 'very unpleasant' sound that Portsmouth made when he tried to sing, but he had never dared to suggest that this should stop him from coming to services.

Both letters came back to haunt Portsmouth. In the context of a Commission that produced so much evidence of her violence and cruelty, Mary Ann may have hoped that Portsmouth's letter to her would demonstrate his affection towards her. Instead, it only showed how deluded Portsmouth could be about the nature of his marriage and the character of Mary Ann. This was not a marriage in which 'absence made the heart grow fonder'. There was similarly no substance to Portsmouth's assessment of the Acton clerk: Antrobus replied with a letter that 'endeavoured quietly to remove the delusion from his Lordship's mind'.

But what was most damning about both letters was when and where they were written. As Wetherell, counsel for the petition of lunacy against Portsmouth, explained in his summing up:

> Instead of listening to one of the ablest addresses ever made, in defence of what was considered by the speaker of it…to be an important attack to the constitution, he was addressing a letter to Mr. Antrobus, to complain of his parish clerk. He was engaged in a trial, but it was of poor Markham, and not of the Queen.

Portsmouth's mind was unfocused. Rather than listening to the evidence that had been gathered against Caroline from her time abroad, 'his Lordship's mind was wandering in the church and churchyard at Acton'. He wasn't paying attention to the debates that had captured the nation's attention, but was obsessing about his own little domestic world. Even this he had got all wrong.[3]

By the time the Lunacy Commission was brought against Portsmouth, Queen Caroline was dead. Her cause was quickly dropped by political radicals after her trial. They no longer saw her as an appropriate symbol for their aims, and her acceptance of an enormous annual pension funded by the taxpayer in March 1821 further alienated her from public support. When she arrived at George IV's lavish coronation in July, she was refused entry to the Abbey, and the doors of Westminster Hall were shut in her face. The crowds outside were hostile to her attempts to gain entry. Only when she died a month later would people again rally to her side, insisting that her coffin made its way through the City of London, much to the government's annoyance. The plaque on her coffin, which read 'Caroline of Brunswick, Injured Queen of England', never made it to her grave, however. Someone removed it the night before her coffin left Harwich, meaning 'she departed England unmarked'.

Some of those who had tried Queen Caroline were also those who judged Portsmouth in February 1823. Eldon was the Chancellor for both Caroline and Portsmouth, and Caroline's lawyer, Brougham, was employed by the Fellowes family to prove Portsmouth was insane. Portsmouth's defence lost little time in reminding Brougham that he had relied upon Portsmouth's vote in the Lords. Once Portsmouth had delivered his verdict on the third reading, Serjeant Pell recalled 'the face of his learned friend beaming with delight at the triumph which he enjoyed from the vote then delivered'. Pell 'could not but marvel now', less than three years later, to see Brougham 'endeavouring to prove that that the person' who delivered that vote 'was a madman'. Portsmouth had been used, just as the radicals had used Caroline, for as long as he had been politically expedient. The hypocrisy that Pell exposed prompted applause from the audience at the Commission, which was joined by some members of the jury.

Outside the Freemasons' Hall, and in the days immediately following the end of the Commission, there was an attempt to make some political mileage out of the fact that Portsmouth had been permitted to sit and vote in Parliament, despite his questionable sanity. On 1 March 1823, some seven to eight thousand 'respectable' people met in Winchester castle-yard to discuss petitioning the government about the 'present alarming state of agricultural interest'. It was one of a series of county meetings that were held in England since the start of the year. Present were the two big names in radical politics, both of whom held land in Hampshire, Cobbett and 'Orator' Hunt. Hunt, who had been held in Ilchester gaol since the Peterloo Massacre, had only been released the previous autumn, and was greeted as a hero with cheers of 'bravo!' Cobbett and Hunt spoke for two different forms of petition, but it was Hunt, with his calls for universal manhood suffrage, and a complete reform of Parliament, who won out.

But Hunt overstepped the mark when he referred to Portsmouth's trial. He 'animadverted on the affliction of Lord Portsmouth, which called forth strong and general marks of disapprobation,' *The Times* reported. Sir Thomas Baring, who was Chairman of the meeting, and also a member of the jury that had tried Portsmouth, rose to speak. Hunt's remarks 'gave him inexpressible pain,' said Baring. It was to him 'a matter of deep regret' that 'any individual should have had so little of human feeling in his composition as to allude to the melancholy case of a noble but hapless person'. Baring told the crowd how he had sat on Portsmouth's Lunacy Commission for the last three weeks:

> harassed in mind and in body by the fatigue and anxiety of such an inquiry, he had travelled all night to be present at this meeting. (Applause)...if Mr Hunt had seen the unhappy nobleman, as he had seen him, examined by 23 gentlemen, and placed in the condition in which he stood, he would, he thought, have forborne from making any allusion to his heavy and bitter calamity. (Hear). The spectacle was calculated to have drawn tears from any man, even had he a heart of adamant. (Hear, hear).

Hunt, judging the public mood had swung against him, changed his tune. 'In explanation', he responded that 'the mere reading of Lord Portsmouth's case, in the newspapers, had drawn tears from him'. He had only raised the case 'to show one instance of the manner in which votes were given in passing acts of Parliament'. The debate then moved on.

Hunt's words showed a surprising lack of sensitivity in part because he had personal experience of coping with the effects of mental disability. His own brother, described as a 'harmless fool', was confined in Warburton's private madhouse in Hoxton. But, while nobody dared to refer to this, his words were also politically miscalculated. Hunt went too far because he had been critical of an individual member of the House of Lords, who was also a local aristocrat. In Winchester, he might have thought he could bring national politics closer to home by referring to Portsmouth, but his words betrayed a deep misunderstanding of popular sentiment. Whatever he was, and to a great extent however he conducted himself, Portsmouth was the key aristocratic figure in this county's community. As the largest landowner in the county, Portsmouth was perceived as its representative in the House of Lords. He was their man. As such, he would always command respect and loyalty. While many people were critical of the corruption that was endemic in politics, and could yearn for a reform of Parliament, they did not seek a wholesale change in the political system. That would mean revolution, and the recent example in France was enough of a reminder of the horrors that could bring.

Just as the British people came to 'distinguish the person from the office' of monarchy in this period, allowing them to show support for George IV at his coronation, even though this followed a year of public unrest over Queen Caroline, so they could also put the institution before the individual in Parliamentary politics. The personal qualities, and in particular the morals of both George IV and Portsmouth, were manifestly unsuited to their positions of authority. But this did not disqualify them from office. Dr Stephen Lushington, another lawyer who spoke in the Lords for the Queen, and was counsel in legal proceedings involving Portsmouth that followed his Commission, understood the politics of the time all too well. Portsmouth's vote in Caroline's trial proved nothing about his sanity, because, he explained:

> the members of the House of Peers did not undergo a scrutiny as to their capacity before they voted; and without meaning any disrespect to that most honourable house, he thought it possible there might even now be a member of it…who, on inquiry, might be found to possess not a perfectly sound mind. It was not one of the privileges of that house that its members were to be assumed sound by virtue of a seat in it.

Queen Caroline's trial was relegated in history to an 'affair', a 'domestic melodrama' that did no long-term damage to the monarchy. So also, argued Lushington, Portsmouth's distressing case, and any other individuals who might be suffering from similar 'calamities', should not be allowed to affect the strength of the House of Lords. Indeed, to score political points by drawing attention to the personal misfortunes of one man could be regarded as utterly heartless, distasteful, and even cruel. Portsmouth's case invited a display of emotion, and, if the correct response was tears and sympathy, then it lost all its political potency. Hunt was silenced and nobody else attempted to score political points by referring to Portsmouth's case. Such was local sensitivity that neither of Hampshire's newspapers mentioned Hunt's speech, and even the reporter for *The Times* did not go as far as to specify the precise words Hunt used to describe Portsmouth. There might be other members like Portsmouth, but the future of the House of Lords was safe, at least for now.[4]

When the public spotlight was on Portsmouth, he had messed up. His conduct during the Queen Caroline trial earned him unwelcome notoriety. 'So long as he was sane, he took no part in politics', recorded a future editor of *Complete Peerage*, as he noted Portsmouth's vote in the Queen's trial.[5] But so far, aged nearly fifty-three, the only prominent person harmed by Portsmouth's behaviour was himself. All that was about to change.

He 'always expressed much anxiety about his Lady's health'

∽

THE FAMED PROFESSOR James Hamilton was a good choice of doctor for Mary Ann, countess of Portsmouth. Hamilton had been practising midwifery since he was twenty-one years old, working alongside his father, the previous incumbent of the Chair of Midwifery at Edinburgh University, and travelling to study at Leiden and Paris. His expertise in women's health was well known, and he attracted wealthy patients as well as medical students to Edinburgh University, where he campaigned to make midwifery a compulsory subject. His lectures were legendary, and he achieved the considerable feat of filling the lecture theatres where he spoke to eager listeners, despite the non-compulsory nature of his courses. Along with his father, Hamilton founded and funded Edinburgh's Lying-In Hospital for the poor, and it was there that he gained valuable experience observing and delivering many hundreds of babies. As a 'man-midwife', there was little he didn't know about how to see a woman and her child safely through labour.

Along with many other physicians of the day, Hamilton was used to conducting medical consultations with his patients by letter. It meant that he could treat patients from a wide geographical area, and dispense advice without necessarily seeing or examining the patient. This was how Mary Ann first became his patient, possibly corresponding with him after she suffered a miscarriage in August 1821.

Unfortunately, Hamilton's correspondence does not survive, but whatever he wrote was so well received that, when Mary Ann found that she was pregnant again in the autumn of that year, she headed straight for Edinburgh.

She was accompanied on this journey by both Portsmouth and Alder. They stopped on their route north at Harrogate for three weeks, perhaps to benefit from the spa waters. Then they continued to Edinburgh, spending at least a night at Alder's home, Horncliffe Hall in Northumberland, on their way. Initially, suitable lodgings in Edinburgh were difficult to find, and the party stayed in the Union Hotel before and after they rejected a house in North Frederick Street for being too noisy. Finally, they settled upon 32 Great King Street, an elegantly furnished townhouse that had been built recently during the second phase of Edinburgh's New Town development. This was Edinburgh at its best and most exclusive: the streets were wide, there were splendid squares and gardens where the fashionable could promenade, and all was a vision of space and order. Most importantly for Mary Ann, it seemed to offer the calm atmosphere and the quiet that she craved.

From all that she had heard about him, Mary Ann may well have been taken aback when Hamilton made his first visit to her. From first impressions, he did not look like the great doctor that everyone talked about. He was short in height, had a permanent stoop, and didn't even appear well, seeming frail and nervous. When he spoke, he did so in a harsh voice and with a heavy Scottish accent that was seen as unsophisticated for his social position. He rarely looked people in the eye. He insisted on being carried around Edinburgh in a sedan chair, and views were mixed about whether this was because he did not have the strength to walk, or reflected his inflated sense of self-importance.

Mary Ann overcame any initial doubts she had about Hamilton, trusting her care to him. When she arrived in Edinburgh in November 1821, she was only a few weeks pregnant, but after all those miscarriages she was understandably anxious. To Hamilton, she was a demanding patient, insisting that he see her nearly every day. Yet, as a countess, Hamilton calculated that she would also be a lucrative source of income. Hamilton's services did not come cheap. When Mary Ann asked how he would like to be paid (per visit, or after the birth?), he declared that 'he never talked on these little matters', cannily allowing her to decide what would be an appropriate payment for a lady of her social status. This was a shrewd move: one interim payment of £150 was made in April, with a much larger sum expected upon the birth of the baby.

Hamilton paid enough visits to 32 Great King Street to get to see the other members of the household. He was never introduced to Alder, and did not know his name, but upon enquiry was told that he was a wealthy gentleman from Berwickshire. Mary Ann was joined in Edinburgh by her sister, Laura, and her brother, Newton, and in the last weeks of her pregnancy, by her father, John Hanson, who travelled up from London to be there for the birth.

But the person whom Hamilton saw most was Portsmouth. Portsmouth 'always expressed much anxiety about his Lady's health', Hamilton recalled. He seemed to display all the worry typical of a father-to-be. Indeed, Portsmouth's daily questioning about his wife's condition, and sometimes 'urgent' enquiries about when the baby would be born, led Mary Ann to advise Hamilton to try to evade the subject. When Hamilton invited Portsmouth to an evening party at his house, Portsmouth declined the invitation, 'from the apprehension of disturbing Lady Portsmouth'. This was a husband who was treating his wife with every degree of care that her fragility seemed to demand.

When Portsmouth did leave the house, he appeared happy. While in Edinburgh, he took the opportunity to make several calls to see Grace's sister-in-law, Caroline Elizabeth, recently widowed from Fletcher Norton. He may have engaged in a spot of sightseeing, and witnessed preparations for George IV's visit to the city that was scheduled for the summer of 1822. The tone of a letter that he wrote to a friend was relaxed and chatty:

> We are so much delighted with this fine town, that had we been here
> at any other season of the year, we should have made it a point of
> visiting the Highlands.

There were signs that, free from the confines of Fairlawn and the restrictions of London society, Portsmouth was back to his old self. He ran up quite a bill at a sweet shop, the owner not realizing who he was until Portsmouth gave his name for a home delivery after about a month of frequent visits. He contented himself visiting a repository where horses were sometimes sold, and even bought a horse there himself. The owner of the repository, who over the course of several months had many conversations with Portsmouth, considered him 'very intelligent in regard to farming, and a particular good judge of horses'. But a few days after Portsmouth had made his purchase, two men visited the repository and told the owner that Portsmouth was 'not in the way of managing his own affairs' so the horse had to be returned. Portsmouth was not seen at the repository again.

With the progress of Mary Ann's pregnancy, her control over Portsmouth lessened, but there were others to remind him of his responsibilities. Hamilton was not a man to cross. He had a reputation for having furious quarrels with his academic colleagues. His long-standing animosity towards the equally fiery Professor James Gregory, for example, eventually resulted in Gregory attacking Hamilton in the street with his walking stick. When Hamilton issued instructions in his patients' households, he expected them to be followed. So he was sorely irritated on one of his visits when he heard Portsmouth making a great noise in the room below Mary Ann's bedroom. Hamilton rushed downstairs, as Portsmouth's 'screaming out, as if in danger of being hurt' had 'alarmed the Countess'. He found Alder in the room with Portsmouth, and was told that Portsmouth had hit Alder as he sat writing a letter. Alder got up 'to return the compliment', and it was at this point that Portsmouth started screaming. When Hamilton remonstrated with Portsmouth, Portsmouth declared that the whole exchange 'was merely a joke, the consequence of which he had not foreseen'. Hamilton had no interest in why the men were quarrelling; his only care was his patient, and she was 'at that time in such a state, as to require the utmost possible quiet'. Whatever Portsmouth's situation, it was vital that it did not affect the health of his wife.

This time Mary Ann carried her baby to full term. On 7 August

1822, she went into labour, and Hamilton rushed to her assistance. His skills were needed as the labour was not an easy one. The baby girl 'was brought into the world by means of instruments', probably forceps, and 'above an hour elapsed before it breathed so freely as to give it reason to expect its living'. A clergyman was called to baptize the baby when its life looked in danger. 'The resemblance of the infant to your Lordship,' Hamilton told Portsmouth, 'particularly about the lower part of the face, was so remarkable as to strike at once all the attendants.' The baby was given her mother's name, Mary Ann, and her birth in Edinburgh was announced in the standard fashion later that month in the Hampshire papers.

But, while the baby had survived her first few hours of life, her future looked far from certain. For when she was born, the man whom her mother said was her father was hundreds of miles away. Hamilton had to write to tell Portsmouth about her birth because he was not there. His absence immediately raised questions about why Mary Ann had chosen to spend her pregnancy and give birth in Edinburgh. Perhaps Hamilton was the obvious choice not just because he was a great doctor, but because he practised far from the gossiping social circles of Hampshire and London. Mary Ann became a virtual recluse in Edinburgh, and her household went into lockdown, because she wanted to keep her condition private for as long as possible. She yearned for anonymity, seeking no company except that of Alder and her family. Her confinement began long before necessary because anyone who knew her would soon guess that the baby she carried was not Portsmouth's.

Mary Ann was one patient that Hamilton could have done without. The last thing he wanted was a reputation for being a doctor who delivered illegitimate babies. Portsmouth's high-profile Lunacy Commission brought him unwelcome publicity. He regretted his letter to Portsmouth in which he stated what all new fathers want to hear, that their baby looked just like them. In an awkward case of back-tracking, he later claimed that it was only in the first few fragile hours of life, when the baby was struggling to breathe, 'that its resemblance to his Lordship appeared so striking'. Twisted and contorted, hardly an attractive image, the baby looked like Portsmouth. 'He never saw any circumstance which could lead him to suspect improper conduct on the part of Lady Portsmouth,' he asserted. Hamilton made no mention of the anonymous letters that were sent to him in the weeks before the birth, warning him that the baby was a bastard. Yet Hamilton's claim that he was ignorant of all that was going on at 32 Great King Street fell apart when accounts were given of Portsmouth's departure from Edinburgh. It was the events of 2 July that laid bare the truth of this family's situation.[1]

The King of Hampshire

T AROUND 1P.M. on Tuesday, 2 July 1822, Lord Portsmouth, having 'breakfasted with his Countess', left his house in Great King Street to go for a walk. He was in 'perfect good humour', 'telling his Lady he should soon return to her, and take an early dinner at three o'clock'. His meal arrangements sorted, Portsmouth headed down through the New Town towards Princes Street. On reaching Princes Street, Portsmouth turned to walk eastwards towards the Royal Hotel.

But it was then that the leisurely pace of this summertime excursion came to an abrupt end. Out of the hotel, apparently taking Portsmouth by surprise, stepped Fletcher Norton, the son of Caroline Elizabeth, a relation of Portsmouth's first wife whom he had occasionally visited since his arrival in Edinburgh. The two men had a short conversation, after which Portsmouth was 'prevailed' to get into Mrs Norton's coach, which was waiting for them outside Register House. The horses set off at great speed, leaving Edinburgh behind them and heading south. A few miles beyond Haddington, a market town in East Lothian, another coach was waiting for them, this one owned by Fletcher's uncle, William Lord Grantley. The men changed coaches, and waiting inside the second coach was John Draper Coombe. Wasting no time, this coach travelled onwards, through day and night, until it arrived at the house of Lord Grantley in Wonersh, just outside Guildford, in Surrey, on the morning of 4 July. Portsmouth had travelled some 440 miles in just 51 hours.

On that journey south, Portsmouth's version of what had been happening behind the closed doors of 32 Great King Street came pouring out. Portsmouth told Fletcher and Coombe a 'long history' of the 'ill treatment he had received at Edinburgh'. Alder had 'frequently knocked him down,' he said, and his nights had been interrupted by Mary Ann requesting that Portsmouth fetch Alder when she felt unwell. At one or two in the morning, Portsmouth had to bring Alder into her room, and Alder, only partially dressed then got into bed beside Mary Ann to comfort her. Portsmouth squeezed his way into the other side of the bed, with Mary Ann lying between the two men. In the daytime, Mary Ann reduced the numbers of hours he was allowed out of the house, from five to two. Kept a prisoner in his own home, he was 'locked up at six o'clock, as soon as it began to grow dark, in her ladyship's dressing room, and there kept till bedtime'. Laura and Newton Hanson continued their accustomed cruelty towards him, sometimes whipping Portsmouth, and on other occasions simply hitting him until he fell to the floor.

If Mary Ann had hoped her reputation would not follow her to Edinburgh, she was mistaken. The party were forced to change lodgings upon arrival in the city 'in consequence of the scandalous intercourse observed between Mr Alder and the Countess'. On three occasions they had to move, after they were 'discarded for indecencies and improper behaviour'. It was Alder who eventually succeeded in renting the house in Great King Street.

This account of life in Edinburgh was so utterly different from that presented by the Hansons that unsurprisingly it led to some questioning at the Lunacy Commission. Portsmouth was quizzed about it during his examination, and attention was given to the letter home that he wrote, in which there was no mention of any problem. 'We have it in evidence from Lord Portsmouth's own lips,' a juror recorded, 'that he never wrote anything while he was at Edinburgh', without Lady Portsmouth's involvement. Portsmouth claimed that he only survived for so long in Edinburgh because he could talk to Mrs Norton. Indeed, the statement he made afterwards that, had it not been for her, 'he should not have known what to do', may unwittingly have given away the plot to remove him from Edinburgh. It was probably

Mrs Norton who told the rest of Portsmouth's family what was going on in Edinburgh, and it may have been her who advised him to take his walk along Princes Street that afternoon.

The Hanson family had their suspicions that something was up. John Hanson had his contacts in the legal world, even in Edinburgh. For all that Alder was physically strong and a bully, it was always John Hanson, never Alder, who called the shots in Mary Ann's household. In June 1822, John Hanson wrote to John James, the writer of the signet in Edinburgh, who was a senior solicitor in the city. Hanson asked James to deliver a letter to his son, Newton, which gave instructions about how to safeguard Portsmouth. The day after the letter had been delivered, Portsmouth and Newton visited James in his chambers, and Portsmouth said he wanted protection from his brother, who had already tried to declare him a lunatic. With a lot of prompting from Newton, Portsmouth told James 'that his brother had now formed a plan for carrying him off from Lady Portsmouth, who was then in the family way in order to alarm her and produce a miscarriage'. Portsmouth was convinced 'that people employed by his brother were watching and dogging him in the streets, and he was afraid to go much abroad'. Newton 'participated in the conversation', encouraging rather than dispelling these fears. Portsmouth was frightened and he asked for help. James, seeing no signs of derangement or insanity in Portsmouth, ordered that two police officers be stationed at Portsmouth's house.

The police did nothing to prevent Portsmouth being bundled into Mrs Norton's coach, but word of Portsmouth's departure soon got back to the Hanson household. Newton knew he had to move fast. He ordered a coach, persuaded James to come with him by telling him it was 'Lady Portsmouth's wish', and the two men set off in hot pursuit of Portsmouth's coach. They chased Portsmouth across the length of the country, but their horses were no match for Grantley's, and they did not arrive at the gates of Wonersh until early Friday morning.

Refused admission, Newton and John Hanson lost no time in organizing a legal challenge to events. They applied to a judge, John Bayley, at King's Bench for a writ of habeas corpus, which was issued in Mary Ann's name. The writ stated that Portsmouth had been 'forcibly and against his will conveyed away from Edinburgh', and that he was now being confined at Wonersh. Portsmouth was brought to be examined at Bayley's house in Bedford Square on 8 July. Bayley questioned Portsmouth with no one else present, and found that Portsmouth responded 'readily'. Portsmouth 'expressed himself very decided in his unwillingness to return to Edinburgh'. He gave no indication that he had been taken against his will, or that he was now being kept against his will. Although Bayley was clear that his purpose was not to judge Portsmouth's sanity, he later stated that if he had any doubts about his mind he would have taken steps to have him 'watched and attended'. But he 'discovered nothing which approached the character of an unsound mind'. Hence he told Portsmouth that 'he was a free agent, and at liberty to go wherever he pleased'. There were no grounds for the writ of habeas corpus.

Within weeks, Portsmouth had returned to Hurstbourne. There he was 'welcomed with the most cordial congratulation, by the numerous and respectable tenantry, and the population of Andover'. He attended the races that month at Winchester, shaking the hand of one of his friends with the words 'Here I am amongst you again'. He was home.[1]

In the meantime, Mary Ann was in Edinburgh awaiting the birth of her child. It was the 'urgent request' of Professor Hamilton that Portsmouth's departure from Edinburgh should be 'concealed' from her 'as long as possible'. When his absence could not be hidden any longer, a surgeon let blood from her arm an hour or two before she was told the news, in the hope that would prepare her for the shock. On 11 July, Hamilton received a letter from Portsmouth asking that he be kept informed of his wife's health, and told when the baby was born. Hamilton handed the letter to either Mary Ann or John Hanson, and it was not seen again.

The Hansons continued to maintain that Portsmouth had been removed from Edinburgh without his consent. Having failed to achieve their aims through the writ of habeas corpus, they now turned to the press. Newton Hanson wrote a letter to the *Edinburgh Courant*, which was then widely reprinted in other newspapers, in which he represented Portsmouth's departure from Edinburgh as abduction, rather than an escape. The mastermind behind Portsmouth's abduction was his brother, Newton Fellowes, it was claimed. Having written a series of anonymous letters to Hamilton, casting the legitimacy of Mary Ann's baby in doubt, Newton Fellowes, along with fellow trustee Lord Grantley, planned to abduct Portsmouth. Portsmouth had no idea what was going to happen to him the day he stepped out from his house in Great King Street. 'His Lordship had not a change of apparel of any description, nor had made the smallest preparation for such a journey,' the letter declared. The 'secret instrument of taking his Lordship away' was amateur in some aspects: Coombe had decided to travel incognito, assuming the rather unimaginative name of 'Captain Cook'. But its intention was deadly serious. Newton Fellowes was 'presumptive heir', and he had to do all he could to distance Portsmouth from the baby who threatened to deny him his future. Now that Mary Ann's health was in an 'alarming state', the actions of Newton Fellowes might even cause a miscarriage, Hanson warned.

While Newton Fellowes was quick to print a press denial of his authorship of the letters to Hamilton, there was truth to many of the other accusations made by Hanson. Years later, as Coombe tried to secure payment from Fellowes for his part in the scheme, he produced a letter that Fellowes and Lord Grantley had written to him on 24 June 1822 instructing him to remove Portsmouth 'from the custody and control' of the Hansons. A number of previous attempts to achieve this had already failed, they wrote. Portsmouth had been mistreated in Edinburgh, they told Coombe, and so they authorized him 'to act in the manner you may think best for the personal protection, benefit and credit of his Lordship and family'.

The fact was that Portsmouth had been cruelly used by the Hansons and Alder for years. Newton Fellowes had remained a trustee of the Portsmouth estates, and he had never lost sight of the prize that was promised to him as heir. He continued to pursue Chancery actions that sought to protect the property that he saw as his to inherit. This ranged from the seemingly petty injunctions he brought about the felling of trees on the Hurstbourne estate, to the more serious accusations he pursued in the summer of 1821. By then, Newton had become convinced, with some justification, that income from the

English and Irish estates was being siphoned off by the Hanson family before it reached the Portsmouth trustees.

Even when Newton Fellowes first heard that Mary Ann was pregnant, and that she and his brother were in Edinburgh, he may not have been concerned. There was no reason to believe that this pregnancy would end any differently from her others. But as the months went by, and Mrs Norton continued to send news of Mary Ann's advancing pregnancy, for the first time it looked as though this baby would survive. Newton had to act, not just to safeguard his inheritance, but also that of his son, Henry Arthur, who had just come of age. Newton was too convinced, like others, of his brother's impotence to ever entertain the notion that the baby might be legitimate. Fortunately for Newton, Mary Ann had been so blatantly unfaithful with her lover Alder that there was ample evidence to prove that the baby was a bastard. But he had to remove Portsmouth from Mary Ann's clutches first, and before the baby was born.

That Portsmouth wanted to leave Mary Ann helped. The Hansons' accusation of abduction fell apart when they could produce no proof that Portsmouth had been forced into that carriage. In broad daylight, in the middle of the capital city, not a single witness could be produced to say otherwise.

Portsmouth was miserable, and as he travelled away from Edinburgh he could feel relief. He thought he had escaped. But he could not foresee what would happen over the next few months, or know that six months later he would be facing a Commission of Lunacy. While the circumstances of his sudden departure from Edinburgh bore little resemblance to those he had experienced when he had been abducted by Seilaz more than twenty years earlier, the motives of those behind the scheme were remarkably similar. To both his brother, and to his wife and her family, Portsmouth was a valuable asset that neither party was prepared to give up. His wellbeing was always of secondary importance to his financial worth.

Having recovered from childbirth, Mary Ann left Edinburgh. She first used charm to try to win her husband back, writing letters to him. When these letters were withheld, she turned to intimidation. In the late afternoon of 2 October, 'an open carriage and four, with two postilions, followed by two servants wearing the Portsmouth liveries, was seen approaching Whitchurch'. In the carriage was seated Lady Portsmouth, with her nurse and infant daughter. They stopped to rest at the White Hart Inn.

Portsmouth knew they were coming. The previous day, he had received a visit at Hurstbourne from Dr Bankhead and Mr France, a solicitor employed by the Hanson family. Bankhead tried to give Portsmouth a letter from Mary Ann, which Portsmouth angrily refused to accept. 'She has disgraced herself by insulting me,' Portsmouth declared, 'and I will never live with her again.' According to Bankhead, 'the whole park was in a state of siege'. He found Portsmouth walking on the back lawn, accompanied by two or three men, one of whom was armed with a gun. Within sight of Portsmouth were forty or fifty labourers, 'armed with bludgeons'. Portsmouth told Bankhead that the armed people were 'necessary to protect him from the violence of the Hansons'. 'He was afraid to go anywhere, on account of the Hansons,' he said, 'and the day before they had been endeavouring to get at him.'

When Mr France said that Mary Ann was on her way to Hurstbourne, Portsmouth would tolerate his unwelcome visitors no more. Two of Portsmouth's men, followed by his gamekeeper, who was armed, marched France off the premises. After he had passed through the gate, they were closed and chained together, and 'secured by bolts of an uncommon length and strength'. Men were then 'stationed at them day and night, to guard against any new invasion'.

Meanwhile, 'the people at Whitchurch', hearing that Mary Ann had returned, assembled in front of the gates. 'A party of men, dressed in smockfrocks, and others apparently labourers, were drawn up', in order to oppose, by force if necessary, 'that entrance on which her Ladyship was expected to insist'. Just beyond the Lodge on the park driveway, 'two timber carriages were placed, without horses, to obstruct the way'. These obstacles, along with the trees on either side, would make it impossible for any carriage to pass through. Despite this show of loyalty for Lord Portsmouth, local opinion was divided. Some were 'anxious for her Ladyship's success', while others declared that 'she will never enter the mansion of this Noble Lord again'.

Portsmouth had drawn sufficient attention and support to dissuade Mary Ann from attempting to enter the estate. She came no closer than Whitchurch. But the victory in this battle was not all his. Barricaded in his own home, Portsmouth was literally scared out of his wits. The paranoia that had begun in Edinburgh, when the Hansons convinced him that his brother had placed spies on every street corner, had continued at Hurstbourne. Here he believed his wife and her family were intent on ambushing him and returning him to the horrors of their fold. He had enemies everywhere, and from all sides. His brother did nothing to allay his fears, even employing the services of two Bow Street officers at Hurstbourne. Surrounded by armed men, kept 'in a sort of captivity' within his mansion, and afraid to go out, Portsmouth was experiencing even less freedom at Hurstbourne than he had in Edinburgh.

In a constant state of agitation and alarm, with all the drama, disturbance, and disruption of the last few months, Portsmouth faced examination from doctors. It turned out that taking Portsmouth from Edinburgh was just the first step in a much larger plan that Newton Fellowes had for his brother. Just five days after Bayley had dismissed the habeas corpus writ, Newton Fellowes arranged for Portsmouth to be seen by the physician of Bethlem Hospital, George Tuthill. Tuthill, whose occupation was not disclosed to Portsmouth, saw him again at Hurstbourne in October and January 1823. Dr Sutherland, who had cared for Portsmouth's mad aunt, Dorothea, saw Portsmouth for the first time on 10 August. Both Sutherland and Tuthill were convinced that Portsmouth's mind was unsound. Fellowes was gathering the evidence he needed for his son to make a request for a Lunacy Commission that autumn.

But the Hansons were equally capable of gaining medical opinion to show that Portsmouth's mind was sound. Bankhead had been employed by them to examine Portsmouth during his October visit. It was Bankhead who dropped the bombshell to Portsmouth that his nephew, Henry Arthur, had applied to the Chancellor for a Commission of Lunacy against him. At this, Portsmouth seemed 'surprised and indignant', Bankhead remembered. But that Portsmouth was of 'a very nervous habit' was hardly surprising given all he had endured,

Bankhead told the Commission. Bankhead was a man who was not easily frightened, he declared, but with armed men lurking in the bushes, even he found himself very 'alarmed'. No wonder Portsmouth was on edge. Bankhead, who could boast of thirty years' experience, did not believe Portsmouth was insane. 'If Lord Portsmouth were under the protection of humane persons, he would be as well able to attend to the management of his own affairs as any man,' he told the Commission. At Hurstbourne, he had even given Portsmouth a dose of advice: 'I said that if he had an honest agent, an honest steward, and an honest banker, he could manage his affairs.' With good people around him, Portsmouth would be set right.

Bankhead might have added an honest wife to his list, for it was Mary Ann's actions that had undone Portsmouth, and perhaps had even set him on a path towards insanity. In Edinburgh, she had played on his ignorance of sex, telling him that an injury meant Alder was incapable of being the father of her child. At the same time, Portsmouth had worked out that Dr Hamilton was something to do with pregnancies and babies. Mary Ann had 'assured' her husband that, 'if she only saw Dr Hamilton, he should have a child'. Hamilton was 'the cleverest fellow in the world', Portsmouth repeated to a friend, for after just one consultation his wife had become pregnant. It was such a ridiculous notion that, on hearing it, the Commission collapsed into laughter.

Yet Mary Ann also planted the seeds of another idea into Portsmouth's head. Perhaps to mock him for his foolishness, she suggested that after the birth they would return to Hurstbourne, and 'he was to have a throne erected, and to receive his company'. As he travelled south from Edinburgh in Grantley's coach, Portsmouth told Coombe of this idea, and said that it was from this throne that he planned to 'receive the congratulations of the county upon the birth of his child'. He was to be the King of Hampshire.

So appealing was this idea to Portsmouth that he stuck with it, even after he had left Mary Ann. He kept turning it over in his head. Over the months it festered, grew and then developed another purpose. From being intended as a seat of celebration, in his mind Portsmouth constructed a throne of judgement. From his throne, Portsmouth 'should pass judgement on those who had offended him,' he said. Top of his list was Alder, who was to be hanged and gibbeted, followed by both John and Newton Hanson, who were to be hanged. Mary Ann, whom he called Mrs A or Mrs Alder, was to be transported for life. The plans became ever more elaborate. Portsmouth told Dr Ludlow that he thought that it would 'augment the pomp' if the county militia and yeomanry were present when he gave out his sentences. He believed that a firm of London upholsterers were constructing his throne, and he gave a builder at Hurstbourne detailed instructions about what should happen following its delivery. He wanted a gallery to be erected in the dining room where the throne was to sit, and an additional door to be fitted, to 'afford free ingress and egress for the persons who were to come'. Portsmouth was expecting the place to be packed, with all eyes on him as he exacted his revenge. He told all his servants that he was to be 'King of the county of Hants', with specially made robes to match the role. He had written to the Lord Chancellor, he said, and was just waiting for him to give permission for the sentence to be carried out. Portsmouth repeated these assertions again and again, perhaps eight to ten times to one Hurstbourne servant, and each time he did so they became even more real in his mind.

Just a week before the Commission began on 10 February 1823, Portsmouth was still talking about his throne. By then, he was utterly confused. He told doctors he was impotent, yet declared that Mary Ann's child was his. There was concern that Portsmouth did not understand the aim of a Lunacy Commission, and that he thought it had been called by the Chancellor as a trial of the Hansons, not him. He remained convinced that Mary Ann wanted to get him back in order to further harm him. His paranoia was all too evident: he believed that he saw his wife pass in front of a window of the house where he was staying, and saw her 'kissing her hand to him'. He had rejected this advance, he said, by turning away, but, unwilling to take any chances, gave orders that Mary Ann should not be admitted entrance to his house, and that his pistols and guns should be made ready.

Frightened by Mary Ann, Portsmouth's impatience to be questioned

before the jury of the Commission stemmed from his belief that he
was aiding in her prosecution. Emboldened by the success of his first
appearance on 18 February, when Portsmouth gave such a credible
performance of his sanity that the newspapers wondered why the
Chancellor had called a Commission, Portsmouth put himself forward
for a second round of questioning on 26 February. It was then that
Portsmouth was asked about the throne.

Coached by his legal team, Portsmouth was prepared for this line
of questioning, and ready to downplay the significance of his claims
to be the King of Hampshire. 'He answered with very considerable
emotion,' his lawyer reminded the jury. 'At the time he talked of that,'
he said, 'he was labouring under great distress, on account of the loss
of a dear and much respected wife.' Without his wife, Mary Ann, he
had said crazy things. Asked if he thought himself the King of
Hampshire, Portsmouth said that by that 'he only meant that his
fortune and situation in the county were considerable'. In Hampshire,
he argued, 'he was a sort of King'. He was like a King; after all, hadn't
everyone been paying him respect for years? Nobody had tried to
publicly deny his position until now. Next, Portsmouth was asked
how he intended to use the throne. 'To receive the congratulations of
his friends on his return' to his home, he answered. Was a coronation
necessary? 'Oh no,' was his reply.

Stressed by his experiences in Edinburgh he may well have been,
but the explanation that he was upset by his split from his wife was
hardly convincing after all the jury had heard about her. Nevertheless,
it remained difficult to designate Portsmouth's ideas as the delusions
of a madman. It was important to understand how delusions were
created, Dr Ainslie explained to the Commission. Portsmouth's delusions were the result 'either from the fermentations of his own mind,
the errors of his own judgement, or the false impressions produced
from the statements of others'. In the case of the throne, 'his Lordship
first stated his intention to sit in a chair; the chair afterwards grew into
a throne, then it extended to a throne from which to administer justice'.
Remembering all the times he had sat watching the trials of wrongdoers
at assizes and the Old Bailey, Portsmouth had developed an idea that
had perhaps been first suggested to him by his wife. He had built upon

it, adding layer upon layer until it made sense to him. That took brains capable of thought and imagination. Wanting to dispense justice upon those who had so badly used him was perfectly rational. Portsmouth was attracted to the idea of a throne because his mind was weak, but it was no evidence of insanity. 'His Lordship's mind may be restored to almost its original state, by kind and judicious treatment,' Ainslie concluded. Then there would be no need for Portsmouth to be King.[2]

'The attention of the fashionable world has lately been a good deal occupied by the singular manner in which Lord Portsmouth was removed from Edinburgh, and the proceedings consequent thereon,' reported newspapers in July 1822. Portsmouth's dramatic departure from Edinburgh marked the moment when his life story went public. Aided by Mary Ann's attempt to re-enter Hurstbourne Park, and fuelled by the letters submitted to the press by both the Hanson and Fellowes sides, public interest mounted as the legal case for a Commission of Lunacy was submitted, and then accepted. By the time the much anticipated Commission began on 10 February 1823, it was clear that this was going to be a bitter struggle between two families over the future of one man.

Nevertheless, the public was ill-prepared for what they heard. Stories of blood-letting, 'black jobs', abduction, adultery, and cruelty to man and beast took the 'fashionable world' by surprise. As the days of the Commission wore on, and more shocking evidence was produced, seats in the Freemasons' Hall became harder to find, and news of the stories told there reached a larger and wider audience. Byron, perturbed that he was not invited to testify, eagerly awaited letters about the case to reach him in his foreign exile.

Stories about Portsmouth were a revelation because he had put up such a convincing performance of sanity for so long. Many witnesses to the Commission, and no doubt others who had known him, were unwilling to relinquish their view that Portsmouth was weak-minded but not insane. Yet Portsmouth was a disturbing figure, however he was categorized. He had crossed the taboos of sex and death with little sense that he was doing anything wrong. But he had also unsettled this society's confidence in its ability to judge itself. For if

Portsmouth was not the person he first appeared, neither were many others who featured in his life story. His devoted mother was perhaps a harsh disciplinarian; the loyal valet, the schemer with blackmail on his mind; the trustworthy family solicitor, a man who would sacrifice his daughter for personal ambition; the innocent young wife, a harlot; the patient younger brother, a man who put his inheritance before his sibling's happiness. When character could not be known, and when the apparently sane as well as the alleged insane could deceive people, who was left to trust?

After seventeen long days of this trial, it was decision time for the jury. Weighing up the evidence meant determining who had known the truth about Lord Portsmouth: the privileged men and women who shared a similar social status to those on the jury, or the servants and labourers who had worked for Portsmouth. Through the words of more than a hundred witnesses, the jury had been taken on a journey into Portsmouth's past. It had taken many twists and turns. From the awkward, stammering boy who never grew up, to the young man who was easily misled. From the aristocrat who hosted and attended many society functions, to the man who could not relinquish perverted obsessions. From the husband who did not appear to grieve upon the death of his first wife, to the cuckold who failed to react to the adultery and cruelty of his second. Portsmouth attracted sympathy and revulsion in equal measure. He was a man who didn't quite fit, either in the society of the sane, or in that of the insane. After all his secret pleasures had been revealed there could be no turning back to his life before the Commission. Nobody would want his company now, even if the jury judged that he had a weak, rather than unsound mind. Nor did he belong in the world of the insane. His had always been a unique mind, which gave him some remarkable capabilities, as well as profound weaknesses. Even his delusions had logic to them. While much of his behaviour, especially recently, seemed to point to an unsound mind, there was a nagging sense that Portsmouth was not entirely to blame for his condition. Had he been driven to this state of mind by others, and was rescue still possible? Lingering doubts also remained about the real motives for this Commission. Whose best interests would an 'unsound mind' verdict serve?

After the counsel for each side of the Commission had completed their final speeches, the Chief Commissioner, Mr Trower, gave his summary. This had been 'no ordinary case,' he said, as its length had indicated. 'A vast number of medical men' had pronounced that Portsmouth was of unsound mind. Bankhead had not seen Portsmouth since October, and even Dr Latham, who had originally thought Portsmouth sane, had changed his mind on his fourth visit. Dr Ainslie was alone in still insisting that Portsmouth was sane. The Commissioner then reminded the jury of the circumstances of Portsmouth's marriage to the present countess. Portsmouth had been a 'patient sufferer', and the Commissioner asked 'whether a man, capable of submitting to all this, could be considered as of sound mind, and competent to the management of his own affairs'. He referred to Portsmouth's faults, 'his ringing of bells – his attention to black jobs – his familiarities with his servants – his adventures with the female peasants on his estate – his tapes – his lancets, and all the other singularities and weaknesses which he had displayed; and from these,' he asked, 'what conclusion could be drawn as to the state of his Lordship's mind?'

The jury retired at six o'clock. They returned an hour and a quarter later. Fitzroy, the foreman, put to them: 'Those that are of opinion that John Charles Earl of Portsmouth is a man of unsound mind, and incapable of managing himself or his affairs, will hold up their hands.' Every member of the jury 'instantly' held up his hand, and the verdict was pronounced to be unanimous. Portsmouth had been returned a lunatic, not a King.[3]

King

The plan

Is it possible for the country or the world ever to forget it; for never perhaps were scenes unfolded so disgraceful and revolting to humanity.

Morning Post, 19 March 1823

NORMALLY, THE HISTORICAL record falls silent after a Commission of Lunacy, especially when the individual who was its subject was found to be a lunatic. The decision made, lawyers' bills paid, the insane person was expected to retreat into the background, and into the safety of legal protection. Not in Portsmouth's case.

While media attention was never the same again, there was another major court case to be fought to end Portsmouth's marriage, and years more of legal wrangling. Portsmouth himself was never a man to go quietly. He still had the capacity to surprise, and to test his rights, even when most had been taken away from him. For Portsmouth had kept hold of his title, and, more importantly for him, his home, Hurstbourne Park.

Portsmouth was not present in the Freemasons' Hall when the jury pronounced their verdict on 28 February, and we do not know who told him the news. How he reacted is not recorded, and whether he understood what had happened is impossible to tell. All he wanted was to go home. He had been in London since January, and he was restless. Just over two weeks after the end of the Commission, a petition was presented to Chancery. Coombe, the man whom Grace had employed to help manage her husband, and who had sat beside Portsmouth when he appeared at the Commission, had been appointed interim committee to care for Portsmouth. The petition declared that, since the end of the Commission, possibly to avoid further publicity, Portsmouth had been 'kept in so great privacy as to have impaired his health'. Now Portsmouth was 'most anxious to return to his seat in the country, where he alone seems to enjoy any comfort'. Chancery responded by granting Coombe permission to take Portsmouth back to Hurstbourne Park, and to take 'the most indulgent care' of him there.

Portsmouth had been declared a lunatic, but his return to Hurstbourne was marked by formal celebration. Newspapers reported how on 2 July Portsmouth attended a service in the church at Hurstbourne, where there was a large crowd in the congregation. 'At the conclusion' it was recorded that:

> the people proceeded in a body, attended by a band in his Lordship's livery, to the Park, where an excellent and substantial dinner had been provided for the inhabitants of the adjoining parishes. About 1,700 men, women and children partook of his Lordship's hospitality, and were highly delighted, continually rending the air with their shouts. Strangers were admitted at one o'clock, and not less than 5,000 were present. But one sentiment pervaded all classes, joy at Lord Portsmouth's return to his mansion.

Nobody was going to turn down the chance for a good party, but, even when sobriety returned, there was a sense of relief in the local community. Portsmouth was back where he belonged, and that was a symbol of order and stability in these unsettling times.

For Portsmouth, life would never be the same again at Hurstbourne Park. On 10 May 1823, Chancery formally appointed Henry Arthur Fellowes, Portsmouth's twenty-three-year-old nephew and his brother Newton's son, his permanent 'committee'. Henry was a young man, and less than half the age of his uncle, but he took his new responsibilities seriously. Portsmouth's property was his future inheritance, and a substantial one at that, yet Henry did far more than was required. He submitted a scheme of care to Chancery, which was approved. For its focus on the individual needs of Portsmouth and its attention to the detail of his daily life, it is a truly remarkable document. Its recovery by chance among a bundle of parish registers nearly a century later, when it was passed to the 6th earl of Portsmouth, was a moment of rare historical luck.

Portsmouth's care plan outlined where and how he was to live, from the moment he awoke, to the time he went to sleep. Although the Commission had ruled that all Portsmouth's property was in the custody of his committee, it was decided that he should continue to live at Hurstbourne Park. This included all 830 acres of gardens, pleasure grounds, and the park. Furthermore, 'in order to gratify the Earl in his fondness for superintending the operations of the farming', the estate called Home Farm, consisting of 571 acres of adjoining arable, meadow, and pasture land, would be his, under the management of a bailiff, 'as it had been before'. Portsmouth's love of horses was also recognized. He was to have a coach and a phaeton, 'to which latter carriage he had always been partial', and cart horses and waggons 'for his own private use and amusement over and above the farming establishment'.

Far from being kept in isolation, the plan declared that Portsmouth should be allowed to invite 'proper persons' to visit him at Hurstbourne, and that, if he objected to any visitors, they would not be permitted entry. His music band was employed to play for him once or twice a week. Henry would hire and dismiss all his uncle's servants, but no servant would remain should Portsmouth take a 'personal prejudice or dislike' to them. A long list of servants would need to be hired, including a butler, valet, coachmen, cook, housemaids, gamekeepers, and even two 'old men of the parish to chop wood'. As the house and the maintenance of its contents had been neglected since Portsmouth had married Mary Ann, it was now 'necessary' that new articles of furniture should be purchased. Portsmouth would be 'supplied with pocket money', just as he had been when he had lived with his mother or Grace.

Although Henry intended to go to Hurstbourne, and remain there until he was satisfied that the arrangements were in place, he also stated 'that it was part of the plan' to appoint 'a Gentleman of undoubted fitness and respectability' to be resident at Hurstbourne after he returned to London. This gentleman was to 'watch the state of his Lordship's mind', and 'act as a companion, guide and protector'. A book should be kept by this individual, which would be a sort of journal or diary 'of all occurrences in any way affecting or connected with the situation or comfort of Lord Portsmouth or the conduct of any part of his establishment, of his pursuits and employments and of all persons coming to and going from the house'.

The best person to fulfil this kind of role would be a clergyman, Henry thought. A member of the clergy would 'unite the characters of chaplain and companion'. After all, there was a 'beautiful chapel' at Hurstbourne, where morning and evening prayers had been said when Portsmouth's mother had been alive. 'It was a well-known fact that such system was not only very pleasing to his Lordship but had a remarkable effect in producing regularity and an even state of mind.' Attending prayers would take up a portion of the day, and have the practical benefit of bringing dinner and drinking wine to an end before evening prayers began. Both Henry and Portsmouth would have to be satisfied that they had found the right person before the position became a permanent one: the clergyman would spend some time at Hurstbourne to make sure that they knew what the job entailed, and that they were 'agreeable' to Portsmouth.

It was vital, Henry explained in his plan, that this appointment 'would not impose on his Lordship's mind the least suspicion of his being placed there in the character of a keeper or as a person exercising any watch or control'. On the contrary, it was important that Portsmouth felt 'proud of having a chaplain forming part of his establishment', so that his presence would 'tend to support his feelings of personal rank and consequence rather than in any degree to lower them'. In sum, Henry told the Chancellor, 'every possible respect and attention by every member of the household shd be paid to his Lordship'. Above all, 'his unfortunate situation' should be 'concealed from him by every means which could be devised'.

Henry's plan for his uncle was a blueprint of benevolent care. It allowed for Portsmouth to be looked after at home, and by people he liked. Within the vast expanse of his Hurstbourne estate, he could indulge in the more respectable and socially acceptable of his pastimes. He could ride his phaeton, wander the fields, and talk to his farm workers. His life inside his house would be regulated and ordered, with an eye to keeping his mind on a calm and even track. After all the humiliation and indignity that he had endured, for the first time in years, Portsmouth was given the prospect of respect and under-standing. Portsmouth had been declared a lunatic, but Henry had no intention of rubbing his nose in it. Portsmouth needed special care, but he did not need to be constantly reminded of his position. It was a care plan that was positive and optimistic: it offered hope. For it devised humane treatment that might have restored Portsmouth to the man he was.[1]

Plans, as Henry was soon to realize, were one thing on paper, another in reality. He had drawn up the schedule of care for his uncle with the knowledge that the Chancellor wished for Portsmouth to be treated well, and with the hope that he would be appointed Portsmouth's committee. His intentions may have been honourable, but he barely knew his uncle. After only a few weeks of living with Portsmouth at Hurstbourne, Henry began to realize the shortcomings of his plan. 'It is impossible for anyone to take more pains to please than Mr Henry Fellowes does,' Henry Karslake, the Fellowes' solicitor, reported back to Newton, 'but it is kindness thrown away or at all events not productive of the result intended by him.' Henry was now 'conscious', Karslake believed, of the 'absolute insanity' of Portsmouth. As a result, there was a necessity for 'some proper restraint' upon Portsmouth. 'Respectful and indulgent treatment' was not enough.

Karslake had already made enquiries about who might supply that 'restraint'. Back in London, Karslake had visited Dr Thomas Warburton. Warburton made his name as one of the physicians consulted over the treatment of George III, but had secured a reputation for cruelty and greed because of abuses committed in the private madhouse he owned in Hoxton. He did not come cheap: reportedly charging £1,500 a year from 1815 to accommodate the Duke of Atholl's son. Thomas' much kinder son, John, who carried on the madhouse business, would look after Portsmouth's cousin Catherine Gordon in the 1830s, so the Warburtons were well known to the Portsmouth family. Thomas had declared Portsmouth 'so unsound as to be quite incurable' at the Commission, but the proof he offered of his diagnosis was 'of a nature that no one can comprehend', complained one critic. Indeed, it was claimed that Warburton had made use of 'the same words he did upon Lord Portsmouth's trial fifty times over, and applied them to as many different cases'.

Warburton 'smiled at the notion of attempting to manage Ld P. without restraint,' Karslake reported, and suggested that, if he could be procured, Mr Penlington would be a good keeper for Portsmouth. Penlington had attended George III for twelve years, Warburton said, and the Chancellor would be pleased at his appointment for Portsmouth. What Warburton neglected to mention was that Penlington was also his nephew. One former incumbent of the Hoxton madhouse described Penlington as 'obscure, illiterate, and vulgar'; a previous owner of a chandler's shop whose only qualification to look after the insane was his ability to fit straitcoats. Perhaps unaware of these facts, Karslake thought that Penlington, assisted by local Hampshire surgeon Dr Williams, and the current curate at Hurstbourne, might work together to achieve 'some well regulated and well advised restraint'.[2]

Warburton's alternative plan for Portsmouth amounted to control rather than measured freedom, deprivation rather than indulgence, and a draconian regime administered by strangers. It was the life experienced by many of those condemned to private madhouses in the eighteenth and early nineteenth century before their horrors were exposed and official inspection and regulation began. Portsmouth escaped this treatment, and there is no record that Penlington was ever brought to Hurstbourne. But this was not because Henry's plan was favoured over Warburton's. Although Dr Williams was hired to administer to Portsmouth's physical health, and the local cleric became resident at Hurstbourne Park, the new clergyman-companion whom Henry had envisioned providing the mental stability for Portsmouth was never recruited. This was because the stumbling block to achieving any future care plan for Portsmouth was money.

The costs for Portsmouth's Commission of Lunacy were unprecedented. It was estimated at the time that the proceedings cost two
guineas a minute. The Commissioners alone were said to have received
over one thousand pounds in fees, and expenses mounted as each
day passed. The use of the Freemasons' Hall was reported to be twenty
guineas a day; sixty people were provided with dinner each night,
and there were the travelling expenses and maintenance of five or six
hundred witnesses to be met. It had cost anywhere between four and
seven hundred pounds a day to hold the Commission, amounting to
a final sum of at least twenty thousand. Family accounts put the cost
closer to thirty thousand pounds.[3]

Even for a wealthy family like the Portsmouths, this was a huge
bill to pay, and arguments soon broke out about how it would be
settled. A key problem lay with the verdict of the Commission. The
jury had been asked when Portsmouth's mind had become unsound,
and they had been given the choice of three dates: from 1799 when
Portsmouth's estate was handed over to trustees; from 1808 (this date
probably related to the arrival of Coombe); or from 1814, the year
when Portsmouth married Mary Ann. The jury selected the date in
the middle, stating that Portsmouth had been insane from 1 January
1809. This meant that the deed signed in 1799 remained legally valid,
and the four trustees in charge of Portsmouth's estate, Newton
Fellowes, John Hanson, Lord Grantley, and William Draper Best,
continued to share responsibility for its maintenance.

Incredibly, after all that had happened, Newton Fellowes and John
Hanson were forced to meet regularly as fellow trustees. Unsurprisingly,
Newton tried to discharge Hanson as a trustee, and to bring the deed
to an end. But at both he failed. Meeting at Hanson's offices in Chancery
Lane was a painful experience, and it is easy to imagine the hostile
atmosphere in which decisions were made concerning Portsmouth's
estate. Minutes from their meetings survive as late as July 1836, and
it is clear that Hanson did all he could to frustrate Newton's plans,
from refusing to agree to a change of bankers for the estate, to dis-
agreeing over such petty matters as how the cost of an audit of
paintings at Hurstbourne Park should be met. More seriously, Hanson
would not produce the accounts of the trustees or sign any draft that

settled the legal costs relating to the Commission. This left Newton having to meet some of the expenses out of his own income, and facing mounting discontent from lawyers whose bills were not paid.

John Hanson was not the only trustee who presented difficulties for Newton, however. William, 2nd Lord Grantley, had sent his nephew and heir, Fletcher Norton, to rescue Portsmouth from Edinburgh, and had welcomed Portsmouth to Wonersh on his return south. He had died on 12 November 1822, before the Lunacy Commission had met. Its ruling that Portsmouth had become insane from 1809 was a bitter blow to the Norton family because it meant that he was deemed to have been sane when he married Grace in 1799. Her promised marriage portion of twelve thousand pounds had still not been paid. In the face of the cost of the Commission, this looked like a pot of gold to Newton Fellowes. But Fletcher, now 3rd Lord Grantley, was not about to settle the debts of his ancestors. The man who boasted of having fought at Waterloo, but whose military career had in fact come to an abrupt end after he insulted the wife of a fellow officer, proved to be just as troublesome and obstructive as John Hanson when it came to being a trustee. 'There will never be any peace whilst Lord Grantley remains a Trustee,' warned Karslake in November 1823, but so long as the 1799 deed remained in place so did Grantley. Even when Grantley became involved in the messy and very public divorce proceedings of his brother and sister-in-law George and Caroline Norton, he did not give up on his refusal to pay the twelve thousand pounds, fiercely resisting a Chancery suit brought by Henry Fellowes in 1833–4 to try to recover it.[4]

The self-interest that had once bound Portsmouth's trustees together was now tearing them apart. Portsmouth's Commission had not brought about a resolution of family problems, but had unleashed a torrent of new ones. The most devastating impact of the Commission's decision was felt where it was least expected, however. For its verdict pitched Newton's interests against those of his son, Henry.

In August 1823, having agreed Henry's plan for Portsmouth, the Chancellor ruled that six thousand pounds should be paid to Henry per year for the maintenance of Portsmouth at Hurstbourne Park. This annual payment rose to seven thousand pounds from 1829. The problem was that this sum was to be raised from Portsmouth's estate, and that meant securing the agreement of Newton Fellowes and the other trustees. Already feeling hard pressed to settle legal costs, which increased once proceedings to end Portsmouth's marriage to Mary Ann began, the trustees rarely paid the full amount to Henry. Henry, determined to carry out his plan for his uncle, kept up his scheme, but was left to pay for it out of his own pocket, leaving him owed ten thousand pounds by 1841. In effect, Newton Fellowes wanted to preserve the estate, add to its value, and reduce costs, while Henry as Portsmouth's committee wanted to spend it.

Having thought that he would be able to settle matters at Hurstbourne quickly, and delegate the day-to-day care of his uncle to others, Henry discovered that he was required to make Hurstbourne his permanent home. A young man in his twenties when Portsmouth was declared a lunatic, his life stalled. He never married, but his father had remarried in June 1820 within fifteen months of the death of his mother. Newton's new wife was Catherine, daughter of the earl of Fortescue, and she went on to bear four children, including a son, Isaac Newton, born on 11 January 1825. Catherine was important in encouraging Newton to demolish the house at Eggesford in 1832, and to build another on a new position. There is nothing to suggest that Henry and his stepmother did not get on. But his visits to Eggesford were short ones while his responsibilities remained at Hurstbourne. Newton had enough cash to build a new home, but kept his son in a constant state of worry about the funding of Portsmouth's care. While Newton had a new life with Catherine, away in Devon he kept a distance from all the problems at Hurstbourne, only occasionally visiting London for business meetings. By contrast, Henry was face-to-face with the everyday burden of care. All his youthful energy, indeed his future, was sapped away by living with Portsmouth.

Over the years, Henry and his father were increasingly at odds. In February 1827, Karslake wrote to Newton, quoting a letter he had received from Henry. Henry foresaw dire consequences for Portsmouth's welfare if Newton pushed ahead with attempts to reduce the amount paid for his maintenance. 'The whole system here must be altered,' Henry warned, his uncle's 'establishment must be reduced, his amusements curtailed, and all society abandoned'. As a result, Henry would 'certainly oppose' Newton's efforts to cut costs, 'as being injurious to Lord Portsmouth's state of mind by abridging him of his present comforts'.

Both father and son had originally been Karslake's clients, but, since this 'difference of opinion appeared between you, and the Committee', Karslake found himself not knowing whose interests to represent. With prophetic insight, he wrote in 1827 to Newton:

> I confess it does appear to me very extraordinary that two gentlemen circumstanced as you and the committee are cannot come to an understanding of what is fit and proper to be done rather than appear in the very injurious character both to your own interest and that of Ld Portsmouth ~~of appearing~~ in Court and before the public, as opposed to each other.

But opposed they remained, and, some fourteen years later, the exasperated Henry, complaining that he had 'devoted the best portion of his life to the service of Lord Portsmouth and his family', brought Chancery proceedings against his father and the other trustees to try to force them to pay for the maintenance they owed. Henry presented to Chancery his original plan for Portsmouth in all its idealistic detail, and followed it with a point by point description of how all his hopes had been dashed by his father's refusal to finance it. This was a family who could not agree how to care for their most vulnerable member, and whose quarrels had led to a rift between father and son that was never mended.[5]

Ending Portsmouth's marriage to Mary Ann, and declaring her baby illegitimate, had always been part of Newton's plan for his brother. Indeed, there were many who suggested that the Commission of Lunacy was just the first step in this plan. Sure enough, by the autumn of 1823, Newton was receiving legal advice about this matter from the distinguished lawyer Stephen Lushington, who had been one of Queen Caroline's counsel three years earlier. Lushington advised Newton against seeking a marriage termination on the grounds of adultery, since, if it could be shown that Portsmouth knew of Mary Ann's infidelity, then 'his forbearance would amount to connivance which is a legal bar to the suits'. It would be better if an annulment of the marriage was sought. Yet the finding of the Lunacy Commission was not sufficient to produce a nullity of marriage. It had to be proved that Portsmouth was insane on the day of his marriage, and thus was unable to give his legal consent. Insanity on his wedding day, as Lushington later explained to the court, meant that the subsequent relationship was nothing but a 'show or effigy of a marriage', which should be declared null and void, and Mary Ann's baby a bastard.

On 9 November 1825, annulment proceedings began in London consistory court. The case was brought by Henry on behalf of his uncle. The Chancellor had ruled in August 1824 that Henry could bring this case; as a lunatic, Portsmouth himself had no say in the future of his marriage. Henry, like his father, wanted this annulment, but for different reasons. While Portsmouth remained married to Mary Ann, he had to pay £1,500 per year to her and her child, the Chancellor had ruled, and this was an expense that Henry as Portsmouth's committee could well do without.

Procedure in the consistory court, and then the court of Arches, to which the case was transferred by May 1827, was very different from the Lunacy Commission. There was no jury, just a judge. Both husband and wife presented their side of the argument, but as written documents rather than verbal testimony. Neither Portsmouth nor Mary Ann ever had to make a personal appearance in the court. Their written statements, along with those of witnesses were presented to the judge, who then pronounced his sentence. While the newspapers reported the case at its various stages, and printed the opening statements made by Lushington and Dr Jenner, the lawyer who represented Mary Ann, they did not have access to the words of the witnesses that had made accounts of the Commission such compelling reading. Portsmouth and his life story were in the news again, but it was attracting nothing like the same publicity.

If Newton and Henry had hoped that, since Portsmouth had already been proved a lunatic before the Commission, the process of getting his marriage annulled would be straightforward, they were sorely mistaken. Lushington knew they were in for a fight. He had crossed swords with John Hanson once before, since it had been Lushington who had represented Lady Byron when she had sought a private separation from Hanson's client, Lord Byron, back in 1816.

Furthermore, having read the statements made by witnesses during the Commission, Lushington was clear that the annulment was never going to be a done deal. 'I admit,' Lushington privately told Karslake, that 'the evidence in favour of Lord Portsmouth's soundness of mind' is 'very strong, especially the testimony of Dr Ainslie and Mr Justice Burrough'. They might be telling the truth, Lushington thought, but that did not 'disprove the existence of the insane acts and declarations proved by the other witnesses'. It was essential to demonstrate that Portsmouth was a lunatic on the day of his wedding, and the death of Byron on 19 April 1824 certainly helped their case. As Karslake excitedly told Newton, without Byron, not only would they avoid the expense and delay of a legal delegation being sent to examine Byron in Greece, but also the Hanson case 'much relied' upon Byron 'as establishing the fact of Lord Portsmouth's anxiety to be married to Miss Hanson and of the sufficiency of his mind at that time to under-stand the nature of such a contract'.

Nevertheless, Newton and Henry still faced awkward questions about why they had waited so long to raise questions about the legality of Portsmouth's marriage, if they had thought him insane on 7 March 1814. Lushington did not try to answer on the Fellowes' part, but drew attention to the lack of evidence about the state of Portsmouth's mind on his wedding day. He reminded the court that both Byron and the clergyman who officiated were now dead, and hence that it was suspicious that Mr Buckworth, the young man who had acted as a witness at the church, and was still living, was not called to testify at the annulment case. In addition, 'the non-examination of the Hanson family spoke volumes,' he argued; 'why did not Mr Hanson himself – why did not his two sons and his other daughter come forward, if the transaction was a fair one, and they had nothing to fear from cross-examination?'

Without sufficient evidence for the wedding day, both sides instead relied upon accounts of Portsmouth's behaviour both before and after his marriage to Mary Ann. The whole process of describing the history of Portsmouth's mental condition that had been recounted at the Commission was gone through again before the court of Arches. More than a hundred witnesses were called, many of them the same individuals who had testified both in 1814–15 when Newton first called for a Commission, and again in 1823 at the Commission. Their statements were well rehearsed, but new details and stories still emerged, and there were more than a dozen new witnesses who had not testified in any legal proceeding relating to Portsmouth before.

Every aspect of Portsmouth's life was being scrutinized once more because, as Lushington had predicted, despite the Commission's ruling, people were still uncertain about whether Portsmouth was insane. There was evidence both ways. Furthermore, as Godden, the park keeper at Hurstbourne explained, it was unclear whether Portsmouth's strange behaviour 'proceeded from weakness of mind and want of common understanding or from his mind being deranged'. Was Portsmouth an idiot, a lunatic, or neither? After all these years, and following so much legal and medical debate, the difficulty of labelling him remained. He defied all classification.

Taking statements from all these witnesses took time. Witnesses were examined in Hampshire and Edinburgh, as well as where the court sat in London. Whereas the Commission had taken months to organize and weeks to hear Portsmouth's case, the annulment case took years. Beginning in November 1825, the sentence in the court of Arches was not reached until May 1828. While Newton's lawyers reported the progress of the case to him in Devon by letter, there were numerous delays when the parties argued about costs. Ironically, and painfully for Newton and Henry Fellowes, while Portsmouth remained married to Mary Ann, his committee had to pay for her legal costs as well as maintenance. Only if she lost the case would she have to repay the costs. Adding to the difficulties was John Hanson's reluctance to agree to the payment of any costs for the annulment while he was Portsmouth's trustee. Why should he smooth the way for his son-in-law to end his daughter's marriage? For months, the parties were at stalemate, and legal proceedings halted.

Finally, on Saturday, 10 May 1828, all papers relating to the annulment case had been submitted, and the judge, Sir John Nicholl, pronounced his judgment. He had not been convinced of the evidence produced by the Hansons to prove that Portsmouth was sane. He had listened to all the witnesses who had described Portsmouth's conduct in society: 'As to his behaviour at parties, his observations on the weather, on horses, and on farming – his attending at public meetings and county balls – all this was not inconsistent with great imbecility of mind.' The earl, like a child, could be taught to control his behaviour when in public, Nicholl said (hence he could not be an 'idiot' by contemporary definition). 'Lord Portsmouth knew he was peer, and the rights and duties which belonged to that high station,' Nicholl continued, yet he pursued 'the most degrading employments and amusements'. His 'fondness for his servants' society, his carting dung, flogging horses unmercifully', 'his malicious cruelty to man and beast', were what condemned him. Lushington's case that Portsmouth was insane at the point he married Mary Ann, which he had summarized in a speech lasting four hours a few days before, had been a powerful and persuasive one. Nicholl ruled that because Portsmouth had been of 'unsound mind' he was incapable of forming a marriage contract, and hence that his marriage to Mary Ann was null and void. Some fourteen years after his wedding to Mary Ann Hanson, Portsmouth's second marriage was over.[6]

It is hard to believe that Portsmouth felt anything but relief at the news. How he responded to all the negative comment about his life, we do not know. He had hardly been seen in public since the Lunacy Commission. Each summer, he appeared at the county races, but accompanied by his brother or nephew, and kept within his carriage, so that friends could only talk to him through the carriage window. His social life had certainly become more limited and tightly controlled. Quiet dinners with the Reverend Goddard, formerly the headmaster of Winchester College, where Henry had studied, were now the order of the day.

But this retreat into the seclusion of Hurstbourne Park did not mean that Portsmouth was ready to relinquish all control over his life. He remained aware of the legal decisions that were being made about him, and the fiery spirit he inherited from his mother seemed if anything strengthened by the trials he had faced. Portsmouth still had a voice, even if that was now expressed in the letters he wrote, rather than in the courtroom.

On 6 March 1827, Portsmouth wrote to his brother from Hurstbourne. His marriage annulment case should have been reaching its conclusion. But Portsmouth was deeply frustrated. He had not received a response to an earlier letter he had written to Catherine, Newton's wife, about the issue of 'the want of money to pay debts and costs incurred on the business which is at present at a standstill of not having sufficient money to proceed on with it'. All the blame for this delay in the law case was Newton's, Portsmouth forcefully declared: 'You was the Gentleman who first instituted the suit against me and you ought to be at the expense of the money to pay the costs and the debts incurred, as I am not able to pay them.' Newton could expect no brotherly support: 'I hope and trust some steps will be taken' at the next meeting of the court 'to force you to pay them'. If not, 'I am very confident you will be sent to the Fleet prison for contempt of court for a certain time for not paying the costs and also the debts incurred by the opposite party as sure as you are alive that will be the case.' The sum owed, according to Portsmouth, was paltry, a mere sixty-three pounds. Perhaps spurred on by conversations with Henry, who shared Portsmouth's annoyance about the tardiness of funds for their living expenses, Portsmouth was furious with his brother. It was payback time for Newton, Portsmouth decided. Still acting like the King of Hampshire, he judged only a spell in prison would teach his brother a lesson.

Newton owed money and favours to everyone. Doctors, including Monro and Willis, asked for sixty pounds each for appearing at the Commission. Tradesmen who had supplied goods to Hurstbourne Park, and servants who had worked there and whose wages were long overdue, all demanded payment. Most distressing of all, old ally Coombe turned against him. Perhaps realizing how valuable his testimony and support had been, Coombe grew impatient when he was not rewarded for his part in taking Portsmouth from Edinburgh, and taking care of him until the Commission. He began to seek compensation from June 1824, claiming the 'preposterous' sum of three thousand pounds.

Coombe's threats to expose Newton as the sole survivor of the instruction to remove Portsmouth from Edinburgh caused concern. The Chancery case would be eagerly watched by the Hansons, Karslake warned, for any 'disclosures' that 'might throw a doubt or suspicion upon the proceedings in the Lunacy'. Coombe pressed ahead with his case against Newton, being awarded £1,250 for his trouble, and refunded nearly £270 for his expenses caring for Portsmouth. Almost as soon as this case was over, Coombe started looking for a refund of expenses, itemized down to the bills he had paid to wine merchants, for the few months he had spent as Portsmouth's interim committee before Henry's appointment. Even with Coombe's death in September 1829, his case could not be forgotten: his widow continued to pursue Newton in the courts the following year.[7]

While his fellow trustees refused to cooperate, Newton was left to settle many of these demands for money out of his own pocket. He knew that this was a situation that could not continue indefinitely, and from 1827 he and his faithful solicitor, Karslake, looked for ways to raise funds. They had Portsmouth assessed for life insurance. Several companies turned Portsmouth down 'by reason of his unsoundness of mind'. But not all were so prejudiced. In December 1828, the Globe Insurance Company had Portsmouth examined in London by its own physician, Dr Latham, as well as Sir George Tuthill, and Dr Warburton. All were specialists in mental health, and each had testified at Portsmouth's Commission. But this time they were judging life expectancy, and, with Portsmouth about to turn sixty-one years old, they all 'reported favourably of his health'. Subsequent financial negotiations with the Globe led to the sale of an annuity on Portsmouth's life for fifty thousand pounds. For once, Portsmouth's health was good news for his family.

While Portsmouth remained a valuable asset, he was also vulnerable. Just over a month after his marriage had been annulled in May 1828, Newton received a letter offering information about a plot to abduct Portsmouth. Newton took this threat seriously enough to write a reply, with Karslake's advice. Given the recent decision of the courts, it was impossible that Portsmouth could be married again, Newton wrote, so he asked for clarification of the claim that 'he shall not be seen or heard of till he is both a husband and a father'. But who knows what Portsmouth would do if he got in the wrong hands.[8]

Nothing more was heard from the letter writer or the plot, but this was not the end of threatening letters. On 23 February 1831, Ralph Etwall, long-time steward to Portsmouth's estates, received an anonymous letter, which he forwarded to Newton. Postmarked Winchester, the letter claimed that Etwall and Newton had already received several petitions from their tenant farmers asking them to lower rents. Without lower rents, the farmers were unable to pay 'us, as their labourers, our wages'. The letter writers gave Etwall and Newton one month to act, or 'we will be revenged'. 'We don't want to hurt the farmers nor destroy anything of other people's,' the letter explained, but the state of the harvests over the last two to three years had made payment of rent at the current rates impossible. If Etwall and Newton did not respond to this request for a fairer economy, then 'prepare yourselves for the worst':

> we will level all your farms and Lord Portsmouth's to the ground before next harvest – and if we can't be revenged on you living we are determined to have you after you are dead.

The authors did not need to underline their threat to set the alarm bells ringing for its recipients, for their letter was received in the months following the most widespread popular disturbances Hampshire had ever seen. Known as the Swing Riots, protests by agricultural workers had begun in Kent during the summer of 1830, and had then spread to other counties in southern England. Well over a thousand incidents were recorded. Following an appalling harvest in 1829, labourers faced unemployment and underemployment. Turning to the Poor Law for support, they found relief much harder to obtain, as parish authorities struggled to cope with the numbers of claimants, and, most humiliatingly of all, because landowners such as Hampshire's Sir Thomas Baring had taken steps to reduce the value of their allowances.

Fuelled by the politically radical ideas of local man Cobbett, protests in Hampshire were concentrated in the week 18–25 November 1830, and focused in the area just where Hurstbourne Park was situated, between Andover, Winchester, and Basingstoke. The largest crowd, of some eight hundred to one thousand men, gathered on 19 November in the village of Sutton Scotney, less than eight miles south of Hurstbourne Priors. While more numerous than many groups of workers who protested that autumn, they followed the same course of action, breaking the threshing machines that they believed were robbing them of work, and demanding food, drink, and money from the farmers and landowners they confronted. Heading eastwards along the Dever Valley, the protestors reached Stratton Park, Baring's seat. They broke machinery, and then requested, and were given, ten pounds from Baring's steward not to go up to the house, and this they honoured. Protests continued to be orderly, and, although the men were armed with their tools, including axes, hammers, and sticks, there was little violence. The day ended peacefully when Reverend Dr Newbolt, a local magistrate, consented to mediate with the farmers on the workers' behalf, agreeing that the wage increase they desired was 'extremely reasonable'.

But the authorities were left severely shaken by events like these. Landowners like Baring were terrified that they marked the beginnings of a social revolution. 'The motive which has operated upon the minds of my people' (note the 'my'), he wrote, 'has not been distress but a revolutionary spirit.' According to one letter written from Hampshire to the Home Department, the 'contagious violence of the lower orders' was spreading so that:

> They who are at the summit of society appear to be on the top of a volcano composed of the physical strength of the pauper population and plentifully surcharged with the sulphur of discontent.

To remain at the 'summit of society', a Special Commission was held in Winchester in December to make an example of the organizers of the protests. Nearly three hundred men faced trial, of whom 101 were sentenced to death, and 117 transported.

The letter to Etwall had not been signed by 'Captain Swing', but it may as well have been. Etwall told Newton of a number of fires that had been caused recently by incendiaries in nearby parishes, including Longparish. It was well known that Robert Mason, one of the leaders of the Sutton Scotney group, had tried to encourage the men of Hurstbourne Priors to petition the King with their grievances. Etwall and Newton feared that in February 1831 it was their turn to face the mob. This was enough to speed up the retirement of Etwall, who had been in his position since the time of the 2nd earl. Perhaps the rents of tenants were renegotiated after the letter was received, as Etwall had been advising since the disturbances in November, for the threats to destroy property were not carried through that year. Two years later, there were arson attacks. Multiple fires were started in the farm buildings and barns belonging to Apsley Farm on Portsmouth's estate, on 9 October 1833. In 1835, more farm buildings owned by Portsmouth were attacked at Tufton. 'Providentially', the newspapers reported, there was little wind that night, as otherwise all the year's harvest might have been destroyed, and the village of Hurstbourne Priors seriously threatened.

Swing menaced, but never struck at Hurstbourne Park. If there was an Achilles heel in the defences of Hampshire's landowners, it was surely at the home of its resident lunatic, Lord Portsmouth. But the 'Hampshire bumpkins', as *The Times* so rudely dismissed the protestors, had a strong sense of morality and decency. It would not do to attack the person or the estates of a lunatic, at least not overtly. The working people of Hampshire were out to achieve a fair society, not a new social hierarchy. The volcano never erupted.[9]

When Sir Henry Halford, President of the Royal College of Physicians, had examined Portsmouth in the month before the Commission, he concluded that he had an unsound mind, and that he had probably been born with 'a puny sickly intellect'. He thought that Portsmouth did not understand what the Commission was about, and had witnessed Coombe and others trying to explain its purpose. Trying to reassure Portsmouth, who remained 'fearful of something which he does not fully understand', Halford told him that 'whatever might be the issue of these proceedings, he would be much more happy and secure'.[10]

Happiness and a feeling of security would have been welcome experiences for Portsmouth after his marriage to Mary Ann. His nephew certainly had these goals in mind when he devised his scheme of care. But all did not go according to plan. Money was in large part to blame, and disputes over Portsmouth's care took their toll upon Newton's relationship with his oldest son. Try as he might, Henry could not schedule friendships for his uncle. Nobody of his own social class wanted to spend time with Portsmouth now, except as a favour to his family. A new set of servants and workers had to be recruited at Hurstbourne because nearly all the previous staff had jeopardized their positions by testifying one way or other in the courts. Once the annulment case began, Portsmouth's past was raked up again, as witness after witness was encouraged to trawl through aspects of his behaviour that he might have once thought were secret, but that now he was told were improper, or even morally reprehensible. Portsmouth did not know the new workers at Hurstbourne, and he was unlikely to trust them. Everyone from his life before the Commission had a story to tell or a financial claim to make.

So, while Portsmouth was safe behind the walls of Hurstbourne Park, and his mental condition may even have helped to protect him from the tumultuous world of Swing outside, he was increasingly isolated. What no plan had anticipated was that, when the verdict was announced at the Commission in February 1823, Portsmouth still had another thirty years to live. Despite predictions at the time, as the years slipped by, the world did forget Portsmouth's trial. But while he was alive and well, Portsmouth was determined to be a man his family could not forget. Loneliness was not an experience that Portsmouth had encountered before and, with so much time on his hands, that would breed trouble.

Family letters

ON 2 FEBRUARY 1851, Portsmouth sat down at his desk to write a letter. Writing was a skill that had always come easily to him, and, now that he was spending much of his time within his mansion at Hurstbourne, sending a letter was a way to communicate with those outside the park gates. What his letters lacked in punctuation (it seems that no teacher had taught him the importance of a comma or full stop), they more than made up for in their confident and clear hand.

For a man like Portsmouth, letter writing was an ideal form of communication. He could choose whom he addressed, and when it suited him. While he might have expected a reply, the decision to initiate or end a correspondence rested with him. He could take his time composing a letter and that gave him more control. Writing from a distance presented him with none of the problems of social awkwardness that meeting someone in person might present. And now that he had been declared a lunatic he could say what he liked: how could he cause offence?

The recipient of this letter was Catherine Fellowes, the second wife of his brother, Newton. Portsmouth seems to have developed a fondness for Catherine, and, while his relationship with Newton would always now be conducted in the shadow of the Lunacy Commission, she carried none of that family baggage. Catherine was remembered by others as the 'deaf and dumb lady from Castle Hill', but, as one descendant recorded, she was 'quite deaf but she was by no means dumb'. For she had been taught by a Frenchman to 'speak and to read the motions of the throat and lips'. She had a 'curious, deep voice', and her children 'spoke to her on their fingers, which her husband never learnt to do'. Her deafness 'cut her off very much' from her family's lives and in her silent world she absorbed herself in needle-work, gardening, and decorating the new house at Eggesford.

Perhaps Portsmouth felt an affinity for this woman whose disability distanced her from society and confined her to the home. He initially viewed letters to her as a way to prompt his brother to action, as in 1827 when he wrote to her to request that she press on Newton the importance of paying the bills owed for his marriage annulment case. But Portsmouth's subsequent letters showed more of a personal interest in her concerns. He wrote condolence letters to Catherine when her sister-in-law and brother-in-law died. Visits by Catherine and Newton to Hurstbourne strengthened their relationship. Theirs was not a regular correspondence (only seven letters written by Portsmouth to Catherine survive, and none from her), but it was reciprocated. The tone of Portsmouth's letters was relaxed, and there was none of the anger found in letters to his brother. Writing in August 1834, for example, Portsmouth explained to Catherine that he had been prompted to send a letter after he had heard from his sister, Henrietta Dorothea, that Newton was gravely ill. Enquiring about Newton's condition, Portsmouth told Catherine to 'keep up your spirits as much as possible'. He then quickly moved on to describe how his summer had been 'quite pleasant', and how many of the younger members of the Fellowes family were currently at Weymouth 'for the benefit of the sea air', while he remained at Hurstbourne with 'old Harry Fellowes'. He finished the letter with a flourish of affection:

I shall be very happy to hear from you as it will give me pleasure to hear from one who loves me as yourself has always professed to do so when you used to be here which I shall never forget it.

I am my Dear Catherine
     yours et al
          Portsmouth
     With our best Love and regards to Newton and your Family wishing him better health

Newton made a full recovery, but what Catherine thought of this letter, or any of the others she received from her brother-in-law we do not know. Portsmouth seized upon her kindness to him and remembered it, but whether she wanted to be reminded of this when her husband was ill seems unlikely. Her priority at this worrying time was Newton, not his emotionally needy older brother.

One thing we can be sure of is that Portsmouth's letters were never regarded by their family recipients as private correspondence. Just like the letters written by his insane aunt and cousins in former times, Portsmouth's letters were passed around the family breakfast table, perhaps even read out aloud and scrutinized for evidence of his mental state. They were carefully kept, in a way that Catherine's letters were not, because they were the words of a man who had been declared insane. Letters could contain the early warning signs of trouble ahead. Any letter Portsmouth wrote to Catherine was passed straight over to Newton.

The letter Portsmouth wrote to Catherine on 2 February 1851 opened with such an explosive blast of news that it must have rocked the Fellowes household to its very core:

> My Dearest Catherine
> I beg leave to inform you of our intention of being married to Miss C. Norton a niece of mine a sister of Lord Grantley she is coming down here tomorrow morning for the occasion...

Portsmouth was eighty-three years old. 'Miss C. Norton' was probably Caroline Elizabeth, at fifty-three years old, the unmarried sister of Fletcher, 3rd Lord Grantley, and the niece of Portsmouth's first wife, Grace. Having announced their marriage, in the same breathless sentence Portsmouth continued:

> ...and on Tuesday next there will be a grand review to take place by all the regiments given to me by the Duke of Wellington which will be a grand thing to take place here in this park on Tuesday next of the Surrey Militia regiment of both horse and foot soldiers under command of me and the rest of the officers in Hants and Surrey...

which will be a grand sight here of my own given to me by Lord Grantley…and Hampshire and Surrey yeomanry regiments…and from all parts of the country of Guildford and Lymington and Andover yeomanry…if the weather should be fine it will be a grand sight in memory of this happy day which I hope will take place tomorrow to this very nice and affectionate young Lady Miss Norton a very nice young Lady she is certainly and very agreeable one I must say she is

Portsmouth was brimming with excitement. This was the most glorious fantasy. The King of Hampshire was to be restored to his rightful place, commanding his troops who would parade over the land that he ruled. It was a scene that he had been dreaming about ever since he told doctors that he wanted the county militia to be present when he tried the Hansons and Alder some thirty years earlier. The Duke of Wellington, who had been hunting in Hurstbourne Park at least once in previous years, and was lord lieutenant of the county, was imagined to have bestowed this honour upon Portsmouth. The occasion was to be grand (repeated twice) because Portsmouth was to be important once more. The forgotten Lord Portsmouth would be remembered. Everyone would take note.

Characteristically, his letter devoted more attention to the details of the celebration that would follow his wedding than to his bride-to-be. Miss Norton might have appeared youthful to the octogenarian Portsmouth but what was more important to him was that she was 'nice', 'agreeable', and 'affectionate'. Perhaps she reminded him of Grace, who had those qualities in bucket-loads. Probably unaware of Portsmouth's intentions, Miss Norton is unlikely to have found the prospect of marriage to Portsmouth attractive, even if she was a spinster of similar age to her aunt when she had married the earl.

In Portsmouth's mind, the marriage was a done deal: poor weather might hamper the military display, but the wedding was going ahead the very next day. His two previous marriages had been arranged for him. Now he was going to make an independent decision about his life, and enjoy doing so. Nearly thirty years after the Commission of Lunacy, Portsmouth was testing his family's resolve. Having been declared a lunatic, Portsmouth could not marry. But what was a legal technicality to a man like Portsmouth? If he could get hold of a willing bride and an ignorant clergyman, then getting married was just the kind of impulsive act of which he was capable. History should have taught Newton that.

But Newton was growing old himself. In February 1851, he was seventy-eight and he had suffered from painful attacks of gout for at least his early forties. Years of travelling to and from Devon to London and Hurstbourne had begun to take their toll. Most significantly, the person whom he had made responsible for taking care of Portsmouth, his oldest son and heir, Henry Arthur, had died in London on 15 February 1847.

Newspapers reported that Henry's death came 'after a long and lingering illness'. His body was transported to be buried at Eggesford. Having remained a bachelor, he had spent his adult life caring for Portsmouth at Hurstbourne. But his father could not bring himself to acknowledge his son's greatest achievement. A handwritten obituary, possibly composed by Newton and read at his funeral, gave an account of Henry's life. It began in standard enough form, describing his education at Eton and Trinity College, Cambridge, and travel abroad. He had been MP for the 'family borough of Andover'. But this role had been cut short:

> Impaired health however and a preference for the…studies of literature and an attachment to the fine arts induced him to withdraw from public life and for many years he has made his residence at Eggesford which he varied by occasional tours on the continent.

For 'occasional tours on the continent' read 'long stretches of time at Hurstbourne'. Disagreements with Henry over funding Portsmouth's care, coupled with a desire that at least in Devon society reminders that this family had connections with a publicly declared lunatic should be minimized, meant that Henry's years of service to his family had no mention. Henry might have inherited a delicate constitution from his sickly mother, but his obituary represented him as a man without distinction. The cover-up about Portsmouth had begun, and Henry was its first victim.

After Henry's death, other arrangements for Portsmouth must have been made, and a new 'committee' appointed by Chancery, although no name has been recorded. It is clear that other members of the Fellowes family visited and stayed at Hurstbourne. But their stays were fleeting, and there was no individual who took overall control. That was Newton's mistake.

So, when Portsmouth's letter to Catherine arrived at the start of February 1851, Newton had to act fast. The Fellowes family scrambled to respond. Since it was received after the date when the wedding was to have taken place (a fact that Portsmouth must have known), Newton first had to establish that there had been no nuptials. Much to their relief, this fact was proved. In the meantime, Isaac Newton, Newton's oldest son by Catherine, and his heir since the death of Henry, was dispatched to Hurstbourne.

Isaac was still there at the end of March. Portsmouth was deluded: he remained convinced that his wedding was going ahead. He wrote a long and rambling letter to Catherine, beginning with the statement that 'I am very much obliged to you for allowing your Son to come up from Eggesford on my wedding which I hope will be soon'. He told Catherine that for the present he was confined to bed with a cold, which had been brought on by the bad weather. His head was 'aching very bad' and he worried about the effect of the weather on the sowing of crops. Many phrases, not just words, were repeated, and his prose became disjointed and difficult to follow. He seemed out of sorts, in both mind and body.

He might have been sent as a rescue party to sort things out, but Isaac had no intention of following in his stepbrother's footsteps and remaining at Hurstbourne indefinitely. Yet at some point that year he seriously offended Portsmouth in a way that the sensitive Henry never did. At the start of November, Portsmouth wrote a letter direct to Newton:

Dear Brother
    I shall never part with this house and premises as long as I live [nor?] for not letting your son Newton come to it at all ever again and I cannot spare it at all as long as I live I will never let your son

have it at all to come to it nor will I be at the expense of the repairs
he has occasioned to defray the expenses at his own expense I will
not send him any money at all to do it it was done unknown to me
quite so

Isaac had crossed a line that never should have been breached with
Portsmouth. Portsmouth was Hurstbourne Park. He was King there.
To threaten his future there was tantamount to treason. To undertake
improvements and then not pay for them was to question the legitimacy of his rule. Hurstbourne Park was all that there was left for
Portsmouth. Everything else had been taken away. The young man
who had been sent to prevent his marriage now seemed to be effecting
a coup, a take-over well before his time. And Isaac had done this
while he had been a guest at Hurstbourne, right under Portsmouth's
nose. But this was a gross misjudgement, which Portsmouth saw as
a direct challenge to his power and legitimacy. Portsmouth still had
his title, and he would be Lord of Hurstbourne for 'as long as I live'.

Fuming, Portsmouth repeated his refusal to pay for the repairs that
he had not ordered, and then turned the page. At that moment, he
seems to have calmed down, and began writing about something quite
different. He told Newton that he had heard from their sister, Henrietta
Dorothea, and that she sent word that one of their cousins was to be
married. This 'I hope will be a good match for her,' Portsmouth wrote.
Writing about the marriage helped to defuse Portsmouth's anger, but
there was still a message about how Portsmouth saw himself. 'I shall
have no objection to it at all,' he wrote. Portsmouth believed he was
still head of the family. He thought Henrietta Dorothea was writing
to seek his permission for the match, not to inform him of it. Even
if he was calmer when he was writing this, Portsmouth intended it
as a reminder to Newton that his older brother was in charge.
Portsmouth might need protection. He had to be prevented from
enacting the wildest of his fantasies, but this did not render him a
weak character, far from it. Portsmouth showed his strength when he
felt most vulnerable, and that strength rested on defending his home:
'I shall never part with this house and premises as long as I live.'

Portsmouth remained at Hurstbourne, and it seems unlikely that while his uncle was alive Isaac ever dared to cross its threshold again. Three more letters were written by Portsmouth to Eggesford, but each was addressed to Catherine, not Newton. The ties between the brothers were now permanently severed, with Portsmouth's angry letter the last time he communicated directly with Newton. Portsmouth remembered Newton's birthday, writing to Catherine on 27 June 1852:

> I must most sincerely congratulate Newton on his Birthday which took place on yesterday in his 80 year of his age. I hope he will continue and enjoy the day for many years to come and yourself.

But he still had the pleasure of reaching this age first. Portsmouth thanked Catherine for her long letter, and described in his remaining letters the weather and how it was affecting the productivity of his farm. This was his world now, and Catherine was the only one whom he privileged with an insight into it.[1]

More than thirty years after the marriage between Portsmouth and Mary Ann had been annulled, the last thing anyone in the Eggesford household expected was a letter from his former wife. By 1859, the family thought they had put the nightmare of the Hansons well behind them. Even if the name of Hanson was never uttered aloud again, there was probably some knowledge about what happened to Mary Ann and her father once Sir John Nicholl had declared his sentence. The Hansons had got their just deserts.

John Hanson's career was in trouble even before his daughter's marriage ended. He was forever falling out with his professional colleagues; two fellow lawyers told the court of Arches that they had ceased contact with Hanson following personal disputes. At some point, he lost his job as solicitor to the Board of Stamps, and there were immediately rumours that he had been dismissed for neglect of duty. Worse followed when government officials tracked a paper trail of missing money back to Hanson. In 1835, the Treasury took Hanson to court to recover £674, with a further sum of £710 judged to be in default.

Most damaging of all was the loss of support from Hanson's most famous client, Lord Byron. This had nothing to do with his daughter's marriage: Byron was never so judgemental (nor hypocritical). For so long the Hanson family had been important to Byron. In April 1816, as he waited in Dover for the ship that took him from England's shores forever, it was to John Hanson that Byron wrote to say a final goodbye. 'I wish you for yourself and family every possible good – and beg remembrances to all – particularly Lady P and Charles.' If the Hansons were his old family, Byron also remembered his new one, adding an emotional 'P.S. Send me some news of my <u>child</u> – every now and then.'

But Byron became disillusioned by Hanson. He had already experienced the effects of Hanson's family concerns when his marriage arrangements to Annabella Milbanke had been put on hold while Hanson fought the first call for a Lunacy Commission. Once abroad, his patience wore thin as Hanson continued to charge huge fees (his bill for selling Byron's Newstead estate came to a staggering twelve thousand pounds), and still took an age to get anything done. Byron lost all respect for Hanson: he started to refer to him as 'Spooney', a slang term for a 'foolish, pretending fellow'. He thought it laughable when he heard that Hanson was trying to become a peer, and he increasingly turned to another solicitor, Douglas Kinnaird, to get his business done. Byron's frustration was palpable. Writing to Kinnaird from Venice in July 1818, Byron wrote that 'Spooney' was:

> a damned tortoise in all his proceeds – I should suspect foul play – in this delay of the man and papers...for God his sake – row the man of law – spur him – kick him on the Crickle, – do something – anything – you are my power of Attorney – and I thereby empower you to use it and abuse Hanson – till the fellow says or does something as a gentleman should do.

Two days later, in another letter to Kinnaird, Hanson was 'that knave or blockhead'. Even a visit to Byron in person by John and Newton Hanson, who travelled to Venice in November of that year, did nothing to salvage the relationship. Writing to his former wife in February 1820 about their legal affairs, he pleaded, 'do let us concur for once', but 'above all – expediate that eternal dawdle Hanson – who has sent me in such a bill!' Byron was done with John Hanson.

When Byron died in Greece on 19 April 1824, his body was brought back to England. After lying in state for two days, Byron's hearse was accompanied by a cortège of forty-seven carriages back to the family vault near Newstead. John Hanson proudly sat in a mourning coach near the front, and, along with Byron's long-time friend Hobhouse, became an executor of Byron's will. For the rest of his life, Hanson was involved with negotiations about the future of Byron's estate. A lengthy and often fraught correspondence was conducted between Hanson and the publisher John Murray.

There seems little doubt that John Hanson dined off his connections with Byron, and relished the attention this gave him. But anyone who knew him would not employ him professionally, and in a business world that relied on personal recommendations this spelled ruin. Hanson had used up all the goodwill of his legal colleagues fighting his daughter's case, and now that she had lost he faced their bills. He stubbornly refused to give the editor Thomas Moore access to Byron's personal papers, arguing that they contained details of people still living, but probably because he had an eye for the profits that could be made if he sold them. Hanson intended to publish a book entitled 'Lord Byron in his Minority', but never got round to it. His son, Newton, wrote a narrative about Byron's life, and joining with his brother Charles entered into negotiations with Murray about its publication. To tempt him, Newton claimed that the Hanson family had a portrait of Byron's mother, and many original documents and personal items belonging to Byron. Murray either didn't believe Newton or refused to offer the price that was being demanded, for Newton's account remained in manuscript form.

The fact was that John Hanson was a 'has been'. Neither he nor his sons could make a living from stories of their past. There could be no turning back. In a bitter twist of fate, their former home in Earl's Court, where Byron had been brought as a boy, and Portsmouth had first met Byron, was turned into a private lunatic asylum. Hanson was reduced to writing a series of letters to Hobhouse asking for money. 'I have no hesitation in telling you that from many unforeseen family causes my circumstances are very different to what they were and I have a huge family upon me,' he wrote on 16 November 1835. Hobhouse probably shared with others the view that only Hanson could have not foreseen the disaster he was inviting when he tried to defraud a wealthy family like the Portsmouths. By February 1838, Hanson was asking Hobhouse for a loan of four thousand pounds, saying he was 'rigorously pressed' and 'threatened with destruction'. He wrote again in March 1840 pleading for money to allow him 'to sustain my position in that station of life I have maintained for upwards of fifty years'. But Hobhouse wasn't listening.

Hanson, the man who had worn a pompous hat to his son's school speech day, courted wealthy clients, fancied himself as a country squire, and had made his daughter a countess, was a broken man. Ill health now beset him. Hanson wrote to ask Murray to visit him at his home, 52 Upper Norton Street, in London, as 'I have not been across the Threshold of my Door for the greatest part of a year', sardonically adding, 'tho' the symbols of the sanity of my mental and bodily health, which you allude to, are certainly strong'. He was the one confined now: 'I am yet a Prisoner and you will be sure to find me at any Time,' he wrote in a further letter. He died in September 1841.[2]

The impact of first the Lunacy Commission and then the marriage annulment case upon John's relationship with his oldest daughter, Mary Ann, were hard to bear. Initially, in November 1822, as each side gathered their evidence for the Commission, John was confident of his daughter's case. He wrote a letter to the editor of the *Salisbury and Winchester Journal*, arrogantly dismissing the attention that other newspapers had given to the scandalously short week-long courtship between his daughter and Portsmouth before their marriage on 7 March 1814. He was certain that once members of the public heard his daughter's version of events they would understand that the Commission was 'one of the most extraordinary conspiracies that ever was contrived against a virtuous, innocent, and helpless woman'.

Even when the Commission found that Portsmouth was a lunatic, the Hanson family continued to protest Mary Ann's innocence. Newton Hanson wrote a lengthy letter to *The Times* in response to 'the foulest and most malignant aspersions' that had been cast upon his sister's 'conduct and reputation'. She had been left a 'heart-broken lady' by the Commission, he said. But while her family continued to support her, and do what they could to salvage her reputation, by the time the case for her marriage annulment was brought to the church courts, it served Mary Ann better to distance herself from her father and brothers. Dr Jenner, the lawyer appointed by Mary Ann to oppose the annulment, represented her as 'the victim of the wicked designs of her own family'. She was the 'unfortunate and devoted girl' who had been reluctantly 'dragged on by her own family' to a marriage of 'fraudulent and cruel iniquity'. By the close of the case, when accounts of her abusing and tormenting her husband had been told, nobody saw Mary Ann in this light. By then she was a social outcast, a figure of public disgust, and an adulteress with a bastard in her arms. Mary Ann wanted nothing more to do with her family, but they felt likewise. It was her wilfulness that had meant she had continued her affair with Alder despite her father's disapproval. Sooner or later one of her pregnancies would go full term, and then it was inevitable that Portsmouth's family would act. If only Mary Ann had not taken a lover, then she would have remained a countess, and the Hansons' gateway into a family fortune would have been secured.

Mary Ann never played by the rules, but she did remain faithful to Alder. In February 1825, she was rumoured to be pregnant again, and, on 10 October 1828, five months to the day since Judge Nicholl had ended her marriage to Portsmouth, she married Alder. Their marriage was announced in the papers, but whether anyone realized that she was the former Lady Portsmouth is unknown. Their wedding took place in Clifton, and it was in Bristol that she gave birth to a third child, a boy, in July 1829. Rumour had it that one of her children was called Byron.[3]

There was a vain and audacious attempt in April 1833 by John Hanson to make the financial terms of his daughter's 1814 marriage settlement stick, even after the relationship had been annulled. Alder made an appearance in Chancery as a witness to the deed. The record of Alder and Mary Ann then falls silent. As Mary Ann rebuilt her life with Alder, her former husband settled into a life of seclusion within

Hurstbourne Park. They never contacted each other again. But on 6 October 1859 Mary Ann, now in her sixties, wrote a letter that was directed to Eggesford. Like a ghost from the past, the spectre of Mary Ann Hanson was alive again.

The letter had come all the way from Canada. Just how Mary Ann had ended up on the other side of the Atlantic, nobody could be sure. But the opening lines of the letter gave some clues. Mary Ann would have preferred to have written to Portsmouth's cousin, William Barton Wallop or his son, she said. It seems that Mary Ann had ingratiated herself with this side of her former husband's family. William had served as a Captain in the Nova Scotia Fencibles, and his wife was from New Brunswick. He had probably first served in Canada during the 1812 war. At some point, Mary Ann had joined the couple and their young family in the small town of Chatham-Kent, in the south-west of Ontario. There she claimed to have looked after William's son during his holidays, and his sister had 'resided with us some years'. As expats living in a foreign land, this branch of the Wallop family might have been glad to have had Mary Ann to lend a helping hand. They may even have pitied the aunt who had become the black sheep of the family.

'I can almost fancy that I see him a Child now,' Mary Ann wrote, remembering her time looking after the little boy, 'but time changes all things and it may be that the thoughts of the Man are far different to those of the free headed and generous boy.' Somewhere along the line Mary Ann had lost touch with the family, and she claimed to not know how to contact them now.

It was almost certainly widowhood and poverty that had prompted Mary Ann to emigrate. Alder had died on 7 February 1847, heavily in debt. He had had to give up his home at Horncliffe, and move his family to the tiny village of Spittal, at the mouth of the River Tweed in Northumberland. The only child mentioned in his will was his youngest son, William Baillie Graham. Mary Ann was probably still being chased for repayment of legal costs so going abroad was one way to escape her debts. Ships regularly sailed to Canada from nearby Berwick. Mary Ann was first recorded as residing in Chatham-Kent in the 1851 census, but there were no other members of the Wallop or Hanson family present. By the 1861 census, two years after Mary Ann wrote her letter, she had been joined in the town by her son, Graham Alder, his wife, M. Alder (born in England), and their four children, aged between ten and one (all born in Canada). Graham gave 'farmer' as his occupation, and was listed in an 1864 business directory for the town. But by the time of the next census in 1871, neither Mary Ann nor any other member of the Alder family resided in Ontario.

Chatham-Kent could not be further removed from the social world of London and Hampshire that Mary Ann had experienced as Lady Portsmouth. Beginning as a naval dockyard in the 1790s, and centred upon the Thames River, Chatham-Kent was surrounded by rich farming land. Known from the 1830s as 'the coloured man's Paris', African-Americans escaped the horrors of slavery and flocked on routes called the Underground Railroad that led to Chatham-Kent. While Mary Ann may also have seen the town as 'a place of refuge', the sight of black faces would have been unfamiliar to her. There is little to suggest that she was able to benefit from the town's sudden wealth when oil was discovered in Bothwell during the 1850s.

Mary Ann's letter was a begging one. She asked for a pitiful '£10 or £20'. She claimed to be 'really and truly in the greatest want of many even common comforts that become necessaries to a person of my years'. In her old age she was now:

> stranded on the shore of adversity without a hope of better days, such is the way with me once the Lady of Hurstbourne Park, now with not sufficient to buy my daily bread for the short remaining time that I may need it.

Hopeful of support, Mary Ann added a postscript to her letter, directing that any bank note should be sent in two halves, and not sent on the same day, 'for safety'.

Her letter sent shivers down the spine at Eggesford, but it is unlikely to have met with any response. Resentment at the cost and suffering she had brought to the Portsmouth family could not be so easily forgotten or forgiven. That she dared to write now was an affront to all decency. She was said to have left the country with a full set of the family's silver that she subsequently sold. Even today, items are being recovered from North America.

In Chatham-Kent, all Mary Ann had left were her memories of being 'once the Lady of Hurstbourne Park'. She lived as a recluse in a rather rundown wooden-frame house on the north-east corner of Adelaide and Murray streets. One neighbour who died in 1943 remembered as a child being scared of the old lady 'who was often seen hobbling about in a crimson velvet cloak trimmed with ermine'. Locals knew her as Lady Alder, and she never tired of telling them that she was once the countess of Portsmouth. She told them a mix of lies (the Prince Regent, later George IV, was at her wedding), as well as truths (so was Byron). After her death in May 1870, she entered the stuff of local myth and legend. 'Spirit walks' in the town still stop by the site of her home to record 'how the Countess of Portsmouth came to Chatham'. She died far from home and alone. She was the misfit now.[4]

Epilogue

IT HAD BEEN a life packed full of stories. From parental disappointment and playground bullies to attempted abduction, blackmail, and suggested homosexuality; from blood-letting and funerals to arranged marriages, adultery, and cruelty. Add madness or idiocy to the mix, and there were enough stories to keep a raft of novelists busy for years. But Portsmouth's life story never made a successful novel because its narrative was too complex. Collected together, stories of Portsmouth did not produce a single picture of him. For over the years layer upon layer of stories had been added, as each storyteller gave their own version of events. There were attempts at family secrecy (not all stories were publicly told), and deliberate lies. The result was such a variety of stories that it was difficult to know fact from fiction. The truth had become so hidden beneath this web of stories that there could be no certainty about Portsmouth: was he sane or insane? An incurable idiot or just weak-minded?

There is, however, usually a thread to someone's life, a clue to their identity that can be traced from the start to the end, no matter how many twists and turns life can take. Portsmouth pointed right at it. At the very moment when his mind was pushed to the limits, as he stood on the precipice of mental breakdown, he gave the clearest articulation of who he was. Brought back to his home from Edinburgh, and rescued from the misery of living with the Hansons, he declared himself to be the King of Hampshire. Hurstbourne

Park, the 'perfect palace' that had been refashioned by his mother, the house where he had spent his youngest years, lived while he was married to Grace, and spent the happiest hours on its farm, and the fields of its estate, was the place he was King. Neither Farleigh Wallop nor the dreaded Fairlawn House bought for Mary Ann was home to him. In times of trouble, and there had been many, Hurstbourne had always been the place to which he had returned, and it was where he retired after the Lunacy Commission had given its verdict.

The tragedy was that even towards the end of his life his own family did not 'get' Portsmouth. Newton's son tried to take Hurstbourne away from him. In so doing, he betrayed a total lack of understanding of everything that was Lord Portsmouth. For most people, a lunacy verdict followed by confinement in their home for the remaining years of their life would feel like a death sentence. But not for Portsmouth. It liberated him from the public duties and social roles of an aristocrat, and it freed him from his wife and any future fortune-seeking opportunist. With a sympathetic 'Committee' on his side, and left alone, Portsmouth could enjoy his kingdom. For more than thirty years, he lived as the King of Hampshire in the grandeur of his estate, undisturbed by its solitude. Hurstbourne was paradise to him.

His was a much anticipated death. Newton had been waiting to become the 4th earl of Portsmouth all his life, and he had been willing to bring a Lunacy Commission against his brother to protect his inheritance. Even the patient Henry Arthur asked Chancery if he might claim his uncle's wine and horses in lieu of the costs of his care if Portsmouth died in his debt. Towards the end, Portsmouth's physical health did deteriorate. Local newspapers reported Portsmouth's ill health in November 1846 and 1850, his 'very precarious state' on the later date leading them to explain that it would be Newton Fellowes, 'one of the relics of a class nearly extinct, that of the "old English gentleman"', who would succeed him if he died. But whatever his mental or physical ailments, Portsmouth proved stubbornly resistant to mortality. He outlived his younger carer, and his lifetime had spanned the reign of three monarchs. Born in the reign of George

III, Victoria was on the throne by the time he died. His death finally came at Hurstbourne on 14 July 1853. He was in his eighty-sixth year.

Death normally signals the start of a new set of life stories. The act of remembering is all about retelling stories of the person that was. But nobody who had known Portsmouth wanted to remember him. For Portsmouth was a man whose life had unsettled, disturbed, and disrupted everyone around him. He had affected not only his own family but also his society's view of itself. In crossing the boundaries of order, decency, and morality he had highlighted the shallowness, hypocrisy, intolerance, and cruelty of his times. His life story turned out to be as much about the inadequacy of others as himself. This was the uglier side of nineteenth-century English society, and, while people might in turn be fascinated and repelled by stories of it during his lifetime, they had no desire to be reminded of it when he was gone. They could instead comfort themselves that his story represented a world that was past, a life of stories that could not be replicated in their more modern, civilized times.

So Portsmouth's family set about forgetting. Portsmouth, the man who delighted in funerals, had started planning his own 'black job' some thirty years or more before his death, discussing with a valet what horses might be used to drive his hearse. He would have been sorely disappointed with what did transpire. There was no grand funeral. His body was transported from Hurstbourne Park to the church at Farleigh Wallop where the rest of his ancestors were interred. No document suggests that it was accompanied by a procession of carriages, or attended by any other family member. There was none of the ceremony that had marked the funeral of Portsmouth's first wife, Grace. No handwritten obituary was filed in family papers, as it had been for his nephew and would be for his brother. His was a burial, not a funeral. Parish registers simply record that his body was buried at Farleigh Wallop on 20 July.

Hampshire newspapers reported his death, but by 1853 most people could not recollect the stories about Portsmouth that had circulated more than three decades earlier. They had to be reminded of who he was. 'Few of our readers will now recollect the famous "Portsmouth case"', wrote one reporter:

Few trials have, in modern times, caused greater interest, and it was said that the cost was 'a guinea a minute.' However this may be, it brought Lord Portsmouth and all his peculiarities into general notoriety. Up to the time of the marriage, these had never been interfered with.

The public could rest assured that since the Lunacy Commission Portsmouth 'passed his time in perfect seclusion, on his Hampshire estate.'

The 4th earl of Portsmouth, the press recorded, was Newton Fellowes. But 'almost contemporaneously' with his succession to his title, Newton fell seriously ill. He lay sick at Eggesford, and died on 9 January 1854. He had never taken his place at the family seat in Hampshire. His wife, Catherine, died the same year, on 12 May. Isaac Newton became the 5th earl of Portsmouth.

Laying the 3rd earl of Portsmouth to rest meant burying his past with him. In a small church stuffed with family memorials, and a graveyard with headstones for his ancestors, Portsmouth was placed in an unmarked grave. We do not know if his wish to be laid alongside his mother and father was fulfilled. His family never wanted to make him a part of their history. No portrait of him was commissioned. He was the faceless man whom his family wanted to forget. Possibly the only material reminders that he had ever existed were the gold watch and eye glass that he left to his sister, Henrietta Dorothea, and that she was careful to will in due course to her children. On New Year's Day 1891, a fire raged through the central part of the mansion at Hurstbourne Park. The family were safely away at Eggesford, but the house and many of its contents were destroyed. This was the end of the Hurstbourne Park that Portsmouth had known. It seemed that all traces of Portsmouth had been removed.[1]

But stories of John Charles Wallop, the 3rd earl of Portsmouth, do remain. They are the many thousands of words that were spoken and recorded in his legal trials, and the letters that were written about him, and by him. Put in storage by court clerks, hundreds of statements by witnesses survive. Kept at Eggesford to be returned by a later generation to Hampshire archives, family letters escaped the ravages of the Hurstbourne fire. Reopening the files, and unfolding the letters, we can bring Portsmouth back to life. We have the full story.

Acknowledgements

This book started with a tip-off. It was July 2000 and I was working in one of my favourite places, Lambeth Palace Library, on a book about marital violence. Surrounded by theologians, whom I am sure were researching worthier things, I was ploughing through the depressing stories of couples whose violent marriages were ended by the church courts during the course of the seventeenth and eighteenth centuries. I was looking for an excuse for a break. Then Melanie Barber, the Senior Archivist, entered the room. I liked Melanie ever since I had first visited the Library as a naive PhD student, and she had responded to my many queries with patience and kindness. As was Melanie's way, she walked around the room, asking each person what they were reading, and taking an interest in their work. Then it was my turn. 'You should take a look at the Portsmouth annulment case,' she told me. 'There are boxes of material and nobody has ever looked at them before.'

I still have the pencil note of this conversation, and the case reference number, but a combination of work and family commitments meant that it was a long time before I opened those boxes. To my great regret, I never got to thank Melanie for her generous advice, as she died in 2012. I hope she would think I have done the archive justice.

The boxes at Lambeth are a treasure trove. Never before have I come across such a volume of words and outpouring of emotion about a historical figure. This cacophony of voices came from well-known figures in nineteenth-century society, but also very humble people who otherwise would have disappeared from history. It seemed as if in the 1820s everyone had an opinion about Lord Portsmouth, but I had never heard of him. Why had his story laid buried in the archives for so long?

The annulment case got me hooked, but it turned out to be just the last of the legal trials that Portsmouth faced. When I traced his story back, I discovered lawyers' notes relating to the first call for a Lunacy Commission in 1815; printed and newspaper accounts of the 1823 Lunacy Commission; legal disputes heard at Chancery; and a cache of personal letters written by family members and Portsmouth himself. Only one historian, Akihito Suzuki, had ever referred to Portsmouth in their academic work. Suzuki has used a printed account of the 1823 Commission as the starting point to an important book about the care of the wealthy insane by their families. But by focusing on just one of Portsmouth's trials, he missed the complexity of his story, and the inaccuracies of that trial account. There is such a volume of material about Portsmouth's life that others have been put off investigating it in its entirety. Fortunately, I was well on the way to completing my research of the records held at Lambeth when I read the following note by a biographer of Byron, 'to condense the actual records' of Portsmouth's annulment case, 'would be a daunting task'.

The first question I am asked about Lord Portsmouth is what was wrong with him. I still find this difficult to answer. In these days of modern science, we rush to diagnosis. But diagnosing the dead can go horribly wrong. For years, historians blindly followed the view held by mother and son psychiatrists, Ida MacAlpine and Richard Hunter, that Portsmouth's famous contemporary, George III, was made ill from the effects of the blood disorder porphyria. They were misled by evidence of the King's urine. In fact, a broader range of evidence proves that George III's fits were the result of mental illness, not a physical complaint.

In Portsmouth's case, it is not just that I don't feel medically qualified to say what troubled him. My problem is more fundamental: I don't think I should. To do so would be to fall into the same trap as his contemporaries. Diagnosing a mind, as they found to their cost, is a tricky business. Even after the finding of the 1823 Lunacy Commission, sufficient doubts remained about its verdict for the whole process to begin again with his marriage annulment case. Much to the frustration of everyone who knew him, Portsmouth never presented a clear-cut case. Portsmouth changed: whatever Portsmouth's mental state in his youth, it was not the same in 1823 or, from what we can tell, at the end of his life. To reduce Portsmouth to the simple black and white categories of sane/insane, retarded/developed would be to demean him. His brain had too much grey matter for that. So in this book I've deliberately resisted labelling and instead tried to understand Portsmouth.

A generous Leverhulme Trust Research Fellowship funded my research, and gave me valuable time free from teaching and administration to write this book. I am enormously grateful to the Trust for their support, and for understanding when my research did not take me down the paths I had originally envisaged. My colleagues at Clare College, Cambridge, were supportive of my period of leave, and I consider myself very fortunate to be teaching such a bright and stimulating group of students. As well as working in Lambeth Palace Library, I have spent substantial periods of time at Hampshire Record Office in Winchester, and I am thankful to the staff there, particularly Sarah Farley, who catalogued the Wallop papers. Alison M. Deveson's research on the Portsmouth family and the Hurstbourne Park estate has been invaluable, and I am grateful to her for answering my queries. Elizabeth Vickers of Elizabeth Vickers Photography kindly supplied photographs of family portraits. Permission to reproduce this material and support for the project was received from Lord and Lady Portsmouth. I much appreciate the trust they demonstrated by allowing me to write a history of their ancestor.

Janelle Andrew at Peters Fraser & Dunlop first saw the potential of this project, and has been hugely helpful in encouraging me to develop it into this book. My writing has benefited significantly from the advice of Janelle, and the careful editing of Sam Carter at Oneworld Publications. Thank you to all the production team at Oneworld.

My former PhD supervisor, Anthony Fletcher, had the mixed pleasure of reading this entire book in its early drafts, and I've enjoyed talking to him during our many Pizza Express lunches. My PhD student, Jake Ladlow, took time out from his important research to read a final draft. I am very grateful to him for his encouragement and good humour at this stage. Fellow historian Jennine Hurl-Eamon, my 'friend in Canada', helped to track down the record of Mary Ann's burial in Chatham-Kent, allowing me to find the final piece of that jigsaw. Thank you.

I've thoroughly enjoyed writing this book, but fitting it around family life has not always been easy. My husband, Peter, has kept me going with his love and support, even if his inability to keep secrets meant that its dedication to our children was revealed before publication. I will never forget James and Emma, clipboards in hand, enthusiastically searching for Portsmouth's grave in the churchyard at Hurstbourne Priors one rainy Saturday (wrong place, Mum). At times this book has been a family endeavour, but it is all the stronger for that.

Abbreviations

BLA	Bedfordshire and Luton Archives and Records Service, Bedford
CAH	Cambridgeshire Archives, Huntingdon
Genuine Report	*A Genuine Report of the Proceedings on the Portsmouth Case* (London, 1823)
HRO	Hampshire Record Office, Winchester
LMA	London Metropolitan Archives
LPL	Lambeth Palace Library, London
NA	National Archives, Kew
NLS	National Library of Scotland, Edinburgh
NRO	Norfolk Record Office, Norwich
ODNB	*Oxford Dictionary of National Biography* (Oxford: Oxford University Press, 2004)

Notes

An unsound mind?

1. *The Morning Post* 25 January 1815; LPL, H997/11, Exhibit 27; H997/32, f.49; H997/35, f.33.
2. Witnesses during Portsmouth's marriage annulment case were asked specifically about his personal appearance, see LPL, H997/29, f.23, 55, 57; H997/31, f.227, 261; H997/32, f.65.
3. The material for much of this chapter is taken from reports in *The Times* and *The Morning Post*, and *Genuine Report*. Notes taken from the first application for a Commission of Lunacy in 1815 and the Chancellor's comments upon it are held at HRO, 15M84/5/4/2.

The gift

1. T. F. T. Baker, D. K. Bolton and P. E. C. Croot, *A History of the County of Middlesex* vol.9 (London: Victoria County History, 1989), pp.51–2; HRO, 15M84/5/3/2/3, Accounts of Coulson Fellowes, April 1731; 15M84/5/3/2/4, Accounts of Coulson Fellowes, May 1765 to January 1769; 15M84/5/9/4/65, Mrs Fellowes bill, 24 November 1766; 15M84/5/3/2/17, Household bills for Coulson Fellowes; 15M84/5/14/19, Family history, 26 January 1803.
2. J. Martin, 'Wallop, John, first earl of Portsmouth (1690–1762)' *ODNB*.
3. HRO, 15M84/F25, Notebook by 6th earl, c.1892.
4. HRO, 15M84/5/3/2/17, Bundle of letters and bills; 15M84/5/3/2/4, Accounts of Coulson Fellowes, May 1765 to January 1769.
5. Alison M. Deveson, *En Suivant La Vérité: A History of the Earls of Portsmouth and the Wallop Family* (Portsmouth Estates, 2008), pp.42–4; Giles Worsley, 'Farleigh House, Hampshire' *Country Life* (16 June 1994), pp.62–5.

6. Edward Wedlake Brayley and John Britton, *The Beauties of England and Wales*, vol.6 (London: Vernor and Hood, 1805), pp.7, 11, 235–6.

7. HRO, 15M84/F321/6, Letter, 25 June 1855; 15M84/F25, Notebook by 6th earl of Portsmouth, c.1892; 15M84/F27, Notebook by 6th countess of Portsmouth, c.1901–5; Brayley and Britton, *The Beauties of England*, vol.6, p.234; William Page (ed.), *A History of the County of Hampshire* vol.4 (London: Victoria County History, 1911), pp.287–91; Deveson, *En Suivant*, pp.34–6, 'Hurstbourne Park: Image and reality' *Hampshire Studies* 59 (2004), 196–209, and 'The lost mansions of Hurstbourne Park' *Hampshire Field Club and Archaeological Society Newsletter* 43 (Spring, 2005), 31–6.

8. *World*, 10 October and 5 December 1788; *Genuine Report*, p.59; HRO, 15M52/T186, Marriage settlement, 12 February 1790.

9. HRO, 15M84/5/3/2/4, Accounts of Coulson Fellowes, May 1765 to January 1769; G. E. C., *The Complete Peerage* revised and enlarged edition (The St Catherine Press: London, 1945), vol.10, p.612.

'Very backward of his Age, but good temper'd and orderly'

1. Many of the descriptions of Steventon and the Austen family in this chapter are taken from Marilyn Butler, 'Austen, Jane (1775–1817)' *ODNB*; Claire Tomalin, *Jane Austen: A Life* (Viking: London, 1997); and Audrey Hawkridge, *Jane Austen and Hampshire* (Hampshire Papers, 2001).

2. Anna's description of Cassandra Austen, and this definition of 'sprack wit' are taken from George Holbert Tucker, *A History of Jane Austen's Family* (Stroud, Glos: Sutton, 1998), p.66.

3. R. A. Austen-Leigh (ed.), *Austen Papers 1704–1856* (Spottiswoode: Ballantyne and Co Ltd, 1942), pp.28–9.

4. W. Austen-Leigh and R. A. Austen-Leigh, *Jane Austen: A Family Record*, Revised and Enlarged by Deirdre Le Faye (London: The British Library, 1989), p.15.

5. *Austen Papers*, pp.28–9.

6. NRO, FEL557, 558x8, Letter from Urania Portsmouth to Robert Fellowes, 21 April 1793.

7. HRO, 15M84/F321/6, Letter from Lady Henrietta Dorothea Churchill to Eveline, Lady Portsmouth, 25 June 1855.

8. Deirdre Le Faye (ed.), *Jane Austen's Letters* 3rd edition (Oxford: Oxford University Press, 1995), pp.196, 409.

9. *Austen Papers*, pp.23, 27.

10. *Austen Papers*, pp.28–9.

11. *History of Jane Austen's Family*, p.117.

12. J. E. Austen-Leigh, *A Memoir of Jane Austen and other Family Recollections*, 1st published 1870 (Oxford: Oxford University Press, 2002, edited by Kathryn Sutherland), pp.16, 205.

'Alarm'd at the Hesitation in his speech'

1. *Morning Chronicle and London Advertiser* 19 November 1773.
2. *Newcastle Courant* 15 February 1752.
3. Samuel Angier, *The Polite Modern Divine* (London, 1756).
4. *Newcastle Courant* 15 February 1752; *Public Ledger* 10 April 1761.
5. Charles Angier, *A Few Observations on the Inconveniences which arise from Impediments and other Defects in Speech* (Dublin, 1804), p.7; *Public Advertiser* 10 January 1772; *London Evening Post* 8–10 September 1774.
6. *Morning Chronicle and London Advertiser* 19 November 1773; *Public Advertiser* 19 February 1761; *Public Advertiser* 10 January 1772; *Morning Post and Daily Advertiser* 18 July 1777; [Charles Angier], *An Address to the Public, Concerning Impediments in Speech* (London, 1786), p.5.
7. Austen-Leigh (ed.), *Austen Papers 1704–1856*, pp.30–1.
8. John Tallis, *London Street Views 1838–40* (London: Nattali and Maurice, with the London Topographical Society, 1969), pp.160–1.
9. Angier, *A Few Observations*, pp.10–12.
10. *Memoirs of the Reverend Dr Joseph Priestley* (London, 1809), p.25.
11. *Public Ledger* 10 April 1761; Denyse Rockey, *Speech Disorder in Nineteenth Century Britain: The History of Stuttering* (London: Croom Helm, 1980), p.193.
12. *Address to the Public*, pp.2, 6–7; and Rockey, *Speech Disorder*, p.225.
13. LPL, H997/32, f.49.
14. Rockey, *Speech Disorder*, pp.23, 30–1, 60, 129.
15. Angier, *A Few Observations*, pp.14–15.
16. *Memoirs of the Reverend Dr Joseph Priestley*, p.20; *Lloyd's Evening Post and British Chronicle* 25–27 March 1761; Angier, *A Few Observations*, pp.13, 6–7; LPL, H997/33, f.186.
17. HRO, 15M84/5/3/2/17, Letters from Urania, Countess of Portsmouth, to her son Newton Fellowes.
18. *Genuine Report*, pp.32, 49; LPL, H997/30, ff.133, 167.

'The laughing stock of the school'

1. William Cobbett, *Rural Rides* (Harmondsworth: Penguin Books, 1967; 1st published 1830), p.39; HRO, 44M69/H1/36, List of boys apprenticed at Odiham school, c.1787; *Oxford Journal* 19 January 1788; *Hampshire Chronicle* 19 January 1789; *Reading Mercury* 26 January 1789.
2. LPL, H997/29, ff.89–90; HRO, 15M84/5/4/4, Evidence to Chancery, 28 January 1815, p.113.
3. LPL, H997/29, ff.25, 89; H997/33, f.174.
4. LPL, H997/35, f.96.

5. *The Times* 25 February 1823; LPL, H997/29, f.25; HRO, 15M84/5/4/4, Evidence to Chancery, 28 January 1815, p.113.
6. LPL, H997/35, ff.91, 95; H997/33, ff.167, 198; H997/35, f.9.
7. HRO, 15M84/5/7, Evidence to Chancery, 30 July 1821; *The Times* 25 February 1823.
8. LPL, H997/29, f.89.
9. LPL, H997/35, f.91; *The Times* 13 February 1823; *Genuine Report*, p.54.
10. LPL, H997/33, ff.173–4; H997/35, ff.91–2; *Genuine Report*, p.64.
11. HRO, 15M84/5/3/1/1, Letters received by the 2nd Countess of Portsmouth, from her son, Newton Wallop.
12. BLA, L30/15/39/3, 16, 27, 30; HRO, 15M84/5/3/1/1; Walter Thornbury, *Old and New London* vol.3 (London: Cassell, Petter and Galpin, 1878), pp.462–83.
13. HRO, 15M84/5/3/1/1; F. M. O'Donoghue, 'Livesay, Richard (1750–1826)' rev. Jill Springall, *ODNB*; Alex Kidson 'Romney, George (1734–1802)' *ODNB*; for other portraits by George Romney, see Linda Colley, *Britons: Forging the Nation* (New Haven and London: Yale, 1992), pp.168–9.

'One of the most sensible women in the Kingdom'

1. HRO, 15M84/5/5/1, Letter from Urania Portsmouth to Newton Fellowes, 15 April 1800.
2. HRO, 15M84/F25, Notebook by the 6th earl of Portsmouth, c.1892.
3. HRO, 15M84/5/4/7, Chancery case, 31 July 1821, f.111; see also copies of accounts submitted by trustees for 1799–1808, which show a similar estate income, LPL, H997/11, Exhibit 2.
4. LPL, H997/33, f.174; H997/12, Exhibit 32.
5. LPL, H997/29, f.28.
6. LPL, H997/33, f.167.
7. LPL, H997/31, f.297; H997/33, ff.185–6.
8. HRO, 15M84/F321/6, Letter from Lady Henrietta Dorothea Churchill to Eveline, Lady Portsmouth, 25 June 1855; LPL, H997/31, f.275.
9. LPL, H997/30, f.143.
10. HRO, 15M84/5/4/7, Chancery case, 30 July 1821, f.23; NA, PROB 11/1543/224; PRO 30/8/168/142–5, Letters to William Pitt from the 2nd earl of Portsmouth.
11. HRO, 15M84/5/3/1/1.
12. HRO, 5M52/T186, Document incorrectly labelled by the archives as the marriage settlement of John earl of Portsmouth and his wife Urania, 12 February 1790.
13. LPL, H997/35, ff.38–45.
14. HRO, 15M84/F27, Notebook by the 6th countess of Portsmouth, c.1901–5.
15. HRO, 15M84/5/3/2/17, Letter from Urania Portsmouth to Newton Fellowes, 30 January 1811.
16. HRO, 15M84/5/3/1/2, List of specific bequests by Urania, 2nd countess of

Portsmouth; HRO, 15M84/F27, Notebook by the 6th countess of Portsmouth, c. 1901–5.

17. LPL, H997/28, ff.232–3.

'His want of ordinary caution'

1. LPL, H997/33, f.187.
2. NA, C13/2833/7 (1803).
3. Comparisons between Ferrers and Portsmouth were made in 1815 when Newton Fellowes first attempted to get a Chancery inquisition of lunacy, HRO, 15M84/5/4/2, pp.139–40. Angus McLaren, *Sexual Blackmail: A Modern History* (Cambridge MA: Harvard University Press, 2002), gives the historical context to attitudes to sodomy and responses to blackmail at this time.
4. LPL, H997/11, Exhibit 5; H997/8; H997/32, ff.39–40, 49; H997/33, ff.110–11; *Morning Chronicle* 8 December 1802; *Hampshire Chronicle* 13 December 1802; *Genuine Report*, p.64. Unfortunately, Portsmouth's affidavits, or sworn statements, to King's Bench do not survive, and we only hear what he said second-hand. Since the Seilaz case became important in later court cases relating to Portsmouth's sanity, it is possible that they were removed from King's Bench files and then mislaid. Given the incriminating evidence and the nature of this case, this loss of documents may not have been entirely accidental.
5. *Genuine Report*, pp.46–7; and *The Times* 17 February 1823, p.2.
6. *Salisbury and Winchester Journal* 26 August 1799.
7. Seilaz's story is given in NA, C13/2833/7 (1803). More limited details are also given in Seilaz's affidavit to King's Bench requesting his papers be returned, KB1/31/6, and the resulting court order, KB21/48.
8. *Morning Chronicle* 8 December 1802.

'Our family greatly indulges secrecy'

1. The marriage separation case in November 1747 was brought on the grounds of John Wallop's cruelty, see LMA DL/C/0551/078–9, 107; HRO, 15M84/5/14/2; I have found no evidence to support the claim that the marriage inspired Hogarth's painting.
2. J. P. C. Roach (ed.), *A History of the County of Cambridge and the Isle of Ely* vol.3 (London: Victoria County History, 1959), pp.450–6; Eamon Duffy, 'Part Three: Late seventeenth to early nineteenth century' in P. Cunich et al, *A History of Magdalene College Cambridge 1428–1988* (Cambridge: Magdalene College Publications, 1994), pp.179–83.
3. British Library, Add MS 89036/1/7, f.58, Letter from John King to William Pitt, 5 August 1800.

4. HRO, 15M84/5/4/2, Evidence to Chancery, 14 January 1815, ff.51, 96–7.
5. *The Times* 13 February 1823.
6. CAH, R35/2/3, Letter from Henry Arthur Fellowes to William Fellowes, 16 August 1785.
7. CAH, R32/7, 'Reasons for confinement', and 5 September 1791, 'List of questions'; 27 August, 28 August, 1 September, 2 September, 10 September 1791, R32/7, 'Vouchers, papers, letters, accounts relative to the affairs of my sister Dorothea Fellowes', 1 June 1789; NRO, FEL 557/1/2, Letter from Henry Arthur Fellowes to Robert Fellowes, 8 January 1791, FEL 652, 554x3, 'Note by Dorothea Fellowes', n.d. and Letter from Dorothea Fellowes to Robert Fellowes, 17 July 1779; FEL 709, 554x9, 'Note by Dorothea Fellowes', 3 May 1786.
8. NRO, FEL 709, 554x9, Letter from John Pridden to Robert Fellowes, 18 January 1819; Richard Riddell, 'Pridden, John (1758–1825)' *ODNB*.
9. CAH, R32/7, 25 August 1791.
10. CAH, R32/7, 31 August 1791.
11. CAH, R35/2/3, Letter from Henry Arthur Fellowes to William Fellowes, 25 October 1788; NRO, FEL 557/1/1, Letter from Henry Arthur Fellowes to Robert Fellowes, 7 December 1788.
12. CAH, R35/2/3, Letter from Henry Arthur Fellowes to William Fellowes, 5 August 1791.
13. NRO, FEL 557/2/20, Letter from Urania Portsmouth to Robert Fellowes, begun 22 June 1792.
14. All these documents are held at CAH, R32/7.
15. CAH, R35/2/3, Letter from Henry Arthur Fellowes to William Fellowes, 21 August 1791.
16. William L. Parry-Jones, *The Trade in Lunacy: A Study of Private Madhouses in England in the Eighteenth and Nineteenth Centuries* (London: Routledge and Kegan Paul, 1972); Charlotte MacKenzie, *Psychiatry for the Rich: A History of Ticehurst Private Asylum, 1792–1917* (London: Routledge, 1992); E. Foyster, 'At the limits of liberty: married women and confinement in eighteenth-century England' *Continuity and Change* 17, 1 (2002), 39–62.
17. Roy Porter, 'Willis, Francis (1718–1807)' *ODNB*.
18. CAH, R32/7, 27 August, 29 August 1791, 'Dr Willis's opinion 29 August 1791'.
19. CAH, R35/2/3, Letter from Henry Arthur Fellowes to William Fellowes, 31 August 1791.
20. CAH, R32/7, 8 and 9 September 1791.
21. Helen Brock, 'Simmons, Samuel Foart (1750–1813)' *ODNB*.
22. CAH, R32/7, 10 September 1791.
23. CAH, R32/7, 11 September 1791.
24. NRO, FEL 653, 554x3.
25. NRO, FEL 557/2/20, Letter from Urania Portsmouth to Robert Fellowes, begun 22 June 1792; FEL 557/1/6, Letter from Urania Portsmouth to Robert Fellowes,

29 August 1792; and FEL 557/1/7, Letter from Urania Portsmouth to Robert Fellowes, 9 September 1792.

26. NRO, FEL 656, 554x4, 'To the Legislature', 3 May, 22 July and 27 September 1799.

27. NRO, FEL 557, 553x8, Letter from Urania Portsmouth to Robert Fellowes, 8 February 1793.

28. NRO, FEL 656, 554x4, Letter from Dorothea Fellowes to Lord Viscount Lymington, 18 November 1800.

29. Evidence of these visits is recorded in Helen Lefroy and Gavin Turner (eds), *The Letters of Mrs Lefroy: Jane Austen's Beloved Friend* (Winchester: The Jane Austen Society, 2007), p.81; and *Genuine Report*, p.30.

30. Loudon Harcourt Gordon, *An Apology for the Conduct of the Gordons* (London, 1804), p.126.

31. Gordon, *An Apology*; *Derby Mercury* 15 March 1804; *Kentish Gazette* 9 March 1804; *Hampshire Chronicle* 12 March 1804.

32. Gordon, *An Apology*, pp.109, 118, 125–6; *A Vindication of Mrs Lee's Conduct Towards the Gordons Written by Herself* (London, 1807); *Northampton Mercury* 28 January 1804; *Kentish Gazette* 13 March 1804; *Stamford Mercury* 25 May 1804. The case was so notorious that it was selected to be included in Peter Burke's *Celebrated Trials Connected with the Upper Classes of Society, in the Relations of Private Life* (London, 1851), pp.231–2.

33. *Kentish Gazette* 13 March 1804; *A Vindication*, pp.20, 44–6.

34. HRO, 15M84/5/5/2, Letter from Urania Portsmouth to Newton and Frances Fellowes, 8 October 1810.

35. HRO, 15M84/5/5/21, Letter from Dr Finch to Newton Fellowes, 27 June 1827; note from Lt. General Gordon to Newton Fellowes, no date; 15M84/5/5/25, Letter from Henry Karslake to Newton Fellowes, 5 January 1828; Parry-Jones, *Trade in Lunacy*, pp.37, 44, 116–17.

36. HRO, 15M84/5/5/2, Letter from Urania Portsmouth to Newton and Frances Fellowes, 8 October 1810.

37. HRO, 15M84/5/5/14, Letter from Dr John Warburton to Newton Fellowes, 27 September 1824; 15M84/5/4/10, Minutes of a meeting of the trustees of the Earl of Portsmouth held on 30 June 1836.

38. NRO, FEL 557, 553x8, Letter from Urania Portsmouth to Robert Fellowes, 14 January 1792.

39. *London Chronicle* 26–28 June 1792.

40. HRO, 15M84/5/14/19, 'Answers of Reverend John Churchill', no date.

41. HRO, 15M84/5/3/2/13, Copy of the will of Henry Arthur Fellowes, 16 September 1789; *Lloyd's Evening Post* 7 May 1792.

42. NRO, FEL 557/2/20, Letter from Urania Portsmouth to Robert Fellowes, begun 22 June 1792; FEL 557, 553x8, Letter from Urania Portsmouth to Robert Fellowes, 18 March 1792.

43. *Lloyd's Evening Post* 7 May 1792.

44. NRO, FEL 557/2/23, Letter from John Hanson to Robert Fellowes, 21 June 1792.

45. For example, *Morning Herald* 8 May 1792, and *London Chronicle* 8–10 May 1792.
46. NRO, FEL 557, 553x8, Letter from Urania Portsmouth to Robert Fellowes, 31 May 1792.
47. For example, NRO, FEL 557, 553x8, Letters from Urania Portsmouth to Robert Fellowes, 18 March 1792 and 31 May 1792.
48. NRO, FEL 557, 553x8, Letter from Urania Portsmouth to Robert Fellowes, 15 June 1792.
49. *Lloyd's Evening Post* 7 May 1792; *London Chronicle* 26–28 June 1792, 9–12 August 1794.
50. NRO, FEL 557/1/7, Letter from Urania Portsmouth to Robert Fellowes, 9 September 1792.
51. LMA, DL/C/549/55/5; LPL, CA, Case 1083, Eee16, testimony of George Ralph; Jonathan Andrews, 'Begging the question of idiocy: the definition and socio-cultural meaning of idiocy in early modern Britain' Part I and 2 *History of Psychiatry* 9 (1998), 65–95, 179–200; David Wright, '"Childlike in his innocence": Lay attitudes to "idiots" and "imbeciles" in Victorian England' in David Wright and Anne Digby (eds), *From Idiocy to Mental Deficiency* (London: Routledge, 1996); Rab Houston and Uta Frith, *Autism in History: The Case of Hugh Blair of Borgue* (Oxford: Blackwell, 2000).

'She was more like a mother to him than a wife'

1. *True Briton* 20 November 1799; Philip Laundy, 'Norton, Fletcher, first Baron Grantley (1716–1789)' *ODNB*; Gideon Mantell, *A Topographical History of Surrey* (London, 1850), pp.150–1; W. Edward Riley and Laurence Gomme (eds) *Survey of London* (London: London County Council, 1912), Vol.3, pp.108–9.
2. *The Times* 13 February 1823.
3. *The Times* 13 February 1823.
4. *Report on the Proceedings*, p.7.
5. *The Times* 13 February 1823.
6. *Report on the Proceedings*, p.7.
7. HRO, 15M84/5/4/7, Chancery case, 31 July and 6 August 1821, pp.110, 128.
8. HRO, 15M84/5/4/3, Chancery case, 24 January 1815, p.35.
9. HRO, 15M84/5/4/7, Chancery case, 30 July 1821, pp.2–3.
10. HRO, 15M84/5/5/16, Letter from Mr Bedford to Newton Fellowes, 16 October 1827; HRO, 15M84/5/4/3, Chancery case, 24 January 1815, p.20.
11. LPL, H997/8 and H997/11, Exhibit 1, 'Plan of settlement proposed in the intended marriage of the Earl of Portsmouth with Grace Norton'.
12. HRO, 15M84/3/1/3/31, Copy of the Will and Codicils of the Right Honourable Grace Dowager Lady Grantley.
13. LPL, H997/33, f.174; H997/30, f.163; H997/31, f.245.
14. LPL, H997/30, ff.124–5.

15. *The Times* 13 February 1823, p.3; LPL, H997/27, ff.9–13.

16. LPL, H997/31, f.264.

17. *Report on the Proceedings*, p.30.

18. HRO, 15M84/5/5/2, Letter from Grace Portsmouth, no date.

19. HRO, 21M69/11/7, Letter from Grace Portsmouth to Charlotte Maria, 8th countess of Banbury, 25 August 1813; for a witness who remembered Grace 'taking tea' in the hayfields with Portsmouth, see LPL, H997/30, f.214.

20. LPL, H997/35, f.57; H997/28, f.191; *The Times* 13 February 1823, p.3.

21. LPL, H997/31, f.296.

22. LPL, H997/29, f.31.

23. LPL, H997/29, f.90; see also H997/30, f.178.

24. LPL, H997/29, f.70; H997/28, f.221.

25. LPL, H997/28, ff.191–2.

26. HRO, 15M84/5/5/1, Letter from Urania Portsmouth to Newton Fellowes, 15 April 1800.

27. HRO, 15M84/5/3/2/17, Letter from Urania Portsmouth to Newton Fellowes, 16 January 1802.

28. HRO, 15M84/5/5/2, Letter from Urania Portsmouth to Newton Fellowes, 18 August 1810.

29. HRO, 15M84/5/3/2/17, Letter from Urania Portsmouth to Newton Fellowes, 30 January 1811.

30. LPL, H997/30, ff.121, 208.

31. LPL, H997/30, ff.121, 137; LPL, H997/31, f.275.

32. HRO, 15M84/5/4/4, Chancery case, 28 January 1815, p.92.

'Lord Portsmouth surpassed the rest in his attentive recollection of you'

1. Le Faye (ed.), *Jane Austen's Letters*, p.53; HRO, 23M93/70/1/8, Pocket book of Eliza Chute, 30 October 1800.

2. Le Faye (ed.), *Jane Austen's Letters*, pp.60–1.

3. Letter from Jane Austen to Martha Lloyd, 12 November 1800, in Austen-Leigh, *A Memoir*, p.58; *Salisbury and Winchester Journal* 27 November 1809.

4. LPL, H997/29, f.48.

5. Lefroy and Turner (eds), *The Letters of Mrs Lefroy*, pp.54–5.

6. Lefroy and Turner (eds), *The Letters of Mrs Lefroy*, pp.92, 179; Anne died after a riding accident the following month.

7. *Oracle and Public Advertiser* 29 June 1797; *Bell's Weekly Messenger* 2 July 1797; *Oracle and Daily Advertiser* 15–16 May 1800.

8. *Oracle and Daily Advertiser* 5 June 1800; *Morning Post and Gazetteer* 5 June 1800.

9. *Oracle and Daily Advertiser* 25 April 1800; *Morning Post and Gazetteer* 25 April 1800.

10. *Morning Post and Gazetteer* 17 May 1800.
11. *Morning Post and Gazetteer* 20 June 1800.
12. LPL, H997/32, ff.21, 105–6.
13. HRO, 23M93/70/1/8, Pocket book of Eliza Chute, 7 October 1800.
14. LPL, H997/33, f.175; H997/35, ff.110–12.
15. LPL, H997/8; H997/11, Exhibit 2; H997/33, f.151; H997/35, f.4.
16. HRO, H15M84/5/4/4, Chancery case, 28 January 1815, ff.137–8; LPL, H997/11, Exhibit 2; LPL, H997/35, f.12.
17. HRO, H15M84/5/4/4, Chancery case, 28 January 1815, f.142.
18. *Salisbury and Winchester Journal*, 11 February and 22 April 1811.
19. LPL, H997/32, ff.91–4, 99–102.
20. LPL, H997/32, f.24; H997/35, f.4.
21. *Salisbury and Winchester Journal* 25 May 1801; www.oldbaileyonline.org, t18010520-8; LPL, H997/33, f.113; Byron knew of the case, L. A. Marchand, *Byron: A Biography* (New York: Alfred A. Knopf, 1957), vol.1, p.441, footnote 6.
22. LPL, H997/32, ff.18, 21.
23. LPL, H997/33, ff.123–4.
24. LPL, H997/32, f.84.
25. *Report on the Proceedings*, p.66.
26. LPL, H997/33, ff.138–9.
27. HRO, 15M84/5/4/4, Chancery case, 28 January 1815, f.89.
28. *The Times* 28 February 1823, p.3.
29. HRO, 15M84/5/4/4, Chancery case, 28 January 1815, f.153.
30. LPL, H997/33, f.116; H997/35, ff.24, 40; H997/27, ff.9–13; *Genuine Report*, pp. 65, 67; *The Times* 24 February 1823, p.3.
31. LPL, H997/33, ff.155–6.

'He must have been quite a natural'

1. LPL, H997/29, ff.14–19; *Genuine Report*, p.20.
2. LPL, H997/29, ff.97–102; *Genuine Report*, pp.20–1.
3. *Genuine Report*, p.20, LPL, H997/29, ff.100–102; John Haslam, *Observations on Madness and Melancholy* 2nd edition (London, 1809), pp.313, 324; McKenzie, *Psychiatry for the Rich*, p.25; Andrews, 'Begging the question of idiocy' Part I, p.84.
4. *The Times* 13 February 1823, p.3.
5. LPL, H997/30, ff.123, 125.
6. *Genuine Report*, p.21; LPL, H997/28, ff.193–4, 200, 224.
7. *Genuine Report*, pp.44–45; LPL, H997/27, ff.14–27; Capy's surname was also spelled Capey in some documents.
8. LPL, H997/27, ff.63, 70.
9. *Genuine Report*, p.58; the case was probably that heard at the Old Bailey and

widely reported in September 1791. Susannah Hill, a London prostitute, was charged with hanging Franz Kotzwara (misspelt as Kutzmanoff in *Genuine Report*), but she was dismissed after it was proven that Kotzwara had sought sexual gratification by being strangled, Julie Peakman, *Lascivious Bodies: A Sexual History of the Eighteenth Century* (London: Atlantic Books, 2004), pp.267–8.

10. L. A. Marchand (ed.), *Byron's Letters and Journals* 12 vols (London: John Murray, 1973–1982), vol.10, pp.125–6.
11. *Genuine Report*, p.54.
12. LPL, H997/27, f.63; H997/29, f.16; H997/30, f.105.
13. HRO, 15M84/5/4/4, Chancery case, 28 January 1815, ff.107, 142.

'Black jobs'

1. LPL, H997/30, ff.108–14; *Genuine Report*, pp.29–30.
2. *Genuine Report*, p.27; LPL, H997/13, unfoliated; H997/27, f.90; H997/28, f.194; H997/31, ff.250–1.
3. *Genuine Report*, p.28; LPL, H997/27, f.91.
4. LPL, H997/28, ff.224–5; H997/29, f.79; HRO, 15M84/5/4/4, Chancery case, 31 January 1815, ff.180–1; LPL, H997/27, ff.9–13.
5. *Genuine Report*, pp.31, 49; *The Times*, 17 February 1823, p.2; LPL, H997/29, ff.64, 80; H997/30, f.146.
6. LPL, H997/30, ff.127–8.
7. HRO, 15M84/5/4/3, Chancery case, 24 January 1815, f.8; LPL, H997/28, f.194; H997/30, f.111; *The Times* 1 March 1823, p.3.
8. LPL, H997/30, f.212.
9. *Genuine Report*, pp.23–4, 30; LPL, H997/31, f.231.
10. *Genuine Report*, pp.24, 66, 69.
11. *Genuine Report*, pp.41, 66; *The Times* 15, 22 and 23 February 1823, p.3; LPL, H997/29, f.65; Richard Burn, *Ecclesiastical Law* 9th edition (London, 1842), vol.2, pp.423–4; intellectuals debated whether idiots had souls and who should be excluded from the communion, C. F. Goodey, *A History of Intelligence and 'Intellectual Disability': The Shaping of Psychology in Early Modern Europe* (Farnham: Ashgate, 2011), pp.201–4.

'I was never with a gentleman of that kind before'

1. *Genuine Report*, p.30; *The Times* 14 February 1823, p.3.
2. LPL, H997/28, f.203; H997/29, f.65; H997/30, ff.146, 168–9, 193; H997/31, ff.250–1; *Genuine Report*, pp.30, 32; *The Times* 14 February 1823, p.3; 17 February 1823, p.2.
3. LPL, H997/27, ff.87–8, 92; H997/28, f.228; H997/29, ff.34–5, 50, 67; H997/30, f.132; H997/31, f.235; H997/35, ff.18, 48; *Genuine Report*, pp.15, 17, 28, 29, 32, 38; HRO,

15M84/5/4/3, Chancery case, 24 January 1815, p.16; G. F. R. Baker, 'Onslow, George, first earl of Onslow (1731–1814)', rev. E. A. Smith, *ODNB*.

4. LPL, H997/1, unfoliated; H997/27, ff.20, 94, 117; H997/28, f.223; H997/29, ff.39–40, 66–68; H997/30, f.133; *Genuine Report*, p.48.

5. HRO, 53 A12/7, Copy of the affidavit of John Pottecary, sworn 23 January 1815; *Genuine Report*, p.24; LPL, H997/29, ff.20–24; H997/30, ff.114, 131, 176.

6. *Genuine Report*, pp.12, 23, 24, 28, 30; *The Times* 14 February 1823, p.3; LPL, H997/31, f.222.

7. HRO, 15M84/5/4/3, Chancery case, 24 January 1815, f.5; 15M84/5/4/6, Chancery case, 1 February 1815, f.100; LPL, H997/27, f.19; H997/29, f.41; H997/30, f.133; H997/31, ff.220–1, 231, 246–51; *Genuine Report*, pp.23, 30; *The Times* 14 February 1823, p.3.

8. *Genuine Report*, pp.26, 30, 32, 39; LPL, H997/36–40, H997/8, H997/30, f.143; *The Times* 14 February 1823, p.3.

The 'company keeper'

1. *The Courier* 28 January 1808; *The Times* 14 February 1823, p.3.

2. Le Faye (ed.), *Jane Austen's Letters*, p.68; HRO, 15M84/5/5/1, Letter from Urania Portsmouth to Newton Fellowes, 15 April 1800; 15M84/5/5/2, Copies of letters from Catharine Wallop (Coulson's wife) to Urania Portsmouth, 17 March 1803; 15M84/5/3/2/17, Letters from Urania Portsmouth to Newton Fellowes: 5 November 1801, 21 July 1801, 16 January 1802, 12 July 1806, 28 July 1806, 2 September 1806, 14 September 1806, 23 December 1806 and 4 December 1807.

3. LPL, H997/30, f.134; HRO, 15M84/5/4/6, Chancery case, 1 February 1815, ff.42, 44.

4. *Genuine Report*, pp.18, 23, 57; *The Times* 13 February 1823, p.3; LPL, H997/28, ff.225–6; H997/31, ff.280–1; HRO, 15M84/5/4/4, Chancery case, 28 January 1815, f.104; 15M84/5/5/12, Letter from Henry Karslake to Newton Fellowes, 18 June 1825.

5. *Genuine Report*, pp.8, 15–17, 21; *The Times* 12 February 1823, p.3; LPL, H997/1; H997/8 (unfoliated); H997/13; H997/28, f.163; H997/29, f.52; H997/35, f.10.

6. *Genuine Report*, pp.8, 13, 24, 25; LPL, H997/27, ff.9–13; H997/28, ff.142–67, 233–4; H997/29, ff.12, 22; H997/30, f.135; *The Times* 12 February 1823, p.3.

7. HRO, 15M84/5/4/6, Chancery case, 1 February 1815, f.43; *Genuine Report*, pp.12–13, 31, 32; LPL, H997/28, ff.125–7, 150; H997/30, f.136.

A lack of 'proper feeling'

1. *Genuine Report*, p.67; *The Times* 24 February 1823, p.3; LPL, H997/35, ff.22–30; John Jones, 'Baillie, Matthew (1761–1823)' *ODNB*.

2. HRO, 15M84/5/4/5, Chancery case, 31 January 1815, ff.180–4; *Genuine Report*,

pp.13, 24, 28–9; *The Times* 24 February 1823, p.3; LPL, H997/1; H997/27, ff.96–8; H997/29, ff.35, 53, 69–70; H997/30, ff.137, 165, 178; H997/32, f.3.

3. HRO, 15M84/5/4/5, Chancery case, 31 January 1815, ff.185–7, 1 February 1815, f.41.

Mad, bad and dangerous to know?

1. Marchand, *Byron*, vol.1, pp.53–4, 440; Marchand (ed.), *Byron's Letters*, vol.1, pp. 61, 63–4,72, 76, 77, vol.2, pp. 25, 36, vol.10, p.129; NLS, Ms. 43537 'Hanson's Narrative' and 'Hanson's Narrative of Lord Byron's Early Life'; Jerome McGann, 'Byron, George Gordon Noel, sixth Baron Byron (1788–1824)' *ODNB*.

2. Marchand, *Byron*, vol.1, p.440; *Byron's Letters*, vol.3, pp.248–9, vol.4, 'Statement concerning Lord Portsmouth', December 1814 (probable date), pp.236–7, vol.10, Letter from Byron to John Cam Hobhouse, 19 March 1823, pp.124–5; NLS, Ms. 43537 'Hanson's Narrative'; *Genuine Report*, pp.13, 31, 35; NA, PROB 11/1291/221, Will of the Right Honourable John Earl of Portsmouth, 24 May 1797; HRO, 15M84/5/4/4, Chancery case, 28 January 1815, f.57; LPL, H997/27, ff.45–7; H997/31, ff.237–8; H997/32, ff.85–6, 95–7; Baron Broughton [J.C. Hobhouse], *Recollections of a Long Life* (London: John Murray, 1909–11), ed. Lady Dorchester, vol.1, p.92–3; *The Times* 15 February 1823, p.3.

3. Marchand, *Byron's Letters*, vol.4, 'Statement concerning Lord Portsmouth', December 1814 (probable date), pp.236–7, vol.10, pp.119–20, 129; NLS, Ms. 43537 'Hanson's Narrative'.

4. Marchand, *Byron's Letters*, vol.1, p.40, vol.4, pp.174–5, 180, 186, 187, 189, 193, 235, 238, 239, 254, 261, 265, 306; vol.10, Letter from Byron to John Cam Hobhouse, 19 March 1823, p.125; Malcolm Elwin, *Lord Byron's Wife* (London: John Murray, 1962), p.240; McGann, 'Byron' *ODNB*.

5. Marchand, *Byron*, vol.2, pp.558–65; Marchand, *Byron's Letters*, vol.10, pp.119–20, 127, 129; John Galt, *The Life of Lord Byron* (London, 1830), cvii; Elwin, *Lord Byron's Wife*, pp.340–1, 346–7; Broughton, *Recollections*, vol.2, pp.250–3; McGann, 'Byron' *ODNB*.

'This unfortunate and devoted girl'

1. HRO, 15M84/5/4/2, Chancery case, 14 January 1815, f.50; 15M84/5/4/4, Chancery case, 28 January 1815, f.57; 15M84/5/4/7, Chancery case, 30 July 1821, ff.22–3; *Genuine Report*, p.9.

2. *St James' Chronicle* or the *British Evening Post*, 9–11 October 1794; Hermione Hobhouse (ed.), *Survey of London: vol.42* (London: London County Council, 1986), pp.196–214; Lefroy and Turner (eds.), *The Letters of Mrs Lefroy*, p.74; HRO, 15M84/5/4/7, Chancery case, 30 July 1821, f.13; LPL, H997/33, ff.156, 161; Marchand (ed.), *Byron's Letters*, vol.1, pp.63–4, 72, 76.

3. *Genuine Report*, pp.34–5, 48, 50; LPL, H997/1; H997/27, ff.1–8; H997/28, ff.215–7; Doris Langley Moore, *Lord Byron Accounts Rendered* (London: John Murray, 1974), pp.462–3.

4. *Bryon's Letters*, vol.10 (1980), pp.125, 129; *The Times* 18 February 1823, p.3; LPL, H997/1; H997/28, ff.235–6; H997/29, ff.82–3; H997/30, ff.179, 199, 201; H997/33, ff.182–4; *Genuine Report*, pp.13, 25, 27, 28, 34.

5. LPL, H997/27, ff.45–7; H997/32, ff.95–8; *Byron's Letters*, vol.10, p.124; HRO, 15M84/5/4/4, Chancery case, 28 January 1815, f.127, 31 January 1815, f.188; 15M84/5/4/8, Bundle of press cuttings; *The Times* 3 December 1825, p.3.

'Heir apparent'

1. HRO, 15M84/5/4/6, Chancery case, 1 February 1815, f.23–5; 15M84/5/4/7, Chancery case, 30 July 1821, f.27.

2. HRO, 15M84/F27, Notebook by the 6th countess of Portsmouth, c.1901–5; 15M84/5/3/2/17, Letter from Urania Portsmouth to Newton Fellowes, 29 May 1797; *Hampshire Chronicle* 22 April 1797; *Norfolk Chronicle* 29 April 1797.

3. Witnesses differed about whether the procession was in April or November 1814; LPL, H997/29, ff.71, 83; H997/30, f.139; HRO, 15M84/5/4/4, Chancery case, 28 January 1815, f.62; 15M84/5/4/7, Chancery case, 30 July 1821, ff.16–7, 40, 46; 15M84/5/4/8; *The Times* 29 July 1819, p.3, 7 August 1819, p.2; LPL, H997/8; H997/14 (unfoliated); H997/32, ff.41–2.

4. LPL, H997/8; H997/12, Exhibits 12 and 27; H997/35, f.33; HRO, 15M84/5/4/2–6, January and February 1815, statements to Chancery; 15M84/F27, Notebook by the 6th countess of Portsmouth, c.1901–5; 15M84/5/4/7, 30 July 1821, ff.27–8, 38.

5. *Morning Post* 25 January and 1 February 1815; *Byron's Letters*, vol.4, p.261; HRO, 15M84/5/4/6, 1 February 1815, f.126; E. A. Smith, 'Scott, John, first earl of Eldon (1751–1838)' *ODNB*; *The Times* 18 February 1823, p.3; LPL, H997/32, f.64; H997/35, ff.18–19; *Genuine Report*, p.63.

Three in a bed

1. For descriptions of Fairlawn Grove, see *The Times* 8 June 1821, p.4, and *Morning Post* 24 August 1841; LPL, H997/13; H997/27, ff.16, 19, 21–22; *The Times* 17 February 1823, p.1; *Genuine Report*, pp.44–7.

2. *Genuine Report*, pp.38–9, 45–6; *The Times* 12 November 1822, p.3, 11 March 1823, p.3, 6 May 1828, p.4; LPL, H997/27, f.24; H997/33, ff.127–32; H997/36–40; H997/53.

3. LPL, H997/53; *The Times* report of Capy's testimony to the Commission on 17 February 1823 gives the date of the 'three in a bed incident' as August 1818 not 1817, so there may well have been some genuine confusion over dates.

4. NA, C13/2685/9, Chancery proceedings, answer of William Rowland Alder, 7 May 1833; *Genuine Report*, pp.35–8, 42, 43, 45; *The Times* 15 February 1823, p.3, 17 February 1823, p.1; LPL, H997/27, f.116.

5. *Genuine Report*, pp.10, 11, 43–6, 50–1, 72; LPL, H997/27, ff.23, 70, 106, 111; H997/28, f.144; *The Times* 12 November 1822, p.3, 17 February 1823, pp.1–2, 18 February 1823, p.3, 19 February 1823, p.3.

6. *Genuine Report*, pp.10, 18, 39–40,46; *The Times* 15 February 1823, p.3, 17 February 1823, p.1, 25 February 1823, p.3, 28 February 1823, p.3; LPL, H997/27, f.105; Marchand (ed.), *Byron's Letters*, vol.10, p.125; Roy Porter, 'The secrets of generation display'd: *Aristotle's Master-piece* in Eighteenth-Century England', in R.P. Maccubbin (ed.), *'Tis Nature's Fault: Unauthorized Sexuality during the Enlightenment* (Cambridge: Cambridge University Press, 1987).

7. *Salisbury and Winchester Journal* 4 April 1814; Moore, *Lord Byron's Accounts*, p.468; *The Times* 12 November 1822, p.3; *Genuine Report*, p.70.

'That cursed woman'

1. LPL, H997/31, f.239; *The Times* 15 February 1823, p.3, 18 February 1823, p.3; *Genuine Report*, pp.25, 33–4, 35; Mary Ann denied pushing Portsmouth out of the carriage, LPL, H997/13.

2. HRO, 15M84/5/4/6, 1 February 1815, f.58; *Genuine Report*, pp.24, 44–5; HRO, 15M84/5/4/4, 28 January 1815, ff.127–8; 15M84/5/4/5, 31 January 1815, ff.194–208; *The Times* 21 February 1823, p.3; LPL, H997/1; H997/13.

3. *Genuine Report*, pp.16, 35–6, 42, 45, 46; LPL, H997/13; H997/28, ff.135, 174; H997/29, f.83; H997/30, ff.117, 152, 180, 204; *The Times* 17 February 1823, p.2, 22 February 1823, p.3.

4. *Genuine Report*, pp.61–3; *The Times* 22 February 1823, p.3; LPL, H997/32, ff.60–79.

5. *Genuine Report*, pp.14, 37, 38, 40, 42–3, 46; LPL, H997/1; H997/13; H997/27, ff.28–9, 54, 56; H997/28, ff.139–40, 206; H997/30, ff.157–8; H997/35, f.29; *The Times* 17 February 1823, p.1; T. F. Henderson, 'Birnie, Sir Richard (c.1760–1832)', rev. Catherine Pease-Watkin, *ODNB*.

6. *Genuine Report*, pp.36, 37, 39, 43; LPL, H997/8, f.174; H997/13; H997/28, ff.119, 140; H997/30, f.152; *The Times* 15 February 1823, p.3.

7. LPL, H997/27, f.56; H997/30, f.153; *Genuine Report*, pp.31–2, 60.

'So long as he was sane, he took no part in politics'

1. NA, PRO30/8/168/142–9, 151–8, 160, 162–3; R. Thorne (ed.), *The History of Parliament: The House of Commons 1790–1820* (London: Boydell and Brewer, 1986); D. Cannadine, *Aspects of the Aristocracy: Grandeur and Decline in Modern*

Britain (Harmondsworth: Penguin Books, 1995), p.20; B. Hilton, *A Mad, Bad, and Dangerous People? England 1783–1846* (Oxford: Oxford University Press, 2013), pp.80–1.

2. HRO, 15M84/5/3/2/17, Letter from Urania Portsmouth to Newton Fellowes, 14 September 1806; Gordon L. Teffeteller, 'Beresford, William Carr, Viscount Beresford (1768–1854)' *ODNB*; LPL, H997/28, f.230; H997/29, f.41; H997/33, f.151; H997/35, ff.2–3, 40–2; *Genuine Report*, pp.63, 66, 68–9, 71; there is no record of how Portsmouth or Newton Fellowes voted in Parliament over the issue of Catholic emancipation.

3. *The Times* 13 November 1820, p.2, 12 February 1823, p.2, 22 February 1823, p.3, 1 March 1823, p.3; LPL, H997/27, ff.41–3, 112–15; H997/32, ff.22, 25, 27–8; H997/33, ff.210–15; *Genuine Report*, pp.40–1, 58–9, 63–4; Michael Lobban, 'Burrough, Sir James (1749–1837)' and 'Brougham, Henry Peter, first Baron Brougham and Vaux (1778–1868)' *ODNB*; HRO, 15M84/5/4/8, Bundle of press cuttings; T. C. Hansard, *The Parliamentary Debates* (London, 1821), vol.3, columns 1698,1744–46; Hilton, *Mad, Bad*, p.28. Wetherell got the name of the clerk wrong: it was Maynard not Markham.

4. *Genuine Report*, pp.56–7; John Belchem, 'Hunt, Henry [Orator Hunt] (1773–1835)' *ODNB*; S. M. Waddams, 'Lushington, Stephen (1782–1873)' *ODNB*; *The Times* 3 March 1823, p.3, 6 May 1828, p.4; *Morning Post* 3 March 1823; Hilton, *Mad, Bad*, p.29; John Belchem, '*Orator' Hunt: Henry Hunt and English Working-Class Radicalism* (Oxford: Clarendon Press, 1985); John Mitford, *A Description of the Crimes and Horrors in the Interior of Warburton's Private Mad-House* (London, 1825), pp.2, 26. Much of this chapter is based on three excellent articles about the trial of Queen Caroline: Thomas W. Laqueur, 'The Queen Caroline Affair: Politics as art in the reign of George IV' *Journal of Modern History* 54 (1982), 417–66; T. L. Hunt, 'Morality and monarchy in the Queen Caroline affair' *Albion* 23, 4 (1991), 697–722; and Jonathan Fulcher, 'The loyalist response to the Queen Caroline agitations' *Journal of British Studies* 34 (1995), 481–502.

5. *The Complete Peerage* (1945), vol.10, p.612.

He 'always expressed much anxiety about his Lady's health'

1. G. T. Bettany, 'Hamilton, James, junior (1767–1839)', rev. Ornella Moscucci, *ODNB*; Derek Doyle, 'James Hamilton the younger (1767–1839)' *Journal of the Royal College of Physicians of Edinburgh* 42 (2012); LPL, H997/13; H997/34, ff.1–30; HRO, 15M84/5/4/8, Bundle of press cuttings; *The Times* 25 February 1823, p.3; *Salisbury and Winchester Journal* 19 August 1822; *Caledonian Mercury* 3 August 1822; *Morning Post* 15 August 1822.

The King of Hampshire

1. *Glasgow Herald* 19 July 1822; *Morning Post* 15 August 1822; *Genuine Report*, pp.11, 16, 51, 66, 68, 71; *The Times* 18 February 1823, p.3, 25 February 1823, p.3; LPL, H997/32, ff.48, 50, 53–9; H997/34, ff.31–8; *Caledonian Mercury* 27 July 1822.
2. LPL, H997/34, ff.11–14, H997/35, f.29; *Glasgow Herald* 19 July 1822; *Morning Post* 15 August 1822; *Caledonian Mercury* 3 August 1822; HRO, 15M84/5/5/24, Letter from Henry Karslake to Newton Fellowes, 19 April 1829; 15M84/5/4/7, Chancery case, 30 July to 14 August 1821; *Genuine Report*, pp.11, 16–18, 47–8, 51, 70, 72–4; HRO, 15M84/5/4/8, Bundle of press cuttings; *The Times* 4 November 1822, p.3, 18 February p.3, 19 February 1823, p.3, 27 February 1823, p.3, 1 March 1823, p.3.
3. HRO, 15M84/5/4/8, Bundle of press cuttings; *Genuine Report*, pp.78–9.

The plan

1. *Morning Post* 19 March 1823, 4 July 1823; HRO, 15M84/5/5/24, Letter from Henry Karslake to Newton Fellowes, 19 April 1829; 15M84/5/4/13, Chancery case, 5 July 1841.
2. HRO, 15M84/5/5/8, Letter from Henry Karslake to Newton Fellowes, 13 June 1823; HRO, 15M84/5/4/10, Minutes of a meeting of the trustees of the Earl of Portsmouth, 30 June 1836; *The Times* 19 February 1823, p.3; Mitford, *Description of the Crimes and Horrors*, pp.1–2; MacKenzie, *Psychiatry for the Rich*, p.14.
3. LPL, H997/31, ff.295–9; *Morning Post* 25 February 1823, 13 March 1823, 31 March 1852; *Hampshire Telegraph and Sussex Chronicle* 24 February 1823, 3 March 1823, 17 March 1823; HRO, 15M84/5/4/12, 15M84/5/5/25, Letter from Henry Karslake to Newton Fellowes, 21 July 1828.
4. *Genuine Report*, pp.78–9; HRO, 15M84/5/5/8, Letters from Henry Karslake to Newton Fellowes, 15 November 1823, 19 January 1824, 27 February 1824, 10 April 1824, 17 June 1824; 15M84/5/4/10, Minutes of trustee meetings held on 30 June, 7 and 8 July 1836; 15M84/5/5/25, Letters from Henry Karslake to Newton Fellowes, 27 June 1827, 21 July 1828; 15M84/5/5/11, Letter from Mr Austin of Gray's Inn to Newton Fellowes, 27 July 1824; 15M84/5/5/22, Letter from Henry Karslake to Newton Fellowes, 27 January 1830; NA, C13/1047/19 Portsmouth v. Grantley; Diane Atkinson, *The Criminal Conversation of Mrs Norton* (London: Random House, 2012), p.45.
5. HRO, 15M84/5/4/13, Chancery case, 5 July 1841; White, *Devonshire Directory* (1850); HRO, 15M84/F27, Notebook by the 6th countess of Portsmouth, c.1901–5; 15M84/5/5/18, Letters from Henry Karslake to Newton Fellowes, 13 January 1827, 7 February 1827, 21 February 1827.
6. HRO, 15M84/5/5/8, Letters from Henry Karslake to Newton Fellowes, 18 October 1823, 23 October 1823, 18 May 1824; 15M84/5/4/13, Chancery case, 5 July 1841; 15M84/5/5/16, Letters from Slade Bedford to Newton Fellowes; 15M84/5/5/25,

Letter from Henry Karslake to Newton Fellowes, 27 June 1827; LMA, DL/C/0924
Portsmouth v. Hanson; *The Times* 3 December 1825, 28 April 1828, 6 May 1828;
The Standard 12 May 1828; LPL, H997/1; H997/30, f.121; H997/61; S. M.
Waddams, 'Lushington' *ODNB*, and *Law, Politics and the Church of England: The
Career of Stephen Lushington 1782–1873* (Cambridge: Cambridge University Press,
1992).

7. LPL, H997/28, f.164; H997/35, ff.37, 52; *Salisbury and Winchester Journal* 28 June
1824; HRO, 15M84/5/4/11, Letter from Portsmouth to Catherine Fellowes,
28 February 1827, Letter from Portsmouth to Newton Fellowes, 6 March 1827;
15M84/5/5/8, Letter from Henry Karslake to Newton Fellowes, 19 June 1824;
15M84/5/5/9, Letter from Henry Karslake to Newton Fellowes, 15 December 1824;
15M84/5/5/12, Letters from Henry Karslake to Newton Fellowes, 1 January 1825,
19 January 1825, 22 February 1825, 23 February 1825, 26 February 1825, 2 July 1825,
16 March 1826, 4 April 1826, 3 May 1826; 15M84/5/5/18, Letter from Henry
Karslake to Newton Fellowes, 18 November 1826; 15M84/5/5/24, Letter from
Henry Karslake to Newton Fellowes, 19 April 1829; 15M84/5/5/22, Letter from
Henry Karslake to Newton Fellowes, 29 November 1830.

8. HRO, 15M84/5/5/18, Letter from Henry Karslake to Newton Fellowes, 7 March
1827; 15M84/5/5/25, Letter from Henry Karslake to Newton Fellowes, 4 July 1827;
15M84/5/5/24, Letter from Henry Karslake to Newton Fellowes, 4 December
1828, 14 January 1829; 15M84/5/4/13, Chancery case, 5 July 1841, f.11; 15M84/5/5/19,
Letter from Henry Karslake to Newton Fellowes, 21 June 1828.

9. HRO, 15M84/5/5/9, Letters from Henry Karslake to Newton Fellowes, 22 January
1831, 26 February 1831; 15M84/5/5/22, Letter from Henry Karslake to Newton
Fellowes, 29 November 1830; *Salisbury and Winchester Journal* 3 November 1823;
Morning Post 8 October 1833; *The Times* 7 October 1835; *Hampshire Telegraph
and Sussex Chronicle* 12 October 1835; NA HO64/3/153 f.419; my account of the
Swing disturbances is heavily indebted to David Kent, 'Popular radicalism and
the Swing Riots in Central Hampshire' *Hampshire Papers* 11 (1997); see also
Ruscombe Foster, *The Politics of County Power: Wellington and the Hampshire
Gentlemen 1820–52* (Hemel Hempstead: Harvester Wheatsheaf, 1990), chapter 4.

10. *The Times* 18 February 1823, p.3.

Family letters

1. HRO, 15M84/F27, Notebook by 6th countess of Portsmouth, c. 1901–5; HRO,
15M84/5/4/11, Bundle of correspondence from the 3rd earl of Portsmouth to his
brother Newton Fellowes and Catherine Fellowes 1827–53; *Morning Post*
2 December 1842; HRO, 15M84/5/14/20, Family papers including handwritten
obituary for Henry Arthur W. Fellowes dated 18 February 1847; HRO,
15M84/5/6/4, Pocketbook of Lady Catherine Fellowes, 1847.

2. LPL, H997/32, ff.50, 88; H997/35, f.34; Moore, *Lord Byron's Account*, pp.469–71;

McGann, 'Byron' *ODNB*; Marchand, *Byron: A Biography*, vol.3, p.1260; *Byron's Letters and Journals*, vol.1, p.275, vol.4, p.255, vol.5, p.70, vol.6, pp.59–60, 61, 74, 232, vol.7, p.40; NLS, Ms. 43537 'Hanson's Narrative', Ms. 43537 Draft Letters and Newton Hanson's Narrative of Lord Byron's early life, Ms. 43436 Letters from John, Newton and Charles Hanson to John Murray (1824-49); Hobhouse (ed.), Survey of London vol.42, pp.196–214.

3. *Salisbury and Winchester Journal* 25 November 1822; *The Times* 11 March 1823, p.3, 3 December 1825, p.3; HRO, 15M84/5/5/12, Letter from Henry Karslake to Newton Fellowes, 26 February 1825; *The Standard* 13 October 1828; *Newcastle Courant* 18 July 1829; Moore, *Lord Byron's Accounts*, p.469.

4. NA, C13/2685/8; HRO, 15M84/5/4/14; *The Berwick Advertiser* 11 January and 22 March 1834; Durham University Library Special Collections, DPR1/1/1847/A4; *The County of Kent Gazetteer and General Business Directory* (1864); Victor Lauriston, *Romantic Kent: The Story of a County, 1626–1952* (Chatham, 1952), pp.509–10; Christ Church Anglican burial registers, Chatham, burial register for Mrs Marianne Alder, 80 years, widow, 22 May 1870; Jim and Lisa Gilbert, 'How the Countess of Portsmouth came to Chatham' www.chathamdailynews.ca 10 April 2015, and 'Jane Austen and Lord Byron provide final pieces of the Chatham puzzle' www.chathamdailynews.ca 17 April 2015.

Epilogue

1. HRO, 15M84/5/4/13; 15M84/5/14/19, Will of Henrietta Dorothea Churchill; 15M84/5/14/20, Handwritten obituary for Newton Fellowes; *Salisbury and Winchester Journal* 14 November 1846, 30 November 1850, 30 July 1853; *Hampshire Telegraph and Sussex Chronicle* 23 July 1853, 14 January 1854; LPL, H997/28, f.225; *Morning Post* 19 December 1853; *The Standard* 26 September 1853.

Index

Act for Regulating Private Madhouses
    (1774) 80
Act of Union (1801) 226
Adams, Sarah 121, 123–4, 125, 127, 146
agriculture 44–5, 224, 277–9
Ainslie, Dr 162–3, 254–5
Alder, William Rowland 200–2, 203,
    204–6, 207, 208, 209–10
  and marriage 292
  and violence 216–17, 220, 241, 245
Aliens Act (1793) 62, 71–2
Angier, Charles 23–4, 25–30, 31
Angier, Samuel 24–5, 27–8, 29
annulment 271–4
Antrobus, Rev 232
Austen, Cassandra 15, 16, 17–18, 21
Austen, Edward 15, 17
Austen, George 14, 15–17, 18, 20–1
Austen, George (junior) 21, 22
Austen, James 15, 17, 21, 22
Austen, Jane 15, 20, 22, 109–10

Baillie, Dr Matthew 157–8, 176
Bankhead, Dr 250–2
Baring, Sir Thomas xxiv, xxix, 235, 277,
    278
Baverstock, John 47–8, 107, 150, 151
Bayley, John 246, 247

Best, Justice 99, 100, 152, 164
Bethlem hospital 77, 82
Bird, Robert 195–6
Birmingham Riots 78
Birnie, Sir Richard 217–19
Bishop, John 34, 35
Bishop, Richard 33, 34
blackmail 62–5
blood-letting 119–28
Brougham, Henry 230, 231, 234
Brown, Martha 90–2
Buggery Act (1533) 63
Burrough, Sir James 115, 229, 231
Byron, Lord xxi, 126, 167–77, 180, 181,
    183, 185
  and death 272
  and Hanson 289–90
  and Lunacy Commission 255
  and Mary Ann 186
  and sex 208–9

Canada 293–5
Capy, James 125, 126, 199–200, 201–4,
    206, 209
  and valeting 215
  and violence 213–14
Caroline, Queen 225, 229–32, 233–4,
    236, 237

Chancellor, see Eldon, John Scott, Lord
charity schools 113–14, 155–6
Churchill, Henrietta Dorothea (sister)
        19, 20, 30, 150, 164
Cobbett, William 225, 234, 235, 277
Commission of Lunacy, see Lunacy
        Commission
Conduitt, Catherine 6, 10, 76
Coombe, John Draper xxix, 152–5, 156,
        164, 179, 262
    and abduction 244, 248
    and Newton 275–6
coral 12–13
Corn Law (1815) 224
Crooke, Elizabeth 117–18
Curtis, Hannah 127, 146

Davis, Thomas 155
Dell, John 181–2
Dougall, John 56

Edinburgh 238–41, 242–6, 247–8
Eggesford 4, 5, 89–90, 91, 188
Eldon, John Scott, Lord xxi, xxiv, 36,
        175, 176, 192–3, 196–7
Eton 39
Etwall, Ralph 277, 278–9

Fairlawn Grove 200
Farleigh House 158, 175, 180–1
Fellowes, Catherine 269, 275, 281–3,
        286
Fellowes, Coulson 3–9, 10, 11–13
Fellowes, Dorothea (aunt) 77–84, 89
Fellowes, Henry Arthur (nephew) 176,
        221, 222, 249, 251
    and annulment 271–2
    and care plan 262–5, 266, 268–70
    and death 285
Fellowes, Henry Arthur (uncle) 77, 78,
        79, 80, 81
    and will 89–92

Fellowes, Newton (brother) 15, 32,
        37–40, 187–91, 194–5
    and annulment 270–3
    and death 299
    and Hansons 248–9
    and Hurstbourne Park 191–2
    and inheritance 50, 92, 99, 100–1
    and Lunacy Commission 175, 176,
        192–4, 251
    and marriage plot 170–1
    and Mary Ann 221, 222
    and money 275–6
    and mother 51, 52–3, 106
    and politics 225
    and Seilaz 61–2, 70
    and son 268–70, 285
    and threats 276–7, 278–8
    and trustee 164, 267–8
Fellowes, Robert (cousin) 82, 83
Fellowes, Urania 4–5
Fellowes, William (uncle) 77, 78, 79–80,
        81, 82
Fisher House 82–4
Fitzroy, Lord John xxiv
France, Thomas 29, 215–16
fraud 59–62
French Revolution 78, 224
funerals 131–4, 136, 159–60, 298
Fust, Fanny 92–3

Garnett, Rev John 49–50, 54, 70, 90,
        98
    and death 158
    and trustee 99–100
Garrow, Sir William 64, 65
George III, King xx, 45, 58, 111–12, 122,
        230
    and madness 81, 82, 157, 197, 266
George IV, King xix, 229–30, 231, 233,
        236
Godden, John 31, 107, 124, 133, 150, 156
Goose, Benjamin 219

Gordon, Catherine (aunt) 84–5, 88
Gordon, Catherine (cousin) 85, 88, 89
Gordon, Lockhart (cousin) 85–6, 87, 88
Gordon, Loudoun (cousin) 85–8, 89
Grace, Harvey 45
grand tours 55–6
Grantley, Fletcher Norton, 1st Lord 87, 97–8
Grantley, Fletcher Norton, 3rd Lord 244, 268
Grantley, William Norton, 2nd Lord 98–9, 164, 244
Green, Charles 138, 139, 143, 145, 146, 147

Hadfield, James 112
Halford, Sir Henry 279
Halls, Thomas 173
Hamilton, James 238–40, 241–3, 247
Hampshire xx, 5–7, 188–9, 277–9
Hanson, Charles 181, 184, 214
Hanson, John 50, 90, 211–12, 246, 290–1
    and annulment 272, 273
    and Byron 167–70, 171, 174, 175, 176, 177, 288–90
    and Lunacy Commission 197
    and Mary Ann 181–2, 183, 184, 185, 194
    and Portsmouths 178–81, 190–1
    and Seilaz 61, 64, 70, 71, 73
    and trustee 99–100, 164, 267–8
Hanson, Laura 214, 218
Hanson, Mary Ann, *see* Portsmouth, Mary Ann, Countess of
Hanson, Newton 203, 214, 246, 247–8, 290, 291–2
Hanson, Selina 214, 218
Harrison, John 172, 184–5
Haslam, John 122
Hastings, George 18
Haydn, Joseph 113

Head, Joseph 212–13
Hobhouse, John Cam 172, 173, 174–5, 177, 185, 290–1
horses 140–1, 142
House of Commons 225
House of Lords 225, 228–9
Hunt, Henry 'Orator' 224, 234–6, 237
Hunter, John 168, 169
Hurstbourne Park 9–11, 19, 42, 110–11, 299
    and care plan 262–4, 265, 269
    and John 286–8
    and Newton 191–2

infant mortality 129
insanity xxxi–xxxiii, 77, 92–3, 176–7
Ireland 225–7, 228

James, Elizabeth 30, 182
James, John 246

Karslake, Henry 265, 266, 268, 269–70, 276
King of Hampshire 252–3, 254–5, 296–7
Kinnaird, Douglas 289
Kyte, Rev 37, 38, 39

landed gentry 4, 5, 44
Lawrence, John 115
Lawson, John 56
Lee, Charles 143, 144
Lee, Rachel 85–7
Lefroy, Anne 111
Litchfield, William 129–31, 142, 146
Livesay, Richard 39
Lock, William 144–5
London, William 162
Long, Robert 197–8
Lovett, William 34, 37
Ludlow, Dr Daniel 130, 150, 151, 152, 162, 253

Lunacy Commission xxiii–xxv, xxvii–
xxviii, xxx, 100, 101, 176, 203–4
and adultery 205–7, 208
and blood-letting 126, 127, 128
and costs 267–8
and Mary Ann 221–2
and Newton 193–4
and politics 235–6
and Portsmouth 195–7, 253–6
and servants 146–7, 151–2
and verdict 257, 261
Lushington, Stephen 185, 236–7, 270–3
Lyford, Giles King 35, 36
Lymington, John, Viscount, *see*
Portsmouth, John Charles
Wallop, 3rd Earl of

madhouses 80, 82–4, 87–8
Mason, Robert 279
Milbanke, Annabella 175–7
Monro, Dr Edward Thomas xxxi, 77
Monro, Dr Thomas 77
Murray, John 290, 291

Newbolt, Rev 117
Newton, Isaac (nephew) 286–8, 299
Newton, Sir Isaac 5, 10, 76
Nicholl, Sir John 273–4
North Hants Club 113
Norton, Caroline Elizabeth 283, 284
Norton, Grace, *see* Portsmouth, Grace,
Countess of

Odiham Grammar School 32–5, 37
Onslow, Thomas, 2nd Earl of 140

Palmer, George 215–16
Palmer, James 211, 213
Parker, John 38
Pell, Serjeant xxiv–xxv, xxix, xxvi, 234
Peterloo massacre 224, 234
Phillips, Edward 158, 159

Pitman, William 154
Pitt, William 81, 225, 226, 227
politics 224–6, 234–7
Poore, Richard 134
Pope, Ann 119–20, 123, 127, 146
Portsmouth, Grace, Countess of (1st
wife) 97, 98–9, 100, 102–8, 124
and death 157, 158–61, 162–4
and marriage 148–9, 152, 153, 156
and servants 144, 145, 146, 150–1
and society 112–13
Portsmouth, John Charles Wallop, 3rd Earl
of 11–13, 35–6, 114–15, 130–1, 280
and attacks 216–20, 221–2
and accounts 45–6
and bell-ringing 138–40
and blood-letting 119–28
and care plan 263–6
and charity schools 113–14, 155–6
and church 134–6
and Coombe 153–5
and cuckold 202, 203, 205–6, 209–10
and death 298–9
and Edinburgh 240–1, 244–6, 247
and farming 44–5
and first marriage 97, 98–99, 102–8
and funerals 131–4
and Grace's death 157–64
and King of Hampshire 252–5, 296–7
and letters 281–4, 286–8
and Lunacy Commission 195–6
and mental health xix–xxxiii, 77, 92–3
and mother 42–4, 47–8, 50–2, 53–4
and Newton 274–5
and politics 225, 226–9, 230–3, 236–7
and schooling 14–18, 19–22, 32–5, 37,
39–41
and second marriage 170, 171–4,
183–5, 190, 211–15, 250–1
and Seilaz 55–63, 64–73
and servants 140–7, 151–2
and 1799 settlement 99–102

and sex 74, 206–8
and society 46–7, 111–13, 115–18
and speech 23–4, 26, 27, 28–31
and threats 276–7
and will 215–16
Portsmouth, John Wallop, 1st Earl of
5–6
Portsmouth, John Wallop, 2nd Earl of 5,
6–8, 11, 48–9, 226
Portsmouth, Mary Ann, Countess of
(2nd wife) 170, 171–3, 179, 180,
181, 182–3, 185–6
and adultery 202, 203, 204–6, 209–10
and annulment 270–4, 291–2
and Canada 293–5
and John 249–51, 252
and marriage xxi–xxii, xxv, xxvii, 196,
198, 211–14, 222–3
and pregnancy 206–7, 238–40, 241–2,
247
and vilification 221
and violence 216, 217–18, 219, 220–1
Portsmouth, Urania, Countess of
(mother) 5, 7–8, 9–10, 11, 18–19,
20
and accounts 45–6
and brother 90, 91
and children 39–41, 149–50
and death 158
and Farleigh House 180
and Grace 105–7
and John 42–4, 47–8, 49, 50–2, 53–4,
93
and Loudoun Gordon 87, 88
and Newton 52–3, 188–9
and sister 77–8, 79–80, 82, 83, 84
and speech therapy 23–4, 26, 27
Pottecary, John 142
power of attorney 59–60
press, the xxiii, xxviii
Pridden, John 78–9, 82–3
Priestley, Joseph 27–8, 29, 78

Prince Regent, *see* George IV, King
public interest 255–6

religion 134–6

Seilaz, Jean 55, 56–73, 74–5, 93, 101
servants 138, 139–40, 141–2, 143–7,
150–2, 219–20
1799 settlement 99–102, 108
shell work 53
Sherard, Frances 189
Simmons, Dr Samuel 82, 83
Soane, John xxiv
society 116–17, 118, 255–6, 298
sodomy 63–6, 74–5
South Sea Bubble 3–4
speech therapy 23–6, 27–30
Steventon 14–15, 19–21
Sutherland, Dr Alexander Robert 89,
125, 251
Swing Riots 277–9

Tahourdin, Gabriel 59, 60, 61, 69, 70, 71
Thomas, Edward 77
Turner, Oliver 181
Tuthill, Sir George 207, 251
Twynam, George 140, 197

United Irishmen 226

Wallop, Barton 20, 76
Wallop, Coulson (brother) 32, 39, 40,
76, 149
and politics 225, 227
Wallop, Newton, *see* Fellowes, Newton
Wallop, Sir Henry 225
Wallop, William Barton 293
Want, Charles 219
Warburton, Dr John 88, 265–6
Warburton, Dr Thomas 89, 265–6
Warren, Walter Long 92
Webb, Rev Benjamin 32, 33

Webb, Charles 140, 143, 159, 160, 161
Wellington, Arthur Wellesley, Duke of 230, 283, 284
Wetherell, Charles xxvi, xxviii–xxix
Williams, David 47, 104–5

Willis, Dr Francis 81, 89, 116
Willis, Robert Darling 80–1, 82
Wonersh Park 97–8
Wright, Rev Robert 51–2, 228
Wyatt, James 9–10